CAMBRIDGE
UNIVERSITY PRESS

Physics

for the IB Diploma

WORKBOOK

Mark Farrington

CAMBRIDGE
UNIVERSITY PRESS

Shaftesbury Road, Cambridge CB2 8EA, United Kingdom

One Liberty Plaza, 20th Floor, New York, NY 10006, USA

477 Williamstown Road, Port Melbourne, VIC 3207, Australia

314–321, 3rd Floor, Plot 3, Splendor Forum, Jasola District Centre, New Delhi – 110025, India

103 Penang Road, #05–06/07, Visioncrest Commercial, Singapore 238467

Cambridge University Press is part of Cambridge University Press & Assessment, a department of the University of Cambridge.

We share the University's mission to contribute to society through the pursuit of education, learning and research at the highest international levels of excellence.

www.cambridge.org
Information on this title: www.cambridge.org/9781009071901
DOI: 10.1010/9781009071888

© Cambridge University Press & Assessment 2023

This publication is in copyright. Subject to statutory exception and to the provisions of relevant collective licensing agreements, no reproduction of any part may take place without the written permission of Cambridge University Press & Assessment.

First published 2017
Second edition 2023

20 19 18 17 16 15 14 13 12 11 10 9 8 7 6 5 4

Printed in the Netherlands by Wilco BV

A catalogue record for this publication is available from the British Library

ISBN 9781009071901 Workbook with digital access

Additional resources for this publication at www.cambridge.org/9781009071901

Cambridge University Press & Assessment has no responsibility for the persistence or accuracy of URLs for external or third-party internet websites referred to in this publication and does not guarantee that any content on such websites is, or will remain, accurate or appropriate.

This work has been developed independently from and is not endorsed by the International Baccalaureate Organization. International Baccalaureate, Baccalauréat International, Bachillerato Internacional and IB are registered trademarks owned by the International Baccalaureate Organization.

....

NOTICE TO TEACHERS
It is illegal to reproduce any part of this work in material form (including photocopying and electronic storage) except under the following circumstances:
(i) where you are abiding by a licence granted to your school or institution by the Copyright Licensing Agency;
(ii) where no such licence exists, or where you wish to exceed the terms of a licence, and you have gained the written permission of Cambridge University Press;
(iii) where you are allowed to reproduce without permission under the provisions of Chapter 3 of the Copyright, Designs and Patents Act 1988, which covers, for example, the reproduction of short passages within certain types of educational anthology and reproduction for the purposes of setting examination questions.

2022 CAMBRIDGE DEDICATED TEACHER AWARDS

Teachers play an important part in shaping futures. Our Dedicated Teacher Awards recognise the hard work that teachers put in every day.

Thank you to everyone who nominated this year; we have been inspired and moved by all of your stories. Well done to all of our nominees for your dedication to learning and for inspiring the next generation of thinkers, leaders and innovators.

Congratulations to our incredible winners!

WINNER

Regional Winner
Australia, New Zealand & South-East Asia

Mohd Al Khalifa Bin Mohd Affnan
Keningau Vocational College, Malaysia

Regional Winner
Europe

Dr. Mary Shiny Ponparambil Paul
Little Flower English School, Italy

Regional Winner
North & South America

Noemi Falcon
Zora Neale Hurston Elementary School, United States

Regional Winner
Central & Southern Africa

Temitope Adewuyi
Fountain Heights Secondary School, Nigeria

Regional Winner
Middle East & North Africa

Uroosa Imran
Beaconhouse School System KG-1 branch, Pakistan

Regional Winner
East & South Asia

Jeenath Akther
Chittagong Grammar School, Bangladesh

For more information about our dedicated teachers and their stories, go to
dedicatedteacher.cambridge.org

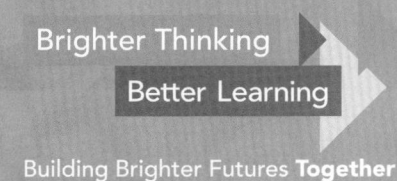

Contents

How to use this series		vi
How to use this book		vii

Unit A   Space, time and motion   1

1   Kinematics   2
- 1.1   Displacement, distance, speed and velocity   3
- 1.2   Uniformly accelerated motion: the equations of kinematics   5
- 1.3   Graphs of motion   6
- 1.4   Projectile motion   10

2   Forces and Newton's laws   19
- 2.1   Forces and their direction   21
- 2.2   Newton's laws of motion   26
- 2.3   Circular motion   28

3   Work, energy and power   36
- 3.1   Work   37
- 3.2   Conservation of mechanical energy   39
- 3.3   Power and efficiency   42
- 3.4   Energy transfers   44

4   Linear momentum   50
- 4.1   Newton's second law in terms of momentum   51
- 4.2   Impulse and force–time graphs   52
- 4.3   Conservation of momentum   54
- 4.4   Kinetic energy and momentum   55

5   Rigid body mechanics   62
- 5.1   Kinematics of rotational motion   64
- 5.2   Rotational equilibrium and Newton's second law   67
- 5.3   Angular momentum   69

6   Relativity   76
- 6.1   Reference frames and Lorentz transformations   78
- 6.2   Effects of relativity   80
- 6.3   Spacetime diagrams   83

Unit B   The particulate nature of matter   93

7   Thermal energy transfers   94
- 7.1   Particles, temperature, and energy   96
- 7.2   Specific heat capacity and change of phase   98
- 7.3   Thermal energy transfer   100

8   The greenhouse effect   110
- 8.1   Radiation from real bodies   111
- 8.2   Energy balance of the Earth   112

9   The gas laws   121
- 9.1   Moles, molar mass and the Avogadro constant   123
- 9.2   Ideal gases   125
- 9.3   The Boltzmann equation   126

10   Thermodynamics   133
- 10.1   Internal energy   135
- 10.2   The first law of thermodynamics   140
- 10.3   The second law of thermodynamics   143
- 10.4   Real systems   149

11   Current and circuits   158
- 11.1   Potential difference, current and resistance   161
- 11.2   Voltage, power and emf   167
- 11.3   Resistors in electrical circuits   170
- 11.4   Analysing circuits   173

| Unit C | Wave behaviour | 185 |

12 Simple harmonic motion — 186
- 12.1 Simple harmonic oscillations — 188
- 12.2 Details of simple harmonic motion — 189
- 12.3 More about energy in simple harmonic motion — 194

13 The wave model — 203
- 13.1 Mechanical waves — 204
- 13.2 Transverse and longitudinal waves — 207
- 13.3 Electromagnetic waves — 211
- 13.4 Waves extension — 212

14 Wave phenomena — 218
- 14.1 Reflection and refraction — 220
- 14.2 The principle of superposition — 226
- 14.3 Diffraction and interference — 229
- 14.4 Single-slit diffraction — 232
- 14.5 Multiple slits — 233

15 Standing waves and resonance — 238
- 15.1 Standing waves — 240
- 15.2 Standing waves on strings — 243
- 15.3 Standing waves in pipes — 244
- 15.4 Resonance and damping — 246

16 The Doppler effect — 252
- 16.1 The Doppler effect at low speeds — 253
- 16.2 The Doppler effect for sound — 256

| Unit D | Fields | 265 |

17 Gravitational fields — 266
- 17.1 Newton's law of gravitation — 267
- 17.2 Gravitational potential and energy — 270
- 17.3 Motion in a gravitational field — 277

18 Electric and magnetic fields — 286
- 18.1 Electric charge, force and field — 289
- 18.2 Magnetic field and force — 293
- 18.3 Electrical potential and electrical potential energy — 296

19 Motion in electric and magnetic fields — 306
- 19.1 Motion in an electric field — 306
- 19.2 Motion in a magnetic field — 309
- 19.3 Motion in perpendicularly orientated electric and magnetic fields — 311

20 Electromagnetic induction — 318
- 20.1 Electromagnetic induction — 319
- 20.2 Generators and alternating current — 323

| Unit E | Nuclear and quantum physics | 335 |

21 Atomic physics — 336
- 21.1 The structure of the atom — 337
- 21.2 Quantisation of angular momentum — 341

22 Quantum physics — 349
- 22.1 Photons and the photoelectric effect — 350
- 22.2 Matter waves — 353

23 and 24 Nuclear physics and Nuclear fission — 362
- 23.1 Mass defect and binding energy — 365
- 23.2 Radioactivity — 368
- 23.3 Nuclear properties and the radioactive decay law — 374
- 24.1 Nuclear fission — 377

25 Nuclear fusion and stars — 385
- 25.1 Nuclear fusion — 387
- 25.2 Stellar properties and the Hertzsprung-Russell diagram — 389
- 25.3 Stellar evolution extension — 393

Glossary — 400

> PHYSICS FOR THE IB DIPLOMA: WORKBOOK

> How to use this series

This suite of resources supports students and teachers of the IB Physics Diploma course. All of the books in the series work together to help students develop the necessary knowledge and scientific skills required for this subject.

The coursebook with digital access provides full coverage of the latest IB Physics Diploma course.

It clearly explains facts, concepts and practical techniques, and uses real world examples of scientific principles. A wealth of formative questions within each chapter help students develop their understanding, and own their learning. A dedicated chapter in the digital coursebook helps teachers and students unpack the new assessment, while exam-style questions provide essential practice and self-assessment. Answers are provided on Cambridge GO, supporting self-study and home-schooling.

The workbook with digital access builds upon the coursebook with digital access with further exercises and exam-style questions, carefully constructed to help students develop the skills that they need as they progress through their IB Physics Diploma course. The exercises also help students develop understanding of the meaning of various command words used in questions, and provide practice in responding appropriately to these.

The Teacher's resource supports and enhances the coursebook with digital access and the workbook with digital access. This resource includes teaching plans, overviews of required background knowledge, learning objectives and success criteria, common misconceptions, and a wealth of ideas to support lesson planning and delivery, assessment and differentiation. It also includes editable worksheets for vocabulary support and exam practice (with answers) and exemplar PowerPoint presentations, to help plan and deliver the best teaching.

> How to use this book

A chapter outline appears at the start of every chapter to introduce the learning aims and help you navigate the content.

> **CHAPTER OUTLINE**
>
> In this chapter you will:
>
> - describe the structure of the atom and the relative charges and masses of protons, neutrons and electrons
> - describe how protons, neutrons and electrons behave in electric fields
> - deduce the number of protons, neutrons and electrons in atoms and ions

> **KEY TERMS**
>
> Definitions of key vocabulary are given when the word is first introduced.
>
> You will also find definitions of these words in the Glossary.

Exercises

Exercises help you to practice skills that are important for studying SL and HL Physics.

The exercises are divided into Standard and Higher Level material. A vertical line runs down the margin of all Higher Level material, allowing you to easily identify Higher Level from Standard material.

Answers to the excercises are available on Cambridge GO.

> **TIP**
>
> Tip boxes will help you complete the exercises, and give you support in areas that you might find difficult.

> **EXAM-STYLE QUESTIONS**
>
> Questions at the end of each chapter are more demanding exam-style questions, some of which may require use of knowledge from previous chapters. Answers to these questions can be found in digital form on Cambridge GO.

Unit A
Space, time and motion

Chapter 1
Kinematics

CHAPTER OUTLINE

In this chapter, you will:

- use the terms *displacement*, *distance*, *speed*, *velocity* and *acceleration* and identify which are *scalar* and which are *vector* quantities.

- determine instantaneous and average values of speed, velocity and acceleration.

- use the equations of kinematics to solve problems with uniformly accelerated motion.

- use and analyse appropriate graphs to represent the motion of objects; this will include

    - constructing displacement–time, velocity–time and acceleration–time graphs.

    - estimating gradients of displacement–time graphs to find velocity, and velocity–time graphs to find acceleration.

    - calculating areas under velocity–time graphs to find displacement and under acceleration–time graphs to find change of velocity.

- use error bars on graphs of *displacement* against *time* to estimate the maximum and the minimum velocities, and on graphs of *velocity* against *time* to estimate the maximum and minimum accelerations.

- resolve the motion of projectiles into horizontal and vertical components and use them to solve problems.

- examine the qualitative effect of fluid resistance on the motion of projectiles.

KEY TERMS

position: the coordinate on the number line

displacement: change in position

distance: length of path followed

uniform motion: motion with constant velocity

average velocity: the displacement divided by the time to achieve that displacement: $\bar{v} = \frac{\Delta s}{\Delta t}$

(instantaneous) velocity: the rate of change of position; it is a vector

1 Kinematics

> **CONTINUED**
>
> **(instantaneous) speed:** the magnitude of the instantaneous velocity
>
> **acceleration:** the rate of change of velocity; it is a vector: $a = \frac{\Delta v}{\Delta t}$ or $\frac{v - u}{t}$
>
> **acceleration of free fall:** the acceleration, g, due to the pull of the Earth on a body; $g = 9.8$ ms^{-2} near the surface of the Earth
>
> **position vector:** the vector from the origin of a coordinate system to the position of a particle
>
> **fluid resistance force:** a speed-dependent force opposing the motion of a body through a fluid
>
> **terminal speed:** the constant speed attained when the resistance force becomes equal to the force pushing the body
>
> **equations of kinematics:** $v = u + at$, $\Delta s = ut + \frac{1}{2}at^2$, $\Delta s = \left(\frac{u+v}{2}\right)t$, $v^2 = u^2 + 2a\Delta s$ where, u = initial velocity, v = final velocity, s = displacement/distance moved, a = acceleration, t = time
>
> **components of a vector:** two (or three in three dimensions) mutually perpendicular vectors that, when added together, form the vector itself—in practice, this usually involves the use of trigonometry:
>
> $v_x = v \cos \theta$
>
> $v_y = v \sin \theta$
>
> where θ is the angle between the vector and the x-axis

Exercise 1.1 Displacement, distance, speed and velocity

The following questions will help you to improve your skill with calculations involving displacement, speed, velocity and acceleration.

1. **a** Explain the difference between *distance* and *displacement*.

   b Explain the difference between *speed* and *velocity*.

2. Calculate the speed, in ms^{-1}, of a:

   a car that travels 200 km in 90 minutes; suggest why your answer is an average speed

   b sound wave that reaches an observer's ears having travelled 1.5 km in 4.5 s

   c transatlantic liner that takes five days to travel 6000 km.

3 A high-speed train travels between Beijing and Tianjin. If the train travels at a speed of 97 ms^{-1}, calculate the time it takes for the train to travel the 117 km journey.

4 Proxima Centauri is the closest star to our Sun. It is 3.78×10^{16} m from the Earth. (The speed of light, $c = 3.0 \times 10^8$ ms^{-1})

   a Calculate the time it takes for light to travel from Proxima Centauri to the Earth.

   b How else could the distance from Proxima Centauri to the Earth be stated?

5 Calculate the acceleration in the following situations:

   a A boy walking along the road changes his speed from 0.6 ms^{-1} to 1.2 ms^{-1} in a time of 1 minute.

   b The velocity of an electron changes from 0.0 ms^{-1} to 2×10^7 ms^{-1} in a time of 4.0 ns.

   c An aeroplane approaching an airport changes its speed from 90 ms^{-1} to 30 ms^{-1} in a time of 20 minutes.

6 An athlete running at a constant speed moves around a bend in the track. Explain why the athlete has accelerated even though his speed has not changed.

7 A molecule of nitrogen in the air travels 3 cm horizontally and 4 cm vertically in a time of 100 μs.

   a Calculate the magnitude of the overall displacement of the molecule.

   b Calculate the average speed of the molecule.

   c Calculate the direction in which it has travelled relative to the horizontal.

   d State its average velocity during the 100 μs period.

8 On the horizontal surface of a flat table, the co-ordinates, in cm, of a ball change uniformly from (1, −1) to (5, 5) during a time of 4.0 s.

   a Calculate the magnitude of the overall displacement of the ball.

   b Calculate the average speed of the ball.

   c By writing the overall displacement of the ball as the *x*- and *y*-components of a vector, calculate the angle to the *x*-axis of the motion of the ball.

   d State the velocity of the ball during the 4.0 s period.

> **TIP**
>
> To solve calculation questions, begin by writing the equation you want to use; then put in the numbers and then write the answer. Don't forget to use the correct amount of significant figures and don't forget to include the correct units.

Exercise 1.2 Uniformly accelerated motion: the equations of kinematics

The following questions will help you perfect your ability to use the equations of kinematics (sometimes called *suvat* equations) to solve problems involving uniformly accelerated motion.

1   Figure 1.1 shows a velocity–time graph for part of a journey made by an electric train.

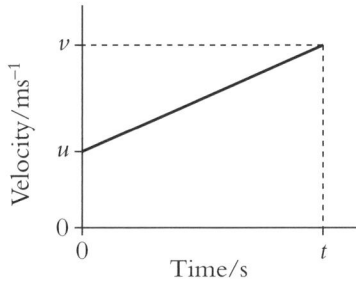

Figure 1.1

   a   If the train had travelled at the same speed as its initial speed throughout the journey, state an algebraic expression for how far the train would have travelled.

   b   Copy the graph and shade in the region of the graph that represents your answer to part **a**.

The remaining part of the graph shows the extra distance travelled by the train because it was accelerating.

   c   Show that the acceleration, a, of the train can be given as $a = \frac{v-u}{t}$.

   d   Show that the extra distance travelled by the train due to its acceleration can be expressed as $\frac{1}{2}at^2$.

   e   Shade this region on your copy of the graph.

   f   State the algebraic expression for the total distance travelled during the journey.

2   A passenger in a car starts a stopwatch when the car is travelling at 28.8 km hour^{-1}. The car accelerates with a constant acceleration of 2.0 ms^{-2} for the next 10 s.

   Calculate the:

   a   speed of the car after 10 s of acceleration (give your answer in ms^{-1})

   b   distance that the car has travelled during the 10 s period (give your answer in m).

3   A girl drops her mobile phone from a window that is 15 m above the ground. Taking the acceleration of the Earth's gravitational field to be 10 ms^{-2} and ignoring any effects of air friction:

   a   Sketch a velocity–time graph for the phone from when it leaves the girl's hand to when it hits the ground.

   b   Calculate the time it takes for the phone to hit the ground.

   c   Calculate the phone's velocity just before it hits the ground.

4   A baseball pitcher practises by throwing a ball vertically into the air with an initial velocity of 30 ms^{-1} and catching it when it falls back.

   Ignoring any effects of air resistance, and using $g = 10$ ms^{-2}, calculate:

   a   how much time it will take for the ball to reach its highest point

   b   how far above the pitcher the ball reaches.

5   When a parachutist jumps from an aeroplane, he hits the ground with a landing speed of 6.0 ms^{-1}.

   What is the minimum jump height required to simulate this landing speed?

6   As of July 2020, the world 100 m and 200 m athletics records were both held by Usain Bolt. His times for these two events are 9.58 s for the 100 m and 19.19 s for the 200 m.

   If we model Usain Bolt's running in both events by a uniform acceleration to his maximum speed followed by a constant speed to the finish, calculate Usain Bolt's maximum speed. (You may assume that he runs at the same maximum speed in both events and that there are no effects of air friction.)

TIP

If you consider upwards as a positive direction, then acceleration due to gravity, which is downwards, must be negative.

TIP

Consider first sketching graphs of his two journeys and using what you know about speed-time graphs to produce a pair of simultaneous equations.

Exercise 1.3 Graphs of motion

The following questions will help you to improve your use of graphs and solve problems about journeys.

1   a   Figure 1.2 shows a journey made by a pedestrian.

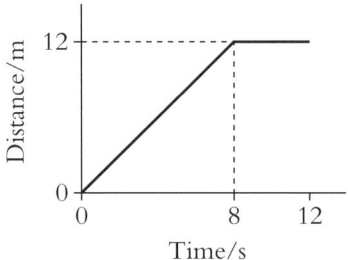

Figure 1.2

Use the graph to find the:

i average speed of the pedestrian for the whole journey

ii speed of the pedestrian during the first 8 s.

b Figure 1.3 shows a velocity–time graph for a journey.

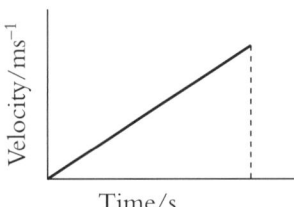

Figure 1.3

What aspect of the journey is shown by the:

i gradient of the graph

ii area under the graph?

2 In an experiment, Lucy measures the displacement of a moving object. Her measurements are shown in Table 1.1. All of Lucy's measurements of displacement have an uncertainty of ±1.0 cm.

Time / s	0.0	1.0	2.0	3.0	4.0	5.0	6.0
Displacement / cm	0.0	2.0	4.0	6.0	8.0	10.0	12.0

Table 1.1

a Use the results in the table to draw a graph of displacement against time.

b Add to your graph appropriate error bars for all points.

c Find, from the graph, the speed at which the object was moving.

d Use the error bars you have drawn to find the maximum and minimum speed of the object.

e Hence state the speed of the object and its uncertainty.

TIP

When drawing graphs, make sure you always label the axes with the correct title and units.

3   The graph in Figure 1.4 shows the velocity of a projectile that is fired vertically upwards from the ground until it momentarily comes to a stop. There are no effects due to air friction.

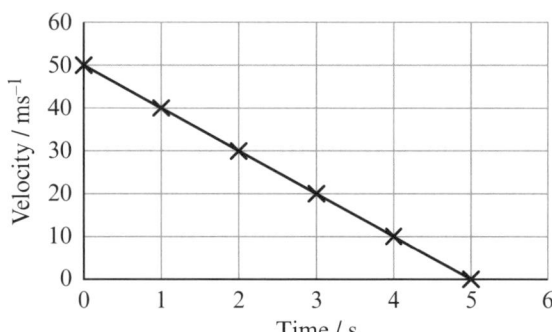

Figure 1.4

   a   Show that the graph is consistent with the Earth's gravitational acceleration, g, having the value 10 ms^{-2} (1 s.f.)

   b   Use the graph to calculate the height at which the projectile came to a stop.

   c   Copy and add to the graph a line to show how the projectile's velocity would change as it returns to the ground.

4   A speedboat moves at a constant speed of 9 ms^{-1} for 5 s, at which time it accelerates at 2 ms^{-2} for 4 s.

   a   Sketch a graph of the speedboats journey over the 14 s period.

   b   Use the graph to calculate the distance travelled by the speedboat.

   c   Show that your answer to part b is consistent with the equation:
       $s = ut + \frac{1}{2}at^2$

5   Figure 1.5 shows how the velocity of child's toy varies during a 20 s period. At $t = 0$, the toy's velocity = 5 cms^{-1} and at $t = 20$ s, the toy's velocity = -7.5 cms^{-1}.

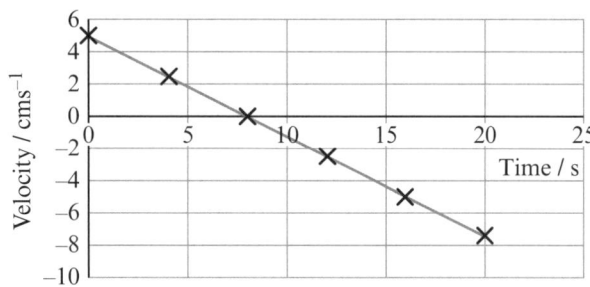

Figure 1.5

   a   Describe the motion of the toy during the 20 s period.

   b   Use the graph to calculate the acceleration of the toy.

c Use the graph to find the total displacement of the toy.

d i How far did the toy actually travel during the 20 s period?

   ii Explain why your answers to c and d are different.

6 Table 1.2 shows how the velocity of an object varied during a period of 80 s.

Time / s	0	10	20	30	40	50	60	70	80
Velocity / ms^{-1}	0	2.0	4.0	6.0	6.0	6.0	6.0	3.0	0

Table 1.2

All of the velocity values in the table have an uncertainty of ± 0.5 ms^{-1}.

a Draw a graph of *velocity* against *time* for the motion of the object.

b Use the graph to calculate the total displacement of the object.

c Calculate the acceleration of the object during the first 30 s.

d By adding suitable error bars to your graph find the maximum and minimum values of the acceleration during the first 30 s.

7 Figure 1.6 shows how the acceleration of an initially stationary object varies with time during a 30 s period.

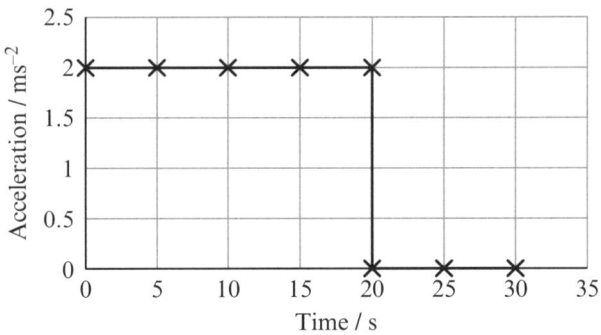

Figure 1.6

a Use the graph to determine the change of velocity of the object during the first 20 s.

b Sketch a graph of *velocity of the object* against *time* for the 30 s period.

c Using your sketch, or otherwise, determine the total displacement of the object.

PHYSICS FOR THE IB DIPLOMA: WORKBOOK

Exercise 1.4 Projectile motion

This exercise contains questions to help you solve problems associated with projectile motion without the effect of fluid resistance. Projectiles subject to the effects of fluid resistance are examined qualitatively only.

1. A glass marble, rolling at 1.0 ms^{-1} along a table top, reaches the edge of the table and falls to the floor. The height of the table top is 1.0 m above the floor. Ignore any effects due to air friction and use $g = 10$ ms^{-2}.

    a   Sketch a simple diagram to show the path that the marble takes after it leaves the table top until it hits the floor.

    b   Explain the shape of the path you have drawn by considering the horizontal and vertical components of the marble's velocity.

    c   Calculate the time it takes for the marble to reach the floor after it leaves the edge of the table.

    d   When the marble hits the floor, calculate how far from the edge of the table the marble has travellled.

2. A plane flying horizontally at a speed of 70 ms^{-1} releases a crate of supplies for some charity workers at their base on the ground below.

    a   If the plane had been 80 m above the ground when it released the crate, using $g = 10$ ms^{-2} and assuming no effects due to air friction:

        i   calculate the vertical component of the crate's velocity just before it hits the ground,

        ii hence determine the magnitude and direction of the crate's velocity just before it hits the ground.

    b   Where will the plane be relative to the crate when the crate hits the ground?

3. At a shooting gallery, a man fires a bullet from a rifle horizontally at a target.

    The target is 75.00 m away.

    The bullet leaves the rifle at a speed of 150.0 ms^{-1}.

    Ignoring any effects of air friction on the bullet, and using $g = 10$ ms^{-2}:

    a   calculate the time it takes for the bullet to hit the target,

    b   using the equation $v^2 = u^2 + 2as$, with the appropriate value for v, show that the bullet hits the target 1.25 m below the horizontal,

    c   calculate the total velocity vector for the bullet just as it hits the target.

4. Mercurio, the human cannonball in a circus show, is fired from a cannon at an initial velocity of 20 ms^{-1} at an angle of 30° above the horizontal.

    How far away from the cannon should the net be placed to catch Mercurio if he is to land at the same horizontal level as the cannon?

    Assume no effects due to air friction and use $g = 10$ ms^{-2}.

5 Two cricketers practise by throwing a cricket ball to each other, as shown in Figure 1.7

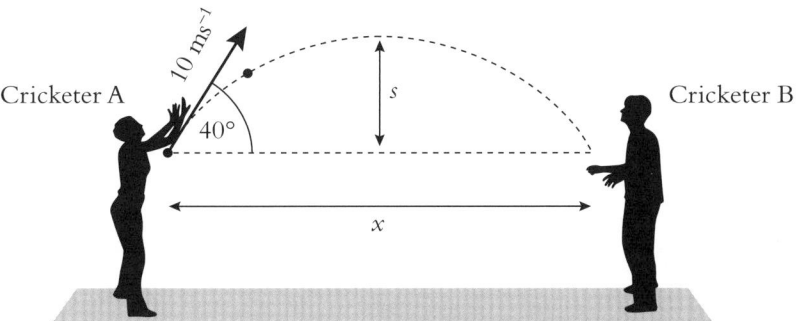

Figure 1.7

Ignoring any effects of air friction and using $g = 9.81\ \text{ms}^{-2}$, calculate:

a   the vertical component of the ball's velocity as it leaves cricketer A's hands,

b   the time it takes for the ball to reach its highest point,

c   the height, s, that the ball reaches above the cricketer's hands,

d   how far apart, x, the two cricketers are.

6 A projectile is fired from ground level to the top of a building which is 200 m away and 150 m high. If the projectile lands on the roof of the building 8.0 s later, ignoring any effects due to air friction, determine the initial velocity of the projectile. Use $g = 10\ \text{ms}^{-2}$.

> **TIP**
>
> With questions like this, sketch a diagram to help you visualise what is happening.

7 Physics questions about the motion of projectiles usually make the assumption that there are no effects due to fluid resistance. It is a simplification that allows physicists to model the motion of projectiles easily. Sometimes, however, the simple model and what happens in real life are not the same.

Figure 1.8 shows two ways in which the velocity of an object changes when it is dropped from a large height above the ground. Line A shows the simple model that assumes no effects due to fluid resistance, and curve B shows what actually happens in real life. Use $g = 10\ \text{ms}^{-2}$.

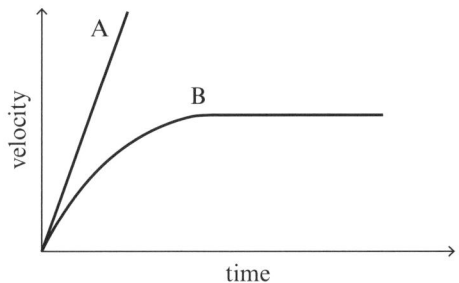

Figure 1.8

a State what the gradient of line A should be.

b Suggest why curve B is the shape it is. Your answer should make reference to the gradient of the curve and why it is not constant.

c Suggest why curve B flattens out to a horizontal line. How do physicists describe this motion?

d Sketch, on Figure 1.8, possible curves for an object of the:

   i   same mass but less density, labelled curve C,

   ii same mass but greater density, labeled curve D.

8 Abdul is playing a game of lawn tennis. When he serves, he tries to hit the ball from a height of 2.5 m. He wants the ball to travel 18.2 m horizontally before landing on the other side of the net. The net is 0.91 m high at its lowest point and is 11.9 m from Abdul.

Assume that the tennis ball travels horizontally from Abdul's racket, and there are no effects due to air friction. Use $g = 10$ ms^{-2}.

a Show that the time it takes for an object to fall, from rest, a distance of 2.5 m is 0.707 s.

b What does this suggest the initial horizontal speed of the tennis ball to be as it leaves Abdul's racket?

c How much time will the tennis ball have taken to reach the net?

d Show that the tennis ball will pass over the net.

In fact, according to the Lawn Tennis Association, the tennis ball may leave a server's racket at a speed of up to 230 km hr^{-1}.

e Calculate the (faster) speed of the tennis ball in ms^{-1}.

f How much time would this serve take for the ball to travel 18.2 m from the server?

g Is the time you calculated in part **f** sufficient for the ball to travel the vertical distance of 2.5 m in order to land in the serving box on the other side of the net?

h Suggest how a real serve in a tennis game differs from Abdul's 'ideal' serve described in this question. Outline what the effects of any differences are.

EXAM-STYLE QUESTIONS

Multiple choice questions

1. The following are three quantities used to describe the motion of a body:
   i   Displacement
   ii Velocity
   iii Acceleration
   Which of the following correctly describes the vector nature of the quantities?
   A i only
   B i and ii only
   C ii and iii only
   D i, ii and iii

2. The following are three statements about the motion of a body:
   i   A body moving with constant speed cannot be accelerating.
   ii A body moving always in the same direction could be accelerating.
   iii A body moving with a changing direction must be accelerating.
   Which of the following is/are true?
   A i only
   B ii only
   C iii only
   D i and iii

3. Which of the following statements about the motion of a body is **false**?
   A It is not possible to travel at a constant speed for 1 minute and have a displacement of zero.
   B It is not possible to travel at a constant velocity for 1 minute and have a displacement that is zero.
   C A body travelling for 1 minute with a changing velocity can have a final displacement of zero.
   D A body travelling with a constant velocity for 1 minute must have a non-zero displacement.

4. A man walks eastwards a distance of 4.0 km and then moves northwards a distance of 3.0 km.
   Which of the following statements correctly describes the overall displacement of the man?
   A 7 km in a direction that is 53° north of eastwards
   B 7 km in a direction that is 37° north of eastwards
   C 5 km in a direction that is 37° north of eastwards
   D 5 km in a direction that is 53° north of eastwards

5. A racing car accelerates from rest at 4 ms^{-2} until it has travelled a distance of 50 m. The final speed of the car is:
   A 10 ms^{-1}
   B 12.5 ms^{-1}
   C 20 ms^{-1}
   D 25 ms^{-1}

CONTINUED

6 In 1969 Neil Armstrong dropped a spanner whilst standing on the surface of the Moon, where acceleration due to gravity is $\frac{1}{6}$ of the Earth's. The time it took to fall to the Moon's surface was:

A $\frac{1}{6}$ of the time it would have taken on the Earth

B $\sqrt{\frac{1}{6}}$ times the time it would have taken on the Earth

C 6 times the time it would have taken on the Earth

D $\sqrt{6}$ times the time it would have taken on the Earth

7 Figure 1.9 shows four different journeys on the same velocity–time axes.

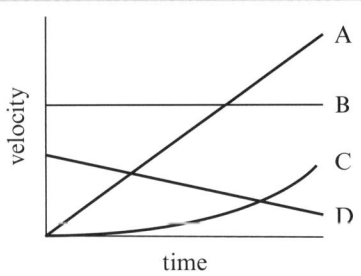

Figure 1.9

Which of the journeys shows an increasing acceleration?

8 The area under an acceleration–time graph is:

A Distance travelled

B Displacement

C Average velocity

D Change of velocity

Short answer questions

9 When a golfer hits a golf ball, the club head makes contact with the golf ball for a time of 0.4 ms. During this time, the speed of the golf ball increases from rest to 80 ms^{-1}.

   a Determine the average acceleration of the golf ball whilst in contact with the club head. [1]

   b Determine the distance that the golf ball travels during this time. [2]

   c High-speed photography has shown that during the contact between the club head and the ball, the ball squashes rather than remaining rigid. Suggest a reason why your answer to part **b** is supported by this observation. [1]

CONTINUED

10 Learning to drive a car usually involves understanding how far a car will travel when a driver applies the brakes in order to stop. This distance is called the stopping distance. It is made up of two components: the thinking distance and the braking distance.

thinking distance = initial speed × driver reaction time

braking distance = distance travelled whilst coming to a stop

A typical healthy driver has a reaction time of about 0.5 s and a typical family car can decelerate at about 5 ms^{-2}.

  a Complete Table 1.3. Some of the values have been calculated for you. [2]

Initial speed / ms^{-1}	Thinking distance / m	Braking distance / m	Stopping distance / m
0	0	0	0
5	2.5	2.5	5
10		10	
15			30
20	10		

Table 1.3

  b Use the data in your completed table to construct a graph of *stopping distance* against *initial speed*. [2]

  c Use your graph to estimate the initial speed of a car that requires 40 m of stopping distance. [1]

11 Figure 1.10 shows the velocity–time graph for a ball thrown vertically into the air and then caught by the thrower.

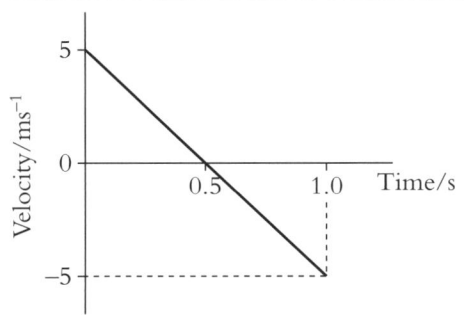

Figure 1.10

  a Show on the graph where the ball has reached its highest point. [1]
  b Use the graph to determine how high the ball reaches. [2]
  c Explain how the graph shows that the overall displacement of the ball is zero. [2]

CONTINUED

12 A firework rocket shoots vertically from the ground with a constant acceleration of 20 ms⁻² for 3.0 s, after which the rocket stops burning its fuel. The rocket continues upwards until it reaches its maximum height and then falls back to the ground. Assume there are no effects due to air friction and use $g = 9.81$ ms⁻².

    a Sketch a velocity–time graph for the rocket's journey. (It is not necessary to include any values on the axes of your graph; only the shape is required.) [1]

    b Calculate the maximum height reached by the rocket. [2]

    c Calculate the total flght time of the rocket. [2]

13 A projectile is launched horizontally at a speed of 40 ms⁻¹ from the top of a hill, 50 m above the ground. Ignoring the effects of air friction, and using $g = 9.81$ ms⁻², calculate the:

    a time it takes for the projectile to hit the ground, [1]

    b horizontal distance from the hill that the projectile travels, [1]

    c **total** velocity vector of the projectile **just before** it hits the ground. [3]

14 Figure 1.11 shows a velocity–time graph for a moving object.

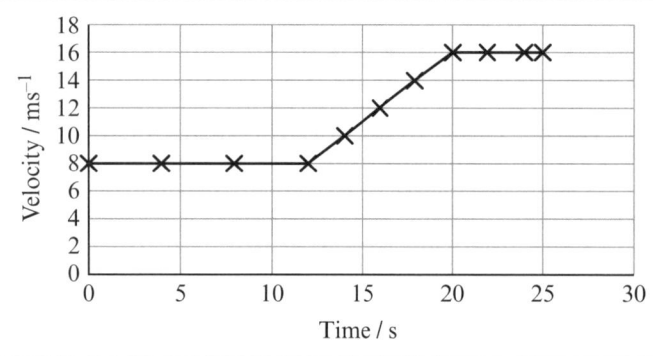

Figure 1.11

    a Determine the acceleration of the object between $t = 12$ s and $t = 20$ s [1]

    b Determine the total displacement of the object during its 25 s journey. [2]

    c Use your answer to part **b** to determine the average velocity of the object. [1]

CONTINUED

15 Figure 1.12 shows how the displacement of an object varies with time.

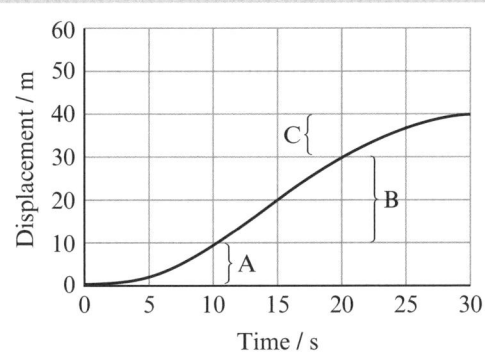

Figure 1.12

   a Describe how the velocity of the object is varying during each of the labelled sections of the graph, A, B and C. [3]
   b Estimate the velocity of the object during the section of the graph labelled B. [1]
   c Calculate the average velocity of the object during its 30 s journey. [1]

16 Figure 1.13 shows how the velocity of a wandering wild elephant varies with time.

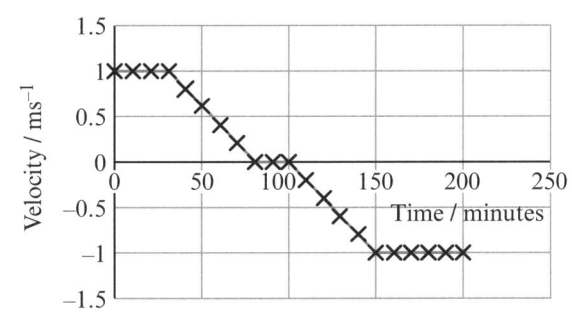

Figure 1.13

Use the graph to:
   a Estimate the acceleration (in ms^{-2}) of the elephant during the period 30 minutes to 80 minutes. [2]
   b Determine the total displacement (in metres) of the elephant during the 200 minute journey. [2]
   c Determine the average velocity (in ms^{-1}) of the elephant for the whole journey. [1]

CONTINUED

17 Figure 1.14 shows how the acceleration of an initially stationary object varies with time.

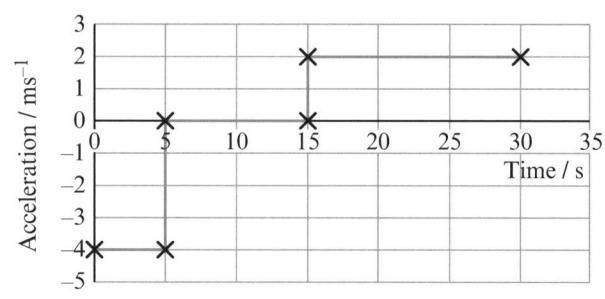

Figure 1.14

a Calculate how far the object moved in the first 5 s. [1]
b Draw a graph of *velocity of the object* against *time*. [2]
c Use your graph to determine the total displacement of the object during the 30 s journey. [2]

18 Figure 1.15 shows the graph of velocity against time for a moving object.

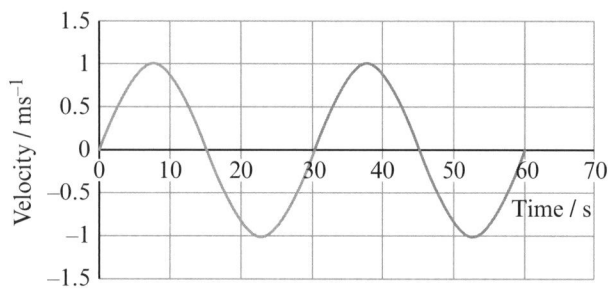

Figure 1.15

a Estimate the maximum acceleration of the object. [2]
b State the total displacement of the object during the 60 s period. [1]
c Describe the way in which the object is moving. [1]

Chapter 2
Forces and Newton's laws

CHAPTER OUTLINE

In this chapter, you will:

- consider forces as vector quantities.
- resolve forces into their components and reconstruct force vectors from their components.
- identify and draw diagrams of the forces that act on objects.
- use vector diagrams and trigonometry to solve problems about equilibrium.
- use Newton's laws of motion.
- identify the nature of some contact forces.
- examine the nature of circular motion.
- solve problems involving uniform circular motion and centripetal force.

KEY TERMS

force: the action of one body on a second body; unbalanced forces cause changes in speed, shape or direction

weight: the force of attraction between the mass of a planet and a body:
$W = mg$
where m is the mass of the body and g is the gravitational field strength of the planet

equilibrium: the state when the net force on a system is zero

net force: the one force whose effect is the same as that of a number of forces combined

tension: the force arising when a body is being stretched or compressed

normal contact force: the force between two touching bodies that is perpendicular to the touching surface

Hooke's Law: the tension in a spring is proportional to the extension or compression

CONTINUED

Newton's first law of motion: when the net force on a body is zero, the body will move with constant velocity (which may be zero); in other words, it will move on a straight line with constant speed (which may be zero)

Newton's second law of motion: the net force on a body of constant mass is proportional to that body's acceleration and is in the same direction as the acceleration)

Newton's third law of motion: if body X exerts a force on body Y, then body Y will exert an equal and opposite force on body X

dynamic friction: a force opposing motion when a body moves

static friction: a force opposing the tendency to motion when a body is at rest

coefficient of static friction: the ratio of the maximum force of friction between two bodies to the normal contact force when an object is at rest

coefficient of dynamic friction: the ratio of the force of friction to the normal contact force on a body that is sliding along a surface

drag force: the force acting against the motion of an object that is moving through a fluid (gas or liquid)

bouyant force: the force acting on an object in a fluid because the object is displacing some of the fluid

Archimedes' principle: When a body is wholly or partly immersed in a fluid it experiences an upward bouyant force, F_b, which is equal to the weight of the fluid displaced: $F_b = \rho V g$, where ρ is the density of the fluid being displaced, V the volume of displaced fluid and g the gravitational field strength.

time period, T: the time it takes for an orbiting object to make one complete orbit

frequency, f: the number of complete orbits made in one second

angular displacement: the angle through which an object has moved during its circular motion/orbit

angular speed: the angle through which an object moves per second when following a circular path:
$\omega = 2\pi f = \frac{v}{r} = \frac{2\pi}{T}$,
where f is the frequency of the rotation, r is the radius of the circular path and T is the time taken to move through one complete circle

centripetal force: the force, directed towards the centre of a circular orbit, necessary for a body to move in orbit; given as $F = \frac{mv^2}{r} = mr\omega^2 = mv\omega$

> **CONTINUED**
>
> **centripetal acceleration:** the rate of change of velocity of a body in orbit; given as $a = \frac{\Delta v}{\Delta t} = \frac{v^2}{r} = r\omega^2 = v\omega$ and is directed towards the centre of the circular orbit
>
> **free-body force diagram:** a diagram showing a body in isolation with all forces acting on it drawn as arrows

Exercise 2.1 Forces and their direction

The questions in this section will help you use vectors in diagrams and calculations and use the vector nature of forces to solve problems.

1   A force, F, has a magnitude of 6.0 N and is directed at an angle of 40° above the horizontal. Find

   a   the horizontal component of F.

   b   the vertical component of F.

2   Vector **X** has components: $\mathbf{X}_{horizontal}$ = 5 N and $\mathbf{X}_{vertical}$ = 4 N. Calculate

   a   the magnitude of **X**.

   b   the angle **X** makes with the horizontal.

3   Force F has components of (5, 3), Force G has components of (−3, 4) and Force H has components of (−2, −7). All three forces act on a point body.

   a   Draw a scale diagram to show that the net force on the point body is zero.

   b   Show, algebraically, that the net force on the point body is zero.

4   An object has three forces acting on it simultaneously:

   An upwards vertical force of 6 N, a left-to-right force of 3 N and another, unspecified force.

   If the object is in equilibrium, find the

   a   magnitude of the unspecified force.

   b   direction of the unspecified force.

> **TIP**
>
> To solve problems of this kind, first draw a diagram and then use trigonometry.

5 Figure 2.1 shows a mass hanging on a string at a particular moment.

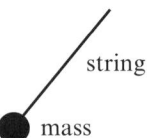

Figure 2.1

   a Copy the diagram and add to it all of the forces acting on the mass.

   b Explain why the mass is not in equilibrium.

6 A picture hangs on a wall by two strings. Each string makes an angle of 35° to the vertical. The tension in each string is 60 N.

   a Draw a labelled free-body force diagram for the picture.

   b Calculate the weight of the picture.

7 Figure 2.2 is a free-body force diagram showing three forces acting on a body.

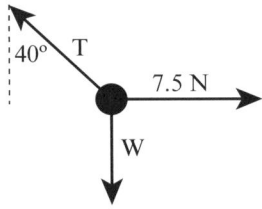

Figure 2.2

If the body is in equilibrium, find

   a the value of T.

   b the value of W.

8 Figure 2.3 shows how the length of a spring changes as it is stretched by a force.

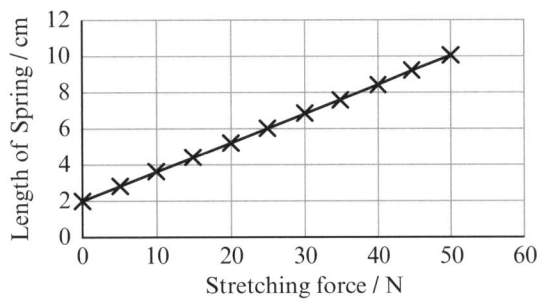

Figure 2.3

a Explain how the graph shows that the spring obeys Hooke's law.

b State the unstretched length of the spring.

c Use the graph to determine the spring constant of the spring.

9 Figure 2.4 shows a free-body force diagram for a book resting on an inclined slope. The book is not moving.

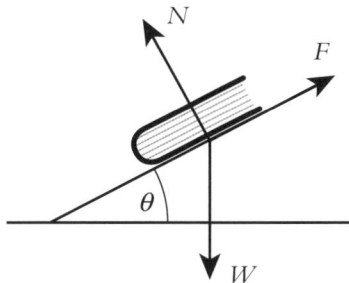

Figure 2.4

a By taking components of the forces along the slope and perpendicular to the slope, determine how F is related to N.

b How does your answer to **a** relate to the coefficient of static friction, μ_s?

c Explain why the book will eventually slip down the slope if the angle of the slope to the horizontal is gradually increased.

10 Air freight is off-loaded from an aeroplane by allowing the containers to slide down an inclined ramp at an angle of 30° to the horizontal. The coefficient of static friction between the containers and the ramp is 0.45.

Show that the containers are able to slide.

11 A box of mass 25 kg is being pulled across a horizontal surface at a constant speed by a rope at an angle of 40° to the horizontal. The tension in the rope is 150 N.

Determine the coefficient of dynamic friction, μ_d, between the box and the horizontal surface. ($g = 9.81$ Nkg^{-1})

12 a State Hooke's Law.

b For springs that obey Hooke's Law, calculate the tension in a

   i spring of spring constant 25 Nm^{-1} that has been extended by 30 cm.

   ii spring of spring constant 0.30 Nm^{-1} that has been extended by 2.5 mm.

c The overall spring constant of three identical springs in series is 12 Nm^{-1}. Determine the spring constant of one spring.

d The overall spring constant of two springs in parallel is 50 Nm^{-1}. Determine the spring constant of one spring.

13 A children's toy comprises a plastic semi-sphere mounted on top of a spring of spring constant 5×10^3 Nm^{-1}. The total mass of the toy is 25 g. The toy is used by compressing the spring by 1 cm. When it is let go, the toy jumps into the air. ($g = 10$ ms^{-2})

    a   Calculate the force in the fully compressed spring.

    b   Calculate the initial acceleration of the toy as the spring starts its return to its uncompressed length.

    c   Once the spring has regained its uncompressed length, the toy experiences only its downwards acceleration due to gravity. The time for this to happen is 4.5 ms. If we consider that the initial acceleration upwards decreases linearly with the compressed length of the spring, show that the initial speed at which the toy moves upwards is 4.48 ms^{-1}.

> **TIP**
>
> Use your knowledge of an acceleration–time graph to find the change in velocity of the toy.

    d   Calculate how high the toy can jump into the air.

14 a   State Archimedes' principle.

    b   Consider a cylinder of cross-sectional area A and height h immersed in a liquid of density ρ. The top of the cylinder is level with the surface of the liquid. The bottom of the cylinder is a distance h below the surface.

        i   Give an expression for the pressure in the liquid just underneath the cylinder at point P.

        ii   Give an expression for the upwards force on the underside of the cylinder due to the pressure in the liquid at a depth, h.

        iii   State an expression for the downwards force on the cylinder due to the atmospheric pressure, P_o.

        iv   Derive an expression for the buoyancy force; that is, the net upwards force on the cylinder due to the liquid.

        v   By finding an expression for the weight of the liquid displaced by the cylinder, show Archimedes' principle to be true.

        vi   If the cylinder just floats, what must its density be?

    c   A block of wood of density 1.1×10^3 kgm^{-3} has a mass of 100 kg. It is completely immersed in water.

        i   Determine the net force on the block of wood.

        ii   Does the block of wood float or sink?

15 Stokes' law states that the viscous drag force, F_d, acting on a sphere moving through a viscous fluid is $F_d = 6\pi \eta r v$, where η is the viscosity of the fluid, r the radius of the moving object and v the speed at which the object is moving through the fluid.

A sphere of lead of radius 1.5 mm falls at a constant velocity vertically through water of a viscosity 1.0×10^{-3} Nsm^{-2}.

a   Draw a free-body force diagram of the sphere showing the forces acting on the sphere.

b   By equating the weight of the sphere with its buoyancy force and its drag force, show that the terminal velocity of the sphere is given by the expression:

$$V_{terminal} = \frac{2r^2 g(\rho_{lead} - \rho_{water})}{9\eta},$$

where ρ_{lead} is the density of lead and ρ_{water} is the density of the fluid through which it is falling.

c   Given that the density of lead is 1.14×10^4 kgm^{-3}, calculate the speed at which the sphere is falling. ($g = 9.81$ Nkg^{-1})

d   In practice, such a sphere falling through water falls with a terminal velocity that is smaller than the value that Stokes' law predicts. Suggest a reason why this is.

e   If the same sphere were to fall through water of a higher temperature, state what would happen to the terminal velocity of the sphere and suggest a reason to support your statement.

> **TIP**
>
> Remember that there are two upwards forces acting on a falling body in a fluid.

16 A typical family car, of mass 1.2×10^3 kg, driving along a road is subject to two forces that act in the opposite direction to its motion. These two forces are dynamic friction between the tyres and the road and a frictional drag force caused by the car moving through the air.

   a   i   If the coefficient of dynamic friction, μ_k, is 0.02, calculate the dynamic friction force acting on the moving car. ($g = 9.81$ Nkg^{-1})

       ii How does this dynamic friction force change when the car's speed increases?

       The frictional drag force, F_d, acting on the car is given by

       $$F_d = \frac{1}{2} CA\rho v^2,$$

       where C is the drag coefficient (a value influenced by the design of the car), A is the cross-sectional area of the car, ρ is the density of the air and v is the speed of the car.

   b   For a typical family car, $C = 0.3$ and $A = 2.0$ m². Given that the density of air is 1.3 kgm^{-3}, calculate the speed at which frictional drag force is equal to the dynamic frictional force.

   c   Hence, determine the driving force from the engine necessary to maintain this constant speed.

   d   Most family cars are capable of travelling at 45 ms^{-1} (in most countries, this speed would be faster than the legal speed limit). With reference to the two frictional forces examined in this question, suggest why typical family cars are not designed to travel at speeds higher than this.

   e   Higher-performance cars and some high-end sports cars are designed to be able to travel at speeds higher than 45 ms^{-1}. Suggest how the design of these cars enables them to travel at such high speeds.

Exercise 2.2 Newton's laws of motion

The questions in this section will help you to learn and use Newton's three laws of motion.

1 a State Newton's first law of motion.

  b State what is meant by the term *equilibrium*.

  c Is it possible for a body to be in equilibrium if it is moving?

2 In which of the following situations is the body in equilibrium?

  a A helicopter is hovering 10 m above a landing site.

  b A car is travelling along a straight road at a constant speed.

  c A cyclist is riding around a bend in the road with a constant speed.

  d A skydiver is free-falling from an aeroplane at their terminal velocity.

3 a State Newton's second law of motion.

  b Use Newton's second law to define the unit of force, the Newton.

  c Use Newton's second law to complete the following table.

Net force / N	Mass / kg	Acceleration / ms^{-2}
120	50	
900		4.5
	6	0.25

Table 2.2.1

> **TIP**
>
> Try to learn formal definitions, such as Newton's laws of motion, word for word. They are often required in exams.

4 A bullet accelerates along the barrel of a rifle. Its speed changes from 0 ms^{-1} to 1500 ms^{-1} in a time of 0.1 s.

   The mass of the bullet is 0.05 kg. Calculate the average force acting on the bullet.

5 Figure 2.5 shows the free-body force diagram for a 12 g paper cone falling through the air.

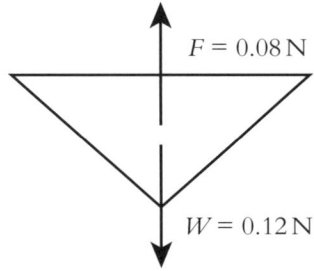

Figure 2.5

a Calculate the acceleration of the paper cone.

b Sketch a graph of *acceleration of the cone* against *time* for the next few seconds of its fall.

c Explain the shape of your graph using Newton's laws of motion.

6 a State Newton's third law of motion.

b Comment on whether the following pairs of forces are examples of Newton's third law pairs.

    i The gravitational force of the Moon on the Earth and the gravitational force of the Earth on the Moon

    ii The weight of a book resting on a table and the normal contact force of the table on the book

    iii The electrical force exerted by a proton on an electron in a hydrogen atom and the electrical force exerted by the electron on the proton

    iv The force exerted by a raindrop as it hits the ground and the force of the ground on the raindrop

7 Consider a person of mass 60 kg standing on a set of weighing scales in an elevator.

a If the elevator is moving at a constant speed, determine the reading on the weighing scales.

b i If the elevator is accelerating downwards with an acceleration of $0.25g$, determine the reading on the weighing scales. ($g = 9.81$ ms^{-2})

    ii How does this make the person feel?

c i If the elevator is accelerating upwards with an acceleration of $0.2g$, determine the reading on the weighing scales. ($g = 9.81$ ms^{-2})

    ii How does this make the person feel?

8 a Outline the way in which we are able to *know* things in the natural sciences.

b Outline what is meant by the term *law* in the natural sciences.

c Is it ever possible to *prove* a law in the natural sciences?

d How has our understanding of Newton's laws of motion changed as a result of Einstein's ideas about relativity?

Exercise 2.3 Circular motion

The questions in this exercise will help you improve your calculations and problem-solving involving circular motion.

1   The angular displacement made in one second is also called the angular speed, ω.

   a   i   Write the equation to show how ω is related to the time period, T, of rotation.

      ii   Write the equation to show how ω is related to the frequency, f, of the rotations.

   b   Calculate the angular speed, ω, of

      i   the Earth in its orbit around the Sun.

      ii   a children's carousel that makes one rotation in one minute.

      iii   the Moon that makes 13 rotations of the Earth in one year.

   c   The Singapore Flyer is a large Ferris wheel of radius 75 m, with observation pods for spectators on the circumference. It takes 30 minutes to make one complete rotation. Calculate the

      i   frequency of the Singapore Flyer's rotation.

      ii   angular speed of the Singapore Flyer.

      iii   linear speed at which one of the observation pods travels.

2   a   Any body that is performing circular motion is accelerating. Explain why this statement must be true.

   b   When a body is rotating in a circular motion, in which direction **must** there be an unbalanced force?

   c   What is the name of this unbalanced force that produces circular motion?

   d   Write the equation for the necessary force, F, required for a body to make a circular motion. Be sure to note what each of the terms in the equation means.

3   a   Sketch graphs to show how the acceleration of a body in circular motion depends on the

      i   body's mass, m.

      ii   body's linear speed, v.

      iii   radius of the circle in which it is moving.

> **TIP**
>
> Use the equations for centripetal acceleration and centripetal force.

b Sketch graphs to show how the force on a body undergoing circular motion varies with the

   i body's mass.

   ii body's linear speed.

   iii radius of the circle in which the body is moving.

4 The necessary centripetal force has to be provided by a real force occurring in the motion of an object. For each of the following examples, outline what the real force is that is providing the necessary centripetal force for circular motion.

   a The Moon in its orbit around the Earth

   b An electron in its orbit around a nucleus

   c A proton in its orbit around the Large Hadron Collider at CERN

   d A car moving on an arc of a circle on a bend in a road

   e A ball attached to light string being rotated in a horizontal plane

5 In one model of a hydrogen atom, the electron is considered to orbit the nucleus at a distance of 5.29×10^{-11} m. The electrostatic force between the proton and the electron is 8.23×10^{-7} N and the mass of the electron is 9.1×10^{-31} kg. Calculate the speed of the electron in its orbit around the proton.

6 a Consider a car travelling on a circular road at a constant speed.

   i How does the friction force between the road and the car's tyres depend on the car's mass?

   ii Derive an expression for the maximum speed of the car around the circular road. Show that this must apply to all cars, large or small.

   iii Explain why the maximum speed at which a car can travel safely on a circular road is likely to be slower when the road is wet or icy.

   b The exit road from a major motorway is usually an arc of a circle. The speed limit on this part of the road is always clearly shown as a motorist leaves the motorway.

   i Explain why the speed limit on the exit road of the motorway is always lower than the speed limit on the carriageway of the motorway.

   ii If the average coefficient of friction between the exit road and a car's tyres is 0.75 and the radius of the circular arc is 80 m, calculate the maximum speed at which a car can travel safely on the exit road without skidding.

   c The tyres of a car are worn. This has halved the coefficient of static friction between the road and the car's tyres. How has the maximum speed at which the car can travel safely around a bend changed?

7   A student attaches a small ball of mass 100 g to the end of a string of length 60 cm. The student makes the ball execute circular motion in the horizontal plane with a frequency of 2.5 Hz.

   a   Calculate the

      i   linear speed of the ball.

      ii   tension in the string.

   b   In fact, it is not possible for anyone to make a ball on the end of a string execute circular motion in an exactly horizontal plane.

      i   Explain why this must be the case.

      ii   Draw a free-body force diagram for such a ball on the end of a string being rotated.

   c   Must the actual tension in the string be smaller, the same or larger than when the string is perfectly horizontal?

   d   Which component of the tension is acting as the centripetal force?

   e   What is the other component of the tension force doing?

8   Consider a cyclist on a banked section of a circular track.

   a   Draw a free-body force diagram for the cyclist. (You do not need to think about the friction force between the cycle's tyres and the track.)

   b   Use your free-body force diagram to derive an expression for the angle, θ, of the banked track in terms of the speed of the cyclist, v, and the radius of the circular track, r.

   c   Explain why the angle of banking for an Olympic cyclist track is likely to be larger than that for an amateur cyclist track.

9   Figure 2.6 shows the path of a mass, m, which is being swung around by a light string in a vertical circle of radius r.

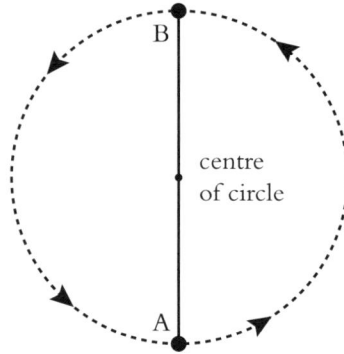

Figure 2.6

TIP

Remember that it is the net unbalanced force that acts as the centripetal force.

a Copy the diagram and add arrows to show the forces acting on the mass at position A.

b Derive an expression for the tension, T, in the string at position A.

c Derive an expression for the tension in the string at position B.

d What do you notice about the tension in the string as the mass moves in a vertical circle?

EXAM-STYLE QUESTIONS

Multiple-choice questions

1 An object of mass 2.5 kg falls vertically through the air with a downwards acceleration of 4.81 ms^{-2}. Taking $g = 9.81$ ms^{-2}, the size of the air resistance force acting on the object is
   A Zero.
   B 5.81 N.
   C 12.5 N.
   D 24.5 N.

2 Here are three statements about an object in motion:
   One: An object that is not accelerating must have a constant speed.
   Two: An object that is travelling at a constant speed cannot be accelerating.
   Three: An object that travels at a constant speed for a period of time cannot have zero displacement.
   Which of the following combinations of these three statements is **true**?
   A One only
   B One and Three only
   C Two and Three only
   D One, Two and Three

3 Here are three statements about an object:
   One: When all the forces acting on an object are balanced, the object must be stationary.
   Two: When all the forces acting on an object are balanced, the object cannot be accelerating.
   Three: When all the forces acting on an object are balanced, the object can be changing direction as long as its speed is not changing.
   Which of the following combinations of the statements is correct?
   A One only
   B Two only
   C One and Two only
   D Two and Three only

CONTINUED

4 An object starts from rest and accelerates uniformly at a rate of 5 ms^{-2} for 6 s. The distance travelled by the object after 6 s is

A 15 m.

B 30 m.

C 90 m.

D 180 m.

5 An object of mass 25 kg collides with, and exerts a force of 900 N on, an object of mass 100 kg. Which of the following gives the magnitude of the force that the 100 kg mass exerts on the 25 kg mass?

A Zero

B 225 N

C 900 N

D 3600 N

6 A block of wood floats on the surface of some water. Which of the following statements about the block may be incorrect?

A The net vertical force on the block is zero.

B The density of the block is the same as the density of water.

C The buoyancy force acting on the block is equal in size to the weight of the block.

D The density of the block cannot be greater than the density of water.

7 Figure 2.7 shows a block of stone resting on a slope. The weight of the block is W, and the normal contact force between the block and the slope is N. The frictional force between the block and the slope is F. At the angle θ, the block just starts to slide down the slope. If the coefficient of static friction between the block and the slope is μ, which of the following statements is correct?

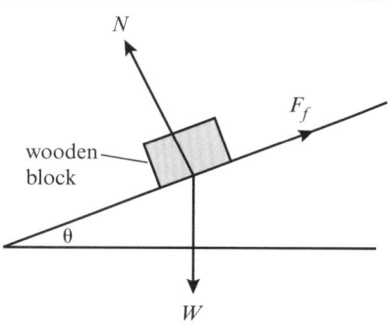

Figure 2.7

A $W = \mu N$

B $W \cos \theta = \mu N$

C $W \sin \theta = \mu N$

D $W \sin \theta = N$

CONTINUED

8 A mass of 300 g is hung from a spring of unstretched length 12.0 cm. The mass causes the spring's length to become 16.0 cm.

Which of the following is the best estimate of the spring constant of the spring?

A 0.8 Nm^{-1}

B 1.9 Nm^{-1}

C 7.5 Nm^{-1}

D 75 Nm^{-1}

9 Callisto and Europa are both moons of Jupiter. Here are some data about the two moons and their circular orbits:

- Europa's average speed in orbit is 1.7 times that of Callisto's average speed in orbit.
- Europa's mass is 0.43 times that of Callisto's mass.
- Europa's orbital radius is 0.35 times that of Callisto's orbital radius.

Which of the following is the best estimate of the ratio of the centripetal force acting on Europa to the centripetal force acting on Callisto?

A 0.28

B 1.0

C 2.1

D 3.6

10 A ball of mass m is attached to the end of a light string. The ball is made to rotate in a vertical circle of radius r so that it makes one complete rotation in a time T. When the ball is directly above the centre of the circular path, which of the following expressions gives the tension in the string?

A $\dfrac{4\pi^2 mr}{T^2}$

B $m\left(g - \dfrac{4\pi^2 r}{T^2}\right)$

C $m\left(g + \dfrac{4\pi^2 r}{T^2}\right)$

D $m\left(\dfrac{4\pi^2 r}{T^2} - g\right)$

Short-answer questions

11 A coal barge travels along a canal at a constant speed in the direction shown by the dotted line in Figure 2.8. The barge is pulled by two ropes, A and B such that the tension in rope A is 4.0 kN.

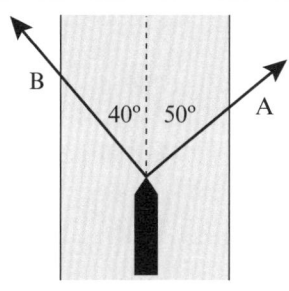

Figure 2.8

PHYSICS FOR THE IB DIPLOMA: WORKBOOK

CONTINUED

    a Calculate the size of the tension in rope B. [2]

    b Calculate the frictional drag force, F_d, between the barge and the water in the canal. [1]

    c The same barge is now pulled by two ropes in the same direction as those in Figure 2.8 during a very hot day (when the temperature of the water is increased) so that the speed of the barge is the same as it had been before.

        i State how the tension in the two ropes would have to differ. [1]

        ii Give a reason to support your statement. [1]

12 A spring of unstretched length 4.0 cm has a spring constant of 25 Nm^{-1}.

    a Calculate the length of the spring when a stretching force of 5 N is applied to it. [2]

    b If four such springs were connected end to end to make a longer spring of new length 16.0 cm, determine the extension of the longer spring if a stretching force of 5 N is applied to it. [1]

    c Calculate how many such springs would be required to be connected in parallel if a stretching force of 8 N causes an extension of 2 cm. [1]

13 A 4.0 kg mass rests on a set of weighing scales on the floor of an elevator. Complete the following table to show the reading you would expect from the weighing scales under the conditions of motion given. ($g = 10$ Nkg^{-1}) [5]

Motion of elevator	Reading on weighing scales / N
Stationary	
Moving upwards at 2.5 ms^{-1}	
Moving downwards at 2.5 ms^{-1}	
Accelerating upwards at 2.5 ms^{-2}	
Accelerating downwards at 2.5 ms^{-2}	

14 An amulet of mass 120 g hangs on a light necklace which is attached to the rear-view mirror of a car. When the car accelerates, the amulet moves backwards so that the necklace makes an angle of 20° with the vertical.

    a Calculate the tension in the necklace when the car is accelerating. [2]

    b Calculate the car's acceleration. [1]

    After travelling at a constant speed for a while, the car now decelerates at 5 ms^{-2}.

    c Determine what would happen to the amulet and necklace. [2]

15 A cricket ball of mass 125 g travelling at 40 ms^{-1} is caught by an inexperienced fielder. The fielder holds his hands, each of mass 400 g, rigidly still during the catch, which takes 0.2 s.

    a Calculate the average force applied by the fielder's hands to catch the ball. [2]

    b State the size of the force exerted by the ball on the fielder's hands. [1]

    One of the fielder's teammates suggests that next time he takes a catch, he should allow his hands to move backwards a little during the catch.

    c With reference to Newton's second and third laws, explain why the fielder should follow his teammate's advice. [2]

CONTINUED

16 Figure 2.9 shows a rectangular block of mass 12 kg sitting on a rough inclined plane.

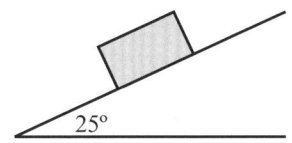

Figure 2.9

- **a** Add to the diagram to show all of the forces acting on the block. [2]
- **b** If the angle that the inclined plane makes with the horizontal were to be increased—even by a very small amount—the block will start to slide down the slope. Determine the coefficient of static friction between the block and the inclined plane. [1]
- **c** If the block were replaced by another block of the same material but of twice the mass, would the block still remain static? Explain your answer. [2]

17 During a thunderstorm a spherical hail stone of radius 3 mm falls through the air at a constant speed.
- **a** Calculate the weight of the hailstone. (density of ice = 920 kgm^{-3} and g = 9.81 Nkg^{-1}) [1]
- **b** If the viscosity of air is 1.8×10^{-5} Nsm^{-2}, calculate the speed at which the hailstone is falling. [2]
- **c** The frictional forces between the hailstone and the air cause the hailstone to melt without any loss of mass during its journey downwards, turning it into a raindrop.
  - **i** Given that the density of water is 1000 kgm^{-3}, would you expect the raindrop to fall at a smaller speed, the same speed or a higher speed compared to the hailstone? [1]
  - **ii** Justify your answer. [1]

18 A geostationary satellite has an orbital radius of 4.23×10^7 m and takes exactly one day to orbit the Earth. Calculate
- **a** the angular speed of the satellite, ω. [1]
- **b** the linear speed at which the satellite is travelling, v. [1]
- **c** the value of the Earth's gravitational field strength at this distance from the Earth. [2]

19 A car of mass 1250 kg travels at a constant speed along a curve in the road which is the arc of a circle of radius 75 m.
- **a** State the force that provides the centripetal force necessary for the circular motion of the car. [1]
- **b** Calculate the maximum speed at which the car can travel without skidding. (μ_s = 0.7) [2]
- **c** A truck, of double the mass of the car, follows the same path as the car.
If the coefficient of static friction remains the same, state the maximum speed at which the truck can travel without skidding. [1]

20 Sometimes, in competition ice skating, a male skater swings his partner around in a circle.
If the skater's arm makes an angle of 30° with the horizontal, and his 60 kg partner rotates around a circle of radius 2.2 m, calculate
- **a** the tension in the male skater's arm. [2]
- **b** the angular speed of his partner. [2]
- **c** the linear speed of his partner. [1]

Chapter 3
Work, energy and power

CHAPTER OUTLINE

In this chapter, you will:

- explore examples of work done by a constant force.
- use graphs of force against distance to determine work done.
- consider how work done on a system changes its kinetic energy.
- consider mechanical energy as the sum of kinetic and potential energies.
- examine examples of the conservation of mechanical energy.
- explore the different kinds of mechanical energy.
- solve problems involving the rate of work done by bodies.
- explore the efficiency of systems in terms of energy transfer or power generated.

KEY TERMS

work done: the product of the force in the direction of the displacement multiplied by the distance travelled:

$W = Fs \cos \theta$,

where θ is the angle between the direction of the force, F, and the direction of the displacement, s

work-energy principle: the net work done on a system is equal to the change in kinetic energy of the system

total mechanical energy: the sum of the kinetic energy, gravitational potential energy and elastic potential energy of a body

kinetic energy (E_K): the energy possessed by a body that is moving:

$E_K = \frac{1}{2}mv^2$,

where m is the mass of the body and v is its velocity

elastic potential energy (E_H): the energy stored in a body that has been stretched:

$E_H = \frac{1}{2}kx^2$,

where k is the spring constant of the body being stretched and x is the amount by which the body has been stretched.

> **CONTINUED**
>
> **gravitational potential energy (E_p):** the work done by a force in moving a body to a position above its initial position; for an Earth-mass system:
>
> $E_p = mgh$,
>
> where m is the mass of the body, g is the gravitational field strength near the surface of the Earth and h is the height above the body's initial position
>
> **power:** the rate at which work is being done (or energy is being dissipated):
>
> $P = \dfrac{W}{t}$,
>
> where W is the work done and t the time taken
>
> **efficiency, ε:** the ratio of useful work or power to input work or power:
>
> $\varepsilon = \dfrac{\text{useful energy out}}{\text{actual energy in}}$ or $\dfrac{\text{useful power out}}{\text{actual power in}}$
>
> **centripetal force:** a force pointing to the centre of a circular path

Exercise 3.1 Work

The questions in this section will help you become more familiar with the concepts of work and energy.

1. **a** Define what a Joule is.

   b State the principle of conservation of energy.

   c A pupil picks up a book from the floor and places the book on a table.

      i Has the book gained energy? Explain your answer.

      ii Has the pupil lost energy? Explain your answer.

      iii Why is it likely that the energy lost by the pupil is not the same magnitude as the energy gained by the book?

2. A mass of 300 g attached to the end of a light string is made to travel in a circular path of radius 1.2 m by a centripetal force of 4 N.

   a Calculate the distance travelled by the mass in one complete circle.

   b State the work done on the mass by the centripetal force during one complete circle. Explain your answer.

3   Figure 3.1 shows how the force required to push a thumbtack into a poster board varies with distance (how far it is pushed into the board).

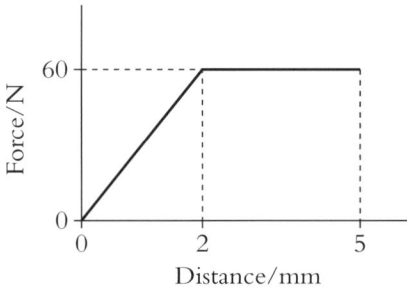

Figure 3.1

Use the graph to calculate the work done when pushing the thumbtack 5 mm into the board.

4   A driver applies the brakes of his 1400 kg car while travelling at 20 ms^{-1}. The car begins to slow down. If the average force of the brakes is 9 kN, calculate how far the car will travel until it comes to a stop.

5   Consider a body of mass m, on which a force, F, is applied for a time, t.

   a   Suggest **six** ways in which the force could affect the mass, and for each way, give an example.

   b   How does the principle of conservation of energy apply to this?

> **TIP**
>
> Think about the various different kinds of potential energy into which the work done can be transferred.

6   A net force is applied to a body of mass 25 kg. The body's speed changes from 10 ms^{-1} to 20 ms^{-1}.

   a   State the work–energy principle.

   b   Use the work–energy principle to calculate the net work done on the body.

   c   Suggest why the net work done on the body cannot be calculated using another method; for example, using the equations of kinematics (*SUVAT* equations).

7   An electron of mass 9.1×10^{-31} kg is travelling at 4×10^{6} ms^{-1}.

   a   Calculate the kinetic energy of the electron.

   b   How much work must be done on the electron to speed it up to double its original speed?

> **TIP**
>
> For questions like this, use the work-energy principle to solve the problem.

8   A toy train of mass 750 g moving at 1.5 ms^{-1} is brought to rest by a constant force over a distance of 8.0 m.

   a   Calculate the work done by the force.

   b   Calculate the size of the force.

9   A box of mass 12 kg is pushed from rest in a straight line along a frictionless surface. The box is pushed with a horizontal constant force of 36 N for 5 s.

   a   Calculate

       i   the acceleration of the box.

       ii the speed of the box after 5 s.

       iii the work done on the box during the 5 s period.

       iv the kinetic energy gained by the box.

   b   What does the principle of conservation of energy say about your answers to **parts iii** and **iv**?

10 In a game of cricket, a fast bowler releases the ball at 140 kmhr^{-1}. The ball has a mass of 160 g. Slow-motion cameras show that the ball loses about 15% of its kinetic energy during the 15 m distance from the bowler to the batsman.

   a   Determine the speed of the ball at its release in ms^{-1}.

   b   Calculate how much work is done on the ball by the friction of the air.

   c   Calculate the average force of air friction acting on the ball.

Exercise 3.2 Conservation of mechanical energy

The following questions will consolidate your use of the conservation of mechanical energy principle.

1   Calculate

   a   the kinetic energy of a tennis ball of mass 58 g travelling at 25 ms^{-1}.

   b   the gravitational potential energy of a bird of mass 40 mg flying at a height of 15 m above the ground ($g = 10$ Nkg^{-1}).

   c   the elastic potential energy stored in a spring stretched by a force of 3.5 N to an extension of 1.5 cm.

2   The total mechanical energy of a body is the sum of its kinetic energy and its potential energy.

   Calculate the total mechanical energy of a:

   a   5 kg mass moving at 2 ms^{-1} along the ground.

   b   4 kg mass sitting stationary on top of a cupboard at a height of 2 m.

   c   3 kg mass moving horizontally through the air at a speed of 4 ms^{-1}, 5 m above the ground.

d spring of spring constant 18 Nm⁻¹ stretched by a distance 8 cm, lying stationary on the floor.

e spring, of mass 20 g, stretched by 60 cm by a force of 5 N, moving horizontally at 2 ms⁻¹ 1.8 m above the ground.

3 It is said that Isaac Newton was inspired to develop the theory of gravitation by watching an apple fall from a tree.

   a Ignoring any effects due to air friction and taking $g = 10$ Nkg⁻¹, calculate the gravitational potential energy of a 100 g apple on a tree branch that is 6.0 m above the ground.

   b If the apple falls to the ground, use equations of kinematics to calculate

      i the time it would take to land on the ground.

      ii the speed of the apple just before it hits the ground.

   c Now use the conservation of mechanical energy to calculate the speed of the apple just before it hits the ground.

4 Figure 3.2 shows a large block of stone, of mass 3×10^3 kg, being pushed up a slope.

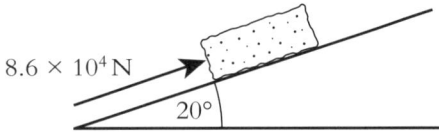

Figure 3.2

The slope is 15 m long. The force used to push the block of stone is 8.6×10^4 N.

   a Calculate the work done in moving the block of stone.

   b Calculate the gravitational potential energy gained by the block of stone.

   c How do you account for the difference between your answers to **parts a** and **b**?

5 A teacher drops his cup of coffee from a height of 1.5 m. The mass of the cup of coffee was 0.45 kg. Ignoring any effects of air friction:

   a Calculate the work done by the Earth's gravitational field on the cup of coffee.

   b Without referring to the principle of conservation of energy, show that the kinetic energy of the cup of coffee just before it hits the ground equals the work done by the Earth's gravitational field on the cup of coffee.

   c Verify that the gravitational potential energy lost by the cup of coffee is transferred into kinetic energy.

d When the cup of coffee hits the floor, it breaks and the pieces of the cup eventually stop moving. With reference to the principle of conservation of energy, suggest what has happened to the gravitational potential energy that the cup once had.

6 A children's toy comprises a plastic semi-sphere mounted on top of a spring of spring constant 5×10^3 Nm^{-1}. The total mass of the toy is 25 g. The toy is used by compressing the spring by 1 cm. When it is let go, the toy jumps into the air. ($g = 10$ ms^{-2})

a Calculate the total mechanical energy of the toy when the spring is fully compressed.

b By applying the conservation of mechanical energy, calculate the initial speed at which the toy moves upwards.

c Hence, calculate how high the toy can jump.

7 An athlete jumps on a trampoline. During a jump, the athlete, of mass 60.0 kg, reaches a height of 8.0 m above the trampoline bed, and when she lands back on the bed, the elastic surface deforms downwards by a distance of 0.7 m. Taking $g = 10$ Nkg^{-1} and ignoring any effects due to air friction, determine the spring constant of the trampoline bed.

> **TIP**
>
> In question 7, you will need to use SUVAT and the conservation of mechanical energy.

8 At Victoria Falls on the border between Zimbabwe and Zambia, there is a bridge over the Zambezi River, from which people bungee jump. Advertising literature states that the jumper falls a distance of 74 m before the stretched bungee cord halts their descent some 40 m or so above the river. The bungee cord is advertised as being 20 m long unstretched.

a Taking $g = 10$ Nkg^{-1}, and ignoring any effects due to air friction, calculate

  i the speed of a 70 kg jumper at the moment the bungee cord just starts to stretch.

  ii the time taken for the jumper to reach this point.

b The bungee cord stretches by 54 m.

  i Calculate the average acceleration of the jumper during the stretching of the bungee cord.

  ii Hence, calculate the time taken for the jumper to come to a stop at the bottom of his fall.

c Assuming that the bungee cord behaves according to Hooke's law, calculate the spring constant of the bungee cord.

9 A student wants to drive a spike into the ground by dropping a large mass onto it. If the necessary work done by the spike in being driven into the ground is 420 J, calculate the mass required by the student if he is going to drop the mass fom a height of 1.5 m. What assumptions have you needed to make?

Exercise 3.3 Power and efficiency

The questions in this section will help you improve solving problems involving power and efficiency.

1   In a water well, a motor lifts a 40 kg bucket 30 m in 12 s. Calculate the

    a   work done by the motor.

    b   output power of the motor.

2   A small car, whose engine is rated at 15 kW, travels at a constant speed of 20 ms^{-1}. Calculate the effective driving force of the engine.

3   Three boys are arguing about who is the most powerful. They each time themselves to do some work. Their results are given in Table 3.1.

Boy's name	Work done / J	Time taken
Anton	3.25×10^3	15 minutes
Ravi	90	25 s
Joshua	11.5×10^3	1 hour

Table 3.1

Which boy is the most powerful?

4   An athlete trains by running up a set of steps. The athlete, of mass 65 kg, runs up 5 m of steps in a time of 6 s.

    a   Calculate the power of the athlete.

    b   If the athlete's efficiency is 20%, how much energy has the athlete used?

5   Mount Snowdon in North Wales is 1085 m high. A popular way of reaching the summit is to walk along the Pyg Track, which is about 5 km long and takes a typical climber about 5 hours to complete.

If a chocolate bar contains 1.1 MJ of chemical energy and the human body is 25% efficient,

    a   calculate how many chocolate bars a typical climber of mass 75 kg would have to eat in order to be able to climb Mount Snowdon. ($g = 10$ Nkg^{-1})

    b   suggest why, in practice, it might require more than this.

    c   calculate the average power that a typical climber must develop during his ascent.

6   Garry and Anatoly are two boys using the gym. They both have a mass of 70 kg. Garry does 20 step-ups in 45 s, raising his centre of mass by 25 cm each time, whilst Anatoly does 12 pull-ups in 20 s, raising his centre of mass by 35 cm each time.

   a   Calculate

       i   Garry's power output.

       ii   Anatoly's power output.

   b   Which of the boys is likely to be out of breath after their exercise?

7   In a healthy human heart, blood is pumped into arteries 72 times per minute. 20 g of blood is accelerated from a speed of 0.20 ms^{-1} to a speed of 0.34 ms^{-1} in every heart beat. Calculate the power generated by a healthy human heart.

8   A crane on a construction site operates at an output power of 2.2 kW and has an operating efficiency of 0.35. If a steel girder of mass 400 kg is to be lifted to a height of 45 m, show that it would take the crane about 4 minutes to lift the girder. ($g = 10$ Nkg^{-1})

9   In 79 CE, Mount Vesuvius erupted, destroying the Roman towns of Pompeii and Herculaneum. Historical and scientific records have suggested that 1.36 Gkg of hot ash and rock were ejected per second to a height of 33.0 km—well into the stratosphere.

   a   Ignoring any effects due to air friction, at what speed must the ejected material have left the volcano?

   b   Calculate the power output of Mount Vesuvius.

   c   The Koeberg nuclear power station in South Africa has an output power of 1.86 GW.

       i   How many times more powerful was the volcanic eruption of Vesuvius in 79 CE than the Koeberg power station?

       ii   According to the *Washington Post*, there are about 62 500 power stations around the world. If the output of the Koeberg power station is considered to be typical of other power stations, how many times more powerful was the Vesuvius eruption than the total power output of the world's power stations?

Exercise 3.4 Energy transfers

1. A firework rocket of mass 50 g is set off from the ground. It travels vertically upwards until it explodes in a shower of brightly coloured sparkles.
   (Use $g = 10$ ms^{-2}.)

   a   Outline the energy transformations taking place as the rocket sets off and moves vertically upwards.

   b   When the rocket explodes at the top of its trajectory, what energy transformation(s) occur?

   c   If the rocket reaches 150 m above the ground when it explodes,

      i   what is the minimum amount of chemical energy the rocket stored before it was set off?

      ii   why is your answer to **part i** a minimum?

2. A worker pushes a large block of stone horizontally along some rough ground at a constant speed.

   a   Outline the energy transformations taking place.

   b   How does the horizontal component of the force being applied by the worker compare to the kinetic frictional force between the block and the ground?

   c   Suggest why the actual force applied by the worker is larger than the kinetic frictional force between the block and the ground.

3. A pendulum consisting of an inelastic string attached to a mass is made to oscillate to-and-fro with a large amplitude.

   a   Outline the energy transformations that occur during one compete oscillation.

   b   How might your answer to **part a** differ if the string were replaced by an elastic string?

4. Comets move in highly elliptical orbits around the Sun. Outline any energy transformations that take place during a comet's orbit.

5. A car is driving at a constant speed up an incline that is covered with loose gravel.

   List as many energy transformations that are occurring as you can.

6. Lord Rutherford and his research team of Hans Geiger and Ernest Marsden fired alpha particles (the nuclei of helium atoms) at nuclei of gold atoms to investigate the structure of atoms.

   Outline any energy transformations that occurred during the paths that the alpha particles followed as they approached and were deflected by the helium nuclei.

> **TIP**
>
> You may find this question easier to answer *after* you have worked through Unit D.

7 a Consider a mass tethered between two horizontal springs that is oscillating from side to side. Outline the energy transformations that take place during one complete oscillation. You may assume no friction.

b Now consider a mass oscillating in a vertical plane on the end of a spring. Outline the energy transformations taking place during one complete oscillation.

8 Outline the main energy transformations that take place in a hydroelectric power station.

9 a As far as we know, is the principle of conservation of energy universal? That is, can it be shown not to apply to all events and circumstances?

b Does the principle of conservation of energy suggest that the total energy of the universe is constant? Is it possible for us test this scientifically?

c The existence of friction forces (which we might understand to be really just electrostatic forces between electrons in atoms) means that bodies that move have some of their kinetic energy transformed into internal energy.

  i The whole universe is moving—and in some places (like here on the Earth) frictional forces can be quite large. Does this suggest that our universe must be getting warmer?

  ii Doesn't our current understanding of the evolution of the universe tell us that the universe is getting cooler, not warmer?

  iii How might you reconcile your answers to **parts i** and **ii**?

  iv Will there be a limit as to how warm—or cold—the universe can become?

  v What might the principle of conservation of energy imply if the universe actually reaches a constant temperature at some stage in the future?

> **TIP**
> This question may form the basis of a nice TOK-type lesson and should produce a good variety of responses from students.

EXAM-STYLE QUESTIONS

Multiple-choice questions

1. Which of the following statements is a correct definition for work done?
   - A The product of force and distance
   - B The product of force and distance moved in the direction of the force
   - C The product of force and displacement
   - D The product of power and time

2. A child pushes with a force of 100 N on a wall of mass 250 kg. The wall does not move. The work done by the child on the wall is
   - A 0 J.
   - B 100 J.
   - C 25 kJ.
   - D 250 kJ.

3. The best estimate of the kinetic energy of a hydrogen atom of mass 1.67×10^{-24} g moving at 500 ms^{-1} is
   - A 4×10^{-25} J.
   - B 2×10^{-22} J.
   - C 4×10^{-22} J.
   - D 2×10^{-19} J.

4. The best estimate of the tension in a piece of elastic of spring constant 30 Nm^{-1} stretched by 12.5 cm is
   - A 1.9 N.
   - B 3.8 N.
   - C 190 N.
   - D 380 N.

5. A centripetal force of 45 N causes a mass to move in a circular path of circumference 12.0 m. The work done on the mass by the centripetal force is
   - A 0 J.
   - B 45 J.
   - C 540 J.
   - D 5.4 kJ.

6. A book of mass 0.80 kg is pulled along a smooth surface by a force of 6.0 N applied at an angle of 60° to the horizontal. The book slides along the surface a distance of 1.5 m. The work done on the book by the force is
   - A 0 J.
   - B 4.5 J.
   - C 7.2 J.
   - D 9.0 J.

CONTINUED

7 A moving body has kinetic energy of E. How much work must be done on the body to increase its speed by a factor of three?

A $\frac{1}{3}E$

B $3E$

C $8E$

D $9E$

8 If a car's engine provides a driving force, F, and the car travels a distance, s, at a speed, v, during a time, t, which of the following statements about the power, P, developed by the engine is correct:

A $P = \frac{Fs^2}{t}$

B $P = Ft$

C $P = Fv$

D $P = \frac{Fv^2}{2}$

9 A firework rocket of mass 100 g uses 150 J of chemical energy to reach a height of 60 m. Which of the following is the best estimate of the efficiency of the rocket?

A 0.2

B 0.3

C 0.4

D 0.5

10 The human body is about 25% efficient. If an athlete accelerates a 7.3 kg shot from rest to a speed of 14 ms^{-1} in a time of 1.5 s, the power he needs to generate is approximately:

A 120 W

B 480 W

C 960 W

D 1900 W

Short-answer questions

11 A hammer of mass 1.6 kg moving at 2.0 ms^{-1} hits the head of a nail, comes to a stop, and drives the nail into a block of wood by a distance of 1.2 cm.

    a Calculate the kinetic energy lost by the hammer. [2]

    b Calculate the average force applied to the nail. [2]

12 A 5 kg mass is moving at 6 ms^{-1}.

    a Calculate the kinetic energy of the mass. [2]

    b Determine how much work must be done on the mass to increase its kinetic energy to 200 J. [1]

    c Calculate the speed of the mass if its kinetic energy = 200 J. [2]

CONTINUED

13 Figure 3.3 shows the force required to extend a spring plotted against the spring's extension.

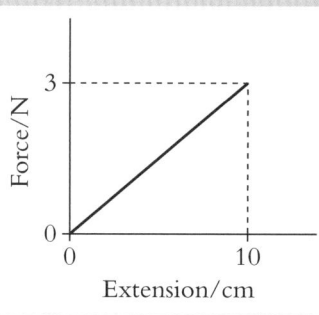

Figure 3.3

    a Outline how the graph shows that the spring obeys Hooke's law. [1]

    b Use the graph to calculate the

        i spring constant of the spring. [2]

        ii amount of elastic potential energy stored in the spring when it has been extended by 10 cm. [2]

14 A drinking glass falls to the floor from a table of height 1.2 m. Manufacturing statistics claim that the glass is likely to break if it hits the floor at a speed of more than 3.0 ms^{-1}. If the drinking glass has a mass of 150 g, taking $g = 9.81$ ms^{-2} and ignoring any effects due to air friction,

    a show that the glass loses about 1.8 J of gravitational potential energy in falling to the floor. [1]

    b state the kinetic energy of the glass just before it hits the floor. [1]

    c determine whether the glass is likely to break. [2]

15 A bow has an effective spring constant of 270 Nm^{-1}, and its string is drawn back a distance of 12 cm. When released, the bow fires an arrow of mass 30 g at an initial speed of X ms^{-1}.

    a Calculate the elastic potential energy stored in the bow when its string is drawn back. [1]

    b Calculate the kinetic energy of the arrow when the string is released. [1]

    c Calculate the efficiency of the bow. [1]

    d Suggest in which forms the 'lost' energy has been transferred. [2]

16 A librarian is filling a shelf with Physics books, each of which has a weight of 19.0 N. The librarian lifts each book a distance of 1.4 m, using up 798 J of energy in a time of 8 minutes.

    a Calculate how many books the librarian is able to put on the shelf. ($g = 10$ Nkg^{-1}) [2]

    b Calculate the useful power developed by the librarian. [1]

    c Suggest why the actual power developed by the librarian is likely to be significantly higher than your answer to **part b**. [2]

CONTINUED

17 a Define what is meant by the term *power*. [1]

    b A boy, of mass 50 kg, climbing a ladder, reaches a height of 4.5 m in a time of 12 s. Calculate the power developed by the boy. [2]

    c If the boy is 25% efficient, determine how much energy he used up to make the climb. [2]

18 A keen engineering student wants to build a set of weighing scales to find his own weight—and that of his friends. He has a large bag full of springs of spring constant 250 Nm^{-1}

    a Suggest how the student can determine his weight using the springs he has as well as any other equipment he will require. [3]

    b If the maximum amount that one of his springs can compress is 5.0 cm and the student's mass is 65 kg, calculate the minimum number of springs he will need to use. ($g = 9.81$ Nkg^{-1}) [2]

19 Three boys are trying to find out who is the most powerful. Table 3.2 shows some data on how they performed during a climbing test. ($g = 10$ Nkg^{-1})

Name	Mass / kg	Height climbed / m	Time taken / s
George	75.0	4.5	8.0
Remy	68.0	5.5	9.0
Andreas	82.0	4.0	7.0

Table 3.2

    a Which boy does the most work? [3]

    b Which boy is the most powerful? [2]

Chapter 4
Linear momentum

CHAPTER OUTLINE

In this chapter, you will:

- look at linear momentum as a vector quantity.
- consider Newton's second law in terms of a rate of change of momentum.
- relate impulse to a change in momentum.
- use force–time graphs to find an impulse.
- explore the conservation of linear momentum.
- solve problems involving a body's change in mass.
- solve problems in one- and two-dimensions involving collisions of two bodies.
- examine elastic and inelastic collisions between two bodies.
- look at problems involving explosions.

KEY TERMS

linear momentum: in the absence of an external force, linear momentum, $\vec{p}$, is the product of the mass of a body and its velocity:

$\vec{p} = m\vec{v}$,

where p is the momentum, m the mass of the body and v is the velocity of the body; note that the direction of the momentum is the direction of the velocity

impulse: the product of force and the time interval for which the force acts; it equals the change in momentum:

$J = \Delta p = \int F \, dt$

impulse = area under a graph of *force* against *time*

conservation of momentum: when the net force on a system is zero, the total momentum of the system remains constant

elastic collision: A collision in which the total kinetic energy before the collision equals the total kinetic energy after the collision; that is, E_K is conserved

inelastic collision: A collision in which the total kinetic energy after a collision is less than the total kinetic energy before the collision; that is, some E_K is lost during the collision.

Exercise 4.1 Newton's second law in terms of momentum

The questions in this section will help you to become familiar with the concept of linear momentum and the more formal definition of Newton's second law of motion.

1   a   Define the term *linear momentum*.

    b   Show that the units for momentum, kgms^{-1}, can also be written as Ns.

    c   Calculate the momentum of

        i   a girl of mass 50 kg running westwards at a speed of 6 ms^{-1}.

        ii   an electron of mass 9.1×10^{-31} kg travelling at a speed of 2.0×10^7 ms^{-1} towards an anode.

        iii a hockey ball of mass 110 g travelling at 60 ms^{-1} towards a goal.

> **TIP**
>
> Remember that momentum is a vector quantity and so it needs a direction.

2   Two bodies, A of mass 3.2 kg, and B of mass 5.0 kg, are both moving. A moves northwards at 2.5 ms^{-1} whilst B moves southwards at 1.5 ms^{-1}.

    a   Determine the total linear momentum of the system.

    b   A 400 = g mass moves horizontally at a speed of 3 ms^{-1}, and a 250 g mass moves vertically upwards at 4 ms^{-1}. Determine the total linear momentum of the system.

3   A mass of 4.0 kg, moving horizontally at 2.5 ms^{-1}, is acted on by a force for a time of 5.0 s, which makes the mass come to a stop. Use your knowledge of SUVAT equations to answer the following:

    a   What was the change in the velocity of the mass?

    b   What was the acceleration of the mass?

    c   Calculate the size of the force that acted on the mass.

    d   How does your answer show the direction of the force?

4   a   State Newton's second law in terms of momentum.

    b   Show that, if a body's mass does not change during an interaction, Newton's second law can be written $F = ma$.

5   A mass of 4.0 kg, moving horizontally at 2.5 ms^{-1}, is acted on by a force for a time of 5.0 s, which makes the mass come to a stop. Answer the following questions **without** referring to SUVAT equations.

    a   Determine the change in the momentum of the mass.

    b   Hence use Newton's second law to find the size of the force.

6   A mass of 12.0 kg experiences a force of 180 N for a time of 2.5 s. By how much will the speed of the mass change?

7 A mass of 600 g moving at 3.0 ms⁻¹ horizontally experiences a force of 180 N in the same direction as its travel. The mass accelerates to a speed of 4.5 ms⁻¹. Calculate the time for which the force acted on the mass.

8 A car travelling at 10 ms⁻¹ accelerates under a driving force of 5200 N for 5 s until its speed has increased to 30 ms⁻¹. Calculate the mass of the car.

9 A hose pipe squirts water horizontally at a wall. If the water jet has a cross-sectional area of A and the water, of density, ρ, hits the wall at a speed of v—and then falls off vertically:

   a Give an expression for the mass of the water that hits the wall per second

   b Hence determine an expression for the size of the force exerted by the wall on the water.

   c State the force—and its direction—exerted by the water on the wall.

   d A high-pressure washer emits water at a speed of 100 ms⁻¹ from a nozzle that is 1.5 mm in diameter. Calculate the size of this force. (ρ_{water} = 1000 kgm⁻³) Assume that the jet of water does not spread out after leaving the nozzle.

   e The pressure due to the atmosphere is about 1.0×10^5 Pa. How does the pressure exerted by the water jet compare to the atmospheric pressure?

> **TIP**
> Remember that
> pressure = $\frac{force}{area}$.

10 Photons of sunlight have a momentum of 1.3×10^{-27} N s and a kinetic energy of 2.5×10^{-9} J.

   If the received power of a solar panel is 1.0 kWm⁻²,

   a calculate the number of photons hitting the solar panel per second.

   b calculate the average force exerted on a square metre of the solar panel due to the photons.

   c if a typical solar panel has a collecting area of 12 m², calculate the total force on the solar panel.

   d should one be concerned about the force from the sunlight on an array of 10 solar panels fitted to the flat roof of a house?

Exercise 4.2 Impulse and force–time graphs

In this section the questions will help you become more familiar with the identity $J = F\,t$ and to use force–time graphs to solve problems involving impulses.

1 a State what is meant by the term *impulse*.

   b State the units of impulse.

2   Table 4.1 shows the momentum of a body before and after an interaction. For each example, determine the impulse.

	Momentum before interaction	Momentum after interaction
a	4.0 kgms⁻¹ vertically upwards	6.5 kgms⁻¹ vertically upwards
b	3.0 kgms⁻¹ vertically upwards	2 kgms⁻¹ vertically downwards
c	12.0 kgms⁻¹ horizontally	9.0 kgms⁻¹ vertically upwards

Table 4.1

> **TIP**
> Since momentum is a vector quantity, drawing a vector diagram may help to visualise the problem—and hence solve it.

3   A stationary pool ball, of mass 200 g, is struck by a cue with an average horizontal force of 60 N. If the contact time between the cue and the ball is 12 ms, calculate:

   a   the impulse felt by the ball.

   b   the speed of the ball immediately after impact.

4   A 60 kg woman jumps off a 3 m high wall onto the hard ground. Taking $g = 10$ Nkg⁻¹,

   a   calculate the impulse felt by the woman as she lands on the ground.

   b   when the woman lands, her body moves a distance of 1.5 cm. Calculate the average force exerted on the woman's feet and legs by the hard ground.

   c   if the woman had bent her legs whilst landing, her body would have moved a distance of 50 cm. Compare the force she would have experienced whilst bending her legs to the force you calculated in **part b**.

   d   Comment on why it is sensible to bend one's legs when landing on the ground from a jump.

5   Explain, with reference to the terms *impulse*, *force* and *time*, how crumple zones on a modern car reduce the chance of injury to its passengers.

6   A force of 3.2 N acting on a mass of 600 g decreases uniformly over a period of 8.0 s until it becomes zero.

   a   Sketch a graph of the force acting on the 600 g mass.

   b   Use your graph to determine the impulse felt by the mass.

   c   Hence, calculate the final speed of the mass.

7   Figure 4.1 shows how the unbalanced force on an initially stationary object of mass 3 kg varies with time.

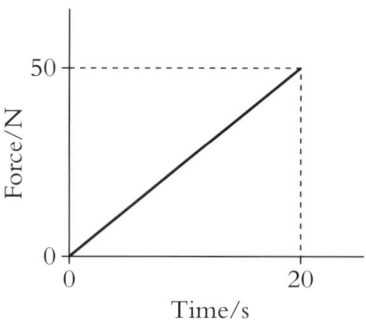

Figure 4.1

a   Use the graph to determine the impulse experienced by the object.

b   Sketch a graph of how the velocity of the object may be changing.

c   Calculate the final velocity of the object.

Exercise 4.3 Conservation of momentum

This section will help you perfect your problem-solving using the principle of conservation of momentum.

1   a   State the principle of conservation of linear momentum.

    b   Is the principle of conservation of momentum a universal law? Explain your answer.

2   A bullet of mass 25 g travelling at 120 ms^{-1} penetrates an initially stationary 1.5 kg block of wood and passes through, emerging with a speed of 85 ms^{-1}. If the block of wood is on a frictionless surface, use the principle of conservation of momentum to calculate the speed of the block of wood immediately after the bullet emerges.

3   A 4.5 kg block sliding along a horizontal frictionless surface at a speed of 4.0 ms^{-1} strikes and sticks to a stationary block of mass 1.5 kg. Use the principle of conservation of momentum to calculate the speed at which the two stuck-together blocks move.

4   A truck of mass 3.2×10^3 kg, including its load, is travelling along a road at a constant speed of 15.0 ms^{-1} when its load, of mass 800 kg, falls vertically from the back of the truck hitting the ground and stopping immediately. Calculate the speed at which the truck then travels.

5   A mass, X, of 450 g moving at a speed of 3.0 ms^{-1} collides head-on with a stationary mass, Y. Mass X stops and mass Y moves onwards at a speed of 5.0 ms^{-1}. Calculate the mass of Y.

6   A hummingbird of mass 5.0 g hovers by forcing air, of density 1.3 kgm^{-3}, downwards at a speed, v, below its wings of area 1.6×10^{-3} m^2. Calculate the value of v.

7   A mass, A, of 3.0 kg moving at 5.0 ms^{-1} collides head-on with a mass, B, of 2.5 kg moving towards it at a speed of 4.0 ms^{-1}. If the two masses stick together after the impact, calculate the speed at which they move after the collision.

8   Some chat on social media has suggested that if the total population of China were to jump to the ground from a height of 1.0 m at the same time, the motion of the Earth would change. Examine this claim using your knowledge of the conservation of momentum. (You may take the population of China to be 1.4×10^9, the mass of the Earth to be 6.0×10^{24} kg and make any other sensible assumptions necessary.)

9   To sustain nuclear fission in a nuclear power station 'fast' neutrons can be slowed down by their head-on bombardment elastically with stationary carbon nuclei. If the relative masses of neutrons and carbon nuclei are 1 and 12, respectively, determine the percentage by which a neutron slows down due to a collision with a carbon nucleus.

> **TIP**
>
> Question 9 is a more challenging question that requires the application of conservation of momentum and conservation of kinetic energy as well as some careful mathematical manipulation.

Exercise 4.4 Kinetic energy and momentum

In this section of questions, you will bring together your understanding of kinetic energy (which you explored in Chapter 3) and momentum to solve problems about collisions, interactions and explosions.

1   a   Show that the kinetic energy of a body of mass, m, and momentum, p, can be expressed as $E_K = \frac{p^2}{2m}$.

    b   Calculate the kinetic energy of
        i   a 3.0 kg mass with momentum 12.0 kgms^{-1}.
        ii an electron of mass 9.11×10^{-31} kg with a momentum of 5.4×10^{-24} kgms^{-1}.

    c   Calculate the momentum of
        i   a mass of 0.60 kg with a E_K of 30.0 J. (Direction not required.)
        ii a tennis ball of mass 58 g with a E_K of 26.1 J. (Direction not required.)

2   A body of mass 3 kg travelling horizontally at 4 ms^{-1} collides with, and sticks to, a stationary mass of 1 kg. Use the principle of conservation of momentum to calculate the speed of the combined masses after the collision.

3   A falling ball of mass 0.4 kg and speed 8 ms⁻¹ hits the ground and bounces back upwards with a speed of 5 ms⁻¹.

   a   Calculate the momentum of the ball *before* its collision with the ground.

   b   Calculate the momentum of the ball *after* its collision with the ground.

   c   How do you reconcile the principle of conservation of momentum?

4   A typical molecule of gas in the air has a mass of 4.8×10^{-26} kg and moves at 500 ms⁻¹. If such a molecule collides with, and rebounds elastically from, a flat surface,

   a   calculate the impulse felt by the molecule.

   b   state the impulse felt by the flat surface.

   c   if 2.1×10^{27} molecules collide with, and bounce off, 1 m² of the surface every second, calculate the pressure that the air exerts on the surface.

> **TIP**
>
> Remember that $1 \text{ Pa} \equiv 1 \text{ Nm}^{-2}$.

5   Marcus is at a shooting range, firing bullets at bales of hay with targets on them. He uses bullets with a mass of 250 g. The bullets travel at 450 ms⁻¹ when fired.

   a   Calculate the momentum of the bullet after it has been fired from the gun.

   Marcus hits the target. The bullet lodges inside the bale of hay in a time of 0.1 s. The bale of hay has a mass of 70 kg.

   b   Calculate the speed of the bale of hay just after it has been hit.

   c   Now calculate the force that the bullet exerted on the bale of hay.

   d   What do your answers to **parts b** and **c** tell you about the subsequent motion of the bale of hay?

6   One of the most famous experiments in the history of physics is the Rutherford α-particle scattering experiment. In this experiment, which helped Rutherford to formulate a new model for the structure of an atom, α-particles of mass 6.64×10^{-27} kg and kinetic energy 8.0×10^{-13} J were fired at gold nuclei of mass 3.29×10^{-25} kg. Very occasionally, an α-particle bounced backwards from its interaction with a gold nucleus. Such collisions were thought to be elastic.

   a   Calculate the speed of an α-particle as it starts to approach a gold nucleus

   b   Hence, calculate the impulse felt by the α-particle during its interaction with the gold nucleus.

   c   Calculate the recoil speed of the gold nucleus.

   d   Hence, calculate the E_K of the gold nucleus after the collision.

   e   Comment on the validity of the assumption that the collisions between the α-particles and gold nuclei were elastic.

7   Consider a steel sphere, of mass, m, colliding elastically head-on at a speed, u, with a stationary identical steel sphere.

   a   Use conservation of linear momentum to write a general expression for the total momentum before and after the collision.

   b   If the collision is elastic, write a general expression for the total kinetic energy before and after the collision.

   c   Show that the initially stationary sphere moves off at speed, u, and the initially moving sphere stops.

8   On take-off, a space rocket expels gas of speed 3.0×10^4 ms^{-1} at a rate of 1250 kgs^{-1}. Calculate the force exerted on the rocket by the expelled gas.

9   An eagle of mass 3.9 kg flying horizontally eastwards at a speed of 7.5 ms^{-1} collides with a seagull of mass 1.8 kg flying horizontally southwards at a speed of 3.0 ms^{-1}. On collision, the eagle holds the seagull firmly in its claws.

   a   Calculate the speed at which the two birds move after the collision.

   b   In which direction do the two birds move after the collision?

   c   Determine whether the collision was elastic or inelastic.

> **TIP**
>
> Draw a vector diagram to help you visualise what is happening.

10   A rifle of mass 2.970 kg fires a cartridge of mass 32.0 g at a speed of 500 ms^{-1}.

   a   Calculate the recoil speed of the rifle when firing.

   b   What is the minimum amount of chemical energy that must be available from the cartridge during firing?

EXAM-STYLE QUESTIONS

Multiple-choice questions

1   Which of the following statements about momentum, p, is correct?

   A $p = \frac{1}{2}mv^2$

   B $p = Ft$

   C $p = mv$

   D $p = \frac{F}{t}$

2   When two objects collide elastically, which of the following combinations of kinetic energy and momentum is correct?

   A   Kinetic energy = conserved; momentum = conserved

   B   Kinetic energy = not conserved; momentum = conserved

   C   Kinetic energy = conserved; momentum = not conserved

   D   Kinetic energy = not conserved; momentum = not conserved

CONTINUED

3   A car of mass 1250 kg accelerates from 10 ms⁻¹ to 24 ms⁻¹ in 7.0 s. The impulse felt by the car is

   A   2500 N s.

   B   8750 N s.

   C   17 500 N s.

   D   122 500 N s.

4   Which of the following expressions gives the correct units for impulse?

   A   N

   B   Ns⁻¹

   C   Nms⁻¹

   D   N s

5   Which of the following gives the correct units for power?

   A   kgms⁻²

   B   kgm²s⁻²

   C   kgm²s⁻³

   D   kgm³s⁻³

6   The area under a graph of *force* against *time* gives

   A   final velocity.

   B   final momentum.

   C   impulse.

   D   power.

7   The gradient of a graph of *momentum* against *time* gives

   A   force.

   B   impulse.

   C   average momentum.

   D   acceleration.

8   A rubber ball, of mass 250 g, travelling at 4.0 ms⁻¹ hits a wall perpendicularly and bounces off with a speed of 3.0 ms⁻¹. The time of impact is 0.2 s.

   Which of the following gives the best estimate of the average force exerted by the wall on the rubber ball?

   A   0.25 N

   B   1.25 N

   C   8.75 N

   D   50.0 N

9   Which of the following expressions is a correct relationship between kinetic energy, E_K, and momentum, p?

   A $E_K = \dfrac{mp^2}{2}$

   B $E_K = \left(\dfrac{p}{2m}\right)^2$

   C $E_K = \dfrac{p^2}{m}$

   D $E_K = \dfrac{p^2}{2m}$

CONTINUED

10 The momentum of a 4.0 kg mass with a kinetic energy of 200 J is

  A 20 kgms^{-1}.

  B 40 kgms^{-1}.

  C 60 kgms^{-1}.

  D 80 kgms^{-1}.

Short-answer questions

11 In a vehicle test centre, a car of mass 1200 kg crashes into a solid wall at a speed of 18 ms^{-1}. The car is not equipped with crumple zones. If the average stopping force exerted by the wall on the car is 3.0×10^5 N,

  a calculate the time it takes for the car to come to a stop. [2]

  b calculate how far a passenger not wearing a seatbelt would have travelled during the stopping of the car. [1]

  c discuss why the wearing of seatbelts in a car is compulsory. [1]

12 A body of mass 6 kg moving horizontally at a speed of 6 ms^{-1} collides with, and sticks to, a stationary mass of 3 kg. The collision between the two masses lasted for a time of 0.2 s.

  a Calculate the speed of the combined masses after the collision. [2]

  b Show that the force experienced by the 3 kg mass was 60 N. [1]

  c Determine whether the collision was elastic or inelastic. [2]

13 A car and a truck, both travelling at the same speed of 60 kmh^{-1} but in opposite directions, collide head-on. The truck has **twice** the mass of the car.

  a During the collision, how does the force experienced by the truck compare to the force experienced by the car? Explain your answer using one of Newton's laws of motion. [1]

  b If the two vehicles become entangled during the collision, calculate the speed of the vehicles immediately after the collision. [2]

  c Show that the collision was inelastic. [2]

14 The momentum of a 3.0 kg mass increases uniformly from zero to 15 kg ms^{-1} in a time of 20 s. Calculate the:

  a average force being experienced by the object. [2]

  b change in kinetic energy of the object during the 20 s period. [2]

15 In the alpha-decay of an Americium-241 nucleus, a $^{237}_{93}$Np nucleus moves away at a speed, v, while the alpha-particle moves away at a speed of 1.6×10^7 ms^{-1} in the opposite direction. The relative masses of the two particles are 237 and 4.

  a Determine the speed at which the $^{237}_{93}$Np nucleus moves after the emission of the alpha-particle. [2]

  b How does the kinetic energy of the alpha particle compare with the kinetic energy of the $^{237}_{93}$Np nucleus? [2]

CONTINUED

16 A stationary tennis ball of mass 58 g is struck by a racket. The way in which the force applied by the racket to the ball varies with time is shown in the simplified Figure 4.2.

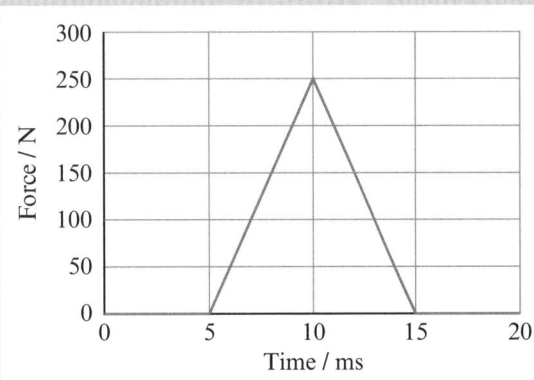

Figure 4.2

a Use the graph to determine the impulse felt by the tennis ball. [2]

b Hence, calculate the speed of the tennis ball after being struck by the racket. [1]

c If another racket with looser strings were to strike the tennis ball with the same maximum force, suggest how the speed of the tennis ball would be different, if at all, to your answer in **part b**. [2]

17 The graph in Figure 4.3 shows how the force acting on a toy train of mass 2.2 kg varies with time.

a Calculate the total impulse felt by the toy train. [2]

b Calculate the final speed of the train. [1]

c Calculate the average power developed by the force. [2]

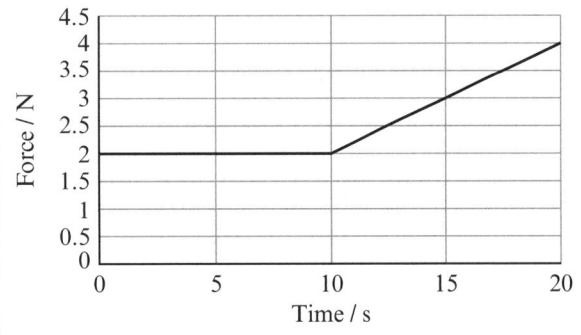

Figure 4.3

CONTINUED

18 In a desalination plant, salt is deposited vertically, with no appreciable kinetic energy, at a uniform rate of 30.0 kgs^{-1} onto a conveyor belt moving horizontally at a constant speed of 2.5 ms^{-1}. Giving your answers to an appropriate number of significant figures, calculate

    a the force required to keep the conveyor belt moving at a constant speed. [1]

    b the power required to maintain this constant speed. [2]

    c change of kinetic energy of the salt after landing onto the conveyor belt. [1]

19 A spacecraft, of mass 12500 kg, has a rocket engine that ejects 4.0 kg of hot gas every second at a speed of 250 ms^{-1}. Calculate

    a the force on the spacecraft. [1]

    b the acceleration of the spacecraft. [1]

    c the impulse felt by the spacecraft if the rocket engine were used for a time of 20 s. [1]

    d the change in speed of the spacecraft. [1]

20 In the radioactive process of β$^+$ emission, a positron, of momentum 9.2×10^{-23} N s, and a neutrino, of momentum 5.3×10^{-23} N s are emitted at right angles to each other from an unstable nucleus of mass 3.9×10^{-25} kg. Calculate

    a the momentum of the new nucleus. [3]

    b the velocity of the new nucleus. [1]

    c the E_K of the new nucleus. [1]

> Chapter 5
Rigid body mechanics

CHAPTER OUTLINE

In this chapter, you will:

> use the terms *angular displacement*, θ; *angular velocity*, ω; and *angular acceleration*, α.

> learn and use the equations of motion for uniform angular acceleration.

> use graphs to represent motion with uniform, or non-uniform, angular acceleration.

> learn about the torque, τ, of a force about an axis.

> examine examples of rotational equilibrium.

> examine the rotational acceleration caused by an unbalanced torque.

> learn and use the term moment of inertia, I.

> use Newton's second law for rotation to solve problems involving torque, moment of inertia and angular acceleration.

> look at the conservation of angular momentum, L.

> examine the term *angular impulse*, ΔL, and how to determine it from a torque–time graph.

> use the equation $\Delta L = \Delta(I\omega)$ to solve problems involving angular momentum, angular impulse, changes of moment of inertia and coupled pairs of objects.

> solve problems involving the kinetic energy of rotational motion.

KEY TERMS

angular displacement: the angle through which something has rotated; measured in rad

angular velocity: the rate at which something is rotating: $\overline{\omega} = \frac{\Delta \theta}{\Delta t}$; measured in rads^{-1}

angular acceleration: the rate of change of angular speed; $\overline{\alpha} = \frac{\Delta \omega}{\Delta t}$; measured in rads^{-2}

CONTINUED

These definitions are analogous to definitions of linear quantities:

Linear quantity	Angular quantity
Position, s	Anglular displacement, θ
Linear velocity, v	Angular velocity, ω
Acceleration, a	Angular acceleration, α

So, if a formula applies to the linear quantities, a similar formula will apply to the angular quantities:

Linear quantity	Angular quantity
$s = ut + \frac{1}{2}at^2$	$\theta = \omega_i t + \frac{1}{2}\alpha t^2$
$s = \frac{u+v}{2}t$	$\theta = \frac{\omega_i + \omega_f}{2}t$
$v = u + at$	$\omega_f = \omega_i + \alpha t$
$v^2 = u^2 + 2as$	$\omega_f^2 = \omega_i^2 + 2\alpha\theta$

torque: the product of the magnitude of the force and the perpendicular distance between the line of action of the force and the axis of rotation: $\tau = Fd$ or $\tau = Fd\sin\theta$

translational equilibrium: the net force of the body is zero

rotational equilibrium: the net torque on the body is zero

moment of inertia: the distribution of mass of an extended body about an axis of rotation: $I = \sum m_i r_i^2$

angular momentum: the product of mass, speed and orbit radius of a particle; $L = I\omega$

conservation of angular momentum: when the net torque on a system is zero, the angular momentum is conserved; that is, it stays constant

angular impulse: the change in angular momentum

kinetic energy of rotational motion: $E_K = \frac{1}{2}I\omega^2$

Newton's second law for rotational motion: $\tau_{net} = I\alpha$

Exercise 5.1 Kinematics of rotational motion

The questions in this section will help you solve problems involving the rotational motion of objects.

1   a   Define the terms

    i   *angular displacement*.

    ii *angular velocity*.

  b   Calculate the angular velocity, ω, of the

    i   second hand of a clock.

    ii minute hand of a clock.

    iii hour hand of a clock.

  c   The hour hand of a clock is 1.5 cm long, its minute hand is 2.0 cm long and its second hand is 2.5 cm long. Calculate the linear speed of the tip of the

    i   second hand.

    ii minute hand.

    iii hour hand.

> **TIP**
> It's always a good idea to show all your work when doing calculations.

2   On a children's funfair ride, Lek sits on a unicorn, which is 2.5 m from the axis of rotation. Lek's brother, Yai, sits on a tiger, which is 4.5 m from the axis of rotation. The merry-go-round completes ten rotations during their 5-minute ride.

  a   Calculate the angular velocity, ω, of the funfair ride.

  b   Calculate

    i   the linear speed of Lek's unicorn.

    ii the linear speed of Yai's tiger.

3   a   Define the term *angular acceleration*.

  b   A cylinder making 300 rotations in one minute slows down. After 5 s, it makes 120 rotations per minute. Calculate the cylinder's

    i   initial angular velocity.

    ii final angular velocity.

    iii angular acceleration.

4   A disc rotating with an angular velocity of $\omega = 40$ radians s^{-1} is subject to an angular acceleration of 5 radians s^{-2} for 6 s.

a Sketch a graph to show how the angular velocity of the disc varies with time.

b Determine the

    i final angular velocity of the disc.

    ii total number of rotations that the disc makes during the 6 s period.

5 The Sun has an equatorial radius of 6.96×10^5 km. It rotates with a period, at the equator, of 24.47 days. The Earth's equatorial radius is 6.37×10^3 km.

Calculate the ratio of the Sun's

a angular velocity at the equator to the Earth's angular velocity at the equator, $\frac{\omega_S}{\omega_E}$.

b linear speed at its equator to the Earth's linear speed at its equator, $\frac{v_S}{v_E}$.

6 Calculate the

a angular acceleration of a rotating object that takes 4.0 s to change its angular velocity from 20.0 radians s^{-1} to 15 radians s^{-1}.

b time it takes for an initially non-rotating object to reach an angular velocity of 600 radians s^{-1} if its angular acceleration is 15 radians s^{-2}.

c total angle turned through if an object initially rotating with an angular velocity of 15 radians s^{-1} is subject to a constant angular acceleration of 2.0 radians s^{-2} until it reaches a final angular velocity of 40 radians s^{-1}.

7 A car travelling at 10.0 ms^{-1} decelerates to rest at a constant rate over a distance of 50.0 m. The wheels, with their tyres, have a radius of 40.0 cm. Calculate the

a initial angular velocity of the wheels.

b number of rotations that the wheels make whilst the car is slowing down.

c angular acceleration of the wheels.

d time it took the car to stop.

> **TIP**
>
> Use the equations of motion for rotational motion in the same way you would use the equations of motion for linear motion.

8 The graph in Figure 5.1 shows how the angular velocity of the hard drive of a laptop computer changes with time when the laptop is switched on.

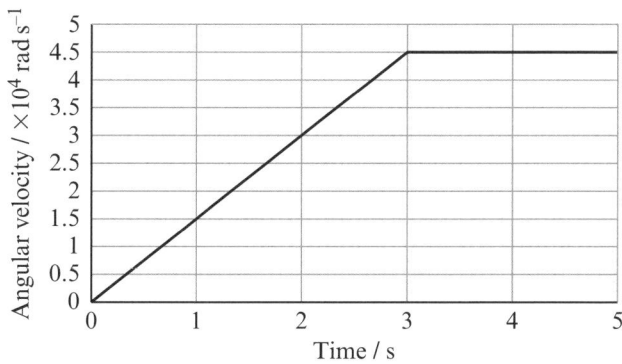

Figure 5.1

Use the graph to find

a the angular acceleration of the hard drive during the first 3 s.

b the total number of revolutions made by the hard drive during the 5 s period.

9 This question will solve a problem in rotational kinematics by two methods: graphically and mathematically.

Figure 5.2 shows how the angular velocity of a fan blade changes with time when it is first switched on.

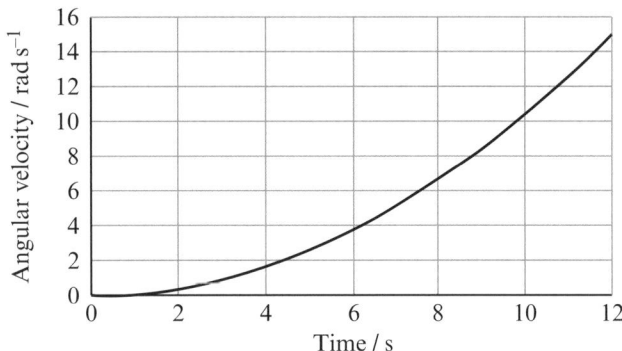

Figure 5.2

a First, we will solve the problem graphically.

   i Use the graph to estimate the instantaneous angular acceleration of the fan blade after 6.0 s.

   ii Use the graph to estimate the average angular velocity of the blades during the 12 s period.

b Now we will solve the problem mathematically.

   The equation for the angular velocity, as shown in Figure 5.2, is $\omega = \frac{2\pi}{60}t^2$.

   i By differentiating the equation for ω, find the instantaneous angular acceleration of the fan blade after 6.0 s.

   ii By integrating the equation for ω over the 12 s period, find the total angle through which the fan blade rotated and hence the average angular velocity during the 12 s period.

Exercise 5.2 Rotational equilibrium and Newton's second law

The questions here will help you to perfect your solving of problems associated with how Newton's second law applies to rotational motion.

1   a   Define the term *torque*.

    b   State the units for torque.

    c   Calculate the torque produced by a

        i   perpendicular force of 250 N acting at a distance of 60 cm from an axis of rotation.

        ii force of 400 N acting 3.0 m from an axis of rotation at an angle of 30° to the line joining the axis of rotation and the point where the force is applied.

2   a   Explain what is meant by a *couple*.

    b   Explain why an object subjected to a couple will be in translational equilibrium but not in rotational equilibrium.

    c   What will happen to the angular velocity of a rotating object if it is subject to a constant couple?

3   The lid of a jar of preserves has a radius of 3.5 cm. To unscrew the lid requires a couple of 15 Nm.

    a   If the lid is to be opened by hand, calculate the minimum force that must be applied to each side of the lid if it is to turn.

    b   A kitchen gadget, with 15-cm-long handles, can clamp onto the lid. Calculate the minimum force that must be applied to the gadget's handles to unscrew the lid.

    c   Suggest why consumers are happy to buy such a gadget rather than just use their hands.

> **TIP**
>
> Think about how what you have learned and how it relates to you—and other people.

4   Figure 5.3 shows a ladder standing against a frictionless wall. The ladder is 8.0 m long. The coefficient of static friction between the foot of the ladder and the ground is 0.25 and W = 500 N.

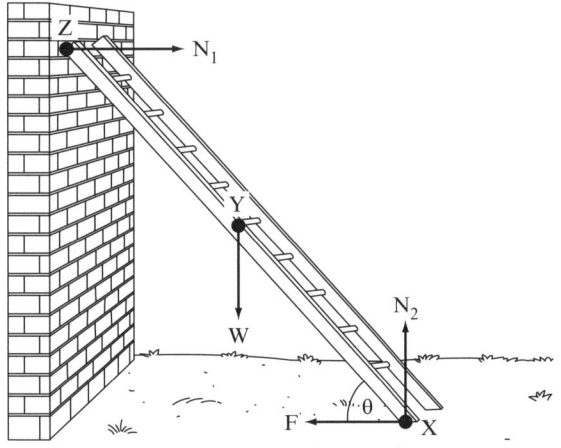

Figure 5.3

a   i   State the condition necessary for translational equilibrium.

    ii State the condition necessary for rotational equilibrium.

b   i   Identify the four forces labelled in Figure 5.3.

    ii Use your answer to **part a i** to find two equalities relating the four labelled forces.

c   Now apply the condition for rotational equilibrium: By taking the axis of rotation to be the point X, find the minimum angle, θ, that will allow the ladder not to fall to the ground.

d   Repeat **part c** but, this time, take the axis of rotation to be point Y.

e   Repeat **part c** again but, this time, take the axis of rotation to be point Z.

f   What do you learn from this?

5   a   Define the term *moment of inertia*, *I*.

    b   Outline why *I* is often thought of as analogous to the mass of an object.

    c   State the equivalence of Newton's second law of linear motion for rotational motion.

6   Determine the moment of inertia, *I*, of

    a   the point mass of 0.20 kg rotating about a centre of rotation of radius 0.40 m.

    b   two point masses, each of 0.20 kg, each rotating in the same way around an axis of rotation of radius 0.40 m.

    c   two point masses, each of mass 0.20 kg, each rotating in the same way about an axis of rotation of radius 0.80 m.

    d   What do you notice about how the

        i   mass of a point mass affects its moment of inertia?

        ii   distance from the axis of rotation affects the moment of inertia?

7   A circus performer rotates a 300 g flat plate on a thin rod by applying a force of 20 N tangentially to its rim. The plate's radius is 20.0 cm.

    a   The moment of inertia of the plate is given by $I = \frac{1}{2}MR^2$. Calculate the angular acceleration of the plate.

    b   As the plate rotates, the circus performer drops a 120 g lump of mashed potato onto it, 12 cm from the axis of rotation. The potato sticks to the plate. He continues to apply the same force. Calculate the new angular acceleration.

8   A cylinder of mass 6.0 kg and radius 0.3 m can rotate around an axis of rotation that passes through its centre of mass. If a constant force of 4.0 N is applied tangentially to the edge of the cylinder, calculate the angular velocity of the cylinder after 8.0 s.

Exercise 5.3 Angular momentum

The questions in this exercise will help you become more familiar with angular momentum and how to use the conservation of momentum to solve problems in rotational dynamics.

1   **a**   **i**   Define the term *angular momentum* for a body rotating about a fixed axis.

        ii   Give the units of angular momentum.

    b   **i**   Define the term *angular impulse*.

        ii   Give the units for angular impulse.

    c   For translational motion, Newton's second law is $F_{net} = \frac{\Delta p}{\Delta t}$. For rotational motion, Newton's second law is $\tau_{net} = \frac{\Delta L}{\Delta t}$.

        i   State what each of the terms in Newton's second law for rotational motion are.

        ii   Show that if the moment of inertia of a body remains constant then Newton's second law for rotational motion can be given as $\tau_{net} = I\alpha$.

        iii   What is the translational motion equivalent to $\tau_{net} = I\alpha$?

> **TIP**
>
> Exam questions frequently ask for definitions. Make sure you learn definitions by heart.

2   Calculate the angular momenta of

   a a mass of 450 g rotating on the end of a string of length 1.5 m at 2 revolutions s^{-1}.

   b a homogeneous sphere of radius 3.0 cm and mass 0.25 kg spinning at 50 revolutions s^{-1} about an axis that passes through its centre of mass.

   c a uniform cylinder of mass 4.0 kg and radius 4.0 cm spinning about its long axis at 20 revolutions s^{-1}.

3   The Earth has a mass of 6.0×10^{24} kg. If we model the Earth as a uniform sphere of radius 6400 km that spins on its axis once per day,

   a calculate the Earth's angular momentum.

   b calculate the force required, if applied tangentially, and continuously, at the surface of the Earth to bring the Earth to a stop within 1 year. (1 year is 3.15×10^7 s.)

4   Figure 5.4 shows how the torque acting on a cylinder of radius 3.0 cm and mass 4.0 kg varies with time. The torque is directed to increase the rotation rate of the cylinder.

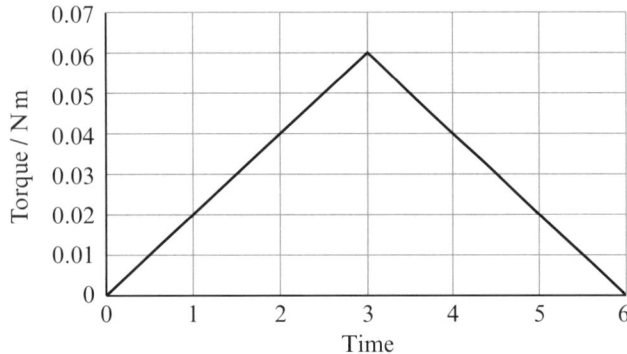

Figure 5.4

   a Use the graph to determine the angular impulse felt by the cylinder.

   b If the cylinder had been rotating at 15 revolutions s^{-1}, calculate the new rotation rate of the cylinder. ($I = \frac{1}{2}MR^2$ for a cylinder)

   c Calculate the rotational kinetic energy of the cylinder after speeding up its rotation.

5   A simple model of a clutch assembly for a motorbike consists of two coaxial circular discs, X and Y, each of radius 12.0 cm. Both discs can rotate without friction. Disc X, of mass 2.5 kg, is made to rotate, from rest, to 3 revolutions s^{-1} by a torque, τ, in a time of 1.5 s. ($I = \frac{1}{2}MR^2$ for a disc.)

   a Calculate the angular momentum gained by disc X.

TIP

Use the conservation of angular momentum.

b Hence, calculate the torque, τ, required to accelerate the disc.

c When a gear is engaged, disc Y, of mass 4.5 kg, which had previously been at rest, is pushed against disc X so that the two discs stick together due to the friction between the disc faces. Calculate the new new number of revolutions that the two-disc system makes per second.

6 a State the equation for the kinetic energy of a body of mass, M, moving along with a linear speed, v.

b State the equation for the rotational kinetic energy of a body of mass, M, rotating at an angular velocity, ω.

c Calculate the total kinetic energy of a cricket ball of radius 3.5 cm and mass 163 g rolling along a horizontal surface without slipping at a linear speed of 4.0 ms^{-1}.

(The moment of inertia of a sphere of mass, M, and radius, R, is $\frac{2}{5}MR^2$.)

7 A sphere of mass, M, and radius of 5.0 cm rolls, without slipping, down a sloping surface of length 1.5 m in a time of 6.0 s.

(The moment of inertia of a sphere of mass, M, and radius, R, is $\frac{2}{5}MR^2$.)

a Use the equations of linear kinematics to determine the speed of the sphere when it reaches the end of the sloping surface.

b Calculate the angular velocity of the sphere at the end of the sloping surface.

c Show that $gh = \frac{7}{10}v^2$ where h is the height of the top of the sloping surface above its bottom.

d Calculate h.

8 Consider two solid cylinders, A and B. A has a radius of 0.20 m and a mass of 1.25 kg, and B has a radius of 0.80 m and a mass of 20.0 kg. Both cylinders are released at the same time, from rest, to roll down a sloping surface, without slipping, so that they both end up 0.20 m below where they began.

a Show that both cylinders will reach the bottom of the sloping surface travelling at the same speed.

b Calculate the final speed of the cylinders at the bottom of the sloping surface.

c Which famous experiment does this make you think of?

d How might you explain this to a young physics student?

EXAM-STYLE QUESTIONS

Multiple-choice questions

1 Which of the following gives the units used by physicists and engineers for the quantity torque?
   A Nm
   B J
   C Nm^{-1}
   D kgm^2

2 The correct units for angular momentum are
   A kgms^{-1}.
   B Nms^{-1}.
   C kgms^{-2}.
   D kgm^{2}s^{-1}.

3 The angular velocity of the minute hand on a clock is
   A $\frac{2\pi}{60^2}$.
   B $\frac{2\pi}{60}$.
   C $\frac{\pi}{6}$.
   D 2π.

4 The London Eye is a cantilevered observation wheel of radius 60 m, which rotates once every 30 minutes. The best estimate of the linear speed of one of its observation pods on the circumference of the wheel is
   A 3 cms^{-1}.
   B 20 cms^{-1}.
   C 2 ms^{-1}.
   D 3 ms^{-1}.

5 If a net torque of 2.5 N m is applied constantly to an initially stationary wheel of moment of inertia 12 kgm^2, the angular velocity of the wheel after 1 minute will be
   A 0.21 rads^{-1}.
   B 1.25 rads^{-1}.
   C 1.99 rads^{-1}.
   D 12.5 rads^{-1}.

6 A mass of 400 g, attached to a light string of length 60 cm, follows a circular path that takes 0.5 s for one complete revolution. The angular momentum of the mass–string system is
   A 0.29 kgm^{2}s^{-1}.
   B 0.48 kgm^{2}s^{-1}.
   C 0.90 kgm^{2}s^{-1}.
   D 1.8 kgm^{2}s^{-1}.

CONTINUED

7 A solid cylinder of mass, M, and radius, R, rolls from rest down an incline without slipping through a vertical height, h. Given that the moment of inertia of a cylinder is $\frac{1}{2}MR^2$, the linear speed of the cylinder at the bottom of the incline is

- A $\sqrt{\frac{2}{3}gh}$.
- B $\sqrt{\frac{3}{4}gh}$.
- C $\sqrt{\frac{4}{3}gh}$.
- D $\sqrt{2gh}$.

8 The rotational kinetic energy of a rotating disc is E. If the same disc now rotates at twice the previous rate, its rotational kinetic energy will be

- A $\frac{E}{2}$.
- B E.
- C $2E$.
- D $4E$.

9 The moment of inertia of a sphere is $\frac{2}{5}MR^2$ where M is the mass and R the radius of the sphere. When rolling, without slipping, the ratio of the sphere's translational kinetic energy to its rotational kinetic energy is

- A $\frac{2}{5}$.
- B $\frac{5}{2}$.
- C $\frac{5M}{2}$.
- D $\frac{2R}{2}$.

10 A rotating disc of moment of inertia, I, and initial angular velocity, ω, is slowed down by a constant torque, τ, until it comes to rest. The number of revolutions made by the disc whilst slowing down is

- A $\frac{I\omega^2}{4\pi\tau}$.
- B $\frac{I\omega^2}{2\pi\tau}$.
- C $\frac{\pi I\omega^2}{\tau}$.
- D $\frac{2\pi I\omega^2}{\tau}$.

Short-answer questions

11 The Earth spins on its axis once per day and orbits the Sun once per year. The radius of the Earth is 6.37×10^6 m and its average distance from the Sun is 1.5×10^{11} m. If we model the Earth as a homogeneous sphere in a circular orbit around the Sun,

   a calculate the angular velocity of

      i the Earth spinning on its axis. [1]

      ii the Earth in its orbit around the Sun. [1]

   b Calculate the ratio of the linear speed of a point on the equator to the linear speed of the Earth in its orbit around the Sun. [2]

CONTINUED

12 A car travelling at 20 ms⁻¹ has wheels (tyres included) of radius 30 cm.
   a Calculate the angular velocity of the wheels. [2]
   b If the car slows down at a uniform rate of 2.5 ms⁻² until it stops, calculate how many revolutions the wheels will make whilst stopping. [2]
   c Calculate the angular acceleration of the wheels whilst stopping. [1]

13 A constant torque of 30 N m acts on a bicycle wheel of radius 40 cm and moment of inertia 850 kgm².
   a Calculate the angular acceleration caused by the torque. [1]
   b Calculate how many revolutions the wheel makes per second if the torque acts for 5 minutes. [2]
   c Calculate the linear speed of the bicycle after 5 minutes. [1]

14 A metal disc of radius 0.25 m is made to rotate from rest by applying a tangential force of 0.5 N to the edge of the disc. If the disc takes 3.0 s to make its first complete rotation, calculate
   a the angular acceleration of the disc. [1]
   b the moment of inertia of the disc. [2]
   c the mass of the disc. $\left(I = \frac{1}{2}Mr^2\right)$ [1]

15 A glass marble of radius 1.25 cm and mass 20 g rolls, without slipping, a distance of 30 cm down a slope of gradient 15°.
   a Calculate how much GPE the marble loses at the bottom of its roll. ($g = 9.81$ Nkg⁻¹) [1]
   b Calculate the translational speed of the marble at the bottom of its roll. (The moment of inertia of a sphere is $\frac{2}{5}MR^2$.) [3]
   c Hence, calculate the time the marble takes to complete its roll. [1]

16 A mass of 1.5 kg attached to a light string of length 60 cm is made to rotate from rest to an angular velocity of 30 rads⁻¹ in a time of 4.5 s.
   a Calculate the final angular momentum of the mass on the string. [2]
   b Calculate the kinetic energy gained by the mass. [1]
   c Calculate the torque required to make the mass rotate at this angular velocity. [1]

17 a A sphere of mass 20 kg and radius 40 cm is spinning about its axis at 300 rotations per minute. Calculate the sphere's
      i angular velocity.
      ii angular momentum. [2]
   b State the principle of conservation of angular momentum. [1]
   c Suppose that, while spinning, a point mass of 4.0 kg fell onto the sphere and attached itself to the sphere's surface. Calculate the new rotation rate of the sphere with the mass attached. [2]

CONTINUED

18 An ice skater with her arms outstretched has a moment of inertia of 4.5 kgm². She spins about a vertical axis at 0.8 revolutions s⁻¹. She then pulls her arms inwards so that they are flat against her body, making her moment of inertia change to 0.8 kgm².

    a Outline why the skater's angular momentum is conserved. [1]

    b Suggest what will happen to her angular velocity. [1]

    c Calculate the skater's new angular velocity. [1]

    d Calculate the change in the skater's rotational kinetic energy. [2]

19 A mother of mass 65 kg stands at the centre of a children's roundabout. The roundabout has a radius of 3.5 m and moment of inertia of 1100 kgm². It is rotating at 1.5 rads⁻¹. The mother walks radially outwards towards her daughter, who is sitting on the edge of the roundabout.

    a Calculate the angular velocity of the roundabout when the mother reaches her daughter. [2]

    b Calculate

        i the rotational kinetic energy of the roundabout when the mother is standing at the centre. [1]

        ii the rotational kinetic energy of the roundabout when the mother is standing at the edge. [2]

Chapter 6
Relativity

CHAPTER OUTLINE

In this chapter, you will:

> understand the meaning and use of the terms *reference frame* and *inertial reference frame*.

> explore Galilean relativity and its transformation equations for position, time and velocity.

> learn Einstein's two postulates of special relativity.

> see how the postulates of special relativity lead to the Lorentz transformation equations for events occurring in two reference frames.

> explore how to use the Lorentz transformation for relativistic velocity addition.

> learn that a spacetime interval between two events is an invariant quantity.

> learn and use the terms *proper time interval* and *proper length*.

> solve problems involving time dilation and length contraction.

> explore relativistic simultaneity.

> learn about and use spacetime, or Minkowski, diagrams.

> relate the angle between a worldline and the time axis on a spacetime diagram to a particle's speed.

> see how muon decay provides experimental evidence for time dilation and length contraction.

KEY TERMS

event: something that happens at a particular point in space and time

reference frame: a set of coordinate axes and a set of clocks at every point in space

inertial reference frame: a reference frame in which Newton's first law of motion is obeyed

CONTINUED

Galilean transformation equations:

$x = x' + vt$

$x' = x - vt$

$t' = t$

$u' = u - v$

Einstein's postulates: 1. all the laws of physics are the same in all inertial frames; 2. the speed of light in a vacuum is the same for all inertial observers

Lorentz transformations:

$\gamma = \dfrac{1}{\sqrt{1 - \dfrac{v^2}{c^2}}}$

$x' = \gamma(x - vt)$

$x = \gamma(x' + vt')$

$t' = \gamma\left(t - \dfrac{v}{c^2}x\right)$

$t = \gamma\left(t' + \dfrac{v}{c^2}x'\right)$

spacetime interval: $(\Delta s)^2 = (c\Delta t)^2 - (\Delta x)^2$

proper time interval: the time interval between two events that occur in a reference frame in which both events occur at the same position

proper length: the length of an object measured by an observer in a frame of reference in which the object is stationary with respect to the observer

time dilation: an observer with respect to whom a clock moves, measures a longer time interval between the ticks of the clock than the observer at rest relative to that clock; $\Delta t = \gamma \Delta t'$

length contraction: the length of an object that moves past an observer is shorter than the length of the object in a frame where it is at rest; $L' = \dfrac{L}{\gamma}$

simultaneity: events that take place at the same time are said to be simultaneous

spacetime diagram: a graph in which the y-axis represents time (although it is more usually given as ct), and the x-axis represents position, x; single events are then shown by a dot on the diagram

worldline: a line on a spacetime diagram relating a sequence of events, the angle of which is related to the speed at which something is moving:

$\tan \theta = \dfrac{x}{ct} = \dfrac{v}{c}$,

where θ is the angle between the worldine and the ct axis

Exercise 6.1 Reference frames and Lorentz transformations

The questions in this section will help you learn how objects moving very quickly do not follow the Galilean transformation equations and require the use of special relativity transformation equations involving the Lorentz transformation.

1   Use the Galilean transformations to solve the following examples.

   a   A student standing by a two-lane road sees a truck travelling at 12 ms^{-1}. A car is travelling at 18 ms^{-1} in the same direction. Determine the velocity of the:

   i   car as observed by the truck driver

   ii truck as observed by the car driver.

   b   A nitrogen molecule moving vertically upwards at 500 ms^{-1} passes an oxygen molecule travelling vertically downwards at 438 ms^{-1}. Determine the velocity of the

   i   nitrogen molecule as observed by the oxygen molecule.

   ii oxygen molecule as observed by the nitrogen molecule.

2   The Michelson–Morley experiment is important for the history of physics.

   a   Sketch a diagram of the apparatus used by Michelson and Morley. Add rays of light to show how an interference pattern is formed for the observer.

   b   In part of the experiment, the whole set of apparatus was rotated through 90°. Why did Michelson and Morley do this?

   c   Explain the purpose of the moveable mirror.

   d   What did Michelson and Morley notice from their results?

   e   Explain how their results helped to confirm what Einstein and Maxwell had predicted for the speed of light.

> **TIP**
>
> Make sure you have learnt about this famous experiment; it is so important in the history of physics.

3   Pete and Jonathan are sitting on a bus travelling forwards at 15 ms^{-1}. Pete is 3 m behind Jonathan. Pete throws a chocolate bar to Jonathan at a speed of 6 ms^{-1}.

   Ellie and Oscar saw Pete throw the chocolate bar: Ellie was sitting on the bus, and Oscar was standing on the road watching the bus pass by.

   a   i   Explain what is meant by *a frame of reference*.

       ii Explain what is meant by *an inertial frame of reference*.

   b   At what speed does Ellie see the chocolate bar travelling?

   c   Does the bus's speed affect Ellie's observation of the chocolate bar's speed? Explain your answer.

d At what speed does Oscar see the chocolate travelling?

e Does the bus's speed affect Oscar's observation of the chocolate bar's speed? Explain your answer.

f In Ellie's frame of reference, how far did the chocolate bar travel?

g Show that, in Ellie's frame of reference, the time taken for the chocolate bar to complete its journey from Pete to Jonathan is 0.5 s.

h Oscar also measures the time of the chocolate bar's journey as 0.5 s. How far did Oscar see the chocolate bar travel?

i Have Ellie and Oscar used the same physics laws to find the distance, speed and time for the chocolate bar?

j How was Newton able to explain why the laws of physics are the same for different frames of reference, even if two observers see the same event differently?

k Write Einstein's first postulate of special relativity.

4 An observer in an inertial frame of reference, S, observes an event occur at (x, t). An observer in a reference frame, S', moving with a speed, v, relative to S, observes the same event occur at (x', t')

    a Use the Lorentz transformations to show how:

        i x' is related to v, x and t

        ii x is related to v, x' and t'

        iii t' is related to v, t and x

        iv t is related to v, t' and x'.

    b What assumption is made in expressing these equations?

5 An observer in an inertial frame of reference, S, wants to measure the length of an object. They would find the position of one end of the object, x_1, at a time t_1, and the position of the other end of the object, x_2, at a time t_2, and then say that the length of the object, Δx, is $x_2 - x_1$.

Another observer in frame S', moving at a speed, v, relative to S, wants to measure the length of the same object.

    a Using the Lorentz transformation, write expressions for x_1' and x_2'.

    b If $\Delta x' = x_2' - x_1'$, show that $\Delta x' = \gamma (\Delta x - v\Delta t)$.

6 An observer in frame S wants to measure how long something takes to occur. They will measure the start time of an event, t_1, at a place x_1, measure the end time of the event, t_2, at a place x_2 and then say that the event took a time of $\Delta t = t_2 - t_1$.

Another observer in frame S', moving at a speed, v, relative to S, wants to measure how much time the event has taken.

    a Using the Lorentz transformation, write expressions for t_1' and t_2'.

    b If $\Delta t' = t_2' - t_1'$, show that $\Delta t' = \gamma \left(\Delta t - \frac{v}{c^2} \Delta x \right)$.

7 An observer on Earth sees a rocket travelling away from Earth at a speed of $0.7c$. The rocket fires a projectile forwards at a speed of $0.3c$ relative to it.

    a Calculate the speed that the observer on the Earth measures for the projectile.

    b Suppose that, instead of firing a projectile, the rocket fired a laser. By calculating the speed that the observer on the Earth measures for the leading edge of the laser beam from the rocket, show that the relativistic addition of velocities is consistent with the second postulate of relativity.

8 A spacecraft launches two pods in opposite directions. Pod A leaves the spacecraft at a speed of $0.6c$, and pod B leaves the spacecraft at a speed of $0.7c$. What speed does pod A measure for pod B?

Exercise 6.2 Effects of relativity

In this exercise you can practise solving a range of problems using the Lorentz transformation.

1 **a** Explain what is meant by the term *invariant*.

    b **i** Define the spacetime interval, Δs.

        ii By using the Lorentz transformations show that the spacetime interval is invariant.

    c Define the following terms:

        i Rest mass

        ii Proper length

        iii Proper time

2 Figure 6.1 shows a light source on the floor of a closed container of height H. The container is initially at rest with respect to the ground. An observer inside the container uses a clock to measure the time it takes for light to travel from the source to the top of the container.

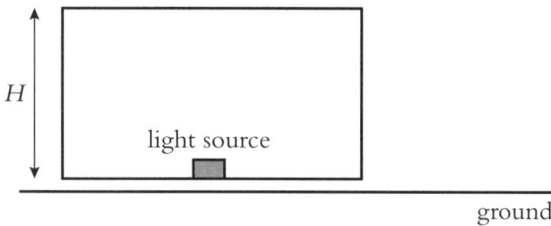

Figure 6.1

a i Write an expression for the time it takes for light to travel from the source to the top of the container to give the value that the observer inside the container measures. Call this t.

   ii If another observer, outside the container, also measures the time it takes for the light to reach the top of the container, will this observer measure the same time? Explain your answer.

b Assume that the container is set in motion so that it moves sideways at a constant speed of v relative to the ground, as shown in Figure 6.2.

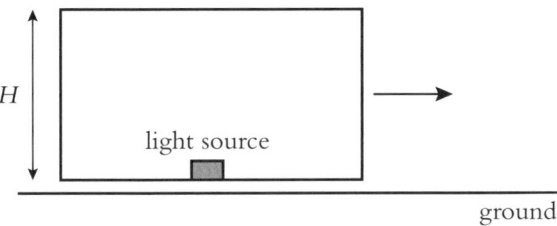

Figure 6.2

   i For the observer inside the container, is the time it takes for the light to reach the top of the container the same as when the container was at rest? Explain your answer.

   ii For the observer outside the container, the light beam now has to travel a horizontal distance as well as a vertical distance to reach the top of the container. If this observer measures the time for the light beam to reach the top of the container as t', write an expression for the total distance that the light beam has travelled.

   iii This total distance travelled is measured by the observer outside the container as taking a time t'. Show that $t'^2 = \dfrac{t^2}{1 - \dfrac{v^2}{c^2}}$ and that $t' = \gamma t$.

c Explain why this phenomenon is called *time dilation*.

3 In the frame of reference, S, the two ends of a table are located at the coordinates x_1 and x_2 such that the proper length of the table, $L = x_2 - x_1$. An observer in the frame of reference, S', moving with a speed, v, relative to S measures, at the same time, the coordinates of the ends of the table to be at x_1' and x_2' such that the length of the table measured in S' is $L' = x_2' - x_1'$.

   a Using the Lorentz transformations, show that $L = \gamma (x_2' - x_1')$.

   b Hence, show that $L' = \dfrac{L}{\gamma}$.

   c Suggest why this phenomenon is called *length contraction*.

4 A relativistic red car is observed by an observer on the road to be travelling at $0.5c$. The driver in the car observes a relativistic blue car passing him at a speed of $0.5c$. Determine the speed that the observer on the road measures for the blue car.

5 An observer on the ground measures a building to be 100 m long. Calculate the length of the building measured by another observer sitting in a car travelling at $0.85c$ relative to the ground.

6 A fast-moving particle travels through the air at a speed of $0.85c$. Kenny, standing on the surface of the Earth, sees the particle travel a distance of 12.5 km. How far does the particle travel in its own frame of reference?

7 A spaceship moves at a speed of $0.9c$. The driver in the spaceship measures that it takes the spaceship 20 ns to pass over a golf course. A golfer standing on the golf course observes the spaceship passing. How much time does the golfer think it takes for the spaceship to pass over the golf course?

8 a Outline what is meant by *the twin paradox*.

   b Which of the two twins actually ages the most?

   c Explain why the observations of the ages of the twins in the two frames of reference are not symmetrical.

9 A muon is a sub-atomic particle (a member of the lepton family) that is unstable. It has a half-life of $t_{\frac{1}{2}} = 3.1 \ \mu s$ when measured in a frame of reference where the muon is at rest.

   Muons are produced in large numbers in the Earth's upper atmosphere, at an altitude of about 15 km, by cosmic rays colliding with atoms to produce pions. These pions then decay into muons (and muon neutrinos). When produced, muons travel at a speed of $0.97c$ towards the Earth's surface, where they are detected.

   a According to an observer on the Earth, what is the muon's half-life?

   b According to an observer on the Earth, how far do muons travel through the atmosphere in one half-life?

   c Show that, in the muon's frame of reference, the muon's proper half-life and the distance it travels in this time are consistent with it moving at a speed of $0.97c$ relative to the Earth.

   d How many half-lives must pass before the muons reach the Earth's surface?

   e Outline why so many muons are observed at the Earth's surface.

Exercise 6.3 Spacetime diagrams

In this exercise, you will be able to improve your familiarity with spacetime diagrams and feel more confident of using them to solve problems.

1   Figure 6.3 shows three examples in a spacetime diagram for particles, p, q and w.

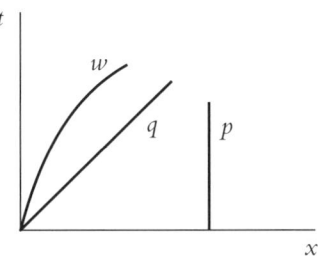

Figure 6.3

   a   Describe what is happening to p.

   b   Describe what is happening to q.

   c   Describe what is happening to w.

> **TIP**
>
> Think of the y-axis as being time and the x-axis as being position.

2   Figure 6.4 shows an example of a spacetime diagram in which a particle, r, and a photon, s, have their worldlines.

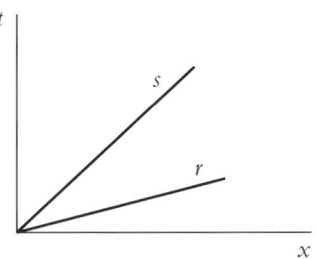

Figure 6.4

   a   State what the gradient of the worldline for s shows.

   b   Explain why the worldline for r is not possible.

3   Figure 6.5 shows a spacetime diagram on which two worldlines, A and B, are shown.

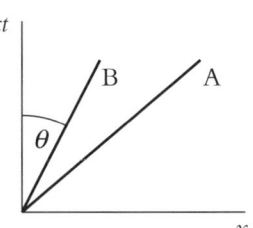

Figure 6.5

a   Worldline A represents a photon. Show that the gradient of this worldline must be 1.

b   Worldline B represents a particle travelling at a constant speed, v. Show that the angle that the worldline B makes with the ct-axis is given by the expression

$$\theta = \tan^{-1}\left(\frac{v}{c}\right).$$

TIP

Think about at what angle a world line would be for a photon travelling at a speed of c.

c   With reference to the angle, θ, that a worldline makes with the y-axis, outline why it is a good idea to plot ct on the y-axis of the Minkowski diagram.

d   What is the maximum angle, θ_{max}, that a worldline can have? Explain your answer.

4   Draw a spacetime diagram to include a worldline for

a   a photon moving in the positive x direction; label this P^+.

b   a photon moving in the negative x direction; label this P^-.

c   an object moving in the positive x direction with a speed of $v = 0.3c$ (and show the angle, θ^+, that this worldline makes with the ct axis); label this Q^+.

d   an object moving in the negative x direction with a speed of $0.8c$ (and show the angle, θ^-, that this worldline makes with the ct axis); label this Q^-.

5   Figure 6.6 shows a spacetime diagram with two sets of axes for two inertial reference frames, S and S', where S' moves with a constant speed, v, relative to S. A single event, M, is shown.

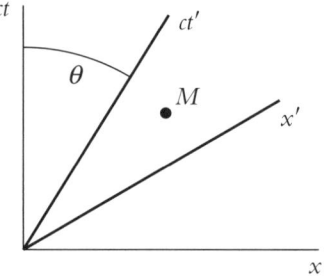

Figure 6.6

a   State an expression for the angle, θ, between the ct-axis and the ct'-axis.

b   Copy Figure 6.6 and show how to find the coordinates of

   i M in S.

   ii M in S'.

c   State an expression for how

   i x' is related to x.

   ii ct' is related to ct.

6 Figure 6.7 shows a spacetime diagram with two sets of axes for the reference frames S and S'. Five events are shown, labelled A, B, C, D and E.

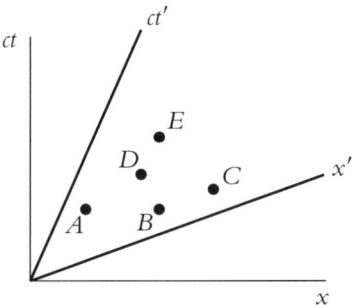

Figure 6.7

a i In S, which two events occur simultaneously?

 ii Outline why it is obvious that these two events do not occur simultaneously in S'.

b i In S, which two events occur at the same place?

 ii Outline why it is obvious that these two events do not occur in the same place in S'.

c i In S', which two events occur simultaneously?

 ii Outline why it is obvious that these two events do not occur simultaneously in S.

d i In S', which two events occur in the same place?

 ii Outline why it is obvious that these two events do not occur in the same place in S.

e Between which two events, and in which reference frames, is it possible to measure a proper

 i time.

 ii length.

7   Figure 6.8 shows a spacetime diagram in which a car, of proper length 5 m in S, is stationary in S. S′ moves with a constant speed, v, with respect to S.

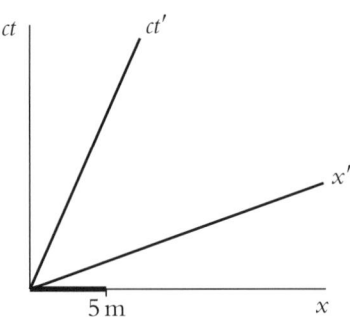

Figure 6.8

a   Copy Figure 6.8 and show what its length will be when measured in S′.

b   Is the length of the car in S′ longer, the same or shorter than its length in S?

c   What can you say about the scale of the axes in S and S′?

8   Figure 6.9 shows a spacetime diagram showing two events, E_1 and E_2, which occur at the same place ($x = 0$) in S. A passing observer, travelling at a constant speed, v, relative to S also observes the two events in S′.

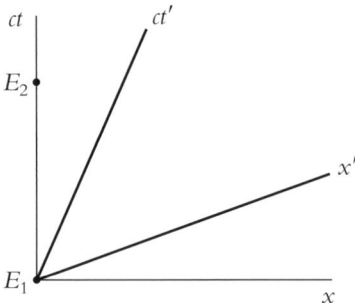

Figure 6.9

a   Copy Figure 6.9 and show the time that the observer in S′ measures between E_1 and E_2.

b   Is the time interval in S′ longer, the same or shorter than it is in S?

9   Two identical twins, Minky and Som, conduct their own twin paradox. Minky stays at home on Earth, whilst Som travels to a nearby star, Fazer, which is 10 light-years away, at a speed of $0.9c$. When Som reaches Fazer, she turns around and returns to the Earth, once again at a speed of $0.9c$.

a   Calculate how much time Minky measures for Som to reach Fazer.

b   Calculate how much Som has aged in her reference frame of the moving spaceship.

c In Som's reference frame, she sees that Minky has been on a journey. How much has Minky aged according to Som when Som reaches Fazer?

d Why is it necessary for Som to begin with a new reference frame, S'', when she turns around at Fazer to head back to the Earth?

e Draw a Minkowski diagram to illustrate Som's journey as observed by Minky in S and by Som in S' and S''.

f What happens to Som's measurement of the Earth clocks when she turns around at Fazer?

g When Som returns to Minky, how much older has Minky become than Som?

EXAM-STYLE QUESTIONS

Multiple-choice questions

1 Einstein's Theory of Special Relativity allows the laws of physics to be formulated based on
  A inertial frames of reference.
  B non-inertial frames of reference.
  C both inertial and non-inertial frames of reference.
  D quantum states only.

2 If it were possible for you to travel at a speed very close to the speed of light, you would notice
  A your pulse rate would have decreased.
  B your smartphone plays music more slowly.
  C Both **A** and **B**.
  D Neither **A** nor **B**.

3 Which of the following quantities is not invariant in all inertial frames of reference?
  A Mass
  B Spacetime interval
  C Proper time
  D Proper length

4 Some radioactive nuclei are observed by 4 different observers, each travelling at a different speed with respect to the nuclei. The observer who measures the half-life of the nuclei to be the shortest has a speed, relative to the nuclei, of
  A zero.
  B $0.33c$.
  C $0.66c$.
  D $0.99c$.

CONTINUED

5 A 'super bird' of proper length 1.0 m flies past a stationary observer on the Earth's surface at a speed of 0.8c. The observer measures the time it takes for the super bird to pass by to be

A 1.6 ns.
B 2.5 ns.
C 4.2 ns.
D 6.9 ns.

6 In a high-energy physics establishment, unstable sub-atomic particles travel with a speed of 0.8c. If the particles have a proper lifetime of 2.2 μs, the distance travelled by the particles is

A 550 m.
B 660 m.
C 770 m.
D 880 m.

7 A passenger aboard an intergalactic transport travelling at 0.94c past a planet measures the length of the transport to be 150 m. An observer on the planet measures the length of the transport to be

A 51 m.
B 141 m.
C 150 m.
D 440 m.

8 Figure 6.10 shows a spacetime diagram, on which are five events, labelled A, B, C, D and P.

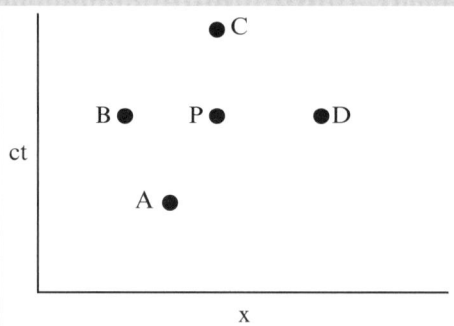

Figure 6.10

Referring to Figure 6.10, which event could be **caused by** event P?

A
B
C
D

9 Referring to Figure 6.10, which event could **cause** event P?

A
B
C
D

CONTINUED

10 Referring to Figure 6.10, which event occurs in the same place as event P?
   A
   B
   C
   D

Short-answer questions

11 A spacecraft, travelling at a speed of $0.95c$, passes the Earth on its way to Mars. In the frame of reference of the Earth, Mars and the Sun, all of which can be considered to be stationary with respect to each other, Earth and Mars are separated by a distance of 2.4×10^{11} m.
   a In the Earth–Mars–Sun reference frame, calculate the time it takes for the spacecraft to travel from the Earth to Mars. [1]
   b In the frame of reference of the moving spacecraft, state the speed at which the Earth and Mars travelling? [1]
   c In the frame of reference of the spacecraft, how far apart are the Earth and Mars? [2]
   d In the frame of reference of the spacecraft, how much time does it take to travel from the earth to Mars? [1]

12 An observer in the inertial reference frame S notices that the relativity express train is passing along the train tracks at a speed of $0.75c$. At a time of $t = 3.0$ s, the observer in S notices that a friend drops his mobile phone at a position of $x = 500$ m. Another observer sitting inside the relativity express also observes the dropped mobile phone.
   a Calculate the value of the gamma factor, γ. [2]
   b Assuming that both observers have clocks that read zero when the origins of their reference frames coincide, determine the
      i position, x', where the observer in S' sees the dropped phone. [1]
      ii time at which the observer in the S' sees the dropped phone. [1]

13 According to NASA, Proxima Centauri, a red dwarf star, is 4.244 light-years from the Earth. According to a spaceman in a rocket moving between the Earth and Proxima Centauri, the star is 0.65 light-years from the Earth.
   a Outline why the distance quoted by Nasa to Proxima Centauri is a proper length. [1]
   b Calculate the Lorentz factor, γ, for the rocket. [2]
   c Calculate the speed of the rocket relative to the speed of light. [2]

14 A fast train is travelling at a speed of $0.6c$ relative to the ground. An observer travelling at the back of the train measures the train to be 400 m long. The observer in the train switches on a torch so that the light beam travels towards the front of the train.
   a Determine how much time the light takes to reach the front of the train as observed by the observer on the train? [1]
   b Calculate how long the train is as observed by the observer on the ground. [2]
   c Calculate how much time an observer on the ground measures for the light from the torch to reach the front of the train. [2]

CONTINUED

15 Anand is on board a space rocket travelling towards Proxima Centauri when he passes Louis observing from the Earth. Louis observes that Anand's space rocket is travelling at $0.9c$ with respect to the Earth. Proxima Centauri is 4.0 light-years from the Earth.

   a Calculate the time it takes for Anand's space rocket to reach Proxima Centauri as measured by Louis on the Earth. (You may assume that the Earth remains stationary during this time.) [2]

   b Calculate the time that Anand measures for him to reach Proxima Centauri. [2]

   c Which of your answers to **parts a** and **b** is a proper time? [1]

16 A student standing on the Earth's surface observes that it takes two minutes for a nearby kettle to boil. Overhead, one of the student's friends passes by in a space rocket travelling at a speed of $0.8c$.

   a Explain why the student on the Earth measures a proper time interval. [1]

   b Calculate the value of γ for the space rocket. [2]

   c Determine how much time the student's friend in the space rocket measures for the kettle to boil. [2]

17 The relativity express intergalactic transport travels a distance of 4.00 light-years at a speed of $0.9995c$.

   a Calculate the value of γ for the transport. [1]

   b Calculate the time taken for the journey as measured by an observer at rest on the Earth. [1]

   c Calculate the time taken for the journey as measured by a passenger inside the transport. [2]

18 Figure 6.11 shows a spacetime diagram in which there are three events, A, B and C. A stationary observer at the origin in S and another observer, in the frame S', who is passing by in a space rocket travelling at a constant speed relative to S, both observe the three events.

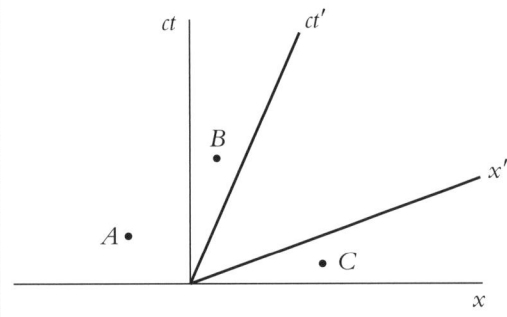

Figure 6.11

   a According to the observer in S, which event is observed
      i first? [1]
      ii last? [1]
   b According to the observer in S', which event is observed
      i first? [1]
      ii last? [1]

CONTINUED

19 The average lifetime of a π-meson in its own frame of reference is 26.0 ns. Suppose a π-meson travels at a speed of $0.95c$ with respect to the Earth.

    a Calculate γ for the moving π-meson. [1]

    b Calculate the lifetime of the π-meson as measured by an observer at rest on the Earth. [2]

    c Calculate the average distance the π-meson travels during its lifetime as measured by an observer at rest on the Earth. [2]

Unit B
The particulate nature of matter

Chapter 7
Thermal energy transfers

CHAPTER OUTLINE

In this chapter, you will:

- identify the ways that atoms are arranged in solids, liquids and gases.
- use the equation density = $\frac{mass}{volume}$.
- learn that absolute temperature is a measure of the average kinetic energy of atoms.
- convert between the Celsius and Kelvin temperature scales.
- link differences in temperature to the direction of net thermal energy transfer.
- identify the internal energy of a sample as the sum of the potential and kinetic energies of the atoms in the sample.
- identify the phase changes: boiling (or vaporising), freezing (or solidifying), melting and condensing.
- use temperature–time graphs to identify changes in phase.
- use graphs of cooling to estimate the rate at which energy is being lost.
- identify the terms *specific heat capacity*, *heat capacity* and *specific latent heat*.
- solve problems about heating and cooling.
- identify the nature of the processes: conduction, convection and radiation.
- solve problems about conduction using the equation: $\frac{\Delta Q}{\Delta t} = kA\frac{\Delta T}{l}$.
- examine qualitatively the process of convection.
- use the Stefan–Boltzmann law to examine the radiative losses of a hot object.
- examine and use the emission spectrum of a black body using Wien's displacement law.

KEY TERMS

states of matter: matter can exist in one of three states: solid, liquid or gaseous form

temperature: a measure of the average random kinetic energy of particles

absolute zero: the temperature at which all random motion of molecules stops

transfer of thermal energy (heat): the transfer of energy from one body to another as a result of a temperature difference

internal energy: the sum of the random kinetic energy of particles and the inter-particle potential energy

specific heat capacity: the energy required to change the temperature of a unit mass by one degree

phase: the state of a substance depending on the separation of its molecules; we consider the solid, liquid and vapour phase in this course

melting: when a solid changes to a liquid (thermal energy is transferred to the solid)

freezing: when a liquid changes into a solid (thermal energy is transferred away from the liquid)

vaporisation (or boiling): when a liquid changes into vapour (thermal energy is transferred to the liquid)

condensation: when a vapour changes into a liquid (thermal energy is transferred away from the vapour)

specific latent heat of fusion: the energy needed to change a unit mass from the solid to the liquid phase at a constant temperature

specific latent heat of vaporisation: the energy needed to change a unit mass from the liquid to the vapour phase at a constant temperature

conduction: method of thermal energy transfer based on collisions of electrons with atoms

convection: method of thermal energy transfer due to the rising of lower density hot fluids

convection currents: motion of a fluid as a result of differences in fluid density

radiation: method of thermal energy transfer through the emission of electromagnetic waves from a hot surface

Stefan–Boltzmann law: the radiated intensity is proportional to the fourth power of the kelvin temperature

intensity: power per unit area

black body: a theoretical body that absorbs all the radiation incident on it and radiates the maximum possible intensity for a given temperature

> PHYSICS FOR THE IB DIPLOMA: WORKBOOK

> CONTINUED
>
> **peak wavelength:** the wavelength corresponding to the peak of the black body spectrum curve
>
> **Wien's law:** the peak wavelength is inversely proportional to the kelvin temperature

Exercise 7.1 Particles, temperature, and energy

The questions in this section will help you consolidate your knowledge and understanding of how a body's internal energy and temperature is linked to the kinetic energy and potential energy of its atoms and molecules.

1   Solve the following problems about density:

   a   A block of iron is 30 cm long, 12 cm wide and 8 cm high. It has a mass of 22.5 kg. Calculate the density of iron.

   b   The Toi Gold Museum in Izu, Japan, displays the world's largest gold bar. The gold bar's makers say it has a volume of 15 730 cm^3 and a mass of 250.000 kg. Given that the density of pure gold is 19 300 kgm^{-3}, show that the world's largest gold bar is not 100% pure gold.

   c   Arun is shopping at a supermarket. He wants to buy 5 kg of potatoes but is concerned that his shopping bag is too small. If the density of potatoes is 660 kgm^{-3} and Arun's shopping bag can hold a volume of 7600 cm^3, is he right to be concerned?

> TIP
>
> Think about what a potato looks like.

2   The Sun has a mass of 2.0×10^{30} kg, and its radius is 7.0×10^8 m.

   a   Calculate the average density of the Sun.

   b   Why is your answer to part a an average?

   c   The Earth has a mass of 6.0×10^{24} kg and a radius of 6.4×10^6 m. How does the density of the Earth compare with the density of the Sun?

3   In our everyday lives we often use the words *hot* and *cold* when we talk about *temperature*. In our exploration of these terms, we will ask some thought-provoking questions.

   a   How can we know when something is hot or cold?

   b   When we use the terms hot and cold, are they *absolute*, or are they *relative* to something else?

   c   Is it reasonable to describe temperature as a measure of hotness, or coldness?

   d   When we touch a hot object, how does a physicist explain the sensation of it being hot?

e   How does a physicist explain the sensation of something feeling cold?

f   How is it possible for a person to touch an object and make a reasonable estimate of its temperature? Give an example to illustrate your answer.

g   If you touch steam at a temperature of 100 °C and an equal mass of water at the same temperature, do they feel the same? If not, why do they feel different?

h   Does your answer to **part g** suggest that our sense of touch is sometimes wrong? Should we be concerned?

i   How does a physicist explain what is happening when we touch something that is hot or cold?

j   Is it reasonable, therefore, to consider that a difference in temperature causes a net flow of energy—in a similar way to a difference in electrical potential causing an electrical current?

k   So, how would a physicist describe that two objects in thermal contact with each other are at the same temperature?

> **TIP**
>
> You may like to discuss these questions with some classmates.

4
a   State what is meant by the term *internal energy*, U, of a sample of material.

b   In what ways can the internal energy of a sample of material be changed?

5 The triple point of water is the temperature at which all three phases of water can exist simultaneously. This temperature is 0.01 °C.

Sample A is 50 g of ice, sample B is 50 g of liquid water and sample C is 50 g of water vapour. All three samples are at the triple point.

a   Which sample has the most internal energy? Explain your answer.

b   Which sample has the least internal energy? Explain your answer.

6 Consider a sample of material at a temperature of 30 °C.

a   Does every atom, or molecule, of the material have exactly the same amount of energy?

b   Does your answer to **part a** depend on the phase of the material?

c   Generally, what two energy stores will atoms, or molecules, of the material have?

d   If the material is heated (in other words, the material is given thermal energy) without the material changing phase, what will happen to the energy stores you stated in **part c**?

e   Suppose that the sample of material contains N atoms, or molecules. Write a mathematical expression for the average amount of random kinetic energy that an atom, or molecule, has.

f Write a mathematical expression for the root mean square speed, c, of the atoms, or molecules.

g Hence show that we can write the average random kinetic energy of an atom, or molecule, of the material as

$$\overline{E_K} = \frac{1}{2}mc^2,$$

where c is the root mean square speed of the atoms or molecules.

7 The Kelvin temperature scale dictates that the average random kinetic energy of the atoms, or molecules, is proportional to the absolute temperature of the material.

a In terms of the average random kinetic energy of the atoms, or molecules, what does a temperature of 0 K—which we call absolute zero—mean?

b Is it possible to have a Kelvin temperature that is less than 0?

c What temperature on the Celsius temperature scale is absolute zero?

d Is the difference between T and T+1 on the Kelvin temperature scale the same as the difference between T and T+1 on the Celsius temperature scale?

e Write an equation to show how to convert between the Celsius temperature scale and the Kelvin temperature scale.

Exercise 7.2 Specific heat capacity and change of phase

In this exercise, you practise solving problems about heating, cooling and changes of phase.

1 Define the terms *specific heat capacity (SHC)* and *heat capacity*.

2 a 300 J of energy is added to an object. Its temperature increases by 0.5 °C. What is the heat capacity of the object?

b A sample of a substance has a heat capacity of 450 J°C^{-1}. If 3.6 kJ of energy are added to the object, calculate the change in temperature of the object.

c Object A has a heat capacity of 375 J°C^{-1}. Object B has a heat capacity of 500 J°C^{-1}. If both objects are given the same amount of energy, which object's temperature will increase the most?

d The SHC of iron is 420 Jkg^{-1}°C^{-1}. Calculate the amount of energy required to heat 5000 kg of iron from a temperature of 15 °C to its melting temperature of 1540 °C. Give your answer in standard form.

e A squash ball (made of rubber) of mass 50 g is heated from an initial temperature of 15 °C to a higher, working temperature. If the amount of energy given to the ball is 2.5 kJ, calculate the final temperature of the squash ball. (The SHC of rubber is 1600 Jkg^{-1}°C^{-1}.)

3   a   Describe what is happening to a sample of material undergoing the following changes of phase:

   i   vaporising

   ii condensing

   iii freezing

   iv melting

   b   The following table lists some changes of phase for a sample of material. Complete the table to show what happens to the average kinetic energy (E_K) and the potential energy (E_P) of the sample's atoms and molecules: use the phrases, *increases, stays the same* or *decreases*.

Change of phase	E_K	E_P
melting		
vaporising		
soldifying		
condensing		

4   The specific latent heat of vaporisation of water is about 2.3×10^6 Jkg^{-1}. Calculate the amount of energy required to change the state of 1.5 litres of water from liquid to gas at a temperature of 100 °C.

5   Figure 7.1 shows how the temperature of a 2.0 kg sample of liquid material changes as it is being cooled.

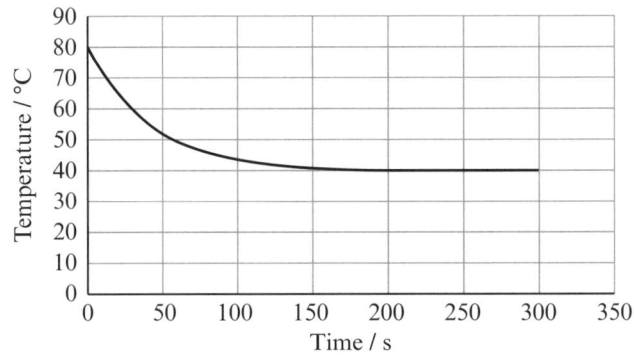

Figure 7.1

   a   Describe how the rate at which the material is losing energy is changing.

   b   Identify the melting temperature of the material.

c   From the graph, estimate the rate at which the temperature is changing when the temperature of the material is 80 °C.

d   If the specific heat capacity of the material is 680 J°C^{-1}kg^{-1}, use your answer to **part c** to calculate the rate at which energy is being lost from the material when its temperature is 80 °C.

6   A 400 g lump of aluminium, of SHC 900 Jkg^{-1}°C^{-1} at a temperature of 800 °C, is added to 2.5 kg of water at 20 °C. After a short time, the aluminium and the water are in thermal equilibrium.

   a   Write an equation for how much energy the aluminium loses. Call the final temperature of the aluminium T_{final}.

   b   Write an equation for how much energy the water has to gain. Call the final temperature of the water T_{final}.

   c   Calculate the final temperature of the water/aluminium.

   d   What assumption has been made in this question?

7   A kettle contains 1.5 litres of water at an initial temperature of 15 °C. The kettle is supplied with energy at a rate of 1.5 kW.

   • specific heat capacity of water = 4.2 kJ°C^{-1}kg^{-1}

   • specific latent heat of vaporisation of water = 2.3 MJkg^{-1}

   Calculate the time it takes for all the water to have boiled away so that there is no water left in the kettle. Assume that no energy is lost to the kettle itself or to the surroundings.

8   A glass containing 250 cm^3 of water at 12 °C is cooled by inserting an ice cube of mass 50 g at a temperature of −18 °C.

   • specific heat capacity of ice = 2100 Jkg^{-1}°C^{-1}

   • specific latent heat of fusion of ice = 3.3 × 10^5 Jkg^{-1}

   Calculate the final temperature of the glass of water.

> **TIP**
>
> The energy required by the ice to melt and then warm up must come from the energy lost by the cooling water.

Exercise 7.3 Thermal energy transfer

In this exercise, you will examine the nature of the three ways in which thermal energy may be transferred and solve problems using some important equations.

1   Look at Figure 7.2. It shows the arrangement of some atoms in a solid object at a temperature of 20 °C.

Figure 7.2

a   Describe the general motion of the individual atoms in the solid object.

Suppose that the left-hand edge of the material is brought into contact with a source of thermal energy, such as an object at a very high temperature.

b   What would you expect to happen to the atoms at the left-hand edge of the object?

c   If some of the atoms at the left-hand edge of the object collide with other atoms farther to the right, what will happen these further atoms?

d   Suggest why it may take a long time before the atoms at the right-hand edge of the object start to vibrate more violently than they had previously.

e   This process of thermal energy transfer is called conduction. Is conduction a fast way of transferring energy or a slow way?

Now consider Figure 7.3, which shows a similar arrangement of atoms, but this time the object is made of a metal, say, iron. In a metal, there are many free electrons which can move freely between the atoms. These are shown in the figure.

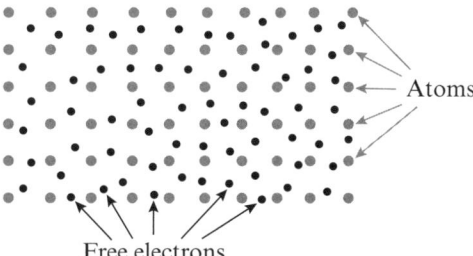

Figure 7.3

f   If the left-hand edge of the metal object is brought into contact with another source of thermal energy, what may happen to the free electrons when they collide with the vibrating atoms?

g   How does your answer to **part e** explain why thermal energy transfer by conduction in metals occurs more quickly than in non-metals?

Now consider the general arrangement of atoms in solids, liquids and gases.

h In which of the three phases would you generally expect thermal energy transfer by conduction to be

  i most effective; explain your answer.

  ii least effective; explain your answer.

  iii Outline why people often wear woollen sweaters to keep them warm on a cold day.

2 When we touch an object, thermal energy is transferred between the object and our fingers.

Suppose that you are sitting on a chair in a classroom. The chair has metal legs and a soft fabric seat. Both the legs of the chair and the soft fabric seat are at the same temperature—the temperature of your classroom.

  a When you touch the fabric seat of the chair, will it 'feel' hot, cold or neither? Explain your answer by referring to what you know about conduction.

  b When you touch the metal legs of the chair, will they 'feel' hot, cold or neither? Explain your answer by referring to what you know about conduction.

3 Suppose we have a conductor that has a length, l, and a cross-sectional area, A. One end of the conductor is at a temperature of T_1 and the other end is at a lower temperature, T_2. The ability of the material of the conductor to allow conduction to occur is called its thermal conductivity, k.

  a Suggest some factors, specific to the material of the conductor, that might affect its thermal conductivity.

  b The rate at which thermal energy is transferred through the conductor, $\frac{\Delta Q}{\Delta t}$. Suggest how $\frac{\Delta Q}{\Delta t}$ depends on

  i l.

  ii A.

  iii k.

  iv $\Delta T = (T_1 - T_2)$.

  c Hence, write an equation for $\frac{\Delta Q}{\Delta t}$.

4 Using the equation for thermal conduction, calculate the following:

  a The rate of thermal energy transfer through a conductor of cross-sectional area 8 cm² and conductivity 200 Js⁻¹°C⁻¹m⁻¹ if the temperature gradient across the conductor is 2.0 °Cm⁻¹

  b The cross-sectional area of a conductor of length 65 cm and conductivity 420 Js⁻¹°C⁻¹m⁻¹ if the difference in temperature between its ends of 40 °C makes thermal conduction occur at a rate of 52 W

c The temperature gradient necessary to cause conduction to occur at a rate of 3.5 W through a conductor of cross-sectional area 25 cm² and thermal conductivity 40 Js⁻¹°C⁻¹m⁻¹

d The thermal conductivity of glass, if conduction occurs at a rate of 600 W through a window of length 2.0 m, height 1.6 m and thickness 4.0 mm when the temperatures on either side of the window are 30 °C and 30.9 °C.

5 a Lots of people think convector heaters are a good way to warm a cold room. Convector heaters take air in through a vent at their base and release the heated air from a vent at their top.

Using your knowledge of convection, explain why a convector heater is so good at warming up a cold room.

b Many weather forecasters use the expression 'wind chill factor' when describing how the temperature feels colder than it actually is.

Use your knowledge of convection to explain what 'wind chill factor' is and why it makes the temperature seem colder.

6 Marathon des Sables is described as 'the toughest footrace on Earth'. Competitors have to run across more than 150 miles of desert. They must carry all their supplies while running—and they have to do it in five days. The average daily temperature is more than 40 °C.

a Outline the problems that runners face in trying to maintain a working body temperature (37 °C).

b Suggest how they are able to prevent themselves from overheating.

7 a State the Stefan–Boltzmann law for power being radiated from a hot object.

b The Sun has a surface temperature of about 5770 K and a radius of 6.96×10^8 m. If we assume that the Sun behaves like a black body (i.e. its emissivity is one) calculate the total power being radiated into space by the Sun.

c The Earth orbits the Sun at a mean distance of 1.496×10^{11} m. Calculate the solar power per square metre incident on the upper atmosphere of the Earth.

8 Typical European houses have a central heating system. The system has radiators that are usually made of two sheets of steel of thickness 2 mm. The radiators are 1.0 m long and 0.5 m high. Hot water at a temperature of 60 °C is constantly fed into the radiator by the heating pump.

a Calculate the net rate at which energy is radiated by the radiator if the room it is in is at an initial temperature of 20 °C. (Take the emissivity of the radiator to be 0.55.)

b Suggest a reason why such radiators are painted white.

9   The emission spectrum of a hot body shows a maximum at a wavelength of 800 nm.

   a   In which part of the electromagnetic spectrum does the wavelength 800 nm lie?

   b   What is the temperature of the hot body?

   c   If the body is now heated up considerably, what would happen to the wavelength at which maximum intensity is radiated?

EXAM-STYLE QUESTIONS

Multiple-choice questions

1   Which of the following statements about temperature scales is **false**?
    A   The smallest value on the Celsius temperature scale is −273 °C.
    B   The difference between −65 °C and −64 °C is not the same as the difference between 280 K and 281 K.
    C   The smallest value on the Kelvin temperature scale is 0 K.
    D   It is not possible to have a temperature of −300 °C.

2   Which of the following is the best description of absolute temperature?
    A   A measure of how hot a substance is
    B   A measure of how much energy a substance has
    C   A measure of the total kinetic energy the atoms and molecules in a substance have
    D   A measure of the average kinetic energy the atoms and molecules in a substance have

3   In a sample of material at absolute temperature, T, the average random speed of atoms is 500 ms^{-1}. If the temperature of the same sample is doubled to $2T$, which of the following is the best estimate of the average random speed of the atoms?
    A   250 ms^{-1}
    B   500 ms^{-1}
    C   700 ms^{-1}
    D   1000 ms^{-1}

4   When a liquid boils, it changes its state from liquid to gas.
    Which **one** of the following combinations correctly describes the changes to the average kinetic energy and the potential energy of the molecules during the boiling process?
    A   average kinetic energy stays the same; potential energy stays the same
    B   average kinetic energy stays the same; potential energy increases
    C   average kinetic energy increases; potential energy stays the same
    D   average kinetic energy increases; potential energy increases

CONTINUED

5 Two objects next to each other are at the same temperature. Which of the following statements is **false**?

   A Both objects are exchanging energy with each other.

   B There is no net transfer of energy from one object to the other.

   C Both objects have the same internal energy.

   D The average kinetic energy of the atoms in each object is the same.

6 A metal sphere of mass, m, at a temperature of 80 °C is placed into an equal mass of water at 20 °C in an insulated container. The specific heat capacity of water is twice that of the metal. After a short time, the metal and the water are at the same temperature. This new temeprature is

   A 60 °C.

   B 50 °C.

   C 40 °C.

   D 30 °C.

7 After running a marathon in cold conditions, athletes are sometimes wrapped in a thin, shiny, metallic-like blanket. The blanket reduces thermal energy loss from the processes of

   A conduction only.

   B conduction and convection.

   C radiation only.

   D radiation and convection.

8 A metal sphere at a Kelvin temperature, T, radiates energy at a rate of P. If the same sphere is heated until its Kelvin temperature is doubled, it would now radiate energy at a rate of

   A P.

   B $2P$.

   C $4P$.

   D $16P$.

9 The Sun has a surface temperature of about 6000 K and a radius of about 7×10^8 m. Betelgeuse, a red supergiant in the constellation of Orion, has a surface temperature of about 3500 K and a radius of about 6×10^{11} m.

   If the power radiated by the Sun is P, then the power radiated by Betelgeuse is about

   A 300 P.

   B 500 P.

   C 85 000 P.

   D 430 000 P.

CONTINUED

10 Figure 7.4 shows the emission spectra of four similar spheres. Which of the spheres is at the highest temperature?

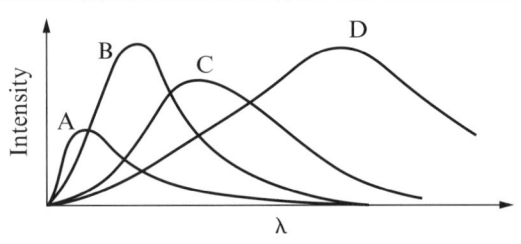

Figure 7.4

Short-answer questions

11 A teacher places a 600 g piece of lead into a sealed card 80 cm cylinder. At one end of the cylinder, there is a small rubber nozzle, where a sensitive thermometer can be placed to measure the temperature of the lead. At the start of the demonstration, the temperature of the lead is 20 °C. The specific heat capacity of the lead is 160 $Jkg^{-1}K^{-1}$.

The teacher holds the cylinder vertically and flips it end to end so that the lead falls to the bottom of the cylinder each time it is flipped. At the end of the demonstration, the teacher measures the temperature of the lead.

  a Calculate the amount of gravitational potential energy that the lead loses each time the cylinder is flipped. ($g = 10\ Nkg^{-1}$) [1]

  b Outline the energy transformation that takes place each time the lead comes to rest at the bottom of the cylinder. [1]

  c If the teacher flips the cylinder 50 times, determine the final temperature of the lead. [3]

12 A teacher sits a beaker of water on a set of electronic scales. The scales read 175 g.

After leaving the beaker untouched for 24 hours, the teacher notices that the reading on the scales is 163 g. The teacher explains to her class that some of the water has evaporated and changed state into water vapour.

Explain why

  a some of the water can change into water vapour without the water needing to be at its boiling temperature. [2]

  b the water cools when some of it evaporates away. [2]

13 A student places a cylindrical block of aluminium of mass 1.0 kg on a protective pad on a desk. The block has two holes, 3 cm apart: the student places a thin electrical heater, rated at 50 W, into one hole and a thermometer into the other. The student switches on the heater and makes these observations.

  - Temperature of aluminium block before switching on the heater: 20 °C.
  - There is no change in the value on the thermometer for 2 minutes.
  - After 6 minutes, the reading on the thermometer is rising by 3.3°Cmin^{-1}.
  - After 25 minutes, the reading on the thermometer is 92 °C.

CONTINUED

a Explain why there is no change in the reading on the thermometer for the first 2 minutes of heating. [2]

b Show that the specific heat capacity of aluminium is 900 Jkg^{-1}°C^{-1}. [2]

c Explain why the reading on the thermometer after 25 minutes of heating is not 103 °C. [2]

14 0.5 kg of ice at its melting temperature is changed into liquid water by the continuous addition of thermal energy. The specific latent heat of fusion of water is 3.3×10^5 Jkg^{-1}.

a The thermal energy is supplied by an electrical heater rated at 100 W. Calculate the time required to melt all the ice. [2]

b The liquid water is now heated until it reaches its boiling temperature. If the same heater is used, calculate the time it takes for the water to boil. The specific heat capacity of water is 4.2 kJkg^{-1}K^{-1}. [2]

c When the water reaches its boiling temperature, the heater continues to supply energy until all the water has changed state into water vapour. Calculate the time it takes for all the water to change into water vapour. You can assume that *all* of the energy supplied by the heater is used to change the state of the water. The specific latent heat of vaporisation of water is 2.26×10^6 Jkg^{-1}. [1]

15 Figure 7.5 shows how the temperature of a sample of 600 g of a solid substance varies with time as it is heated at a constant rate of 100 W.

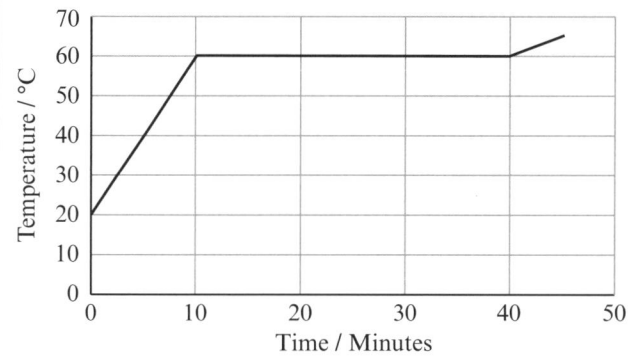

Figure 7.5

Use the information in the graph to

a Identify the melting temperature of the substance. [1]

b The specific heat capacity of the substance. [2]

c The specific latent heat of fusion of the substance. [2]

CONTINUED

16 Figure 7.6 shows how the temperature of a white-coloured cup containing 200 g of warm water, sitting on a table in a room at a constant temperature of 20 °C, changes over a period of two hours.

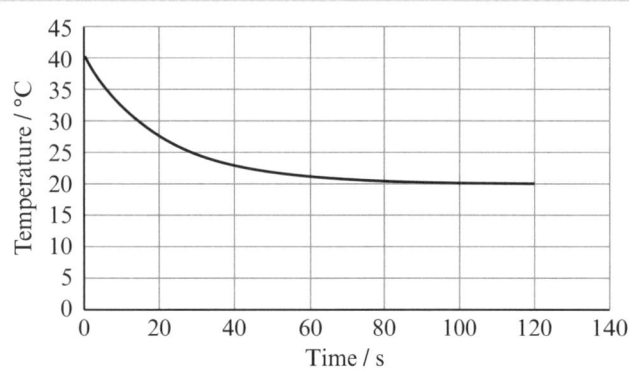

Figure 7.6

    a Explain why the graph in Figure 7.6 has a decreasing gradient. [2]

    b Use the graph to estimate the rate at which the water is losing energy after a time of 40 minutes. (The specific heat capacity of water is 4.2 kJ°C^{-1}kg^{-1}). [2]

    c If the cup had been black-coloured, rather than white, suggest how the graph would differ for the same amount of warm water at the same starting temperature. [1]

17 An insulated cylindrical iron bar of diameter 12 cm and length 50 cm has one of its two ends immersed in boiling water at a temperature of 100 °C. The other end is immersed in a mixture of ice and water at 0 °C. You may assume that the temperatures of the ice/water mixture and the boiling water do not change.

    a Show that the rate at which thermal energy is transferred by conduction along the iron bar is 170 W. (The thermal conductivity of iron is 75 Wm^{-1}K^{-1}.) [2]

    b If the iron bar were replaced by a copper bar of the same diameter but twice the length, calculate the rate at which thermal energy is transferred by conduction through the copper bar. (The thermal conductivity of copper is 390 Wm^{-1}K^{-1}.) [1]

    c If the two bars are now joined end to end, with one end of the copper bar immersed in the boiling water and one end of the iron bar immersed in the ice/water mixture, calculate the rate of thermal energy transfer by conduction at the junction of the two bars. [2]

18 A Leslie cube is a thin-walled cube that can be filled with boiling water in order to demonstrate to physics students how differently coloured surfaces radiate energy at different rates. A typical Leslie cube has faces each of an area 100 cm² and holds 1 kg of water.

    a Calculate the time required for a heater rated at 1000 W to raise the temperature of 1 kg of water from 20 °C to its boiling temperature of 100 °C. (The specific heat capacity of water is 4.2 kJkg^{-1}°C^{-1}.) [2]

    b Outline any assumptions you may have made in answering **part a**. [1]

    c Making the assumption that an insignificantly small amount of energy is required to heat up the walls of the cube to the same temperature as the boiling water, calculate the rate at which energy is being radiated from the matte black face ($\epsilon = 1.0$) of the cube. [2]

CONTINUED

19 A block of tungsten at a temperature of 2000 K radiates energy at a rate of 0.23 MWm^{-2}.

  a Show that the power radiated per unit area of a black body at the same temperature as the tungsten is 0.91 MWm^{-2}. [2]

  b Hence, calculate the emissivity of tungsten at a temperature of 2000 K. [1]

  c Assuming that the emissivity of tungsten is constant up to a temperature of 6000 K, determine the total power radiated by a sphere of tungsten of radius 4.0 cm at a temperature of 6000 K. [2]

20 A typical tungsten filament of a household electric lamp has a working temperature of 2500 K.

  a At what wavelength does the radiated energy from the filament have a maximum intensity? [2]

  b In which part of the electromagnetic spectrum does your answer to **part a** lie? [1]

  c If a star showed a maximum radiated intensity at a wavelength of 50 nm, what would the surface temperature of the star be? [1]

Chapter 8
The greenhouse effect

CHAPTER OUTLINE

In this chapter, you will:

- sketch and Identify black body curves.
- solve problems using the Stefan–Boltzmann law and Wien's law.
- identify and use the terms: emissivity and albedo.
- consider how the Earth's albedo can vary.
- derive and explore the solar constant, S, for the Earth.
- apply the conservation of energy to the energy exchanged by a celestial object.
- examine the absorption of solar infrared radiation by greenhouse gases.
- describe the greenhouse effect.
- consider the effect of fossil fuel burning on the energy balance of the Earth, the enhanced greenhouse effect.

KEY TERMS

emissivity: the ratio of the intensity radiated by a body to the intensity radiated by a black body of the same temperature

albedo: the ratio of reflected-to-incident intensity; it has no unit

solar constant, S: the intensity received in the upper atmosphere of the Earth

energy balance equation: an equation expressing the equality of incoming and outgoing intensities of radiation

greenhouse gases: gases in the atmosphere that are capable of absorbing infrared radiation

greenhouse effect: the phenomenon in which re-radiated energy from the greenhouse gases returns to earth warming the Earth

enhanced greenhouse effect: the augmentation of the greenhouse effect due to human activities

Exercise 8.1 Radiation from real bodies

The questions in this section will help you understand how bodies transfer energy to and from their surroundings.

1   a   Which process of thermal energy transfer is responsible for the transfer of energy between stars and planets, such as the Earth, and their surroundings?

   b   The amount of energy radiated by a hot body depends on four factors. State the four factors.

   c   State the Stefan–Boltzmann law for a radiating body.

   d   i   What is meant by the term *black body*?

      ii   How does a real body differ from a black body?

      iii   How is the term *emissivity* defined?

2   Consider a solid sphere of radius 12 cm hanging on a fine thread from the ceiling of a room.

   a   If the emissivity of the surface of the sphere is 0.75 and the sphere is at a temperature of 150 °C, calculate the power radiated by the sphere.

   b   If the room around the sphere is at a temperature of 20 °C, calculate the rate at which the sphere absorbs energy from the room.

   c   Use your answers to **parts a** and **b** to determine the net exchange of energy per second between the sphere and the room.

> **TIP**
>
> Remember to have temperatures in Kelvin.

3   a   Sketch the black body emission spectrum for a star with a

      i   very hot surface temperature, such as the star Spica.

      ii   low surface temperature, such as the star Betelgeuse.

   b   i   How can you tell the difference between the surface temperatures of two stars by examining their black body emission spectra?

      ii   Which law defines your answer to part *i*? Write this law.

      iii   How does the emissivity of a body's surface affect the wavelength at which its radiated energy is greatest?

   c   Use Wien's displacement law to calculate the surface temperature of a star whose peak wavelength in its emission spectrum is at 650 nm.
       (Wien's constant = 2.9×10^{-3} m K.)

d Arcturus is a star in the constellation of Bootes. Its surface temperature is about 4300 K.

  i Use Wien's displacement law to calculate the peak wavelength in its emission spectrum.

  ii Suggest why astronomers consider the luminosity of Arcturus to be larger than the calculated value of 110 $L_\odot$.

e The cosmic microwave background radiation observed from deep space has an emission spectrum with a peak wavelength of 1.063 mm.
Use Wien's displacement law to calculate the temperature of deep space.

4 A charge-coupled device (CCD) attached to a telescope measures the wavelength at which maximum intensity of radiated energy from a star to be 400 nm and the power received at the Earth's surface per unit area to be 2.8×10^{-10} Wm^{-2}.

  a Show that the surface temperature of the star is about 7300 K.

  b At this temperature, the total power emitted by the star is determined to be 7.2×10^{27} W. Calculate how far away the star is from the Earth. Give your answer in standard form and in light-years.

5 a i State what is meant by the term *albedo*.

  ii What units does albedo have?

  b An isolated body in space, such as a planet or a star, can only absorb and reflect radiation incident upon it. Why are other thermal energy transfer processes not possible for a planet or star?

  c How then, are the emissivity and the albedo of a planet related

  i qualitatively?

  ii quantitatively?

Exercise 8.2 Energy balance of the Earth

This exercise will help you understand the factors responsible for the Earth's energy balance and the roles that the greenhouse effect and the enhanced greenhouse effect play.

1 The Earth and the Moon can be considered to be at equal distances from the Sun. So, both celestial objects will experience the same amount of solar energy incident on them per second per unit area. Yet, averaged over a day, the Moon's surface temperature is about −73 °C, whilst the Earth's is about 15 °C.

  a Suggest a reason why the globally averaged temperature of the Earth's surface is about 90 K more than the Moon's.

  b The Earth and the Moon also have quite different albedos.
  What is the biggest contributing factor to this difference in albedos?

c   The Earth's albedo itself is prone to changes over both short and longer time periods. In addition, the Earth's albedo varies geographically, sometimes by a factor of 300%. Suggest two reasons why the Earth's albedo can vary by so much.

d   i   Which geographical areas of the Earth's surface have high albedos?

   ii What does your answer to **part d i** suggest about any changes that are likely to occur in the surface temperature of such areas?

e   i   Which geographical areas of the Earth's surface have relatively low albedos?

   ii What does your answer to **part e i** suggest about any changes that are likely to occur in the surface temperature of such areas?

f   If the globally averaged albedo of the Earth were to increase, what is its likely effect on the surface temperature?

> **TIP**
>
> Don't forget what you have learnt from Chapter 7 about thermal energy transfers and how substances heat up.

2   This question looks more closely at solar energy incident on a spherical celestial object of radius, R, orbiting the Sun at a mean distance of d.

Suppose that the Sun radiates energy at a rate of P.

a   At a distance, d, from the Sun, how much solar energy arrives per second per unit area? Call this quantity, S.

b   So how much solar energy will be incident on the celestial object per second?

c   Hence give an expression, in terms of S, for the mean power incident on the total surface of the celestial object per unit area.

d   Now suppose that the albedo of the celestial object is α. Give an expression for the mean power per unit area absorbed by the celestial object.

e   Now let us apply this to the case of the Earth. For the Earth. S ≈ 1400 W.

   i   If the average albedo of the Earth is 0.3, show that the Earth would have to radiate 245 Wm^{-2} if it is to be in thermal equilibrium.

   ii   At what temperature would a black body have be if it were to radiate at 245 Wm^{-2}?

   iii In fact, the globally averaged surface temperature of the Earth is 288 K. For the Earth to maintain thermal equilibrium with its surroundings how much more power per unit area must the Earth's surface absorb? You should consider the Earth to radiate as a black body for the sake of this question.

   iv   Since the Earth is in thermal equilibrium with its surroundings, where is this extra power coming from?

   v   By what name is this phenomenon usually known?

3   This question looks into the nature of the incident solar radiation and what happens to some of it as it penetrates the atmosphere.

   a   i   The Sun's surface temperature is about 5700 K. Calculate the wavelength at which the maximum intensity of radiation is emitted.

       ii   In which part of the electromagnetic spectrum is this radiation?

   b   Roughly, at what range of wavelengths is

       i   ultraviolet radiation?

       ii   visible radiation?

       iii infrared radiation?

   c   Do all of the kinds of electromagnetic radiation listed in **part b** occur in the solar radiation incident on the top of the Earth's atmosphere?

   d   As human beings, how do we know that all three kinds of electromagnetic radiation emitted by the Sun, as listed in **part b**, are present at the surface of the Earth?

   e   Between about 15 and 35 km above the Earth's surface, the concentration of ozone molecules is higher than in other regions of the atmosphere.

   Absorption of radiation in the ultraviolet region of the electromagnetic spectrum by ozone molecules can dissociate the molecules into atomic and molecular oxygen.

       i   What is ozone?

       ii   Outline what happens to the atoms of oxygen of an ozone molecule when ultraviolet radiation is absorbed by an ozone molecule in order to cause the molecule to dissociate.

       iii What effect does this molecular dissociation have on the amount of ultraviolet radiation reaching the surface of the Earth?

       iv   Why is this effect so important for life on the Earth?

       v   What would the effect be if the concentration of ozone molecules in the atmosphere were to be reduced?

       vi   Where in the world has this effect already been observed?

       vii Which countries are most at risk from the effects of this 'ozone hole'?

       viii What have scientists—and their influence over governments—done to try to prevent further decreases of ozone in the ozone hole region?

4 In this question, we look at the role that infrared radiation plays in the atmosphere and how it is responsible for the greenhouse effect.

  a The peak intensity of solar radiation occurs at a wavelength that is in the visible part of the electromagnetic spectrum. Given that the globally averaged surface temperature of the Earth is about 15 °C, determine in which part of the electromagnetic spectrum the radiation emitted by the Earth's surface occurs.

  b Atmospheric molecules, held together by covalent atomic bonds, vibrate in quantum states. Such quantum states can be energised (i.e. the molecules vibrate with a larger amplitude) by the absorption of photons of electromagnetic radiation of certain frequencies. In addition, quantum states can fall to lower energies by the emission of photons of the same frequencies. Physicists describe this process of absorption and re-radiation as a resonant process because the energy of the absorbed and emitted photons is the same.

   i Suggest why any given atmospheric molecule will have a set of discrete possible wavelengths of photons that it can absorb and re-radiate.

   ii Such photons have wavelengths that are too large to be visible light. In what part of the electromagnetic spectrum would you find such photons?

   iii Suggest, therefore, why the atmosphere is not transparent to infrared radiation.

  c So, we have established that incoming solar radiation at wavelengths around the Wien peak passes through the atmosphere unaffected whilst outgoing radiation from the Earth's surface is absorbed and re-radiated by some atmospheric gases as described by the greenhouse effect. In fact, only about 62% of the radiation emitted by the Earth's surface is able to pass through the atmosphere out into space.

Show that taking into effect the absorption of infrared radiation by greenhouse gases, the balance between incoming and outgoing radiation from the Earth's surface predicts a surface temperature for the Earth that is in close agreement with the currently measured value of 288 K. For this model, consider the Earth's surface to radiate as a black body.

The next four questions look at the production and removal of four of the main greenhouse gases and the role they play in the greenhouse effect.

5 Water vapour exists in variable amounts in the atmosphere, and it contributes to the greenhouse effect.

  a In which part (or layer) of the atmosphere does water vapour (H_2O_{vap}) exist in its largest concentrations?

  b Suggest some natural origins of atmospheric water vapour.

  c Suggest how water vapour concentrations in the atmosphere might be increased by human activities.

d How does the atmosphere remove water vapour?

e How would you expect an increase in water vapour concentrations in the atmosphere to affect the average surface temperature of the Earth?

6 Nitrous oxide, N_2O, is a highly effective greenhouse gas that can exist in the atmosphere for more than 100 years.

a What natural processes are responsible for about 45% of the nitrous oxide present in the atmosphere?

b About 55% of atmospheric nitrous oxide has man-made origins. Which processes are responsible for this?

c By which natural processes is nitrous oxide removed from the atmosphere?

d How would an increase in nitrous oxide concentrations in the atmosphere affect the greenhouse effect?

e Why has it been difficult for world leaders to come to an agreement on how to try to reduce the man-made production of atmospheric nitrous oxide?

7 Methane is a highly effective greenhouse gas.

a Suggest some natural processes that contribute to the amount of methane in the atmosphere.

b Now suggest some man-made processes that contribute to the amount of methane in the atmosphere.

c With reference to methane, why are environmental scientists concerned about possible global warming?

d How is methane removed naturally from the atmosphere?

e How would an increase in methane concentrations in the atmosphere affect the greenhouse effect?

8 Carbon dioxide can exist in the atmosphere for long periods of time (100 years or more) and is a big contributor to the greenhouse effect.

a List some of the ways by which carbon dioxide can enter the atmosphere naturally.

b Now suggest some of the man-made processes that allow carbon dioxide to enter the atmosphere.

c What attempts have humans made—and continue to make—to reduce the increase in atmospheric carbon dioxide that has been observed over the past two hundred years or so.

d How is carbon dioxide removed from the atmosphere?

e How would an increase in carbon dioxide concentrations in the atmosphere affect the greenhouse effect?

> **TIP**
> Remember what question 8.2.1 examined.

9   a   Outline what is meant by the term *enhanced greenhouse effect*.

    b   Which of the greenhouse gases is/are primarily responsible for the enhanced greenhouse effect?

    c   What do many scientists believe will happen to the Earth if the enhanced greenhouse effect continues?

    d   What proposals have scientists made to reduce the increase in greenhouse gases that contribute to the enhanced greenhouse effect?

EXAM-STYLE QUESTIONS

Multiple-choice questions

1   If the average emissivity of a planet is 0.7, the best estimate of the planet's albedo is
    A 0.1.
    B 0.3.
    C 0.5.
    D 0.7.

2   The best estimate of the Earth's globally averaged albedo is
    A 0.1.
    B 0.3.
    C 0.5.
    D 0.7.

3   Which of the following is not a major factor in the variance of the solar constant, S?
    A Variations in the distance from the Sun to the Earth
    B Variations in the luminosity of the Sun during its 11-year cycle
    C Variations in atmospheric cloud cover
    D Occurrence and frequency of sunspots, solar flares and prominences

4   In which of the following places on the Earth's surface is the albedo likely to be the largest?
    A Tropical rain forest
    B Middle of an ocean
    C Middle of a desert
    D Polar cap

5   Black body X has a surface area of A and an absolute temperature of T. Black body Y has a surface area of $2A$ and a temperature of $\frac{T}{2}$. Which of the following is the best estimate for the ratio of the emitted power of X to Y, $\frac{P_X}{P_Y}$?
    A 16
    B 8
    C 4
    D 1

CONTINUED

6 An isolated sphere of radius, R, and absolute temperature, T, radiates energy with a maximum intensity at wavelength, λ. Another similar sphere of radius $2R$ at the same temperature will radiate energy with a maximum intensity at wavelength

   A $\frac{\lambda}{2}$.

   B λ.

   C 2λ.

   D 4λ.

7 Which of the following is not a major greenhouse gas?

   A N_2O

   B H_2O

   C CH_4

   D NH_3

8 If the greenhouse effect were not present in the Earth's atmosphere, the best estimate of the surface temperature would be

   A $-40\ °C$.

   B $-20\ °C$.

   C $0\ °C$.

   D $20\ °C$.

9 The enhanced greenhouse effect is deemed to be due mostly to

   A CO_2.

   B H_2O.

   C CH_4.

   D O_3.

10 A black body at a constant temperature of 20 °C radiates energy with an intensity, I. If the temperature of the black body were increased to 40 °C, the best estimate of the radiated intensity will be

   A $\frac{1}{2}I$.

   B I.

   C $2I$.

   D $16I$.

Short-answer questions

11 A body at a temperature of 6000 K radiates energy with an intensity, I, of 40 MWm^{-2}.

   a i Show that the wavelength, λ_{max}, at which the maximum intensity of radiated energy lies is about 480 nm. [2]

      ii In which part of the electromagnetic spectrum does this wavelength lie? [1]

   b Calculate the emissivity, ε, of the body. [2]

CONTINUED

12 A joint of meat at a temperature of 300 K with a surface area of 0.01 m² is placed in a butcher's cold room kept at a constant temperature of 4.0 °C. For the purposes of this question, you may assume that the joint of meat behaves as a black body.
   a Calculate the initial net exchange of thermal energy per second between the meat and the cold room. [2]
   b Explain why the meat will not continue to exchange energy at the rate calculated in **part a**. [1]
   c Sketch a graph to show how the temperature of the meat will change with time. [2]

13 The Sun radiates energy to all of the planets in the solar system. Venus orbits the Sun at an average distance of about 70% of the Earth's orbital radius.
   a Calculate the ratio of the solar radiation per second, per unit area, incident on Venus to that for the Earth. [2]
   b The surface temperature of Venus is about 460 °C (733 K), whilst that of the Earth is 15 °C (288 K). Suggest a reason for this. [1]
   c Suggest what gases are present in the atmosphere of Venus. [2]

14 It takes light about 500 s to reach the Earth from the Sun.
   a Determine the average radius of the Earth's orbit around the Sun. (The speed of light is 3×10^8 ms⁻¹). [1]
   b If the Sun's luminosity is $L_\odot = 3.83 \times 10^{26}$ W, show that the solar constant, S, for the Earth is about 1.4 kWm⁻². [2]
   c The average solar power per unit area received by the Earth is only $\frac{1}{4}$ of this value. Suggest a reason for this. (1)
   d The average solar power per unit area incident on the Earth's surface is about 245 Wm². Suggest why this value is less than $\frac{1}{4}$ of 1.4 kWm⁻². [1]

15 This question is about the greenhouse effect on the Earth.
   a State what is meant by the greenhouse effect and what its effect actually is on the Earth's surface temperature. [2]
   b State **two** gases that are responsible for the greenhouse effect **other than water vapour**. [2]
   c It has been suggested that an increase in the amount of water vapour in the atmosphere will actually cause the Earth's surface temperature to fall. Suggest a reason to explain this fall in temperature. [2]

16 The surface temperature of the Sun is about 5700 K.
   a Determine the wavelength, λ_{max}, at which maximum intensity of radiation is emitted from the Sun's surface. [2]
   b Suggest reasons why the Earth's atmosphere
      i **is not** transparent to solar ultraviolet radiation. [1]
      ii **is** transparent to solar visible radiation. [1]
      iii **is not** transparent to infrared radiation. [1]

17 a In which layers of the Earth's atmosphere do you find
      i most of the atmosphere's water vapour. [1]
      ii the ozonosphere. [1]
   b Outline the role that ozone plays in protecting the Earth from potentially harmful radiation. [2]
   c Atmospheric ozone can be depleted by man-made emissions. State one such man-made emission. [1]

CONTINUED

18 A typical white dwarf star has a surface temperature of 20 000 K and a radius of 7000 km. Assuming the star behaves like a black body,

   a show that the total power emitted by the white dwarf is 5.6×10^{24} W. [2]

   b determine the wavelength at which the peak intensity of radiation is emitted. [1]

   c calculate the power received per unit area at the Earth from the white dwarf at a distance of 1.5×10^{11} m away. [2]

19 a State what is meant by the term *albedo*. [1]

   b Suggest **two** factors that cause the albedo of the Earth to change. [2]

   c It has been suggested that, if nuclear weapons were used on Earth, the Earth's surface temperature would decrease, causing a 'nuclear winter'.

   Outline why it is likely that a nuclear winter could follow a nuclear war. [2]

20 The solar constant, S, for the Earth is 1.36 kWm^{-2}. The average distance fom the Earth to the Sun is 1.5×10^{11} m. The Sun's radius is 6.96×10^{8} m.

   a Show that the total power emitted by the Sun is about 3.8×10^{26} W. [2]

   b Determine the surface temperature of the Sun. You may assume that the Sun radiates as a black body. [2]

   c A popular philosophical hypothesis has suggested that human eyes have developed to be sensitive to electromagnetic radiation between the wavelengths of about 400 nm and 700 nm—the part of the electromagnetic spectrum called the visible region—because this is the radiation that is radiated most by the Sun. Comment on whether there is any scientific plausibility to this hypothesis. [1]

Chapter 9
The gas laws

CHAPTER OUTLINE

In this chapter, you will:

- use the equation for pressure: $P = \dfrac{F}{A}$.
- identify and use Avogadro's constant as the number of atoms in a mole.
- define the concept of an Ideal gas and look at the conditions necessary for a real gas to behave as an ideal gas.
- derive the ideal gas law equation from kinetic theory.
- examine the three empirical gas laws and use them to solve problems.
- explore alternative versions of the ideal gas law.
- use the ideal gas law to define the internal energy of an ideal gas.

KEY TERMS

mole: a quantity of a substance containing as many particles as atoms in 12 g of carbon-12; this is equivalent to the Avogadro constant

If a substance contains N particles then the number of moles n is

$n = \dfrac{N}{N_A}$

Avogadro constant: the number of particles in one mole: $6.02214076 \times 10^{23}$

molar mass: the mass in grams of one mole of a substance

pressure: the normal force on an area per unit area; $P = \dfrac{F}{A}$

atmosphere: a non-SI unit of pressure; equal to the average pressure exerted by the Earth's atmosphere.

ideal gas: a theoretical gas in which the particles do not exert forces on each other except during contact

real gas: a gas obeying the gas laws approximately for limited ranges of pressures, volumes and temperatures

state of a gas: a gas with a specific value of pressure, volume, temperature and number of moles

isothermal curve: a curve on a pressure–volume diagram where all points have the same temperature

> **CONTINUED**
>
> **gas constant:** the constant, R, that appears in the equation of state
>
> **equation of state:** equation relating pressure, volume and temperature of an ideal gas: $PV = nRT$
>
> **Boltzmann constant:** the ratio of the gas constant to Avogadro's number
>
> **Ideal Gas Law:**
>
> $PV = \frac{1}{3} Nmc^2$
>
> $PV = NkT$
>
> $PV = nRT$
>
> $P = \frac{1}{3} \rho c^2$
>
> where P is pressure, V is volume, N is the total number of atoms/molecules, m is the mass of an atom/molecule, c^2 is the root-mean-square speed of the atoms/molecules, k is Boltzmann's constant ($k = 1.38 \times 10^{-23}$ JK^{-1}), T is absolute/Kelvin temperature, R is the universal gas constant ($R = 8.31$ JK^{-1}mole^{-1}) and ρ is density.
>
> **Boyle's law:** At constant temperature, the pressure of a fixed mass of gas is inversely proportional to the volume it occupies.
>
> $P \propto \frac{1}{V}$ or $PV = constant$ at a constant temperature.
>
> **Charles' law:** At constant pressure, the temperature of a fixed mass of gas is proportional to the volume it occupies.
>
> $T \propto V$ at constant pressure.
>
> **Pressure law:** At constant volume, the pressure of a fixed mass of gas is proportional to its absolute temperature.
>
> $P \propto T$ at constant volume.
>
> **Avogadro's hypothesis:** Equal volumes of gas at the same temperature and pressure contain an equal number of molecules.
>
> **Kinetic energy and temperature:** $\frac{3}{2} kT = \frac{1}{2} mc^2$
>
> **Internal energy of an ideal gas:** Generally, the internal energy of a substance is the sum of the total kinetic energies and the total potential energies of its atoms/molecules. Since the atoms/molecules in an ideal gas have no potential energy (because there are no forces between them) the internal energy of an ideal gas is the total kinetic energy of its atoms/molecules.
>
> $U = \frac{3}{2} nRT$ or $U = \frac{3}{2} NkT$ or $U = \frac{3}{2} PV$

Exercise 9.1 Moles, molar mass and the Avogadro constant

The questions in this section will help you consolidate your knowledge and understanding of atoms and molecules as the particles that make up a gas.

1   a   How is a *mole* defined?

   b   What do we mean by the term *molar mass*?

   c   Calculate the number of atoms/molecules present in 20 g of

      i ^{56}Fe.

      ii ^{235}U.

      iii water.

> **TIP**
>
> The molar mass of iron is 56 gmole^{-1}, and oxygen has a molar mass of 16 gmole^{-1}

2   The molar mass of ^{12}C is 12 g.

   a   Calculate the mass of one atom of ^{12}C.

   b   The unified atomic mass unit, u, is defined as $\frac{1}{12}$ of the mass of a ^{12}C atom. Show that the value for u is 1.66×10^{-27} kg.

3   The molar mass of zinc is 65.4 gmole^{-1}. A sample of zinc contains 8 moles.

   a   Calculate the mass of the sample of zinc.

   b   Calculate the number of atoms of zinc in the sample.

   c   Calculate the mass of 1 atom of zinc.

4   The mass of a proton is given as 1.673×10^{-27} kg (to 4 s.f.).

   a   Show that the molar mass of hydrogen is 1.0 gmole^{-1}.

   b   Suggest why it is unnecessary to consider the mass of the electron in a hydrogen atom.

5   In March 2021, the United Nations Worldometer estimated the world's population to be 7.9 billion (7.9×10^9) people.

   a   How many worlds, with similar populations, would be required to make a mole of people?

   b   Is it feasible for our galaxy, the Milky Way, to have this many planets similar to Earth?

   c   Is it feasible for the universe to have this many planets similar to Earth?

6   The Earth has a radius of 6400 km, and about 75% of its surface is covered by oceanic water. Making the assumption that the average depth of the oceans is 3.0 km, estimate

   a   the volume of oceanic water on the Earth's surface.

   b   the mass of this oceanic water. How does this compare with the Earth's mass of 6.0×10^{24} kg?

   c   the number of moles in this oceanic water. How does this compare with the estimated number of stars in the known universe?

   d   the number of molecules in this oceanic water.

7   The mass of 1 m³ of air at standard temperature and pressure is about 1.3 kg, about 77% of which is N_2 and 23% is O_2.

   a   i   Calculate the mass of N_2 in 1 m³ of air.

       ii   If the molar mass of N_2 is 28 gmole^{-1}, calculate the number of moles of N_2 in 1 m³ of air.

       iii Hence, calculate the mass of an atom of nitrogen.

   b   i   Calculate the mass of O_2 in 1 m³ of air.

       ii   If the molar mass of O_2 is 32 gmole^{-1}, calculate the number of moles of O_2 in 1 m³ of air.

       iii Hence, calculate the mass of an atom of oxygen.

8   The density of gold is 19 300 kgm^{-3}, and its molar mass is 197 gmole^{-1}.

   The density of copper is 8960 kgm^{-1}, and its molar mass is 63.5 gmole^{-1}.

   a   i   Calculate the number of moles of gold in 1 m³ of gold.

       ii   Hence, calculate the volume taken up by 1 atom of gold.

   b   i   Calculate the number of moles of copper in 1 m³ of copper.

       ii   Hence, calculate the volume taken up by 1 atom of copper.

   c   If we model an atom as a cube, comment on the relative 'size' of atoms of gold and copper.

   d   Using your knowledge of the structure of an atom, suggest why your answer to **part c** is not surprising.

Exercise 9.2 Ideal gases

This exercise will help you become more familiar with the concept of an ideal gas and the three empirical gas laws and to use them to solve problems involving the behaviour of gases.

1   a   Outline what is meant by the term *ideal gas*.

    b   Under what conditions might a real gas behave like an ideal gas?

    c   Outline how the molecules of a gas exert a pressure on their container.

2   a   State Boyle's law as applied to an ideal gas.

    b   Outline an experiment that could verify Boyle's law. Make sure you include

        • the equipment required,

        • the measurements you would make (and the instruments you would use to make them) and

        • how you would manipulate the data to show Boyle's law.

    c   20 cm^3 of an ideal gas at an initial pressure of 100 kPa is compressed slowly into a new volume of 4 cm^3. Use Boyle's law to calculate the new pressure of the gas.

3   When a SCUBA diver breathes out under the water, small bubbles of used air are expelled from the diver's breathing equipment. As the bubbles rise towards the surface of the water, the bubble's volume increases.

    Use your knowledge of Boyle's law to explain why this occurs. State any assumptions you have made.

4   a   The relationship between the pressure of a fixed volume of ideal gas and its absolute temperature is often called 'the pressure law'. State what the pressure law is.

    b   Outline how a demonstration of the pressure law could be used to find a value for absolute zero.

5   Explain why a gas cannot exert a pressure at a temperature of 0 K.

6   A fixed volume container holds 250 cm^3 of air at an initial temperature of 10 °C and pressure of 1.01×10^5 Pa. The container is cooled to a temperature of −60 °C by immersing it for a short time in a bucket of liquid nitrogen at a temperature of −196 °C. Calculate the pressure of the cooled air in the container.

7   a   The relationship between the temperature of some gas and the volume of the gas at a constant pressure is called Charles' law. State what this relationship is.

> **TIP**
>
> The three empirical gas laws featured in this exercise form the basis of many exam questions.

> **TIP**
>
> Use your knowledge of kinetic theory.

b Outline an experiment that could verify Charles' law. Make sure you include

- the equipment required,
- the measurements you would make (and the instruments you would use to make them) and
- how you would manipulate the data to show Charles' law.

8 Outline how you could use the experiment in **question 7** to find a value for absolute zero.

9 An ideal gas at constant pressure is heated so that its volume quadruples.

a What will happen to its absolute temperature?

b What has happened to the average speed of the molecules?

10 150 cm³ of air, kept at a constant pressure, is heated from an initial temperature of 20 °C until its volume has become 300 cm³. Use Charles' law to calculate the final temperature of the gas.

Exercise 9.3 The Boltzmann equation

1 Consider a container in which there are N molecules of an ideal gas at a temperature, T.

  a Do all the molecules have the same amount of kinetic energy?

  b So, do all the molecules have the same speed?

  c Sketch a graph of how the number of molecules with a particular speed varies with the speed of the molecule.

  d Add another line/curve to show the distribution of speeds if the temperature of the gas in the container is larger.

  e What name is usually given to distributions of this kind?

2 a Outline what is meant by the term *root mean square speed of atoms*.

  b Show that the root mean square (rms) speed of an atom can be written as $v_{rms} = \sqrt{\frac{3RT}{M}}$, where R is the molar gas constant, T is the absolute temperature and M is the molar mass.

  c Hence, calculate the rms speed of an oxygen molecule at a temperature of 25 °C.

3 Suppose that, in a very small sample of gas, the following speeds of molecules are observed:

(To make the arithmetic easier, values here are very much smaller than one would expect from real gas molecules.)

5, 4, 8, 7, 5, 6, 6, 5, 3, 4, 5, 9, 8, 6, 7, 6, 5, 9, 10, 5, 6, 7, 7, 8, 5 a   Which speed is most likely? (Another way of asking this question is to ask which is the modal speed.)

b   What is the mean speed?

c   What is the rms speed?

d   What do you deduce about the relative values of the mode, the mean and the rms speeds?

e   Figure 9.1 shows an approximate Maxwell–Boltzmann distribution on which three different speeds, x, y and z, have been indicated.

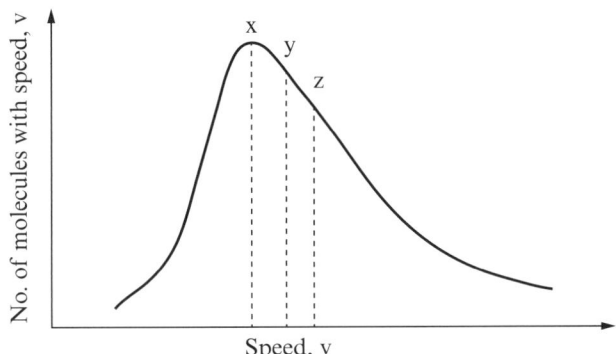

Figure 9.1

Which of the speeds, x or y, are most likely to correspond to

i   the mean speed.

ii the rms speed.

iii the modal speed.

4   This question leads you through the classical derivation of the ideal gas law.

Suppose that in a cubical box of length l, there is an atom of mass m, moving at a speed v, perpendicularly towards one of the faces of the box. For simplicity's sake, we will define the direction towards the face to be negative and the direction away from the face to be positive.

a   What is the momentum of the moving atom?

Now suppose that the atom bounces off the face of the cube elastically.

b   What is the momentum of the moving atom now?

c   So, by how much has the momentum of the atom changed?

d   How much time will it take for the atom to collide with the same face again, assuming that it bounces elastically off the opposite face in the same way as it has bounced off this face?

e   Using Newton's second law, show that the atom exerts a force of $F = \dfrac{mv^2}{l}$ on the face of the cube each time it bounces off.

Now, let us suppose that instead of one atom, there are N atoms, moving with a range of speeds, perpendicular to the faces of the cube.

- **f** How many atoms are likely to be moving towards one particular face?

- **g** Denoting c to be the root mean square speed of the atoms, write an expression for the total force exerted by these N atoms on a particular face.

- **h** What is the area of one face of the cube?

- **i** Now, using the equation for pressure, $P = \frac{F}{A}$, write an expression for the pressure exerted by the moving atoms in the cube.

- **j** What is the volume of the cube?

- **k** Hence, show that one form of the ideal gas equation is $PV = \frac{1}{3}Nmc^2$.

> **TIP**
> Try to make sure you complete this question. It contains many things that are frequently examined.

5 Using the ideal gas equation derived in **question 4**, $PV = \frac{1}{3}Nmc^2$,

- **a** what is the total mass of the atoms in the cube?

- **b** using the equation for density, $\rho = \frac{M}{V}$, show that another way of expressing the ideal gas equations is $P = \frac{1}{3}\rho c^2$.

- **c** At normal atmospheric pressure, $P = 1.01 \times 10^5$ Pa, air has a density of 1.3 kg m^{-3}. Calculate the typical speed of an air molecule.

6 You should have seen already from Chapter 7 that the average kinetic energy of an atom is proportional to its absolute temperature, via the equation

$\overline{KE} = \frac{1}{2}mc^2 = \frac{3}{2}kT$, where k is Boltzmann's constant, T absolute temperature and c the rms speed of the atoms.

- **a** Show that the internal energy, U, of N atoms of an ideal gas can be written as $U = \frac{3}{2}NkT$.

- **b** Notice that in the equation in **part a**, there is no term for m, the mass of the atoms. What does this imply?

- **c** How would you explain to an eager physics student that a mole of hydrogen gas and a mole of oxygen gas (assuming they both behave as an ideal gas), at the same absolute temperature, contain the same amount of internal energy?

7 Calculate the internal energy of 1 mole of an ideal gas at 100 °C.

8 **a** Show that the ideal gas equation can be written as $PV = NkT$.

- **b** Rewrite the equation in **part a** by replacing N with the term n, for how many moles of atoms/molecules are present.

- **c** The expression $N_A k$ can be written as $N_A k = R$, where R is called the universal gas constant. Hence, show that another form of the ideal gas equation is $PV = nRT$, and calculate the value of R and state its units.

d Calculate the temperature of 1 mole of an ideal gas at atmospheric pressure ($P = 1.013 \times 10^5$ Pa) if the volume it occupies is 2.24×10^{-2} m³. Give your answer in Kelvin and in °C.

9 a Show that the internal energy of an ideal gas can be written as $U = \frac{3}{2}PV$.

b Verify numerically that $U = \frac{3}{2}NkT = \frac{3}{2}PV$ for the standard temperature and pressure (STP) values of $N = N_A$, $T = 273$ K, $P = 1.013 \times 10^5$ Pa and $V = 22.4 \times 10^{-3}$ m³.

c For the following changes to a fixed amount of ideal gas (with all other aspects of the gas unchanged), state whether the internal energy of the gas will change a little, a lot or not at all.

   i Its temperature is doubled from 20 °C to 40 °C.

   ii Its temperature is doubled from 200 K to 400 K.

   iii Its pressure is doubled, and its volume is halved.

   iv Its pressure is halved, and its volume is halved.

   v Its pressure is doubled, and its volume is doubled.

EXAM-STYLE QUESTIONS

Multiple-choice questions

1 Which one of the statements about an ideal gas is **incorrect**?
- **A** Atoms always collide elastically.
- **B** No forces exist between atoms.
- **C** All atoms move about in random directions at the same speed.
- **D** The time it takes for an atom to collide is small compared with the time between one collision and the next.

2 Which of the following pairs of properties of a gas would **not** produce a graph that is a straight line passing through the origin?
- **A** Pressure plotted against volume for a fixed temperature
- **B** Volume plotted against Kelvin temperature for a fixed pressure
- **C** Pressure plotted against Kelvin temperature for a fixed volume
- **D** Pressure plotted against $\frac{1}{\text{Volume}}$ for a fixed temperature

3 A fixed mass of gas in a rigid container is heated so that the gas changes its temperature from 20 °C to 30 °C. If the pressure inside the container had been 150 kPa, then the best estimate of the pressure after heating is
- **A** 100 kPa.
- **B** 150 kPa.
- **C** 200 kPa.
- **D** 225 kPa.

CONTINUED

4 If N_A represents Avogadro's constant, the number of molecules in 2 g of H_2 gas is about

  A $\dfrac{N_A}{6}$.

  B $\dfrac{N_A}{2}$.

  C N_A.

  D $2N_A$.

5 The mass of a molecule of oxygen (O_2) is 16 times that of the mass of a molecule of diatomic hydrogen (H_2). If the average speed of an oxygen molecule in the air at a temperature of 20 °C is about 500 ms^{-1}, then the average speed of a diatomic hydrogen molecule in the air at the same temperature is about

  A 30 ms^{-1}.

  B 125 ms^{-1}.

  C 2000 ms^{-1}.

  D 8000 ms^{-1}.

6 Nine molecules have speeds, in kms^{-1}, of 6, 9, 7, 3, 8, 5, 3, 9, 7. Which of the following is the best estimate of their rms speed, in kms^{-1}?

  A 5.8

  B 6.3

  C 6.7

  D 7.0

7 A fixed mass of gas in a container of volume 22.4×10^{-3} m^3 has a pressure of 101 kPa at a temperature of 0 °C. The number of moles of gas present in the container is about

  A 0.1.

  B 1.0.

  C 8.3.

  D 10.

8 A real gas may behave like an ideal gas if

  A its density is low and its temperature is low.

  B its density is low and its temperature is high.

  C its pressure is high and its temperature is low.

  D its pressure is high and its temperature is high.

9 Which of the following expressions for the internal energy of an ideal gas is **incorrect**?

  A $U = \dfrac{3}{2}PV$

  B $U = \dfrac{3}{2}NRT$

  C $U = \dfrac{3}{2}NkT$

  D $U = \dfrac{3}{2}nRT$

CONTINUED

Short-answer questions

10 a State **two** conditions necessary for a gas to be considered *ideal*. [2]

   A fixed amount of ideal gas at a temperature of 20 °C is held in an expandable container of volume 650 cm³. The gas is then heated, at constant pressure, by an amount of thermal energy, Q, which raises the temperature of the gas to 30 °C.

   b Calculate the new volume of the gas. [2]

   c Explain why the change in the internal energy of the gas, $\Delta U \neq Q$. [1]

11 A container of volume 3×10^{-3} m³ contains an ideal gas at a temperature of 27 °C. If the pressure exerted by the gas is 6.0 MPa, calculate

   a the number of moles of gas present. [1]

   b the number of gas atoms present. [1]

   c the average volume occupied by one gas atom. [1]

   d if the radius of one of the gas atoms is 1.3×10^{-10} m, show that the assumption for an ideal gas—that the volume taken up by the atoms themselves is a very small fraction of the volume of the container in which the gas is held—is valid. [2]

12 A container of volume 0.1 m³ contains air at a temperature of 27 °C and a pressure of 1.5 MPa.

   a Calculate the number of moles of air molecules present. [2]

   b If the molar mass of air is 29 gmole⁻¹, calculate the mass of the air in the container. [1]

   c If 20% of the air is made up of oxygen molecules (O_2), calculate how many oxygen atoms are present in the container. [2]

13 A fixed amount of nitrogen gas is held in a rigid container at a temperature of 40 °C and a pressure of 100 kPa. (The density of nitrogen gas can be taken to be 1.2 kgm⁻³.)

   a Calculate the rms speed of the molecules. [2]

   b If the gas is now cooled so that the rms speed is halved, calculate the new temperature of the gas. [2]

14 Bromine gas (Br_2) has a molar mass of 160 g.

   a Show that the mass of an atom of bromine is 1.33×10^{-25} kg.
      ($N_A = 6.02 \times 10^{23}$ mole⁻¹) [1]

   b Calculate the total translational kinetic energy of the molecules of one mole of bromine gas at a temperature of 400 K. [2]

   c Hence, or otherwise, calculate the root mean squared speed of a bromine molecule at a temperature of 400 K. (Boltzmann's constant, $k = 1.38 \times 10^{-23}$ JK⁻¹) [2]

15 0.5 moles of gas are held in a rigid container of volume 0.2 m³ at a pressure of 1.0×10^4 Pa.

   a Calculate the temperature of the gas. [2]

   b Suggest why it is reasonable to assume that the gas behaves like an ideal gas. [1]

   c If the gas is now heated so that the pressure in the container is doubled, with no change in the volume of the container, what will the new temperature of the gas be? [1]

16 The pressure exerted by 2 moles of a monatomic ideal gas in a container of volume 2.5×10^{-2} m³ is measured to be 2.0×10^5 Pa at a temperature of 302 K. ($N_A = 6.02 \times 10^{23}$ mole⁻¹)

   a Calculate the number of atoms of gas present. [1]

   b Show that the value of Boltzmann's constant is 1.38×10^{-23} JK⁻¹. [2]

   c Show that the value of the universal gas constant is 8.31 JK⁻¹mole⁻¹ [1]

CONTINUED

17 A student sets up an experiment to find the value of absolute zero. The student uses a rigid, thin-walled, container, of volume 1.0×10^{-3} m³, that can be immersed in a large beaker of water—or another liquid substance. By changing the temperature of the container and measuring the pressure inside the container, the student produces the results shown in the following table.

Temperature / °C	−196	0	20	40	60	80	100
Pressure / kPa	28	100	107	115	122	129	137

a Using the axes in Figure 9.2, plot a graph of the student's results. [2]

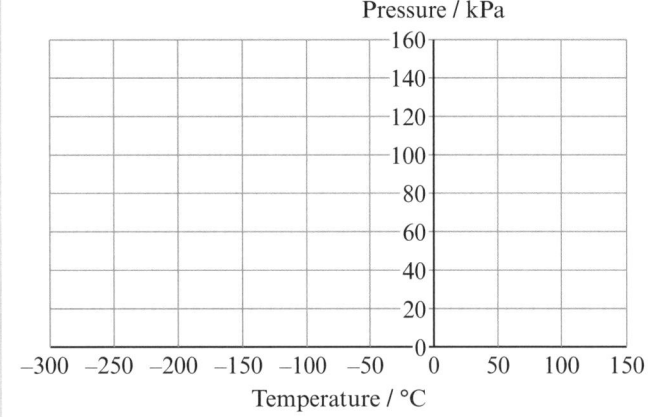

Figure 9.2

b Suggest how the student could have achieved the temperature measurement of −196 °C. [1]

c By using your graph, estimate the value that the student predicted for absolute zero. [2]

18 A constant amount of ideal gas is held in a syringe, one end of which is sealed. The gas is then compressed by pushing the other end of the syringe slowly inwards so that the volume occupied by the gas is halved.

a Before compression, the pressure inside the syringe was 1.0×10^5 Pa. Calculate the pressure inside the syringe after the gas was compressed. [2]

b Outline why it is necessary to compress the ideal gas slowly. [1]

c If the gas were compressed quickly, suggest and explain how the pressure inside the syringe would compare with the value you calculated in **part a**. [2]

> # Chapter 10
Thermodynamics

CHAPTER OUTLINE

In this chapter, you will:

> - consolidate the ideas of internal energy and temperature.
> - realise that changes in temperature are related to changes in internal energy.
> - learn that the addition of thermal energy to a system is related to the change in internal energy of the system and to the mechanical work done on the system.
> - use the conservation of energy to develop the first law of thermodynamics.
> - apply the first law of thermodynamics to solve problems with changes of pressure, volume and temperature of a gas.
> - relate the concept of entropy to the degree of disorder of particles in a system.
> - relate changes in entropy to the addition, or subtraction, of thermal energy and to the thermodynamic temperature of the system.
> - look at how the number of probable ways in which particles may be arranged in a system is related to its entropy.
> - explore four kinds of thermodynamic processes.
> - see how the second law of thermodynamics is related to the change in entropy of an isolated system.
> - explore how the second law of thermodynamics sets constraints on which physical processes are possible and which are not.
> - use graphs to describe the thermodynamic state of gases.
> - develop the concept of a heat engine and relate it to a cyclic gas process.
> - consider the efficiency of a heat engine.
> - see how a Carnot cycle sets a maximum efficiency for a heat engine that is dependent on its two heat reservoirs.

KEY TERMS

closed system: a system that can transfer energy, but not matter (mass), into or from its surroundings

isolated system: a system where no thermal energy or matter (mass) can be transferred into or from its surroundings

entropy: a measure of a system's disorder

heat engine: a device that transfers chemical energy to thermal energy and then to mechanical or electrical energy, which can then be used to do mechanical work

efficiency: the ratio of output work to input energy

Carnot cycle: a thermodynamic cycle consisting of two isothermal and two adiabatic curves

Thermodynamic processes:

Process	Description	Equation
Isothermal	Temperature stays constant	$P_1 V_1 = P_2 V_2$
Isobaric	Pressure stays constant	$\dfrac{P_1}{T_1} = \dfrac{P_2}{T_2}$
Isovolumetric	Volume stays constant	$\dfrac{V_1}{T_1} = \dfrac{V_2}{T_2}$
Adiabatic	No heat enters or leaves the system	$P_1 V_1^{\frac{5}{3}} = P_2 V_2^{\frac{5}{3}}$

Internal energy: the sum of the total kinetic energy and the total potential energy of all the particles in a system

The first law of thermodynamics: When an amount of heat Q is given to a gas, the gas will absorb that energy and use it to change its internal energy and/or to do work. Conservation of energy demands that

$Q = \Delta U + W$,

where ΔU is the change in internal energy and W is the work done.

KEY EQUATIONS

$U = \dfrac{3}{2} NkT = \dfrac{3}{2} nRT = \dfrac{3}{2} PV$

$Q = \Delta U + W$ (the first law of thermodynamics)

$W = P \Delta V$

$\Delta U = \dfrac{3}{2} Nk\Delta T$

10 Thermodynamics

CONTINUED
$\Delta S = \dfrac{\Delta Q}{T}$
$S = k \ln \Omega$
$\eta = \dfrac{\text{useful work done}}{\text{total energy used}}$
where Q is thermal energy transferred, U is internal energy, W is mechanical work done, P is pressure, V is volume, N is the total number of particles in a system, k is Boltzmann's constant ($k = 1.38 \times 10^{-23}$ JK^{-1}), S is entropy, Ω is the number of possible ways in which the particles in a system can be arranged, η is the efficiency of a heat engine and η_c the efficiency of a heat engine following a Carnot cycle.

Exercise 10.1 Internal energy

The questions in this section will help you consolidate your understanding of what internal energy is. By using presure–volume diagrams, you will be able to learn four thermodynamic processes that can change the internal energy of a gas.

1. **a** **i**   What is meant by the term *internal energy* of a gas?

      ii Calculate the internal energy of 3.0 moles of an ideal gas at a temperature of 300 K.

      iii State what will happen to the internal energy of the gas in **part b** if the temperature of the gas is halved.

   b State what is meant by

      i   an *open system*.

      ii a *closed system*.

      iii an *isolated system*.

2. One way of writing the internal energy of a system is $U = \dfrac{3}{2} NkT$.

   a **i**   State what the terms N, k and T refer to.

      ii Show that the internal energy of a system can also be written as $U = \dfrac{3}{2} nRT$.

      iii Show also that the internal energy may be written as $U = \dfrac{3}{2} PV$.

   b Outline **four** ways in which the internal energy of a system may be changed.

3. Outline what is happening to a thermodynamic system when

   a $Q > 0$.

   b $Q < 0$

c $\Delta U > 0$

d $\Delta U < 0$

e $W > 0$

f $W < 0$

4 A fixed amount of ideal gas at a pressure of 2.0×10^6 Pa is compressed from a volume of 0.25 m³ to a volume of 0.15 m³ with no change in pressure.

   a The internal energy, U, of the gas is given by the expression $U = \frac{3}{2} NkT$.

   Show that the change in internal energy of the gas can be expressed by $\Delta U = \frac{3}{2} P \Delta V$.

   b Calculate the change in internal energy of the gas.

   c Calculate the work done, W, on the gas.

5 Figure 10.1 shows a pressure–volume diagram for a sample of 4.0 moles of an ideal gas on which is shown a thermodynamic process, taking the gas from point X to point Y.

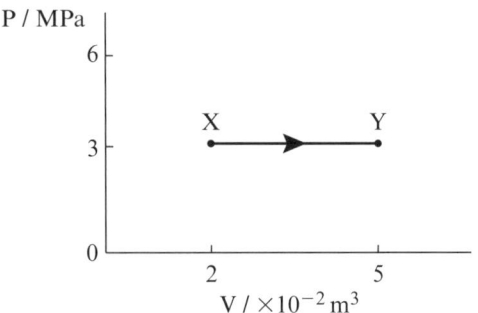

Figure 10.1

   a Identify the type of thermodynamic process that takes the gas from point X to point Y.

   b Calculate the temperature of the gas at

      i   point X.

      ii point Y.

   c i   Calculate the change in internal energy of the gas as it moves from state X to state Y.

      ii Has the internal energy of the gas increased or decreased?

   d How much work has the gas done on its surroundings?

   e If the gas has done work on its surroundings, but its internal energy has increased, what else must have happened to the gas?

> **TIP**
>
> Try to become familiar with the way thermodynamic processes are represented on a pressure–volume graph. Such diagrams frequently form the basis of exam questions.

6 Figure 10.2 shows a pressure–volume diagram on which two thermodynamic processes, A and B, are shown for a fixed amount of 2.0 moles of gas. The temperature at X and Y is 300 K.

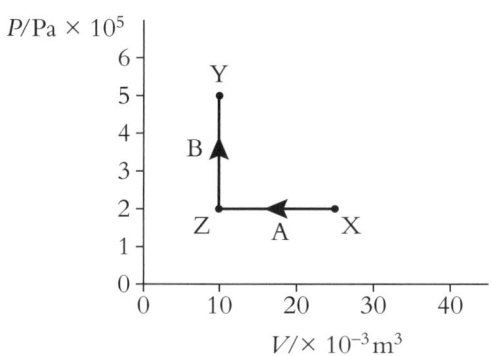

Figure 10.2

- **a**
  - **i** What type of thermodynamic process is process A?
  - **ii** What type of thermodynamic process is process B?
- **b**
  - **i** Calculate the amount of work done on the gas by process A.
  - **ii** Is the gas at Z at a higher or a lower temperature than it is at X? Explain your reasoning.
  - **iii** What can you say about the amount of heat, Q, exchanged between the gas and its surroundings during process A?
- **c**
  - **i** Does process B involve any work being done on or by the gas? Explain your answer.
  - **ii** Since the internal energy, U, of the gas at X and Y is the same (they are at the same temperature) what must be happening during process B?

7 Figure 10.3 shows two more thermodynamic processes, C and D, also acting on a fixed amount of 2.0 moles of ideal gas. The temperature of the gas at X and Y is 300 K.

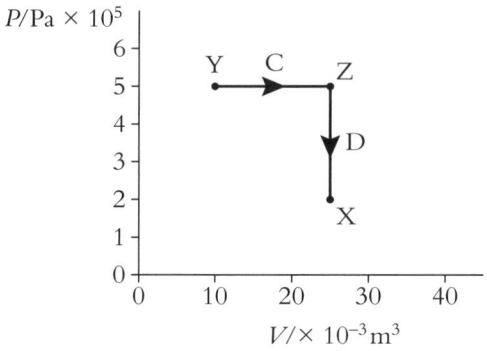

Figure 10.3

a **i** Calculate the amount of work done by the gas during process C.

ii Is the gas at point Z at a higher or a lower temperature than at point Y?

iii What must be happening to the gas during process C?

b **i** Does the gas do any work on its surroundings during process D? Explain your reasoning.

ii What must be happening to the gas during process D?

8 Figure 10.4 shows two thermodynamic processes, A and B. Process A is an isothermal process. Process B is an adiabatic process.

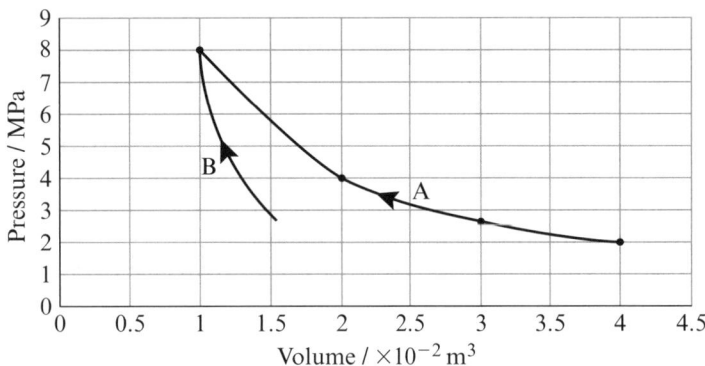

Figure 10.4

a **i** Verify that process A is isothermal.

ii Has the gas done work on its surroundings, or have the surroundings done work on the gas?

iii Hence, deduce whether heat has been exchanged from the gas to the surroundings or from the surroundings to the gas.

b **i** Explain what an *adiabatic* process is.

ii Suggest, with reasoning, whether the adiabatic process, B, occurred quickly or slowly.

iii Has the gas done work on its surroundings, or have the surroundings done work on the gas?

iv Outline how you can find out, by using the pressure–volume diagram, how much work has been done.

v With reference to the conservation of energy, deduce how the work done is related to the change in internal energy.

9   Figure 10.5 shows a thermodynamic cycle consisting of four thermodynamic processes, A, B, C and D, moving a fixed quantity of gas through four thermodynamic states, W, X, Y and Z.

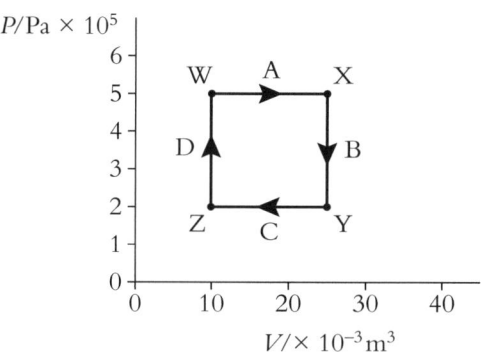

Figure 10.5

a   For process A, calculate the work done by the gas on its surroundings.

b   Do processes B and D involve any work being done on or by the gas?

c   For process C, calculate the work done on the gas.

d   Calculate the net work done by the gas if the gas begins in state W and finishes in state W having undergone processes A, B, C and D.

e   How is this net work done by the gas represented on Figure 10.5?

f   In terms of conservation of energy, how is it possible for the gas to move around the thermodynamic cycle producing a net amount of work done on its surroundings?

10 Figure 10.6 shows pressure–volume diagram for a thermodynamic cycle in which four thermodynamic processes, A, B, C and D act on a fixed mass of gas.

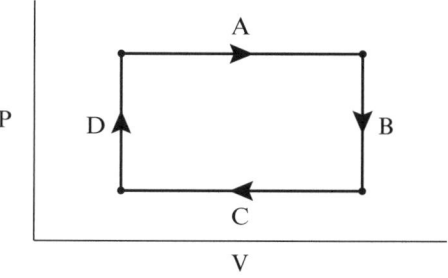

Figure 10.6

a Complete the table to show what is happening to the gas during each of the thermodynamic processes.

Use the words and phrases *added*, *removed*, *increases*, *decreases*, *on the gas*, *by the gas* and *none*.

Process	Q	U	W
A			
B			
C			
D			

b What feature of the thermodynamic cycle represents the net work done by the gas?

Exercise 10.2 The first law of thermodynamics

The questions in this section will help you become more familiar with the first law of thermodynamics and how it can be used to solve problems involving gases and isolated systems.

1 Consider a fixed amount of ideal gas in a container to which can be added an amount of thermal energy, Q.

    a Suppose that when Q is added to the gas, the volume of the container does not change.

        i What will the effect be, on the particles of gas, of adding thermal energy, Q?

        ii What will happen to the internal energy of the gas?

        iii Does the gas do any mechanical work on its surroundings? Explain.

    b Now suppose that, when Q is added to the gas, the pressure exerted by the gas remains constant, but the volume of the container changes.

        i Adding Q to the gas will increase the average speed of the particles of the gas. Explain, using your ideas about kinetic theory, what must be happening for the pressure exerted by the gas to remain constant.

        ii What is SI unit for the product of pressure and volume?

        iii Write an algebraic expression for the work done by the gas on the surroundings in terms of the pressure of the gas and the change in volume of the container.

c i Generally, when thermal energy, Q, is added to some ideal gas, both the internal energy **and** the volume of the gas can change. Use the conservation of energy to write an expression relating Q to U and W.

ii What is the name usually given to your expression?

2 a An ideal gas expands isothermally, doing 5.0 kJ of work on its surroundings.

i By how much does the internal energy of the gas change? Explain your answer.

ii Hence, determine the amount of thermal energy exchanged between the gas and its surroundings.

iii Is the thermal energy you determined in **part b** absorbed by or emitted by the gas?

b An ideal gas is compressed, with no exchange of thermal energy with the surroundings, so that its volume is halved. The amount of work done on the gas is 2.0 kJ.

i How much thermal energy, Q, flows into or out of the gas?

ii By how much does the internal energy of the gas change?

iii Does the temperature of the gas increase or decrease?

3 A frictionless piston, closed at one end, contains a fixed amount of ideal gas at atmospheric pressure. ($P = 1.01 \times 10^5$ Pa.)

4.5 MJ of thermal energy is given to the gas. The volume occupied by the gas changes from 12.0 m³ to 18.0 m³. There is no change to the gas's pressure. Calculate

a the work done by the gas as it expands.

b the change in the internal energy of the gas.

4 3.0 moles of ideal gas of volume 6.0×10^{-2} m³ and pressure 4.0×10^5 Pa expands to a volume of 8.0×10^{-2} m³ at which its pressure becomes 3.0×10^5 Pa.

a Show that the gas undergoes no change in its internal energy.

b Using the first law of thermodynamics,

i is W greater than zero, equal to zero or less than zero?

ii is Q greater than zero, equal to zero or less than zero?

c Rewrite the first law of thermodynamics for a process such as this, that is one in which the internal energy does not change.

5 A sample of ideal gas expands isothermally doing 2.5 kJ of work on its surroundings. Determine the

a change in its internal energy.

b heat exchanged from its surroundings.

6   A sample of ideal gas is compressed by 4.5 kJ of work.

    a   If the process is isothermal, how much heat is exchanged between the gas and its surroundings, and in which direction?

    b   If the process is adiabatic, what happens to the temperature of the gas?

7   Suppose that the volume of 2.5 moles of ideal gas is 1.0 m^3 and its pressure is 5×10^5 Pa.

    a   i   Calculate the temperature of the gas.

        ii Calculate the internal energy, U, of the gas.

    b   The gas is compressed, with no change in pressure, so that its volume becomes 0.25 m^3.

        Calculate

        i   the new temperature of the gas.

        ii the new internal energy of the gas.

        iii the work done on, or by, the gas.

        iv the amount of heat, Q, exchanged with the surroundings.

    c   i   Is the heat you calculated in **part b iv** lost from or gained by the gas?

        ii What do your answers to **part b** suggest about the values of T and Q when a gas is compressed with no change in pressure?

        iii What do you expect will happen to T, U and Q if a gas is allowed to expand with no change in pressure?

8   Consider 4.0 moles of ideal gas of volume 0.15 m^3 at a pressure of 1.0×10^5 Pa.

    a   Calculate

        i   the temperature of the gas.

        ii the internal energy of the gas.

    b   The gas undergoes a change in its thermodynamic state. Its pressure becomes 5.0×10^5 Pa, with no change in its volume.

        Calculate

        i   the new temperature of the gas.

        ii the new internal energy of the gas.

        iii the work done on, or by, the gas.

        iv the amount of heat, Q, exchanged with the surroundings.

c   i   Is the heat you calculated in **part b iv** lost from or gained by the gas?

   ii   What do your answers to **part b** suggest about the values of T and Q when a gas undergoes an increase in pressure with no change in volume?

   iii So, what do you expect will happen to T, U and Q if a gas is allowed to undergo a decrease in pressure with no change to its volume?

9   Consider a fixed amount of ideal gas that undergoes a thermodynamic process in which there is no exchange of heat.

   a   If the gas expands,

      i   what can you say about any work done on or by the gas?

      ii   what can you say about any change in its internal energy?

      iii what happens to the temperature of the gas?

   b   If the gas is compressed,

      i   what can you say about any work done on or by the gas?

      ii   what can you say about any change in its internal energy?

      iii what happens to the temperature of the gas?

10 1.0 kg of water at a temperature of 100 °C has thermal energy supplied to it. All the water changes into steam at the same temperature and at a pressure of 1.01×10^5 Pa. The steam occupies a volume of 1.67 m^3. If the specific latent heat of vaporisation of water is 2.26 MJkg^{-1}, calculate

   a   the thermal energy required.

   b   the work done on its surroundings by the water as it expands.

   c   using the first law of thermodynamics, the change in the internal energy of the water.

Exercise 10.3 The second law of thermodynamics

This exercise will help you explore the importance of the concept of entropy and how it leads to one of the most important laws in all of physics: the second law of thermodynamics.

1   Two physics students decide to play a game of statistics in order to simulate what happens when a hot body is put into thermal contact with a cold body. Amaya models a hot body by having 60 counters, whilst Andrew models a cold body by having six counters. Each counter represents a small amount of energy. When the two bodies are brought into contact, the two students throw a six-sided spinner for each counter they have. If the spinner shows a six, the counter is passed to the other student.

a   After one 'turn' of the game,

   i   how many counters might statistically be expected to be given to Andrew?

   ii how many counters might statistically be expected to be given to Amaya?

   iii how many counters will Amaya and Andrew now have?

   iv what has happened to the 'temperature' of Amaya and of Andrew's bodies?

b   After another 'turn',

   i   how many counters might statistically be expected to be given to Andrew?

   ii how many counters might statistically be expected to be given to Amaya?

   iii how many counters will Amaya and Andrew now have?

   iv what has happened to the 'temperature' of Amaya and of Andrew's bodies?

c   After a large number of turns,

   i   what would you statistically expect to have happened to Amaya's and Andrew's counters?

   ii what would you say has happened to their temperatures?

d   If Amaya and Andrew continued to play the game,

   i   would they still exchange counters on each turn?

   ii how would Amaya and Andrew explain that their two bodies are in thermal equilibrium?

e   After playing the game, Amaya and Andrew are happy that the game does simulate what happens in real life when a hot body is brought into contact with a cold body.

   i   How do the two students explain why the hotter body cools and the colder body warms?

   ii How would the two students explain why the hotter body doesn't become even hotter and the colder body become even colder? That is why isn't there a net transfer of energy from the colder body to the hotter body?

2 This question develops a link between the entropy of a system (often described as the amount of disorder the system has) and the number of ways in which the components of the system can be arranged.

Consider a bookshelf that has some books on it.

a Suppose there are two books: A and B. In how many ways can the two books be arranged on the bookshelf?

Each different way of arranging the books is called a *microstate*. The number of microstates, Ω, is related to the entropy, S, of the system by the equation $S = k \ln \Omega$, where k is Boltzmann's constant.

b Now suppose we add one more book, C.

   i What is the value of Ω now?

   ii By what factor has S increased?

c Now suppose we add another book, D.

   i What is the value of Ω now?

   ii By what factor has S increased?

d If we continue adding books,

   i what happens to the value of Ω?

   ii what happens to the way in which S increases?

Adding books to the bookshelf is like adding energy to a body. So, now we will consider what happens to the body when we add energy to it—and what happens to the body from which we have taken the energy.

e Energy tends to be transferred from a hotter body to a colder body. Suppose we transfer one energy 'unit' from a hot body to a colder body.

   i What will have happened to the value of S for the hotter body?

   ii What will have happened to the value of S for the colder body?

   iii What is the resulting 'net' change in S?

   iv When a hot body and a cold body are brought into contact, energy is transferred from the hot body to the cold body (and not the other way around). Whenever this occurs, what *always* happens to the net value of S?

3 For each of the following situations, state whether the entropy increases or decreases and give a reason to support your answer.

a 10 g of water at 0 °C freezes and becomes an ice cube.

b A sample of ideal gas expands isothermally.

c A glass falls from a table to the floor and shatters.

4 2.0 kg of water at a temperature of 20 °C is mixed with 2.0 kg of water at 80 °C.

    a What will the final temperature of the 4.0 kg of water be?

    b   **i** How much thermal energy will have been lost from the hot water? (The specific heat capacity of water is 4.2 kJK⁻¹kg⁻¹)

        ii How much thermal energy will have been gained by the cold water?

    c   **i** What will the average temperature of the cold water have been while it was warming up?

        ii What will the average temperature of the hot water have been while it was cooling down?

    d The change in entropy for any body is given by the equation

$$\Delta S = \frac{Q}{T},$$

where Q is the thermal energy gained or lost and T the average temperature at which the transfer of energy occurred.

        i Calculate the change in entropy, ΔS_{hot}, for the hot water as it cools.

        ii Calculate the change in entropy, ΔS_{cold}, for the cold water as it warms up.

        iii Show that there has been a positive increase in the total entropy.

> **TIP**
>
> Don't forget to convert temperatures into Kelvin.

5 A mass of 40 kg slides down a slope through a vertical distance of 3.0 m and comes to a stop.

    a Outline the energy transfers that take place as the mass slides down the slope and comes to a stop.

    b Assuming that the temperature of the mass and its surroundings is 20 °C, calculate the change in entropy of the mass and its surroundings.

6 **a** Describe how the net entropy is increasing when

        i a cup of tea is left to cool.

        ii a crystal of sodium chloride grows from a pool of seawater.

        iii an athlete sweats to keep cool.

    b Calculate the net entropy change when 2 kJ of heat is exchanged from a heat source at a temperature of 700 K to a heat sink at a temperature of 300 K.

7   Figure 10.7 shows a pressure–volume diagram for a sample of four moles of an ideal gas. The gas is undergoing an isothermal thermodynamic process to take it from thermodynamic state A to thermodynamic state B.

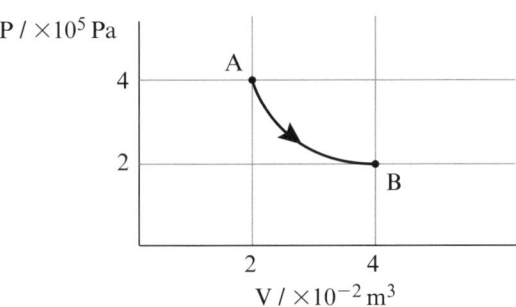

Figure 10.7

- a i   Show that the thermodynamic states, A and B, are at the same temperature.
    - ii What does this imply about the internal energy in states A and B?
- b i   Use the pressure–volume diagram to estimate the work done by the gas on its surroundings.
    - ii Hence, state the heat transferred from the surroundings to the gas.
    - iii Hence, determine the change in entropy of the gas.
- c Since the surroundings have transferred heat to the gas, the surroundings must have undergone a loss of entropy. Suggest why the second law of thermodynamics has not been violated.

8   Figure 10.8 shows a pressure–volume diagram for a sample of 1 mole of ideal gas. The gas is in the thermodynamic state labelled X. Two other thermodynamic states, Y and Z, are shown.

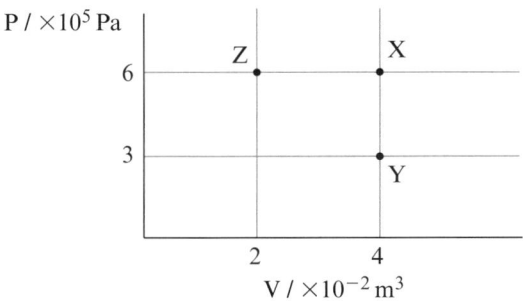

Figure 10.8

a   Calculate the temperature of the sample of gas in the thermodynamic state X.

b   Show that the two thermodynamic states, Y and Z, are isothermal.

c   The gas changes its thermodynamic state from X to Y.

   i   What happens to its temperature?

   ii   What happens to its internal energy?

   iii What happens to its entropy? Explain your answer with reference to the second law of thermodynamics.

d   The gas changes its thermodynamic state from X to Z.

   i   What happens to its temperature?

   ii   What happens to its internal energy?

   iii What happens to its entropy? Explain your answer with reference to the second law of thermodynamics.

9 A physics teacher puts her cup of coffee on a table in a classroom. The coffee has a mass of 250 g and a temperature of 85 °C. The classroom is at a temperature of 20 °C.

The teacher forgets her coffee because a student asks her an interesting question about thermodynamics. The coffee starts to cool down. Calculate

a   the thermal energy lost by the coffee as it cooled to a temperature of 30 °C (the specific heat capacity of the coffee can be taken to be 4.2 kJkg^{-1} °C; you may ignore the cup itself).

b   the average temperature of the coffee during its cooling.

c   the change in entropy of the coffee as a result of cooling.

d   the change in entropy of the classroom (assume that the temperature of the classroom does not change).

e   the net change in entropy of the universe as a result of the coffee cooling.

10 One way of interpreting the second law of thermodynamics is to say that, in any process, the net change in entropy is always positive. We could call this the entropy form of the second law of thermodynamics.

An ice cube sitting on a metal plate will melt quite quickly.

a   Explain why the ice cube will melt quickly.

b   Explain how the net change in entropy is positive despite energy being removed from the surroundings of the ice cube.

c   If the ice cube has a mass of 10 g, calculate the change in entropy of the ice cube. (The specific latent heat of fusion of water is 334 kJkg^{-1}.)

Exercise 10.4 Real systems

1 Figure 10.9 shows a schematic diagram of a heat engine.

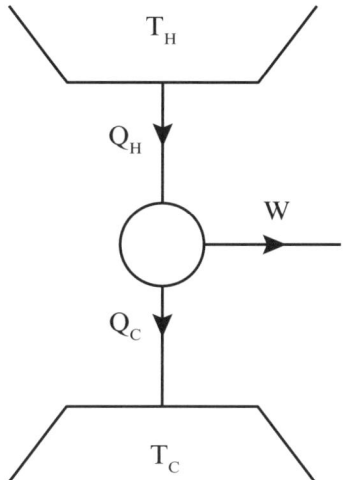

Figure 10.9

   a   Explain the meaning of the term *heat engine*.

   b   With reference to the symbols used in Figure 10.9, outline how the heat engine works.

   c   Using the symbols from Figure 10.9, show that the efficiency of the heat engine can be written as $\eta = 1 - \dfrac{Q_C}{Q_H}$.

2 Entropy has been described by some as a form of thermal energy that is unavailable for doing work. This question examines the validity of this idea.

Consider a car engine.

   a   What is the main idea behind a car engine? That is what energy transfer is a car engine designed to make happen?

   b   Suggest some reasons why a car engine isn't 100% efficient.

   c   In the car engine, suggest some stores of thermal energy that are not available for doing useful work—in other words, energy that doesn't transfer to kinetic energy.

d We can model the car engine as a source of thermal energy, Q_{hot} at a high temperature. It transfers some of this thermal energy to do useful work, W. The engine emits the unavailable thermal energy, Q_{cold}, to the surroundings, which are at a lower temperature.

    i Write an expression for the efficiency of the car engine in terms of Q_{hot} and W.

    ii Hence, show that the efficiency of the car engine could be written as $\eta = 1 - \dfrac{Q_{cold}}{Q_{hot}}$.

    iii Using your answer to **part b**, suggest why the actual efficiency of a car engine is less than that predicted by the equation in **part d ii**.

e For a working car engine, is the total entropy of the car and its surroundings increasing? That is: is the car engine an example of the second law of thermodynamics in practice?

f Is it reasonable, then, to consider that the second law of thermodynamics could be written as 'When thermal energy is transferred into useful work done, some thermal energy is always wasted, making the whole process less than 100% efficient'?

g To which form of the second law of thermodynamics does **part f** refer?

3 A scientific study carried out on a natural gas combined cycle power station showed that the efficiency of the generators decreased as the ambient temperature increased from 8 °C to 23 °C.

  a Outline why this result was to be expected.

  b Calculate the maximum theoretical efficiency of such a power station operating between the temperatures 700 °C and

    i 8 °C.

    ii 23 °C.

  c At the ambient temperature of 8 °C, the electrical energy produced by each generator was 46.0 MW. When the ambient temperature was increased to 23 °C, the electrical energy produced by each generator fell to 40.0 MW. How does the change in electrical energy production compare with the change in the maximum theoretical efficiency of the generators? Comment on your answer.

4   Figure 10.10 shows another kind of thermodynamic cycle on a pressure–volume diagram. In this cycle, there are two adiabatic processes, A and C, and two isovolumetric processes, B and D.

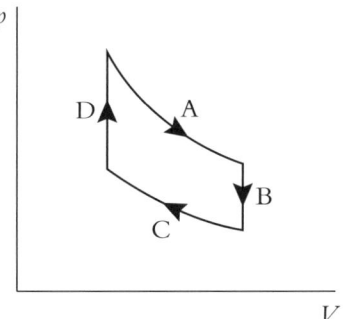

Figure 10.10

a   This cycle describes what happens in an internal combustion engine, such as in a family car. What is the name of this kind of cycle?

b   How can you use the pressure–volume diagram to find the net work done?

c   In which processes does the gas

   i   absorb heat from the surroundings?

   ii release heat to the surroundings?

d   In which of the two processes in **part c** is most heat exchanged?

e   Draw a diagram of a simple heat engine that explains how work can be derived from heat.

f   How does your diagram show that the production of work from heat cannot be 100% efficient?

5   Figure 10.11 shows a theoretical thermodynamic cycle that is deemed to be the most efficient thermodynamic cycle possible.

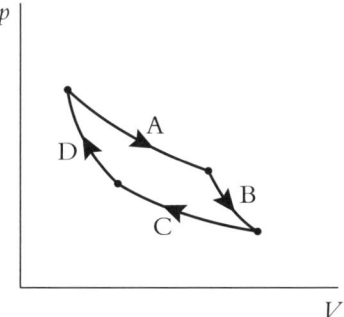

Figure 10.11

a What is the name given to this kind of thermodynamic cycle?

b Identify the thermodynamic processes represented on the diagram by A, B, C and D.

c Along which process is the temperature of the gas highest?

d In which process is heat

   i   absorbed from the surroundings into the gas?

   ii lost to the surroundings from the gas?

e In which of the two processes in **part d** is most heat exchanged?

f Draw a diagram of a heat engine operating between the temperatures T_H and T_C. Use it to show that the efficiency of the heat engine can be given as $\eta = 1 - \dfrac{Q_C}{Q_H}$, where Q_c is the heat exchanged when the temperature of the gas is coldest and Q_H is the heat exchanged when the temperature of the gas is hottest.

g i   Write an expression for the change in entropy of the heat source.

   ii Write an expression for the change in entropy of the heat sink.

   iii Hence, show that the net change in entropy of the system is
       $$\Delta S_{net} = \dfrac{Q_H - W}{T_C} - \dfrac{Q_H}{T_H}$$

   iv Since the second law of thermodynamics states that $\Delta S \geq 0$, show that another way of expressing the efficiency of the heat engine is given by
       $$\eta \leq 1 - \dfrac{T_C}{T_H}.$$

h In a pressurised water reactor (a kind of nuclear power station), pressurised water at a temperature of 327 °C is used to generate work. The cooled water reaches a temperature of 27 °C.

   i   Calculate the maximum theoretical efficiency of such a power station.

   ii In practice, this level of efficiency is not realised. Suggest why it is not possible to replicate this level of efficiency in a real nuclear power station.

   iii How could the theoretical efficiency be increased?

   iv Suggest why your answer is not possible in practice.

6 A steam engine is to operate between the temperatures of 550 °C and 250 °C.

   a Calculate the maximum efficiency of such a steam engine.

   b Suggest why it is likely that the steam engine will operate with an efficiency lower than your answer to **part a**.

7 Figure 10.12 shows the pressure–volume diagram for a Carnot cycle in reverse.

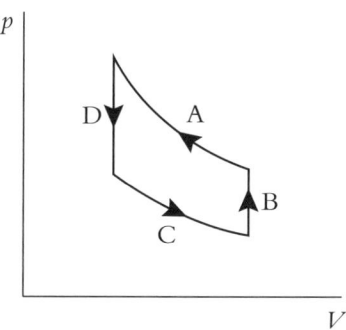

Figure 10.12

a Complete the table to show what is happening to the gas during each of the thermodynamic processes.

Use the words and phrases *added, removed, increases, decreases, on the gas, by the gas* and *none*.

Process	Q	U	W
A			
B			
C			
D			

b Outline what this thermodynamic cycle is achieving.

c Give an example of such a thermodynamic cycle being used in your home.

8 Figure 10.13 shows a heat pump.

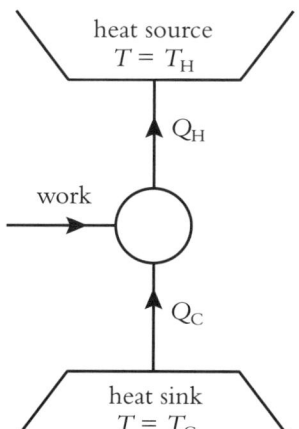

Figure 10.13

a Describe in detail what Figure 10.13 shows.

b Explain how this shows the Clausius form of the second law of thermodynamics.

9 An ideal refrigerator in a kitchen works using a reversible Carnot cycle between the temperatures 4 °C and 25 °C. If 6.0 kJ are extracted from the inside of the fridge, determine

> **TIP**
> Remember to convert temperatures into Kelvin.

a the amount of thermal energy transferred to the kitchen.

b the energy supplied to the fridge as mechanical work done.

EXAM-STYLE QUESTIONS

Multiple-choice questions

1 Which of the following is not a recognised form of the second law of thermodynamics?
   A In any thermodynamic process, the entropy of a sample of gas always increases.
   B It is not possible to make a heat engine that is 100% efficient.
   C You can only transfer heat from a cold object to a hot one if you do some work on the cold object.
   D The entropy of the universe always increases.

2 When a sample of ideal gas expands isothermally, which of the following is false?
   A The pressure of the gas changes.
   B The gas does work on the surroundings.
   C The internal energy of the gas changes.
   D Heat is gained by the gas.

3 What is the Clausius form of the second law of thermodynamics?
   A For an isolated system, $\Delta S \geq 0$.
   B It is not possible to exchange heat from a colder body to a hotter body without the use of mechanical work input.
   C It is not possible to make a heat engine that converts all of the heat exchanged into useful work.
   D A Carnot heat engine is the most efficient of all heat engines operating between the same temperatures.

4 When a cup of hot tea is placed in a cool box, which of the combinations listed in the table is correct?

	Entropy of the cup of tea	Entropy of the cool box
A	Increases	Increases
B	Increases	Decreases
C	Decreases	Increases
D	Decreases	Decreases

CONTINUED

5 Which of the thermodynamic processes in Figure 10.14 is an isobaric process?

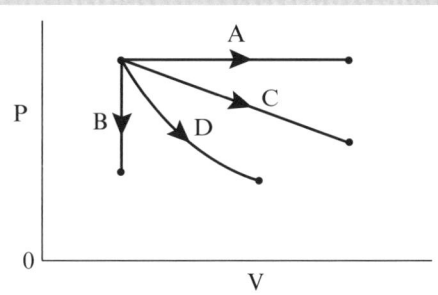

Figure 10.14

6 Which of the thermodynamic processes in Figure 10.14 is an isovolumetric (isochoric) process?
7 Which of the thermodynamic processes in Figure 10.14 could be an isothermal process?
8 In which of the thermodynamic processes in Figure 10.14 is no work done by the gas?
9 Which of the thermodynamic processes in Figure 10.14 results in a decrease in internal energy?
10 The maximum efficiency of a Carnot cycle heat engine operating between the temperatures of 400 °C and 100 °C is

A 55%.
B 65%.
C 75%.
D 85%.

Short-answer questions

11 Figure 10.15 shows a pressure–volume diagram on which is shown a thermodynamic process taking 2.5 moles of ideal gas from state X to state Y.

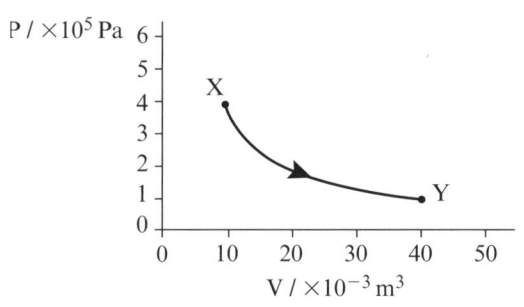

Figure 10.15

a Show that the thermodynamic process shown is isothermal. [2]
b Estimate the work done by the gas in moving from thermodynamic state X to state Y. [2]
c Has the gas received heat from its surroundings or has it lost heat to the surroundings? [1]

CONTINUED

12 The first law of thermodynamics can be written as $Q = \Delta U + W$.

    a Identify what each of the terms represents and, for each, state the conditions under which the term is a positive value. [3]

    b A system exchanges 50 J of heat with its hotter surroundings whilst doing 30 J of work on its surroundings.

        i Calculate the change in the system's internal energy. [1]

        ii Explain why the net entropy of the system and its surroundings has increased. [3]

    a Calculate the number of moles of gas present. [1]

    b Show that the temperature of Y is also 300 K. [1]

    c Calculate the work done by the gas during its expansion. [2]

    d State the value of the heat exchanged between the gas and its surroundings. [1]

13 0.04 moles of ideal gas at a pressure of 8.0×10^4 Pa occupy a volume of 3.0×10^{-3} m^3.

    a Show that the internal energy of the gas is 360 J. [2]

    b Calculate the temperature of the gas. [1]

    c If the gas is now allowed to expand isobarically to a volume of 9.0×10^{-3} m^3, calculate the amount of heat exchanged with the surroundings. [2]

14 **a** Distinguish between an isothermal thermodynamic process and an adiabatic thermodynamic process. [2]

    b A sample of ideal gas, at a pressure of 1.5×10^5 Pa, is compressed isobarically from a volume of 6.0×10^{-2} m^3 to a volume of 4×10^{-3} m^3.

        i Calculate the work done on the gas. [1]

        ii Determine whether the internal energy of the gas has increased or decreased. [1]

        iii Hence, determine whether the gas has gained thermal energy from, or lost thermal energy to, the surroundings. [1]

15 Figure 10.16 shows a pressure–volume diagram for a thermodynamic cycle that takes a fixed amount of gas through four states: A, B, C and D.

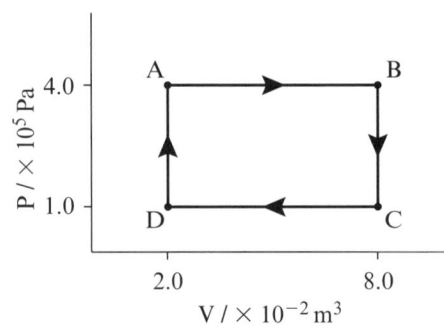

Figure 10.16

CONTINUED

   a   Identify which kind of thermodynamic process takes place when the gas moves from state A to state B. [1]

   b   Calculate the work done by the gas in going through one cycle. [2]

   c   In which of the states, A, B, C or D, is the temperature of the gas greatest? [1]

   d   Calculate the change in internal energy of the gas as it moves from state D to state A. [1]

16 300 g of water at a temperature of 80 °C is placed in a heat sink at a temperature of 10 °C and allowed to cool.

   a   Show that the heat lost from the water is 8.82×10^4 J. (The specific heat capacity of the water is 4.2 kJkg^{-1}°C^{-1}.) [1]

   b   Calculate the decrease in entropy of the water as a result of it cooling. [2]

   c   Explain why the cooling of the water does not contradict the second law of thermodynamics. [2]

17 The first law of thermodynamics can be written as $Q = \Delta U + W$.

   For each of the following thermodynamic processes, state and explain if, and how, Q, ΔU and W change:

   a   A gas in an insulated, rigid, container is heated from 20 °C to 60 °C. [2]

   b   An inflated rubber balloon is dipped in liquid nitrogen (at a temperature of −193 °C) for few seconds. [3]

18 A sample of ideal gas is contained in a frictionless syringe. With reference to the first law of thermodynamics,

   a   if the syringe is pushed in **rapidly**, explain why the temperature of the gas will increase. [2]

   b   if the syringe is pushed in **slowly**, explain why the temperature of the gas will not change. [2]

19 A real heat engine operates between the temperatures 700 °C and 350 °C, delivering 500 J of mechanical work per cycle for a heat input of 2250 J.

   a   Sketch a diagram to represent the heat engine. [2]

   b   Calculate the efficiency of the heat engine. [1]

   c   Calculate the net change in entropy of the engine and its surroundings for one cycle. [2]

Chapter 11
Current and circuits

CHAPTER OUTLINE

In this chapter, you will:

- confirm any pre-existing knowledge of current and potential difference.
- understand that electrical current flows as a result of a potential difference.
- learn that cells provide a source of electromotive force (emf).
- consolidate your knowledge of what an electrical current is.
- consider the two effects of an electrical current.
- consolidate your knowledge of the nature of potential difference.
- learn the function of ammeters and voltmeters in an electrical circuit.
- explore the nature of electrical resistance and its origins.
- explore the role of resistivity.
- consider how the mobility of charge carriers helps describe electrical conductors and insulators.
- look at the similarity between electrical and thermal conductors and insulators.
- solve problems associated with series and parallel electrical circuits.
- examine Ohm's Law and general behaviour of electrical conductors.
- explore the behaviour of some non-Ohmic conductors using V–I graphs.
- see how resistance may be described by its heating effect.
- look at how cells may be characterised by their emf, ε, and internal resistance, r.
- examine how a photovoltaic cell, or solar cell, works

KEY TERMS

potential difference: the work done per unit charge in moving the charge from one point to another

conductors: materials with many free electrons per unit volume, through which thermal energy and electric current can pass easily

insulators: materials with few free electrons per unit volume, through which thermal energy and electric current cannot readily pass

direct current (dc): rate of flow of charge through the cross-sectional area of a conductor

electrical resistance: the ratio of voltage across conductor to the current through it

Ohm's law: at a constant temperature, the current through a metallic conductor is proportional to the voltage across the conductor

thermistor: temperature-dependent resistor where resistance decreases as temperature increases

light dependent resistor (LDR): resistor where resistance decreases as light intensity increases

resistivity: the resistance of a conductor of unit length and unit cross-sectional area

voltage: the potential difference across a conductor

electric power: the energy per unit time dissipated in a conductor

internal resistance: a resistance in series to the cell due to the chemicals in the cell

electromotive force (emf): the work done per unit charge in moving charge across a battery's terminals

parallel connection: resistors connected so that they have the same potential difference across them

series connection: resistors connected one after the other so they take the same current

ammeter: an instrument that measures the electric current through it

voltmeter: an instrument that measures the potential difference across its ends

ideal voltmeter: a voltmeter with infinite resistance (takes no current when connected to a resistor

> ## CONTINUED
>
> **Kirchhoff's first law (the conservation of charge):** the total current flowing into a junction equals the total current flowing out of the junction; $\sum I_{in} = \sum I_{out}$
>
> **Kirchoff's second law (the conservation of energy):** The sum of the IR products in any closed loop is equal to the emf supplied in that loop.

KEY EQUATIONS

Parallel circuits

The potential difference across each parallel branch of a circuit is the same.

$$V_1 = V_2 = V_3 + \ldots$$

$$\frac{1}{R_T} = \frac{1}{R_1} = \frac{1}{R_2} + \ldots$$

Series circuits

The current flowing through each component in a series circuit is the same.

$$I_1 = I_2 = I_3 + \ldots$$

$$R_T = R_1 = R_2 + \ldots$$

Kirchhoff's second law: The emf supplied in any circuital loop is equal to the sum of the potential differences in that loop. Or:

$$\varepsilon = \sum IR$$

$$I = \frac{\Delta q}{\Delta t}$$

$$V = \frac{W}{q}$$

$$R = \frac{V}{I}$$

$$\rho = \frac{RA}{L}$$

$$P = IV = I^2R = \frac{V^2}{R}$$

$$\varepsilon = I(R + r),$$

where I is current, q is charge, t is time, V is potential difference, R is resistance, ρ is resistivity, P power dissipated, ε is emf and r is internal resistance.

Force between two parallel current-carrying wires in a vacuum:

$$\frac{F}{I} = \mu_o \frac{I_1 I_2}{2\pi r},$$

where $\frac{F}{l}$ is the force per unit length of the wires, μ_o the permeability of free space ($\mu_o = 4\pi \times 10^{-7}$ NA^{-2}), I_1 and I_2 are the two currents, and r is the distance between the two wires.)

Exercise 11.1 Potential difference, current and resistance

The questions in this section will help you consolidate your understanding of potential difference, current and resistance.

1 Figure 11.1 shows what it might be like inside a metallic conductor if you could see the atoms and the free electrons around them. There is no current flowing in this conductor.

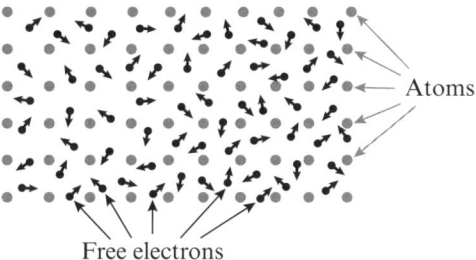

Figure 11.1

   a Suggest how Figure 11.1 shows that there is no current flowing in the conductor despite there being considerable motion of the free electrons.

   b Suggest how Figure 11.1 would have to be changed if there were a current flowing in the conductor.

   c Suggest how Figure 11.1 could be changed to show that the material is made from a better conductor.

2 A conductor of cross-sectional area, A, is made from a material that has n free electrons per unit volume (n would be called the free electron number density). When a current, I, flows, the speed at which the free electrons move in the same direction is v.

   a In 1 s, how far will each free electron move?

   b In 1 s, how many free electrons will pass any point along the conductor.

   c If each free electron carries a charge of e, how much charge passes any given point along the conductor in 1 s?

   d Hence, show that the current, I, flowing in the conductor can be written as $I = nAve$.

   e A conductor of cross-sectional area 1 mm² is made from a material with a free electron number density of 1.0×10^{29} m⁻³. It is carrying a current of 100 mA.

      i Calculate the speed at which the free electrons are moving. (The charge on an electron is -1.6×10^{-19} C.)

      ii Comment on your answer to **part i**.

3   This question shows you how to find the free electron number density for copper. By substituting values of molar mass, density and how many electrons each atom allows to be free for other metals, you can find the free electron density for any metal.

   a   The molar mass of copper is 63.5 gmole^{-1}. How many moles of copper atoms are there in 1 kg of copper?

   b   Calculate how many atoms of copper there are in 1 kg. (Avogadro's number is 6.02×10^{23} mole^{-1}.)

   c   The density of copper is 8900 kgm^{-3}. Calculate how many atoms of copper there are in 1 m^3 of copper.

   d   If each atom of copper donates two electrons to the conduction band (in other words, there are two free electrons for each copper atom), calculate the free electron number density for copper.

> **TIP**
> This is a good method to learn. Try this with the details for some other metals.

4   The SI unit for current is the Ampere, or Amp.

   a   How is an Amp defined?

   b   Show that the definition of an Amp is consistent with the equation
   $$\frac{F}{l} = \mu_o \frac{I_1 I_2}{2\pi r},$$
   where $\frac{F}{l}$ is the force per unit length of the wires, μ_o the permeability of free space ($\mu_o = 4\pi \times 10^{-7}$ NA^{-2}), I_1 and I_2 are the two currents, and r is the distance between the two wires.

   c   i   Calculate the force per unit length experienced by two conductors in a vacuum, each carrying a current of 1 A separated by a distance of 0.25 m.

      ii   If the direction of the currents in **part i** is the same, what will be the effect of the force between the two conductors? What if the currents are in opposite directions?

> **TIP**
> Recalling the definition of the Amp is not usually required in an exam, but it is important for students to see where it has come from.

5   a   Legend has it that Isaac Newton was sitting under a tree when an apple fell on his head. It made him think: 'Why do apples always fall straight down, and not to the side?' He later theorised that this happens because there is a force acting on the apple and that this force causes the apple to move towards the Earth.

   But let us see if we can explain why the apple falls *without* referring to force.

      i   When the apple is on the tree, other than its chemical energy, what store of energy does it possess?

      ii   When the apple falls from the tree what happens to its energy?

      iii   Do apples ever rise from the ground and move upwards to the tree? Why?

      iv   So, without reference to force, why do apples fall from a tree towards the ground?

> **TIP**
> This is a long, involved question, but it is worth persevering with it because its conclusion will give you an important way of thinking about what it is that makes a current flow.

b Now let us use the conclusion from **part a** to see if we can explain why the charged particles in a current are moving. Suppose a wire in which there is a current flowing is lying flat on a table. The current is made up of free electrons drifting along inside the wire.

  i What energy transfer is taking place as the free electrons drift along the wire?

  ii What is it that makes the free electrons move along the wire? Is your answer essentially the same as it had been for **part a iv**?

c The amount of gravitational potential energy possessed by a mass of 1 kg above the ground is called its 'gravitational potential', V_g, and so we can write $V_g = \frac{E_P}{\text{mass}}$.

Similarly, the amount of electrical potential energy possessed by 1 C of charge is called its 'electrical potential', $V_E = \frac{\text{electrical potential energy}}{\text{charge}}$.

  i In the case of the apple, is there a *difference* between the gravitational potential at the tree level and the gravitational potential at the ground level?

  ii So does the apple move from the tree to the ground because there is a gravitational *potential difference*?

  iii And, in the case of the free electrons in the wire, do the electrons move because there is an electrical potential difference?

  iv So, in terms of energy, suggest how *potential difference* might be defined.

  v What is the SI unit for electrical potential difference?

  vi How do we usually create an electrical potential difference?

6 Calculate the potential difference between two points in a circuit if

  a 0.25 C of charge uses up 4.0 J of electrical potential energy.

  b 1.25×10^{18} electrons use up 2.0 J of electrical potential energy.

  c a current of 0.4 A flows for 1 minute transferring 24.0 J of energy to thermal energy.

7 a How much work is done if an electron is moved through a potential difference of 1 V? (The charge on an electron is -1.6×10^{-19} C.)

  b Physicists express this amount of work done as one electronvolt, eV. Calculate the electronvolts equivalent of

  i 6.4×10^{-19} J.

  ii 3.2×10^{-13} J.

  iii 2×10^{-15} J.

c   Calculate the Joules equivalent of

   i   3 eV.

   ii 200 keV.

   iii 7.4 M eV.

8 Look back at Figure 11.1, which shows the atoms and free electrons inside a metallic conductor. Imagine that there is a current flowing in the conductor.

   a i   What happens to the free electrons when they collide with the atoms of the conductor?

      ii   What energy transfer takes place?

      iii Does this help explain why the free electrons drift very slowly along the conductor? Explain your reasoning.

      iv   What happens to the atoms of the conductor when the free electrons collide with them?

      v   What effect does this have on the conductor?

   b Suggest **two** reasons why a greater current will create a greater heating effect in a metallic conductor.

9 a We can consider the heating effect, caused by the collisions of the free electrons, to be due to the conductor having a resistance. Suggest some factors on which the resistance of the conductor might depend. Give a reason for each suggestion.

   b How do your answers to **questions 10b** and **11a** help explain why the filament in an old-fashioned light bulb is

      i   long—it is usually coiled into many small coils.

      ii   very thin—hence the term filament.

      iii usually made of tungsten.

> **TIP**
>
> Think about what the conductor would have to be like if it had no resistance at all, that is if there were no heating effect of a current flowing in it.

10 a Define *resistance* and state the units it is measured in.

   b State the SI base units for resistance.

   c Calculate the resistance of the following resistors:

      i   Current flowing through = 250 mA; voltage across resistor = 0.5 V

      ii   Current flowing through = 50 µA; voltage across resistor = 5 V

      iii Current flowing through = 30 mA; voltage across resistor = 120 V

11 a Define *resistivity*.

   b A resistor is 1 cm long, has a cross-sectional area of 2.0×10^{-6} m² and is made from a material of resistivity 4×10^{-8} Ω m. Calculate its resistance.

c 1 m³ of copper has a resistance of 1.7×10^{-8} Ω. How much resistance would 1 cm³ of copper have?

d 1 m³ of copper is stretched into a rod of cross-sectional area 1 cm². What is the copper rod's

   i   length.

   ii resistance.

e A cylindrical 2.2 kΩ resistor is 2 cm long with a radius of 1.2 mm. Calculate the resistivity of the material it is made from.

f A 100 Ω resistor is 3 cm long. It is made of a material of resistivity 4×10^{-4} Ω m. Calculate its cross-sectional area.

> **TIP**
>
> The definitions of *resistance* and *resistivity* are frequently examined, so try to make sure you have learnt them.

12 Consider two cylindrical resistors made from the same material. Resistor A is twice as long and twice the diameter of resistor B.

   a The resistance of A is 100 Ω. Calculate the resistance B.

   b Resistor A is passed through rollers, reducing its radius to ½ its original. What will its new resistance be?

13 Figure 11.2 shows the electrical characteristic (this means the relationship between the voltage across the component and the current flowing through it in a graphical form) of a component in a circuit.

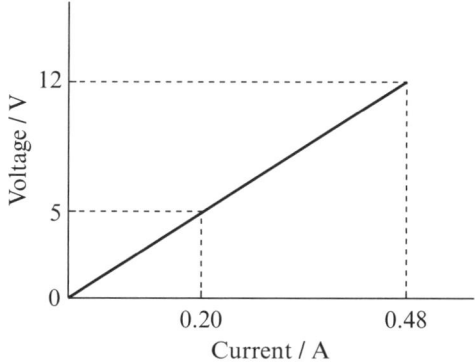

Figure 11.2

   a Outline how the resistance of a component can be found from its electrical characteristic. (Take care with your answer!)

   b Determine the resistance of the component when

      i $V = 5$ V.

      ii $I = 0.48$ A.

   a Explain how the characteristics of the component in Figure 11.2 shows that this component is ohmic.

   b Hence, state Ohm's law.

> **TIP**
>
> It's well worth learning what the electrical characteristics of all the main circuit components are so that you understand how they will work under a variety of conditions.

14 This will look at the similarity between electrical conduction and thermal conduction.

- **a**
  - **i** An electrical current is a flow of electrical charge. What causes a current to flow?
  - **ii** The flow of thermal energy might be considered analogous to the flow of electrical charge. What causes a thermal 'current' to flow?
- **b**
  - **i** Write an equation for the electrical resistance of a component in terms of its physical size and its resistivity.
  - **ii** Write an equation for the thermal resistance of an analogous component.
- **c**
  - **i** In the electrical case, write a simple equation for the current in terms of charge and time.
  - **ii** In the thermal case, write a simple equation for the 'current' in terms of thermal energy and time.
- **d** Combining your answers to **parts a**, **b** and **c**, equate the cause of an electrical current with the current itself and the resistance through which it flows.
- **e** Repeat **part d** for the thermal 'current'.
- **f** Copy and complete the table showing how electrical conduction and thermal conduction are similar.

Term	Electrical case	Thermal case
What makes current flow?		
Expression for current		
Expression for resistance		
Overall equation		

15
- **a** Explain why it is not possible for a filament light bulb to obey Ohm's law.
- **b** Sketch the electrical characteristic (the graph of *voltage* against *current*) for a filament light bulb.
- **c**
  - **i** How does the resistance of a filament light bulb change as the current flowing through it increases?
  - **ii** Suggest why the resistance varies in this way. Your answer should refer to the microscopic behaviour within the resistor.

16 Figure 11.3 shows how the resistance of a negative thermal coefficient thermally sensitive resistor, or NTC thermistor, varies when its temperature is changed.

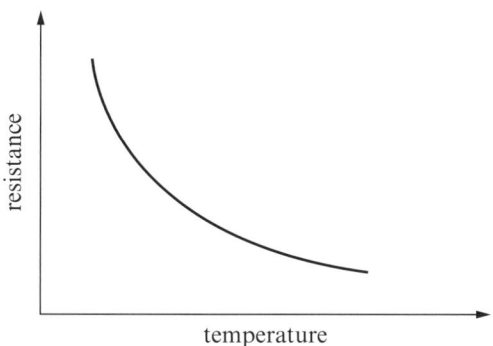

Figure 11.3

Suggest what is happening inside the thermistor to allow its resistance to decrease when the temperature increases.

17 a Sketch a graph to show how the resistance of a light dependent resistor (LDR) varies when the light intensity incident on it varies.

  b Suggest what is happening inside the LDR to allow its resistance to change when the incident light intensity varies.

Exercise 11.2 Voltage, power and emf

1 Consider an electrical current, I, flowing through a resistor of resistance, R, because there is a potential difference, V, across the component.

  a For each Coulomb of charge that flows through the resistor, how many Joules of electrical energy are transferred to thermal energy to increase the temperature of the resistor?

  b In 1 s, how many Coulombs of charge flow past any given point in the resistor?

  c So, write an expression for how many Joules of electrical energy are transfomed into thermal energy every second in the resistor.

  d Hence, show that the power generated in the resistor can be written as

  i $P = I^2 R$.

  ii $P = \dfrac{V^2}{R}$.

2 The energy from a single flash of light from a small strobe lamp is 0.8 J. The voltage across the lamp is 230 V.

  a If the flash of light lasts 10 ms, what is the average current flowing through the lamp?

b It is likely that the actual current flowing through the lamp while the light is flashing is not constant. Explain why.

c Calculate the average power of the lamp.

3 When we buy a 'battery'—such as an AA battery for a television remote control—it is often labelled '1.5 V'.

    a What energy transfer takes place in a battery when it is used in an electrical circuit?

    b What does the label '1.5 V' on the battery really mean?

    c   **i** How is the emf, ε, of the battery usually different to the terminal voltage, V, of the battery.

          ii Under what conditions are the emf and the terminal voltage the same?

> **TIP**
> Physicists usually refer to batteries as cells. A combination of two or more cells is a battery.

4 When a simple cell is placed in a circuit and the circuit is switched on, an energy transfer takes place within the cell.

    a Outline what this energy transfer is.

    b Is this energy transfer likely to occur with 100% efficiency? Explain your answer.

5 **a** When a resistor is placed in a circuit and the circuit is switched on, an energy transfer occurs. Outline what this energy transfer is.

    b Suggest why real cells are considered to have an internal resistance.

6 **a** Outline the difference between a primary cell and a secondary cell.

    b A primary cell is rated as 1200 mA-hours. In its normal usage, the cell delivers a current of 1.6 mA. Calculate how long it will take to stop delivering a current.

> **TIP**
> Think about what you learnt in chapter 10.

7 A cell of emf 5 V and internal resistance 3.0 Ω is connected in series with a variable resistor.

    a Complete this table to show how the power dissipated in the variable resistor varies when the resistance of the variable resistor is varied.

Resistance of variable resistor / Ω	Current in circuit / A	Power dissipated in variable resistor / W
1.0	1.25	1.56
2.0		
3.0		
4.0		
5.0		

    b What can you conclude about the power dissipated in the resistor?

> **TIP**
> The answer to **part b** is a useful general rule to remember.

8   This question is designed to help you understand how a solar cell works.

   a   i   Outline what we mean by the term *semiconductor*.

       ii What do we usually have to do to transform a semiconductor into a conductor?

       iii What is meant by a p-type semiconductor?

       iv What is meant by an n-type semiconductor?

       v   With reference to semiconductors, what is meant by the term *hole*?

   b   In a photovoltaic cell (a solar cell) a very thin layer of silicon is 'doped' with phosphorous. Because silicon has four valence electrons (Si is atomic number 14), all these electrons are locked in place by the atomic bonds that keep the silicon atoms together. Phosphorous is atomic number 15, and so every phosphorous atom bonded to silicon atoms has one electron that is free to move around.

       i   What is meant by the term *doped*?

       ii What type of semiconductor has the silicon doped with phosphorous become, n or p?

   c   Another, slightly thicker, layer of doped silicon is placed underneath the phosphorous-doped silicon layer. This layer is doped with boron (atomic number 5.) Boron atoms have fewer valence electrons than silicon.

       i   What type of semiconductor has the boron-doped silicon become, n or p?

       ii   At the junction of the phosphorous-doped silicon and the boron-doped silicon, what will any free electrons do?

       iii What effect will this have on the phosphorous atoms? And on the upper layer?

       iv   What effect will this have on the boron atoms? And on the lower layer?

       v   Suggest why the region immediately on either side of the junction between the two layers is called a 'depletion zone'.

       vi   Has the upper layer become relatively positively charged or relatively negatively charged?

       vii Has the lower layer become relatively positively charged or relatively negatively charged?

       viii In which direction is there an electric field in the depletion zone?

   d   When light is incident on the photovoltaic cell, its energy is used to create free electrons and holes in the depletion zone.

       i   What effect will the electric field in the depletion zone have on these free electrons and holes?

ii   What will this produce?

iii If the two layers have an external electrical connection, what will happen?

e i   Suggest why the phosphorous-doped silicon layer is both thin and heavily doped.

ii   Suggest why the boron-doped silicon layer is both thick and lightly doped.

iii Suggest why many such photovoltaic cells are usually connected together in series.

iv   Suggest why many such series connections of photovoltaic cells are connected in parallel.

> **TIP**
>
> If you found this question difficult to follow, try looking at some of the very good videos available online about solar cells.

Exercise 11.3 Resistors in electrical circuits

1 Consider the part of an electrical circuit shown in Figure 11.4.

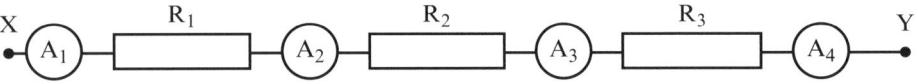

Figure 11.4

a   If ammeter A_1 reads a current, I, what will ammeters A_2, A_3 and A_4 read?

b   What is the potential difference across

   i R_1.

   ii R_2.

   iii R_3.

c   The resistance of an ideal ammeter is considered to be zero. Hence, what is the potential difference between the points X and Y?

d   Hence show that the total resistance of the three resistors, R_1, R_2 and R_3, in series, is given by $R_{total} = R_1 + R_2 + R_3$

2 a   An electrical lead has a copper core of cross-sectional area 1 mm² surrounded by a non-conducting PVC cover. It is 0.75 m long.

   The resistivity of copper is 1.68×10^{-8} Ω m.

   Calculate the resistance of the lead and show that, in a typical circuit, the wire's resistance can be ignored.

b   With reference to your answer in **part a**, would you expect there to be a potential difference across a lead that is part of an electrical circuit? Justify your answer.

c   Look at the circuit in Figure 11.5.

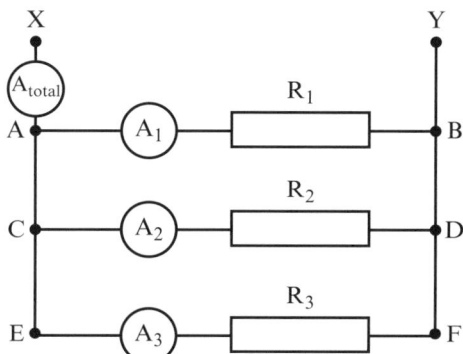

Figure 11.5

If the potential at point X is V and the potential at point Y is 0, what is the potential difference between

i   points A and B.

ii points C and D.

iii points E and F.

d   Hence, determine the current measured by the ideal ammeters A_1, A_2, A_3 and A_{total}.

e   Hence, show that the total resistance in the circuit is given by
$\frac{1}{R_{total}} = \frac{1}{R_1} + \frac{1}{R_2} + \frac{1}{R_3}$.

3   Figure 11.6 shows a cylindrical resistor, of resistance R, made from a material of resistivity ρ. The resistor has a cross-sectional area A, and length l.

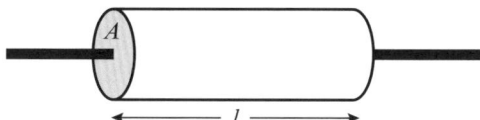

Figure 11.6

a   State R in terms of ρ, l and A.

b   Now suppose that two resistors, identical to the one in Figure 11.5, are placed in series with one another.

i   As established in **question 2 part a**, does the lead joining the two resistors have any resistance?

ii So now, how long is the total resistance?

iii Hence, state what the resistance of the two resistors in series is.

iv What does this suggest about the total resistance of n identical resistors, each of resistance, R, when placed in series?

c Now suppose that two resistors, identical to the one in Figure 11.6 are placed in parallel with one another.

   i What is the effective cross-sectional area of the two resistors in parallel?

   ii Hence, state the resistance of the two resistors in parallel.

   iii What does this suggest about the resistance of n identical resistors in parallel with one another?

4 a Suppose that in a simple series circuit consisting of an emf source, ε, and three resistors: R_1, R_2 and R_3, a current, I, flows.

   Show that the principle of conservation of energy leads to Kirchoff's second law:

   $$\varepsilon = \sum (IR)_i$$

   b Now consider a junction in an electrical circuit at which a current I_{total} flows into the junction and three currents, I_1, I_2 and I_3 flow out of the junction.

   Show that the conservation of charge leads to Kirchoff's first law:

   $$\sum I_i = 0.$$

> **TIP**
>
> Kirchhoff's two laws are very useful for solving problems involving complicated circuits. It's a good idea to know them.

5 a Three resistors, rated 3.0 Ω, 5.2 Ω and 0.3 Ω, are placed in series in a circuit. Calculate the total resistance of the three resistors.

   b Two resistors, rated 3 Ω and 6 Ω, are placed in parallel in a circuit. Calculate the total resistance of the two resistors.

   c You are supplied with four identical 10-Ω resistors. Explore how many different total resistances you can make using some or all of the resistors.

6 Figure 11.7 shows an electrical circuit with an emf source of negligible internal resistance.

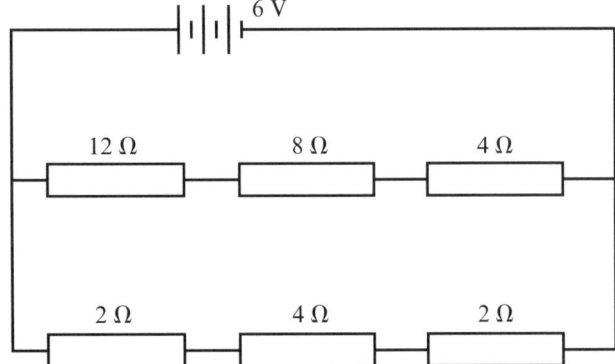

Figure 11.7

- **a** Determine the total resistance in the circuit.
- **b** Hence, determine the current flowing through the emf source.
- **c** Determine the power dissipated by the 8-Ω resistor.

7 A cube is made from 12 identical resistors, each of resistance R. Calculate the resistance of the cube if current flows into one corner and out of the opposite corner of the cube.

Exercise 11.4 Analysing circuits

1 This question examines the use of ammeters in an electrical circuit by considering the effect they might have on the circuit itself.

Consider an electrical circuit containing an emf source and several resistors. Some resistors might be in series with other resistors and some resistors might be in parallel with other resistors.

If we want to measure the current flowing through one particular resistor—let's say of resistance, R—we will need to place an ammeter in the circuit. Suppose that the ammeter has a resistance R_A.

- **a** If the ammeter is placed in series with the resistor,
    - **i** what will the overall resistance of the ammeter and resistor now be?
    - **ii** will the placing of the ammeter have changed the circuit? That is, will the placing of the ammeter have changed the current (which we wanted to measure) flowing through the resistor? Explain your answer.
    - **iii** ideally, what should the resistance of the ammeter be in order to change the circuit by the least amount?
- **b** Now suppose the ammeter is placed in parallel with the resistor.
    - **i** What will the overall resistance of the ammeter and resistor now be?
    - **ii** Will the placing of the ammeter have changed the circuit? That is, will the placing of the ammeter have changed the current (which we wanted to measure) flowing through the resistor? Explain your answer.
- **c** As a conclusion,
    - **i** are ammeters placed in series, or in parallel, with the resistors through which the current flowing is to be measured?
    - **ii** how much resistance should an ideal ammeter have?

2 This question examines the use of voltmeters in an electrical circuit by considering the effect they might have on the circuit itself.

Consider again an electrical circuit containing an emf source and several resistors. Some resistors might be in series with other resistors, and some resistors might be in parallel with other resistors.

If we want to measure the potential difference across one particular resistor—let's say of resistance, R—we will need to place a voltmeter in the circuit. Suppose that the voltmeter has a resistance, R_V. In order for the voltmeter to measure the potential difference across the resistor, it must be placed in parallel with the resistor.

- **a** What will the overall resistance of the voltmeter and resistor now be?

- **b** So, will the placing of the voltmeter have changed the circuit? That is, will the placing of the voltmeter have changed the potential difference (which we wanted to measure) across the resistor? Explain your answer.

- **c** So, ideally, what should the resistance of a voltmeter be?

3 A student sets up a circuit with two 1 kΩ resistors in series with a 6 V emf source of negligible internal resistance. The student is trying to measure the voltage across one of the two 1-kΩ resistors using a voltmeter in the usual way.

- **a** What will the voltmeter read if the resistance of the voltmeter is

    - **i** 1 kΩ.

    - **ii** 100 kΩ.

- **b** Explain why the resistance of an ideal voltmeter is infinite.

- **c** In practice, it is not possible to have a voltmeter with an infinite resistance. Suggest how the resistance of a voltmeter should compare with the value of the resistor, across which it is trying to measure the voltage.

4 A cell used in a circuit has an emf of 1.5 V and an internal resistance of 0.4 Ω.

- **a** Explain what *emf* means.

- **b** If the cell is connected in series with a resistor of resistance 5.6 Ω, calculate the current that will flow in the circuit.

- **c** What will the voltage across the terminals of the cell be?

- **d** What will happen to the terminal voltage of the cell if the resistor is replaced by one of resistance 0.6 Ω?

5 A cell of internal resistance *r* is connected in series with a variable resistor and an ideal ammeter.

- **a** Sketch a graph to show how the terminal voltage of the cell varies with the current flowing in the circuit.

- **b** How can you use your graph to find the value for the internal resistance of the cell, *r*?

- **c** What does the terminal voltage of the cell when no current is flowing tell you?

6 Outline an experiment that could find the emf, ε, and internal resistance, r, of a cell. Make sure you include

- the equipment required (and how to set it up),
- the measurements you need to make and
- how you would manipulate the data to calculate ε and r.

> **TIP**
>
> This is a well-examined idea and an experiment you should make sure you have done.

7 A cell of emf 6.0 V and internal resistance 1.0 Ω is connected in series to a 5.0-Ω resistor. Calculate the

a current flowing in the circuit.

b terminal voltage of the cell.

c power dissipated in the 5.0-Ω resistor.

8 a Figure 11.8 shows three identical ohmic resistors in an electrical circuit. The current flowing through resistor X is 0.4 mA.

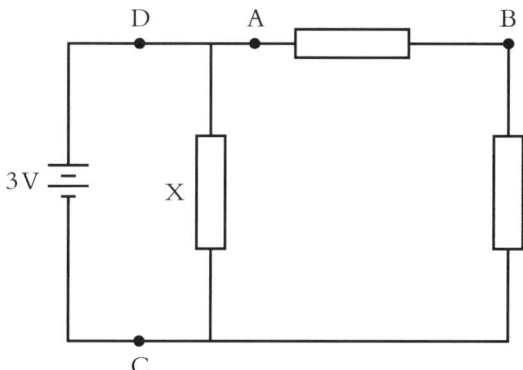

Figure 11.8

i Calculate the resistance of resistor X.

ii What is the current flowing at points A, B, C and D?

iii Show that the total resistance of the three resistors is 5 kΩ.

b Figure 11.9 shows a circuit with three resistors and an emf source of negligible internal resistance.

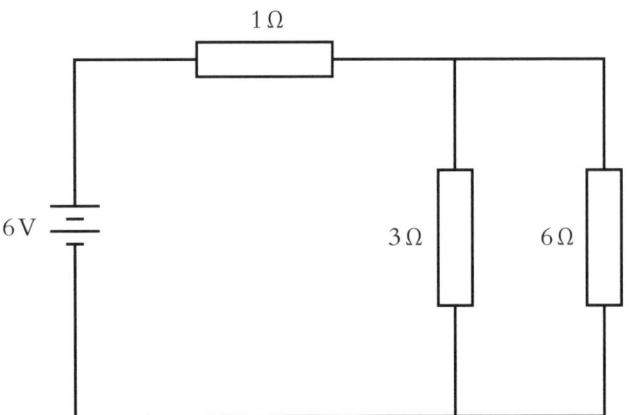

Figure 11.9

Calculate the current flowing through the

i   1-Ω resistor.

ii 6-Ω resistor.

iii 3-Ω resistor.

9 a Consider the circuit shown in Figure 11.10.

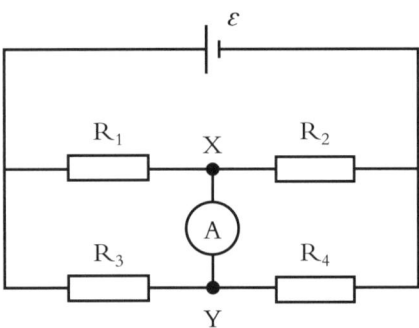

Figure 11.10

i   What is this circuit arrangement of resistors called?

ii Write an algebraic expression for the voltage across resistor R_2.

iii Write an algebraic expression for the voltage across resistor R_4.

iv If the ammeter reads zero, determine how R_1, R_2, R_3 and R_4 are related.

10 a Consider the circuit shown in Figure 11.11.

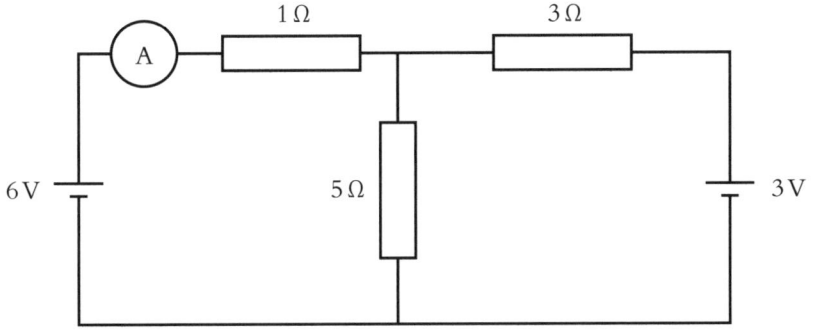

Figure 11.11

Use Kirchhoff's laws to determine the reading on the ammeter.

b Now consider the similar circuit in Figure 11.12.

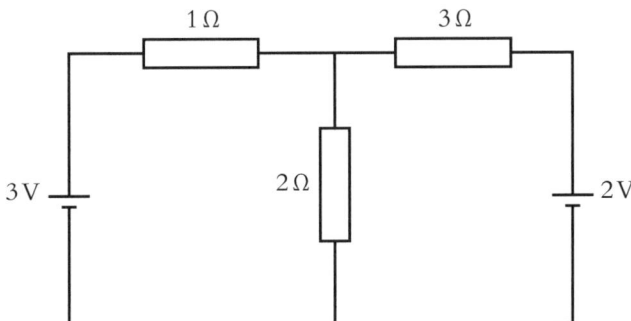

Figure 11.12

Use Kirchhoff's laws to show that

i the current flowing through the 2-Ω resistor is 1 A.

ii there is no current flowing through the 3-Ω resistor.

EXAM-STYLE QUESTIONS

Multiple-choice questions

1. A copper wire, A, of radius 1 mm and length 0.5 m is connected in series to another copper wire, B, of radius 2 mm and length 1.0 m. When a current flows through the two wires, which of the following statements is false?

   A Wire A has a resistance that is twice as large as wire B.

   B The current flowing through wire A is half that of the current flowing through wire B.

   C The potential difference across wire A is twice that of the potential difference across wire B.

   D The power generated in wire A is twice that of the power generated in wire B.

2. Two electrodes separated by a distance d are maintained at a constant potential difference, V. When an electron moves from one of the electrodes to the other, its gain in kinetic energy is E.

   The distance between the two electrodes is increased to $2d$. When an electron moves from one of the electrodes to the other, what will its gain in kinetic energy be?

   A $\frac{E}{4}$

   B $\frac{E}{2}$

   C E

   D $2E$

3. A simple electrical circuit is set up with a resistance, R, in series with an emf source of negligible internal resistance. The power dissipated is P. If the resistance is replaced by a new resistance of $3R$, the power dissipated will be

   A $\frac{P}{9}$.

   B $\frac{P}{3}$.

   C P.

   D $3P$.

4. A copper wire of cross-sectional area 1×10^{-6} m^2 carries a current of 1 A. The free electron number density of copper is about 10^{29} m^{-3}. The charge on an electron is of the order of 10^{-19} C. What is the best estimate for the speed at which the electrons move along the wire?

   A 10^{-4} ms^{-1}

   B 1 ms^{-1}

   C 100 ms^{-1}

   D 10^{4} ms^{-1}

5. A Physics student has three 3-Ω resistors. Which of the following resistances cannot be made using all three of the 3-Ω resistors?

   A $1\,\Omega$

   B $2\,\Omega$

   C $4\,\Omega$

   D $4.5\,\Omega$

CONTINUED

6   Figure 11.13 shows a circuit in which there is a cell of negligible internal resistance, an ideal ammeter and an ideal voltmeter.

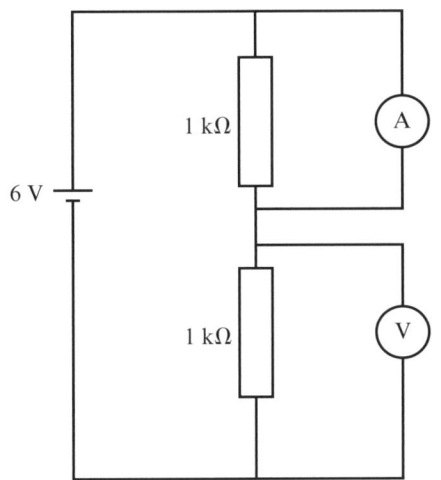

Figure 11.13

Which of the following is likely to be the reading on the voltmeter?

A   0 V
B   2 V
C   3 V
D   6 V

7   Which of the following circuit symbols represents a photovoltaic cell?

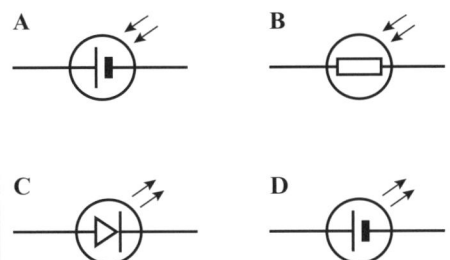

Figure 11.14

8   An emf source, ε, with internal resistance $r = 3\ \Omega$, is connected to a load resistor of resistance R. In which of the following values for R will the power dissipated in R be the largest?

A   1 Ω
B   2 Ω
C   3 Ω
D   5 Ω

CONTINUED

9 Figure 11.15 shows a bridge circuit used to determine the resistance of an unknown resistor.

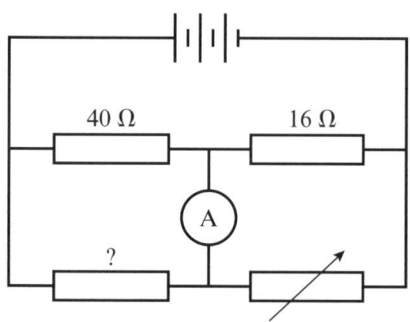

Figure 11.15

When the variable resistor is set to 24 Ω, the ammeter reading is zero. The resistance of the unknown resistor (shown by the question mark) is

A 32 Ω.

B 48 Ω.

C 60 Ω.

D 80 Ω.

Short-answer questions

10 A student plans to set up a circuit to investigate how the voltage across a resistor varies when the current flowing through the resistor changes. The student has a cell (emf 6V; negligible internal resistance), a fixed resistor, an ammeter, a voltmeter, some electrical leads and a variable resistor.

    a Draw a circuit diagram to show how the student should set up the circuit. [2]

    b The student conducts the experiment. The graph of results is shown in Figure 11.16.

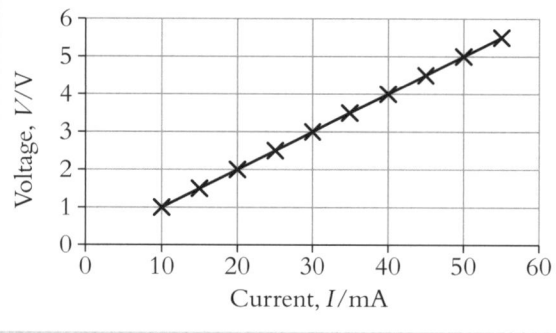

Figure 11.16

CONTINUED

The students says the resistor is an ohmic device. Suggest why the graph supports this suggestion. [1]

c Using the graph, calculate the resistance of the resistor. [2]

11 A cell rated as 6 V, and with negligible internal resistance, is to be connected to four identical resistors.

a Sketch circuit diagrams to show how the circuit should be arranged so that each resistor has a voltage of
  i 1.5 V across it. [1]
  ii 3 V across it. [1]
  iii 6 V across it. [1]

b In which of your three circuits will the cell continue to work for the longest time? Explain your answer. [2]

12 Figure 11.17 shows the electrical characteristics of two components, A and B.

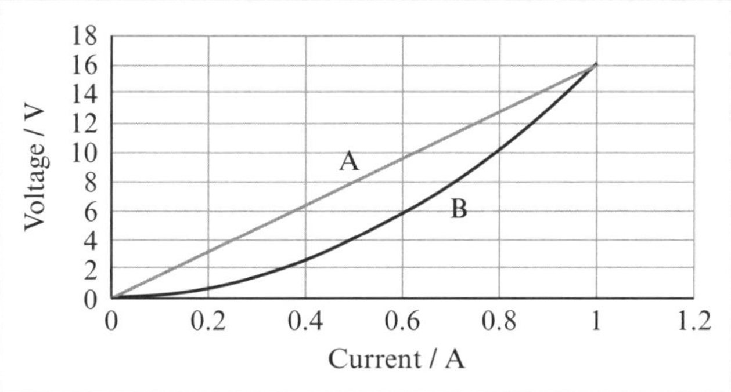

Figure 11.17

a Determine the resistance of component A when its resistance equals that of component B. [2]

b The two components are placed in a simple series circuit along with an ammeter and a cell of emf 12 V and negligible internal resistance.
  i Determine the reading on the ammeter. [2]
  ii Hence calculate the total resistance of the circuit. [1]

13 A 250 mA current flows through a resistor for 1 minute. The potential difference across the resistor is 6.0 V. Calculate:

a How much charge flows through the resistor. [1]

b As the current flows through the resistor, there is an energy transfer. Suggest what the main energy transfer in the resistor is. [2]

c How much energy is transferred by the current during this time. [1]

d The power dissipated by the resistor. [1]

CONTINUED

14 Figure 11.18 shows three resistors and a cell of negligible internal resistance in a circuit.

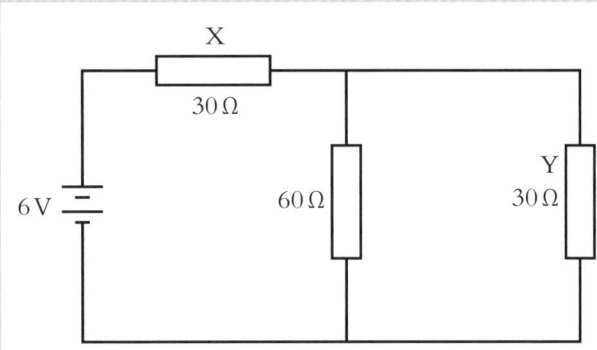

Figure 11.18

a Calculate the total resistance in the circuit. [2]
b Calculate the current flowing through resistor X. [1]
c Calculate the ratio of the powers P_x and P_y dissipated in resistors X and Y, $\frac{P_X}{P_Y}$. [2]

15 Figure 11.19 shows a circuit with a light bulb, two 8 W resistors, a switch and a 12-V cell with negligible internal resistance.

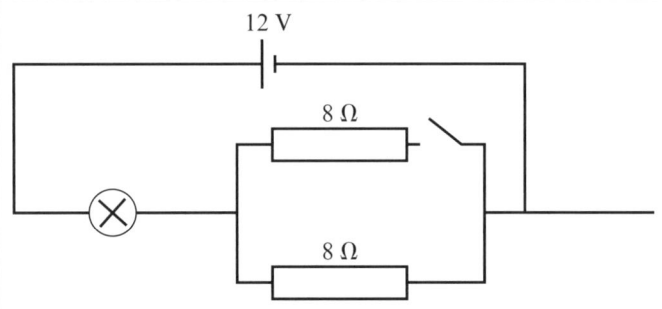

Figure 11.19

a When the switch is open, the current flowing through the bulb is 375 mA. Calculate
   i   the potential difference across the bulb. [2]
   ii the resistance of the bulb. [1]
b If the switch is now closed, explain what will happen to the brightness of the bulb. [2]

CONTINUED

16 Figure 11.20 shows how the power output of a solar panel varies with incident light intensity at low light intensity levels. The emf of the solar panel can be taken to be constant.

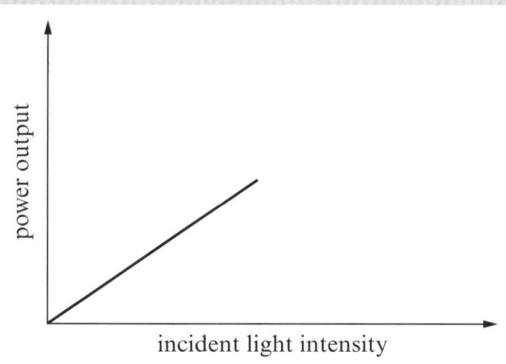

Figure 11.20

- **a** Suggest how the current supplied by the solar panel's emf changes with incident light intensity. [1]
- **b** Outline **briefly** how the solar panel is able to produce an electrical current. [2]
- **c** **i** Add to the graph to show how you would expect the power output of the solar panel to change at much higher levels of incident light intensity. [1]
  - **ii** Justify your answer to **part i**. [2]

Unit C
Wave behaviour

Chapter 12
Simple harmonic motion

CHAPTER OUTLINE

In this chapter, you will:

- explore the conditions required for simple harmonic motion (SHM).
- define *SHM* with the equation $a = -\omega^2 x$.
- understand and use the terms *period, frequency, angular frequency, amplitude, equilibrium, position* and *displacement*.
- represent SHM using graphs of displacement–time, velocity–time, acceleration–time, force–time and force–displacement.
- explore the energy changes during a cycle of an oscillation.
- use graphs of energy-time to describe SHM qualitatively.
- derive and use the equations for the time period of a mass-spring system and a simple pendulum

> understand and use the term *phase difference*.

> solve problems associated with SHM using equations for displacement, velocity, acceleration, kinetic energy and potential energy.

> solve problems associated with kinetic, potential and total energy in SHM.

KEY TERMS

period: the time for one full oscillation

amplitude: the maximum displacement from equilibrium

displacement: the vector distance between the oscillator and its equilibrium position

frequency: the number of full oscillations in 1 s

simple harmonic motion (SHM): oscillations in which the acceleration is opposite and proportional to the displacement

> **CONTINUED**
>
> **angular frequency:** the quantity 2π divided by the period
>
> **phase angle:** the angle that appears in the formula for displacement, determined by the initial position and velocity
>
> **phase difference:** $\Delta\phi = \frac{\Delta t}{T} \times 2\pi$, where T is the period and Δt is the time difference between two neighbouring peaks

> **KEY EQUATIONS**
>
> $a = -\omega^2 x$
>
> $T = \frac{1}{f}$
>
> $\omega = \frac{2\pi}{T} = 2\pi f$
>
> $T = 2\pi\sqrt{\frac{m}{k}}$ for a mass-spring system
>
> $T = 2\pi\sqrt{\frac{l}{g}}$ for a simple pendulum
>
> $x = x_o \sin(\omega t + \phi)$
>
> $v = \omega x_o \cos(\omega t + \phi)$
>
> $E_{total} = \frac{1}{2} m\omega^2 x_o^2$
>
> $E_p = \frac{1}{2} m\omega^2 x^2$,
>
> where a is acceleration, ω is angular frequency, x is displacement from the equilibrium position, T is the time period, f the frequency of oscillations, m is mass, k is the spring constant of a spring, l is the length of a simple pendulum, g is the gravitational field strength, ϕ is the phase difference and x_o is the maximum displacement from the equilibrium position.

Exercise 12.1 Simple harmonic oscillations

The questions in this section explore the nature of oscillations and the conditions necessary for simple harmonic motion (SHM).

1   Explain what is meant by the following terms:

   a   *time period of an oscillator.*

   b   *frequency.*

   c   *amplitude.*

   d   *equilibrium position.*

   e   *displacement.*

   f   *angular frequency.*

2   Consider a body that is oscillating about an equilibrium position.

   a   What does the body experience when it is not at the equilibrium position?

   b   Outline how this experience causes the body to oscillate?

   c   What special condition occurs when the body oscillates in SHM?

   d   Hence, define *SHM*.

3   Figure 12.1 shows the displacement of an oscillating body about its equilibrium position.

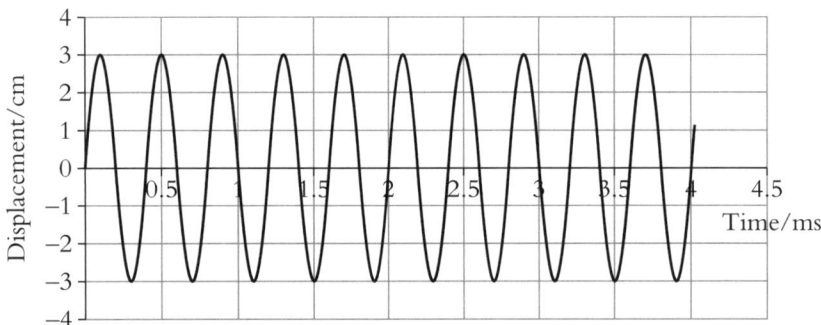

Figure 12.1

   a   What is the period of the oscillations?

   b   What is the frequency of the oscillations?

   c   What is the amplitude of the oscillations?

4   a   With reference to Figure 12.1, outline how to identify on the graph where

  i the speed of the oscillating body is a maximum.

  ii the speed of the oscillating body is zero.

 b What feature of the graph in Figure 12.1 can be used to find the velocity of the oscillating body?

5 Figure 12.2 shows an oscillator performing SHM.

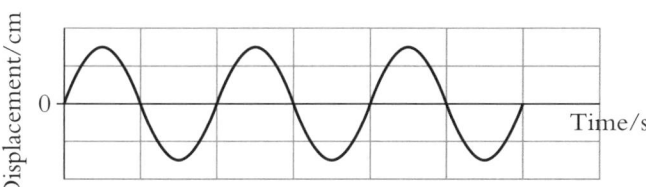

Figure 12.2

> **TIP**
>
> You should try to be very familiar with this kind of graph.

 a Mark two places where the oscillator is in phase. Label them P.

 b Mark two places where the oscillator is out of phase. Label them O.

 c Mark two places where there is a phase difference of $\frac{\pi}{2}$ radians. Label them D.

Exercise 12.2 Details of simple harmonic motion

This exercise will help you derive and use various equations for SHM to solve quantitative problems.

1 A body oscillating about an equilibrium position with an amplitude of x_o and an angular frequency of ω can be described by the equation

$$x = x_o \sin \omega t.$$

 a Sketch a graph of the displacement, x, of the oscillating body against time, t, for three complete oscillations.

 b i Write an equation for the velocity of the oscillating body.

  ii What is the maximum velocity of the body?

 c Sketch a graph of the velocity, v, of the oscillating body against time, t, for three complete oscillations.

 d i Using your answer to **part b**, write an equation for the acceleration of the oscillating body.

  ii What is the maximum acceleration of the body?

 e Sketch a graph of the acceleration, a, of the oscillating body against time, t, for three complete oscillations.

 f Now show that $a = -\omega^2 x$, which gives the definition of SHM.

2 This question is about a body oscillating in SHM.

Figure 12.3 shows how the force acting on a body of mass 500 g varies with its displacement about an equilibrium position.

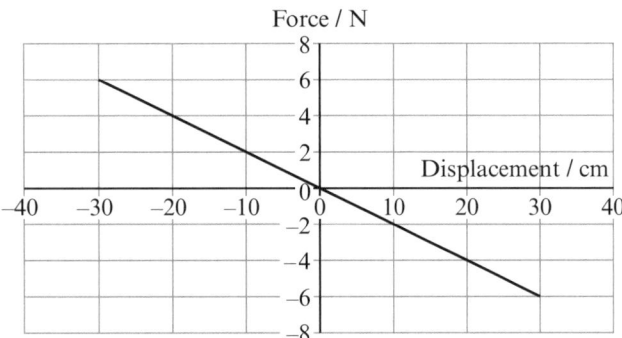

Figure 12.3

a Explain how the graph in Figure 12.3 shows that the body is oscillating in SHM.

b Use the graph in Figure 12.3 to find

   i the amplitude of the oscillations.

   ii the angular frequency of the oscillations.

   iii the frequency of the oscillations.

   iv the time period of the oscillations.

3 This question will derive expressions for the frequency and time period of oscillations of a simple pendulum of length, l.

Figure 12.4 shows a simple pendulum made up of a mass, m, on the end of a light string of length, l. The pendulum has been displaced from the equilibrium position by an angle, θ. The two forces, **q**, and **p**, are the components of the weight, mg, perpendicular and parallel to the tension in the string, T.

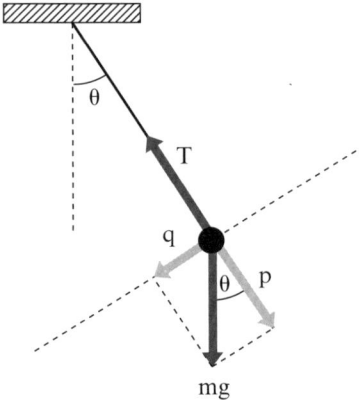

Figure 12.4

- **a** Which force, **p** or **q**, balances with the tension in the string?

- **b** Which force, **p** or **q**, is unbalanced? Write an expression for this force in terms of mg.

- **c** This unbalanced force will cause the pendulum to accelerate. In which direction will the pendulum accelerate?

- **d** Hence, show that the acceleration of the pendulum can be expressed by $a = -g \sin \theta$.

- **e** For small values of θ, $\sin \theta = \theta$.

  Show that $a = -\frac{g}{l} x$.

- **f** Using the definition of SHM, show that the frequency of oscillations is given by the expression

  $f = \frac{1}{2\pi} \sqrt{\frac{g}{l}}$.

- **g** Hence, show that the time period, T, is given by the expression

  $T = 2\pi \sqrt{\frac{l}{g}}$.

4 This question derives expressions for the frequency and time period of oscillations of a mass, m, on a spring of spring constant k.

- **a** State Hooke's law

  Now suppose that a mass, m, is attached to one end of a vertically orientated spring, whose other end is held in a fixed position. When the mass is released, it will oscillate up and down for a short time until coming to a stop. We will call the position of the stationary mass $x = 0$, the equilibrium point.

- **b** **i** What two forces are acting on the mass?

  ii Since the mass is stationary, what can you say about these two forces?

  Now suppose that the mass is pulled downwards a distance of x_o by an external force, F, and then released.

- **c** **i** Using Hooke's law, write an expression for the size of the external force?

  ii Which of the two forces you stated in **part b i** has changed?

  iii In which direction is the net force on the mass?

  iv What will this net force cause the mass to do?

  v Write an expression for the acceleration of the mass when it is displaced from the equilibrium point by a distance x.

  vi Using the definition of SHM, show that the angular frequency, ω, is given by $\omega = \sqrt{\frac{k}{m}}$.

vii Hence, derive an expression for the frequency, f, of the resulting oscillations.

viii Hence, derive an expression for the time period, T, of the resulting oscillations.

5 An opera singer sings a note at a frequency of 250 Hz. It causes a nearby microphone diaphragm to vibrate at the same frequency with an amplitude of 0.2 mm.

> **TIP**
> Remember that the angle in your equations will be in radians.

a What is the angular frequency of the oscillations of the diaphragm?

b i Write an equation for the displacement of the diaphragm as a function of time. (You may assume that at $t = 0$, the displacement is zero.)

ii Hence, determine the displacement of the diaphram at $t = 1.0$ ms.

c i Write an equation for the velocity of the diaphragm as a function of time.

ii Hence, determine the velocity of the diaphragm at $t = 1.0$ ms.

iii What is the maximum speed of the diaphragm?

d i Write an equation for the acceleration of the diaphragm as a function of time.

ii Hence determine the acceleration of the diaphragm at $t = 1.0$ ms.

iii What is the maximum acceleration of the diaphragm?

6 A baby bouncer is a harness attached to two lengths of elastic cord. It enables a baby to bounce up and down gently in SHM.

A one-year-old baby of mass 10 kg is placed in the harness. The elastic cords stretch from 1.2 m to 1.4 m.

a Using $g = 10$ Nkg^{-1}, show that the time period of the vertical oscillations of the baby is just less than 1 s.

b If the amplitude of the baby's oscillations is 20 cm,

i determine the maximum velocity of the baby.

ii show that the maximum acceleration of the baby is about the same value as that caused by gravity.

7 The prong of a tuning fork vibrates in SHM at a frequency of 440 Hz with an amplitude of 2.5 mm. Calculate

a the maximum velocity of the prong.

b the maximum acceleration of the prong.

12 Simple harmonic motion

8 This question looks at how the velocity in a simple harmonic oscillator varies with displacement from the equilibrium position.

a Suppose that a simple harmonic oscillation is described by the equation
$x = x_o \sin \omega t$.

What do the following terms mean?

i x

ii x_o

iii ω

b i Using calculus, differentiate $x = x_o \sin \omega t$ to give an equation for the velocity of the oscillator as a function of time.

ii Using your knowledge of sine and cosine functions, show that the velocity of the oscillator can be given by the expression

$v = \omega \sqrt{x_o^2 - x^2}$.

c For a harmonic oscillator of mass 250 g, oscillating with a frequency of 12 Hz, and an amplitude of 25 cm, calculate

i the maximum velocity.

ii the velocity of the oscillator at $x = \frac{x_o}{2}$.

iii the total energy of the oscillator.

9 The restoring force acting on a simple harmonic oscillator of mass 100 g is given by the equation

$F = 2.7 \times 10^{-2} \sin 3t$.

Determine

a the angular frequency of the oscillations.

b the frequency of the oscillations.

c the amplitude of the oscillations.

d the maximum velocity of the oscillations.

10 a In the Science Museum in London, there is a 22.45-m-long pendulum (known as Foucault's pendulum). It swings, without stopping, in one of the stairwells.

i Calculate the time period of the pendulum. (Take $g = 9.81$ Nkg^{-1})

ii If the pendulum were to be taken to the surface of the moon, where the value of gravitational field strength is $\frac{1}{6}$ of that of the Earth, what would its time period be?

b Now consider a mass of 450 g suspended on a spring of spring constant 20 Nm^{-1} undergoing simple harmonic oscillations.

  i Calculate the time period of the oscillations.

  ii If the mass–spring system were to be taken to the moon, where the value of gravitational field strength is $\frac{1}{6}$ of that of the Earth, what would its time period be?

Exercise 12.3 More about energy in simple harmonic motion

The questions in this section examine the roles that potential energy and kinetic energy play in SHM.

1. This question looks at the energy transformations taking place during simple harmonic oscillations of a mass on the end of a spring.

   Consider a mass, m, oscillating up and down on a spring of spring constant, k. The displacement of the mass from its equilibrium position is shown in Figure 12.5.

   TIP

   Think about which stores (or forms) of energy the mass and the spring have.

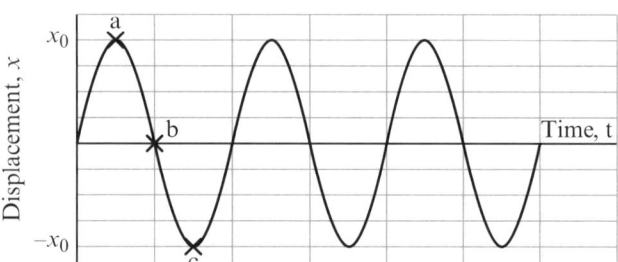

   Figure 12.5

   a Where is the mass at points a, b and c?

   b At which of the points on the graph, a, b and c, is the mass momentarily stationary?

   c At which of the points on the graph, a, b and c, is the mass moving fastest?

   d Hence, outline the energy transfers taking place when the mass moves from the points on the graph

   i a to b.

   ii b to c.

   iii c to b.

   iv b to a.

12 Simple harmonic motion

2 This question looks at the energy transfers taking place during simple harmonic oscillations of a mass on the end of a string, in other words, the SHM of a simple pendulum.

Consider a simple pendulum oscillating back and forth on either side of its equilibrium position. Figure 12.5 also shows how the displacement of the 'bob' on the end of the pendulum varies with time.

> **TIP**
>
> Think about which kinds of energy the bob and the string have.

  a Where is the bob at the points on the graph a, b and c?

  b At which of the points on the graph, a, b and c, is the bob momentarily stationary?

  c At which of the points on the graph, a, b and c, is the bob moving fastest?

  d Hence, outline the energy transfers taking place when the bob moves from the points on the graph

   i a to b.

   ii b to c.

   iii c to b.

   iv b to a.

3 Consider a mass, m, oscillating horizontally on a frictionless surface, held on both sides by springs of spring constant, k, as shown in Figure 12.6. In the figure, both springs are shown neither extended nor contracted.

> **TIP**
>
> Remember that $E_K = \frac{1}{2}mv^2$ and E_P for a spring = $\frac{1}{2}kx^2$.

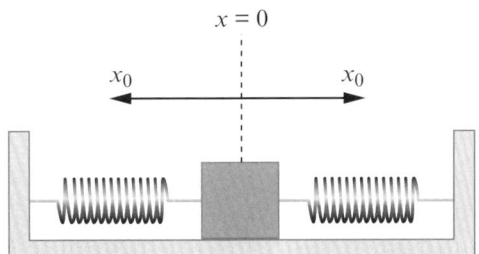

Figure 12.6

  a Where will the mass be when its **velocity** is

   i temporarily zero?

   ii temporarily at a maximum?

  b So, where will the mass be when its **kinetic energy** is

   i temporarily zero?

   ii temporarily a maximum?

  c Using your answers to **part b**, sketch a graph to show how the kinetic energy of the mass varies with its displacement.

  d Now sketch a graph of how the kinetic energy of the mass varies with time during one complete oscillation. You may assume that at $t = 0$, $x = x_o$.

e Where will the mass be when the **potential energy** in the springs is

  i temporarily zero?

  ii temporarily at a maximum?

f In the absence of any friction forces, the conservation of energy states that the total energy of the system remains constant. Using this, and your answers to **parts c** and **d**, sketch a graph of how the potential energy in the springs varies with the displacement of the mass.

g Now sketch a graph of how the potential energy in the springs varies with time for one complete oscillation.

4 This question will look at the energy in an undamped oscillator.

Consider a mass, m, oscillating vertically on a spring of spring constant k, with an amplitude of x_o.

We have seen already that the velocity of the mass at any displacement is given by the equation

$v = \omega\sqrt{x_o^2 - x^2}$.

a **i** Using the equation for v, given earlier, write an equation for the kinetic energy of the mass as a function of its displacement.

  ii Hence, what is the maximum kinetic energy of the mass? Where does this occur?

b Now consider the potential energy on the springs.

  i For an extension, x, write an equation for the potential energy stored in the stretched spring in terms of k and x.

  ii Hence, what is the maximum potential energy stored in the stretched spring?

  iii For the mass–spring system, you should have seen already that $\omega^2 = \frac{k}{m}$.

  Use this identity to show that the maximum potential energy stored in the stretched spring is equal to the maximum kinetic energy of the mass.

c When the kinetic energy of the mass is a maximum,

  i where is the mass?

  ii what is the value of the potential energy stored in the spring?

d When the potential energy stored in the spring is a maximum,

  i where is the mass?

  ii what is the value of the kinetic energy of the mass?

e So, what can you say about the total energy of the mass–spring system?

12 Simple harmonic motion

5 A mass of 150 g oscillates in SHM on the end of a spring with an amplitude of 5.0 cm and a time period of 0.75 s. Calculate

   a the angular frequency, ω, of the oscillations.

   b the spring constant, k, of the spring.

   c the maximum kinetic energy of the mass.

6 A 450 g mass oscillates horizontally on a friction-free surface between two springs whose combined spring constant is 15 Nm^{-1}. The amplitude of the oscillations is 30 cm.

Calculate

   a the time period of the oscillations.

   b the total energy, E_T, of the mass–spring system.

   c the kinetic energy, E_K, of the mass when it is displaced 20 cm from its equilibrium position.

   d the potential energy, E_P, stored in the springs when the mass is displaced 20 cm from its equilibrium position.

7 A mass of 200 g hangs on a light string of length 80 cm. If the mass is displaced horizontally by a distance of 20 cm and then released, calculate

   a the frequency of the resulting oscillations. (You may take $g = 10$ Nkg^{-1}.)

   b the number of oscillations that there will be in 1 minute.

   c the maximum speed of the mass.

   d the total energy of the mass during its oscillations.

8 A body of mass 250 g oscillates in SHM with an amplitude of 4.0 cm completing 24 oscillations in 1 minute.

   a Calculate the angular frequency of the oscillations.

   b Calculate the maximum speed of the body.

   c **i** Calculate the total energy of the body.

   ii If the amplitude of the oscillations were to halve, with the same frequency, what would the total energy of the body now be?

9 A body of mass 1.2 kg is oscillating in SHM with a frequency of 0.4 Hz. If the total energy of the body is 2.0 J, determine the amplitude of its oscillations.

10 a For a mass oscillating on the end of a spring, how does the total energy of the system depend on

   i the mass, m?

   ii the frequency, f, of the oscillations?

    iii   the time period, T, of the oscillations?

    iv   the amplitude, x_o, of the oscillations?

b   For a simple pendulum, consisting of a mass on the end of a string, how does the total energy of the system depend on

    i   the mass, m?

    ii   the frequency, f, of the oscillations?

    iii the time period, T, of the oscillations?

    iv   the amplitude, x_o, of the oscillations?

EXAM-STYLE QUESTIONS

Multiple-choice questions

1   Which of the following statements about a body oscillating in SHM is true?
    A At its maximum displacement from the equilibrium position, its velocity is a maximum.
    B At its maximum displacement from the equilibrium position, its velocity is zero.
    C At its maximum displacement from the equilibrium position, its acceleration is zero.
    D At its maximum displacement from the equilibrium position, its kinetic energy is a maximum.

2   A mass oscillates vertically on a spring with an amplitude of 5.0 cm. If the mass undergoes 50 oscillations, what will the total displacement of the mass be?
    A 0 cm
    B 20 cm
    C 250 cm
    D 500 cm

3   If the length of a simple pendulum is quadrupled, the time period of its oscillations will
    A quarter.
    B halve.
    C double.
    D quadruple.

4   If the mass on the end of a simple pendulum is doubled, the time period of its oscillations will
    A change by a factor of $\sqrt{2}$.
    B change by a factor of $\frac{1}{\sqrt{2}}$.
    C change by a factor of 2.
    D remain unchanged.

CONTINUED

5 A mass suspended on a spring undergoes SHM with a frequency, f. If the amplitude of the oscillations is doubled, what will the frequency of the oscillations be?

   A $\sqrt{2}\,f$

   B $\frac{1}{\sqrt{2}}f$

   C $2f$

   D f

6 A mass suspended on a spring undergoes simple harmonic oscillations such that the velocity of the mass, with respect to time, is described by a sine curve. In the absence of friction, the total energy of the mass–spring system, with respect to time, will be given by

   A a cosine curve.

   B a sine-squared curve.

   C a cosine-squared curve.

   D a horizontal straight line.

7 The time period of a simple pendulum is given by the equation

   $T = 2\pi\sqrt{\frac{l}{g}}.$

   Which of the following plots will produce a straight line graph:

   A T against l.

   B T against l^2.

   C $\sqrt{T}$ against l.

   D T^2 against l.

8 Which of the following expressions gives correctly the velocity of an oscillating mass as a function of its displacement:

   A $v = \omega\sqrt{x_o - x}$.

   B $v = \omega(x_o - x)$.

   C $v = \omega\sqrt{x_o^2 - x^2}$.

   D $v = \omega(x_o^2 - x^2)$.

9 The displacement of an undamped SHM oscillator is given by the expression

   $x = x_o \cos(\omega t)$.

   Which of the following expressions is **false**?

   A The velocity of the oscillator is given by a sine function.

   B The kinetic energy of the oscillator is given by a sine-squared function.

   C The total energy of the oscillator is constant.

   D The acceleration of the oscillator is given by a negative cosine function.

CONTINUED

Short-answer questions

10 Figure 12.7 shows how the displacement of an undamped SHM oscillator varies with time.

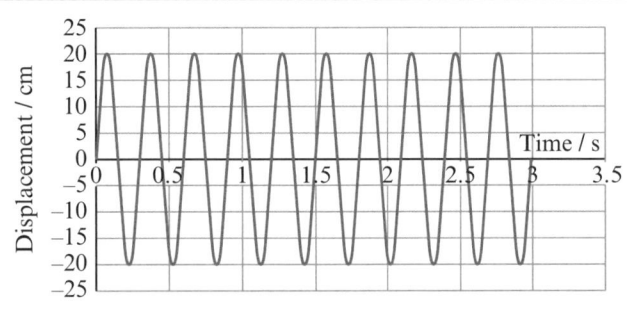

Figure 12.7

Determine
- a the amplitude of the oscillations. [1]
- b the angular frequency of the oscillations. [2]
- c the maximum acceleration of the oscillator. [2]

11 A mass of 1.25 kg is performing simple harmonic oscillations with a time period of 0.80 s and an amplitude of 6.0 cm. Determine
- a the angular frequency of the oscillations. [1]
- b the speed of the mass as it passes through the equilibrium position. [2]
- c the maximum kinetic energy of the mass. [2]

12 a State the conditions necessary for an oscillation to be simple harmonic. [2]
- b For an SHM oscillator with an amplitude of x_o the time period of its oscilations is T.
  - i State how the time period will change if the amplitude of the oscillations decreases linearly to zero with time. [1]
  - ii State, and explain, how the maximum velocity of the oscillator will change if the amplitude of the oscillation decreases linearly with time. [2]

CONTINUED

13 Figure 12.8 shows how the acceleration of an oscillator, of mass 300 g, undergoing SHM, varies with its displacement from the equilibrium position.

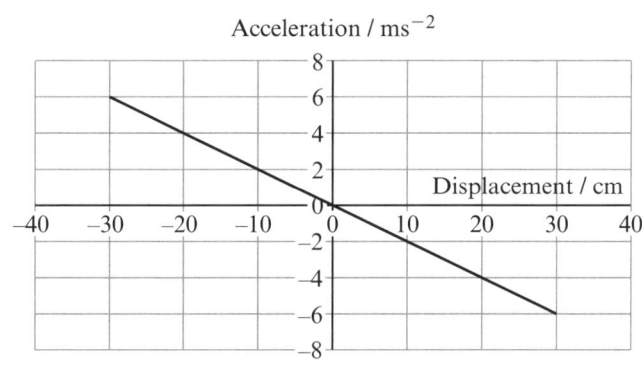

Figure 12.8

- **a** State how the graph shows that the oscillations are simple harmonic. [2]
- **b** Determine the angular frequency of the oscillations. [1]
- **c** Determine the speed of the mass as it passes through the equilibrium poisition. [1]
- **d** Hence, show that the total energy of the oscillator is 0.27 J. [1]

14 The oscillations of a simple harmonic oscillator are described by the equation $x = 0.25 \cos(10\pi t)$, where the amplitude of the oscillations is 0.25 m and a positive displacement is to the right of the equilibrium position.
- **a** State the frequency of the oscillations. [1]
- **b** **i** Determine where, with respect to the equilibrium position, the oscillator will be at a time of $t = 0.3$ s. [1]
  - **ii** State the speed of the oscillator at $t = 0.3$ s. [1]
  - **iii** State any value of t for which the speed of the oscillator is a maximum. [1]
  - **iv** Determine the maximum speed of the oscillator. [1]

15 A mass is suspended at the end of a simple pendulum of length 1.20 m. The mass is pulled sideways to the right-hand side by a distance of 15 cm at time $t = 0$ and released, resulting in the pendulum making simple harmonic oscillations.
- **a** Calculate the period of the oscillations. [2]
- **b** Show that at $t = 1.5$ s, the mass is 6.2 cm to the left of the equilibrium position. [1]
- **c** Calculate the speed of the mass at $t = 1.5$ s. [2]

CONTINUED

16 A mass of 50 g oscillates in SHM with an amplitude of 5.0 cm and an angular frequency of 25 rads s^{-1}.

    a Determine the time period of the oscillations. [1]

    b Show that the total energy of the oscillator is about 40 mJ. [2]

    c Determine where the mass is, with respect to the equilibrium position, when its kinetic energy is 10 mJ. [2]

17 A mass of 500 g oscillates in SHM on the end of a spring of spring constant 20 Nm^{-1} with an amplitude of 25 cm.

    a Calculate the frequency of the oscillations. [1]

    b Calculate the speed of the mass when it is 10 cm from the equilibrium position. [2]

    c If the amplitude of the oscillations is now halved, state

        i by what factor the angular frequency will change. [1]

        ii by what factor the maximum speed of the mass will change. [1]

Chapter 13
The wave model

CHAPTER OUTLINE

In this chapter you will:

- meet the main features that describe waves. Different kinds of waves, both transverse and longitudinal, are examined and the wave equation explored.
- identify the characteristics of a transverse and a longitudinal wave.
- use the terms wavelength, frequency, period and wave speed to describe waves.
- explore mechanical waves, electromagnetic waves and sound waves.
- sketch and interpret graphs of *displacement* against *time* and *displacement* against *distance*.
- use the wave equation to solve problems.

> identify briefly the nature of matter waves and gravitational waves.

KEY TERMS

mechanical wave: a disturbance that transfers energy and momentum through oscillations of the particles of a medium

wavelength: the length of one full wave

period: the time to create one full wave

frequency: the number of full waves per second

amplitude: the maximum displacement

transverse: a wave where the oscillations are at right angles to the direction of energy transfer

longitudinal: a wave where the oscillations are parallel to the direction of energy transfer

rarefaction: a point where the density of the medium is lowest

compression: a point where the density of the medium is highest

electromagnetic (EM) wave: a transverse wave consisting of oscillations of an electric and a magnetic field at right angles to each other

the wave equation: $v = f\lambda$, where v is the wave speed, f is the frequency of the wave and λ is the wavelength of the wave

> **CONTINUED**
>
> **gravitational wave:** a transverse wave, travelling at the speed of light, that stretches and compresses space (by very small amounts)
>
> **matter wave:** a wave corresponding to particles whose displacement is related to the probability of finding the particle at a particular position

Exercise 13.1 Mechanical waves

The questions in this section will help you become familiar with the terms used by physicists to describe waves, illustrate waves with graphs and solve simple problems using the wave equation.

1 a Outline what is meant by the following terms used to describe properties of waves:

    i *wavelength,* λ

    ii *frequency, f*

    iii *time period, T*

    iv *amplitude, A*

    v *wave speed, v*

  b How are frequency and time period related mathematically?

  c On which of the properties listed in **part a** does the energy being transferred by a wave depend?

  d Explain what is meant by the term *mechanical wave*.

2 Waves can be described graphically in two ways: as *displacement* against *time* graphs or as *displacement* against *distance* graphs.

  a i What three features of a wave can be determined from a graph of *displacement* against *time*?

    ii What additional information is required to determine the speed of the wave?

  b i What two features of a wave can be determined from a graph of *displacement* against *distance*?

    ii What additional information is required to determine the speed of the wave?

3 This question is about a wave on a string.

Figure 13.1 shows the variation with distance of the displacement of the string at a particular time. The dotted line shows the position of the string with no wave present. The direction of propagation of the wave is shown by the large arrow.

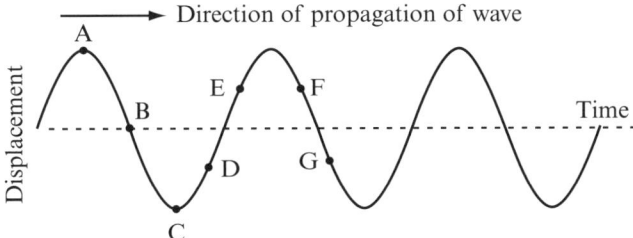

Figure 13.1

Seven positions on the string are marked with the labels: A, B, C, D, E, F and G.

a Which of the positions shows the string at a

   i crest, or peak, of the wave?

   ii trough of the wave?

b The maximum speed at which any part of the string oscillates is v. At which of the three positions shown is the speed of the string

   i v?

   ii 0?

c Add to Figure 13.1 some arrows to show the speed and direction of the part of the string at the positions labelled A to G.

d Now add to Figure 13.1 a double-headed arrow to indicate the wavelength of the wave. Label this 'λ'.

4 Figure 13.2 shows the variation with distance of the displacement of the string. The dotted line shows the position of the string with no wave present. The direction of propagation of the wave is shown by the large arrow.

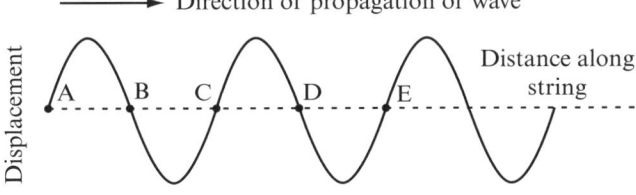

Figure 13.2

a With reference to the letters A to E, between which two letters will the distance be one wavelength, λ?

b In terms of any particular point along the wave, distinguish between the frequency, f, of the wave and the time period, T, of the wave.

c   If the displacement of the string, ABC, moves along to CDE,

   i   how far has the wave moved?

   ii how much time has it taken to move this far?

   iii Hence, show that the speed of the wave is given by $v = f\lambda$.

5 Figure 13.3 shows a snapshot of a wave travelling along a section of a string at a time t.

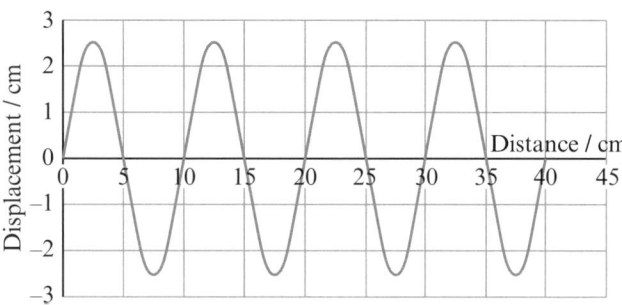

Figure 13.3

a   Use the diagram to find

   i   the amplitude, x_0.

   ii the wavelength, λ.

b   If the frequency of the wave is 2 Hz,

   i   how much time will it take before another snapshot will show the wave to look exactly the same as in Figure 13.1?

   ii determine the speed at which the wave is travelling along the string.

6 Outline an experiment that could measure the speed of sound in air.
   Make sure you include

   - the equipment required,
   - the measurements you need to make (and the instruments you would use to make them),
   - the uncertainty you would expect in each measurement,
   - how you would manipulate the data to calculate the speed of sound in air and
   - how you will find the uncertainty in your value for the speed of sound in air.

Exercise 13.2 Transverse and longitudinal waves

The questions in this section will help you explore the nature of transverse and longitudinal waves.

1   Figure 13.4 shows some atoms ahead of an incident wave. The direction of the wave is shown by the large arrow.

Figure 13.4

   a   On Figure 13.4 draw a double-headed arrow on one of the atoms to show the direction in which the atom will oscillate when the wave passing through is a transverse wave. Label this arrow 'T'.

   b   On Figure 13.4 draw a double-headed arrow on one of the atoms to show the direction in which the atom will oscillate when the wave passing through is a longitudinal wave. Label this arrow 'L'.

   c   Hence, explain briefly the difference between a transverse wave and a longitudinal wave.

   d   Give an example of

      i   a transverse wave.

      ii a longitudinal wave.

2   This question is about a sound wave. Sound waves are longitudinal waves.

Figure 13.5 shows the position of some molecules of air when a sound wave is passing through the air. The direction of motion of the sound wave is shown. Underneath the diagram is a set of axes, with the same *x*-axis of distance, to enable the plotting of the air pressure to be carried out.

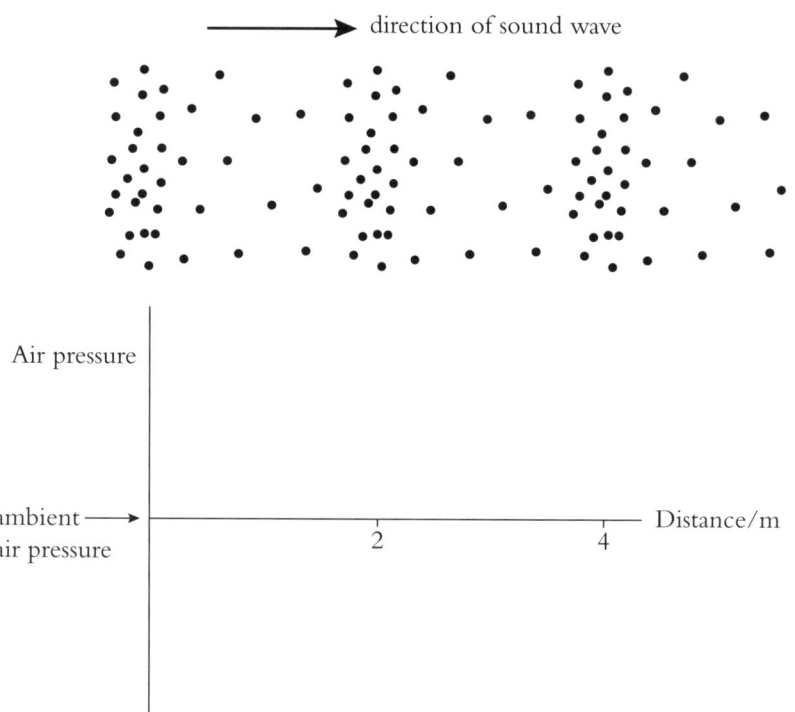

Figure 13.5

a   Indicate on the diagram where the air pressure is

   i   a maximum; label this P_{max}.

   ii a minimum; label this P_{min}.

   iii ambient (in other words, when there is no sound wave present); label this P_{amb}.

b   Sketch the graph, using the axes provided, to show how the air pressure varies with distance.

c   Draw a double-headed arrow on one of the air molecules in Figure 13.5 to show the direction in which the air molecule oscillates when the sound wave is present.

d   The speed of sound in air is 330 ms⁻¹. Use the diagram (or your graph) to calculate the frequency of the sound wave.

3   Figure 13.6 shows the displacement as a function of time of a molecule of nitrogen in the air as a sound wave passes by.

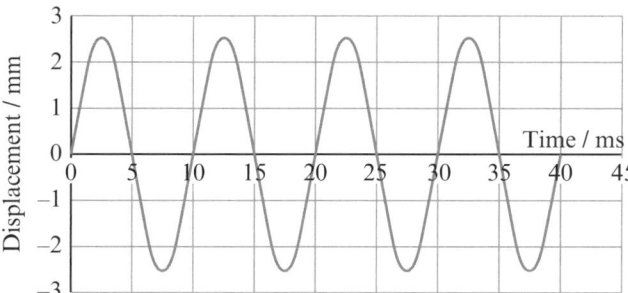

Figure 13.6

a   Is it possible to know—just by looking—that Figure 13.6 represents a longitudinal wave?

b   Use Figure 13.6 to

   i   determine the amplitude of the oscillations of the nitrogen molecule.

   ii   show that the frequency, f, of the sound wave is 100 Hz.

c   If the wavelength of the sound wave is 3.3 m, calculate the speed of sound in air.

d   Explain how Figure 13.6 shows that the speed of the molecule is

   i   momentarily zero at a time of $t = 2.5$ ms.

   ii   a maximum at a time of $t = 10$ ms.

e   Sketch, on the same axes as Figure 13.6, a graph to show another sound wave, which is quieter and of twice the frequency as that of the sound wave in Figure 13.6.

4   The transmission of a mechanical wave through a medium can be modelled with a number of balls all held in a line by unstretched (and uncompressed) springs attached between them. Figure 13.7 shows such a model.

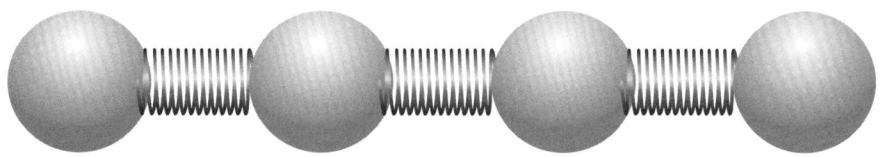

Figure 13.7

Suppose that the ball on the far left-hand side is pushed quickly towards the next ball and then pulled back quickly away from it.

a   What happens to the spring between the first two balls?

b   What effect does this have on the second ball?

c So what then happens to the spring between the second and the third balls?

d What does this eventually do to all the balls in the line?

e When the first ball is then pulled back, away from the second ball, what happens to all the springs and the balls in the line?

f How is this modelling a wave that transfers energy and momentum?

g This is modelling a single pulse of a wave. Is it a pulse from a transverse wave or a longitudinal wave?

h   **i** Suggest **two** factors that will affect the speed at which the pulse moves along the line of balls.

    ii For each of your suggestions in **part i**, explain what the effect on the speed of the pulse is and why.

i From your answers to **part h**, suggest why sound waves travel faster along a steel rod than they do in the air.

5 Look back at Figure 13.7. Suppose that the first ball on the left-hand side is suddenly pulled upwards and then downwards in an oscillatory fashion.

  a Outline what will happen to the springs and balls in the line.

  b Is this a model for a pulse of a transverse wave or for a longitudinal wave.

  c Do your answers to **question 4 part h** still apply to this situation?

6 Suppose that a transverse wave propagates along a string with an amplitude of 5 cm and a frequency of 100 Hz.

  a For any point along the string,

    i what is the period of its oscillations?

    ii what is the net displacement of the point on the string over a time of 1 s?

  b Hence, what is the average velocity of the point on the string?

  c How far does the point on the string actually move during the time of 1 s?

  d Hence, what is the average speed of the point along the string.

  e Explain why your answers to **parts b** and **d** are different.

  f Explain why it is not possible to determine the speed at which the wave is moving.

7 Toothed whales can use sound waves to detect objects around them using echolocation.

  a Outline what is meant by the term *echolocation*.

  b Suppose a whale emits a sound wave of frequency 120 kHz, which travels through the ocean at a speed of 1.4 kms^{-1}.

    i   What is the wavelength of the sound wave emitted by the whale?

    ii   If the whale hears an echo 0.3 s after it has emitted the sound wave, how far away is the object it is locating?

    iii Will the whale be able to detect a squid of length 20 cm at this distance? Explain your answer.

Exercise 13.3 Electromagnetic waves

The questions in this section are designed to help you explore the basic nature of electromagnetic waves and to become familiar with the electromagnetic spectrum.

1 **a** Explain why an electromagnetic wave is not a mechanical wave.

    b Outline briefly the major features of an electromagnetic wave.

    c What do all kinds of electromagnetic waves have in common?

    d List the seven main regions of the electromagnetic spectrum in order of increasing wavelength.

Questions 2–8 explore in more detail the seven regions of the electromagnetic spectrum.

2 **a** How are gamma rays produced?

    b Why are gamma rays considered to be dangerous?

    c State the range of possible wavelengths for gamma rays.

    d The following are a few ways in which gamma rays are useful to us. For each way, try to find out how the gamma rays are used and outline briefly your findings.

        i   Medical applications

        ii   Radio-sterilisation

        iii Gamma ray spectroscopy

        iv Gamma ray astronomy

3 **a** How are X-rays produced?

    b State the range of possible wavelengths for X-rays.

    c List some ways in which X-rays are used by humans.

    d Suggest why we should be careful not to expose ourselves to too much X-ray radiation.

4 **a** Outline how ultraviolet light is produced by atoms.

    b State the range of wavelengths for ultraviolet light.

> **TIP**
>
> You may need to do some research to answer these questions; make sure that, as an absolute minimum, you know the wavelengths of each of the regions of the electromagnetic spectrum.

c Suggest some possible hazards associated with ultraviolet radiation.

d List some ways in which ultra-violet light can be useful to humans.

5 a How is visible light produced by atoms?

b Young children are sometimes taught the mnemonic: Richard Of York Gave Battle In Vain. What does this mnemonic help children to learn?

c For each of the seven major colours in the visible light spectrum, give a typical wavelength for the light.

d To which colour of the visible light spectrum are our eyes most sensitive? Suggest a reason why.

6 a How is infrared radiation produced by atoms?

b State the range of wavelengths for infrared radiation.

c List some ways in which infrared radiation is used by humans.

7 a Outline briefly how microwaves are produced.

b State the range of possible wavelengths for microwaves.

c List some ways in which microwaves are used in everyday life.

8 a Outline how radio waves are produced.

b State the range of wavelengths of radio waves.

c List some ways in which radio waves are used in everyday life.

d What feature of radio waves makes them particularly suitable for communications?

Exercise 13.4 Waves extension

The two questions in this extension section are designed to make students aware of two other kinds of wave: matter waves and gravitational waves.

1 About a hundred years ago, Louis de Broglie proposed that matter that was moving would exhibit wave-like properties.

For this question, consider some particles, each of mass m, moving with a speed v, towards a barrier in which there is a small hole about the same size (or just a little larger) as the particles.

a How much momentum would a particle have?

b Many of the particles arriving at the barrier will be stopped as they collide with (and perhaps bounce off) the barrier. But some of the particles will pass through the hole—and when they do their paths will change a little, causing them to spread out as they move beyond the hole.

i   What wave property is the spreading out of the paths of the particles mimicking?

   ii If the particles had more momentum (perhaps because they move faster), would you expect them to spread out more, or less, as they pass through the hole? Justify your answer.

   iii If the hole in the barrier were made very much larger, (say, more than 10 times the size of the particles) would you expect the spreading out of the particles to be more, or less, than before? Justify your answer.

c So, if the particles show behaviour similar to that of waves, we can assign them a wavelength, λ.

   i   With reference to your answer from **part b ii**, suggest how the wavelength of a moving particle is related to its momentum.

   ii With reference to your answer to **part b iii**, suggest how the amount of spreading out of the paths of the particles is related to the momenta of the particles and to the size of the hole.

d Which of the following particles would you expect to show the greatest amount of wave behaviour? Justify your answer.

   - a fast-moving proton
   - a stationary atomic nucleus
   - a slow-moving electron

e The time-dependent wave function, describing any particle, developed by Erwin Schrödinger can be manipulated to form a probability density function. What does this function tell us about the particle?

2 This question looks briefly at gravitational waves.

a What is the cause of gravitational waves?

b What is it that oscillates in a gravitational wave?

c Are gravitational waves transverse or longitudinal, or both?

d At what speed do gravitational waves travel?

e Outline briefly why it is very difficult to observe gravitational waves

PHYSICS FOR THE IB DIPLOMA: WORKBOOK

EXAM-STYLE QUESTIONS

Multiple-choice questions

1. Look at Figure 13.8. Which arrow—A, B, C or D—represents the wavelength of the wave?

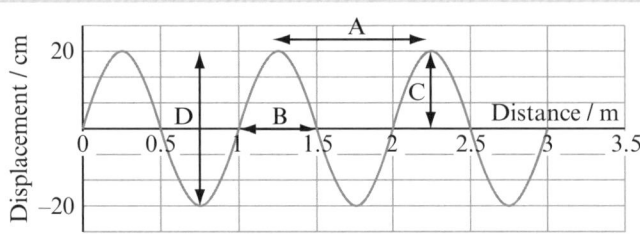

Figure 13.8

2. Look at Figure 13.8. Which arrow—A, B, C or D—represents the amplitude of the wave?

3. The speed of electromagnetic waves in the air is about 3×10^8 ms^{-1}. Which of the following is the best estimate of the frequency of a microwave of wavelength 3 cm?

   A 10 Hz
   B 10 kHz
   C 10 MHz
   D 10 GHz

4. Which of the following kinds of waves is **not** a transverse wave?

   A Sound wave
   B Radio wave
   C Gravity wave
   D Ripples on the surface of some water

5. Figure 13.9 shows a graphical representation of a wave.

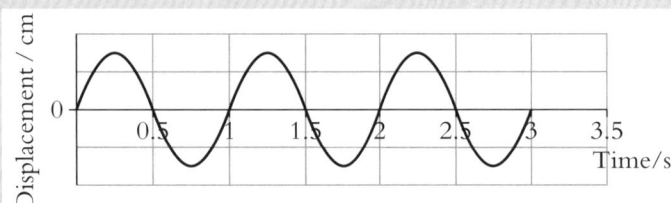

Figure 13.9

What is the frequency of the wave?

   A 0.33 Hz
   B 0.5 Hz
   C 1.0 Hz
   D 3.0 Hz

CONTINUED

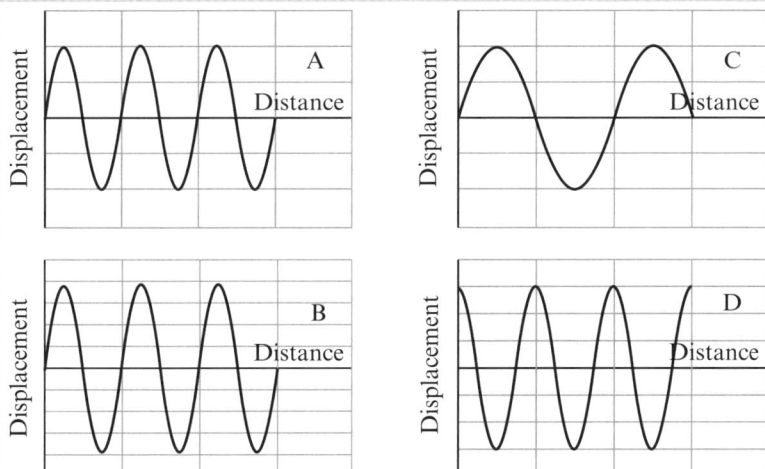

Figure 13.10

6 Look at Figure 13.10. Which wave—A, B, C or D—is transferring the most energy?

7 Look at Figure 13.10. Which wave—A, B, C or D—has the largest time period?

8 Which of the following statements about sound waves is **incorrect**?
   - A Sound waves travel through water faster than they travel through air.
   - B Sound waves travel through empty space slower than they travel through air.
   - C Sound waves are longitudinal waves.
   - D We can see a lightning strike before we hear it because sound waves travel slower than light waves.

Short-answer questions

9 Dolphins can communicate by emitting sound waves that travel through water at $1.5\ kms^{-1}$. The speed of sound waves in air is $330\ ms^{-1}$.
   - a Suggest why sound waves travel faster through water than through air. [2]
   - b If the frequency of a dolphin's sound waves is 200 kHz, calculate
     - i the wavelength of the sound waves in the water. [1]
     - ii the wavelength of the sound waves in the air. [1]
   - c Explain why it is not possible for a human to hear these sound waves. [1]

CONTINUED

10 Figure 13.11 shows a transverse wave travelling along a long spring. The dotted line shows the displacement of the spring at $t = 0$ and the solid line shows the displacement of the spring at $t = 100$ ms.

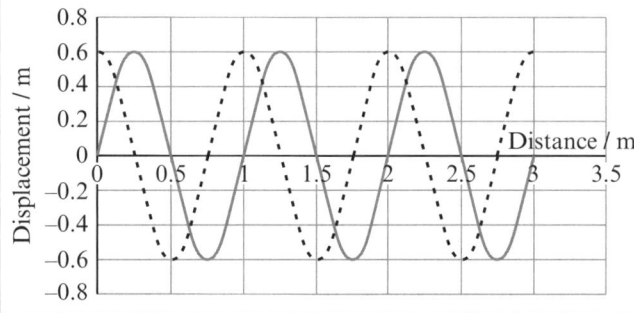

Figure 13.11

Use Figure 13.11 to determine the

- **a** amplitude of the wave. [1]
- **b** wavelength of the wave. [1]
- **c** speed of the wave. [1]
- **d** frequency of the wave. [1]
- **e** time period of the wave. [1]

11 Figure 13.12 shows how the velocity of a particle of matter varies with time as a mechanical wave passes by.

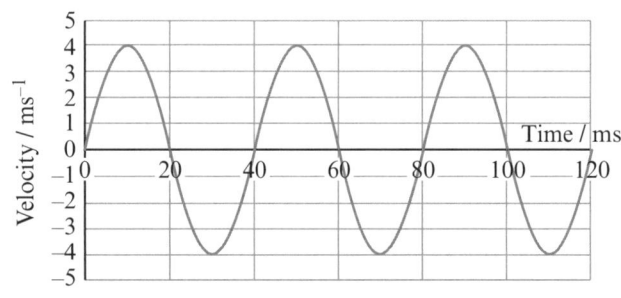

Figure 13.12

- **a** Use Figure 13.12 to determine the frequency of the oscillations of the particle. [2]
- **b** Indicate on the diagram
  - **i** a time at which the particle is momentarily at a maximum distance from its equilibrium position. Mark this with an 'X'. [1]
  - **ii** a time at which the particle is momentarily at its equilibrium position. Mark this with a 'Y'. [1]
- **c** Suggest how the area under the curve from $t = 0$ ms to $t = 22$ ms is related to the amplitude of the oscillations. [1]

CONTINUED

12 Figure 13.13 shows the way in which a particle is oscillating due to a sound wave passing by.

Figure 13.13

    a Indicate, with a suitable arrow on the diagram, the direction in which the sound wave is travelling. [1]

    b The particle makes one complete oscillation in 5.0 ms. The wavelength of the sound wave is 1.65 m.

        i Calculate the frequency of the sound wave. [1]

        ii Calculate the speed at which the sound wave is travelling. [1]

    c A different sound wave, of the same frequency but louder, now causes the particle to oscillate. Outline the changes, if any, to the

        i average speed of the oscillating particle. [1]

        ii time it takes for the particle to make one complete oscillation. [1]

13 A boy throws a pebble into a still pond. The pebble makes circular waves on the surface of the pond that have their crests 10 cm apart with an amplitude of 1.0 cm. The crests move outwards at a speed of 20 cms^{-1}.

Draw graphs to show how the vertical displacement, x, of the surface of the water varies with

    a distance, d, from the centre of the circular waves. (At $d = 0$, $x = -1.0$ cm) [3]

    b time, t. (At $t = 0$, $x = -1.0$ cm) [2]

14 Transverse waves of frequency 2.0 Hz are sent along a long hollow rubber tube, resting on an almost friction-free tabletop, by a teacher holding one end of the tube and moving it sideways back and forth. It is noticed that the distance between a crest and a trough is 0.6 m.

    a Calculate the speed at which the waves move along the hollow rubber tube. [2]

    b The amplitude of the waves is now doubled. State the speed of the waves now moving along the hollor rubber tube. [1]

    c The rubber tube is now filled with sand. If the teacher continues to move one end of the tube sideways back and forth at a frequency of 2.0 Hz, what changes will there be, if any, to

        i the speed of the new transverse waves. [1]

        ii the wavelength of the new transverse waves. [1]

> Chapter 14
Wave phenomena

CHAPTER OUTLINE

In this chapter, you will:

- examine the behaviour of waves at boundaries in terms of reflection, refraction and transmission.
- examine the diffraction of waves around objects and through apertures.
- use wavefront and ray diagrams to show refraction and diffraction
- examine the superposition of pulses and waves
- examine interference from two sources
- become familiar with Young's double source interference

> examine single-slit interference

> explore how double-slit interference is dependent on the single-slit diffraction envelope.

> explore interference patterns from multiple slits and diffraction gratings.

KEY TERMS

reflection: When a wave meets a boundary between two different media, some, or all, of the wave may not pass beyond the boundary and will 'bounce off'. This is called reflection.

refraction: The change in speed (and sometimes direction) when waves pass from one medium into a different medium

refractive index: The ratio of the speed of electromagnetic waves in a vacuum to the speed of the same wave in a different medium;
$n = \frac{v_{vacuum}}{v_{medium}} = \frac{c}{v}$

Snell's law: $_1n_2 = \frac{\sin \theta_1}{\sin \theta_2}$

critical angle, θ_c: The angle at which the refracted ray (from a more dense medium to a less dense medium) travels along the boundary between the two media; $\theta_c = \sin^{-1}\left(\frac{1}{_1n_2}\right)$

diffraction: The spreading out of waves as they pass around an object or through an aperture

CONTINUED

coherent: A term describing when two or more sources are emitting waves in phase or with a constant phase relationship between them

superposition: When two or more waves meet at the same place and time

interference: The effect of two or more waves meeting at the same place and time

wavefront: A line, or surface, showing parts of a wave that are of the same phase as each other (usually shown as wave peaks)

ray diagram: A diagram showing the path, or paths, of waves

diffraction grating: An assembly of many narrow slits, equally spaced a small distance apart, through which waves can travel

KEY EQUATIONS

refractive index: $n = \dfrac{v_{vacuum}}{v_{medium}} = \dfrac{c}{v}$

Snell's law: $_1n_2 = \dfrac{\sin \theta_1}{\sin \theta_2}$

critical angle: $\theta_c = \sin^{-1}\left(\dfrac{1}{_1n_2}\right)$

constructive interference: path difference = $n\lambda$

destructive interference: path difference = $(n + \frac{1}{2})\lambda$

Young's double slit: $s = \dfrac{\lambda D}{d}$

Constructive interference equations

- Single slit: $\qquad n\lambda = b \sin \theta_n$

    (Here, θ_n is the angle between the central maximum, the single slit and the nth minimum.)

- Double slit/2 sources: $\qquad n\lambda = d \sin \theta_n$

    (Here, θ_n is the angle between the central maximum, the single slit and the nth maximum.)

where n is the refractive index, n is an integer, λ the wavelength, s the fringe separation, D the distance from sources to screen, d the separation of two sources and b the width of a single slit.

Author's note: the two n's in these equations are different; the italic n is the refractive index and the normal case n is representing an integer.

> **TIP**
>
> Be careful not to get these two different ns mixed up!!

Exercise 14.1 Reflection and refraction

The questions in this section will develop your understanding of reflection and refraction of waves.

1   Figure 14.1 shows a string attached perpendicularly to a mirror. A pulse is travelling along the string towards the mirror in the direction shown.

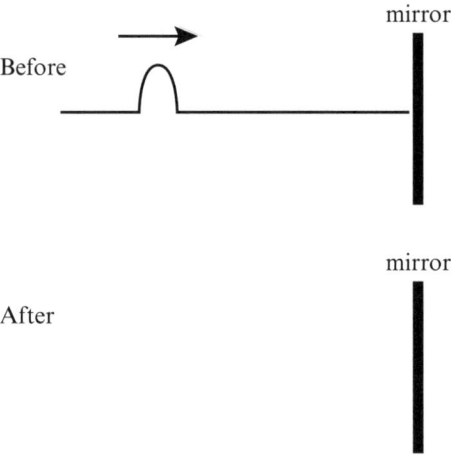

Figure 14.1

a   Complete the diagram in Figure 14.1 to show what happens to the pulse on the string after it has reached the mirror.

b   What can you say has happened to the pulse?

c   By how much has there been a phase change?

2   Figure 14.2 shows two strings attached together. The left-hand string is narrow and has a pulse travelling along it in the direction shown. The right-hand string is made from the same material as the left-hand string, but it is much thicker and so has more mass per unit length.

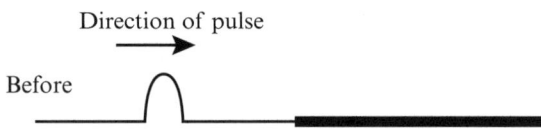

Figure 14.2

a   i   Complete the diagram in Figure 14.2 to show what happens after the pulse has reached the place where the two strings are attached.

   ii   Explain the features of your addition to Figure 14.2.

b   i   How will the speed of the transmitted pulse compare with the speed of the reflected pulse?

   ii   Explain your answer.

    c   Compared with the original incident pulse, comment on the phase of the

          i   transmitted pulse.

          ii   reflected pulse.

    d   Compared with the original incident pulse, comment on the amplitude of the

          i   transmitted pulse.

          ii   reflected pulse.

3   Figure 14.3 shows two strings attached together. The left-hand string is thick and has a pulse travelling along it in the direction shown. The right-hand string is made from the same material as the left-hand string, but it is much thinner and so has less mass per unit length.

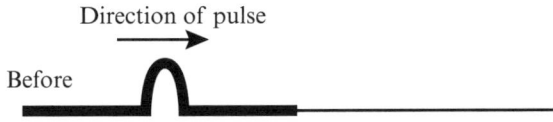

Figure 14.3

    a   i   Complete the diagram in Figure 14.3 to show what happens after the pulse has reached the place where the two strings are attached.

         ii   Explain the features of your addition to Figure 14.3.

    b   i   How will the speed of the transmitted pulse compare with the speed of the reflected pulse?

         ii   Explain your answer.

    c   Compared with the original incident pulse, comment on the phase of the

          i   transmitted pulse.

          ii   reflected pulse.

    d   Compared with the original incident pulse, comment on the amplitude of the

          i   transmitted pulse.

          ii   reflected pulse.

4   Figure 14.4 shows two different ways of representing the same event: some waves incident on a mirror surface at an angle of incidence of θ.

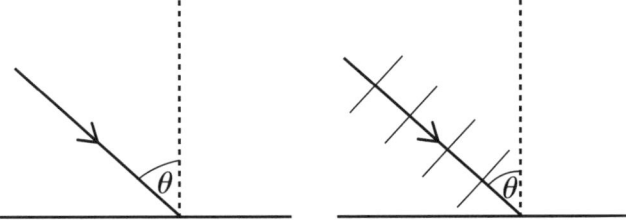

Figure 14.4

a Explain what is meant by the following terms:

　i　*ray*

　ii　*wavefront*

　iii　*normal*

　iv　*angle of incidence*

　v　*angle of reflection*

b Complete the two diagrams in Figure 14.4 to show what happens when the waves are reflected from the mirror surface.

c How are the angle of incidence and the angle of reflection related?

d How are the wavefronts and the rays related?

5 a　i　Explain what is meant by *refraction*.

　　ii　Define the term *refractive index, n,* of a substance.

b Figure 14.5 shows a ray of light incident on the boundary between the air and some water.

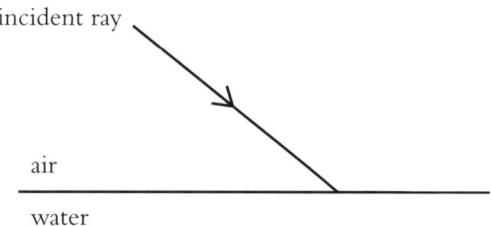

Figure 14.5

Add to the diagram

　i　the normal.

　ii　the reflected ray.

　iii　the refracted ray.

　iv　the angle of incidence.

　v　the angle of refraction.

c How is the angle of refraction, *r*, related to the angle of incidence, *i*? (Take the refractive index of air to be 1.0.)

d What is the name of this law?

14 Wave phenomena

6 Figure 14.6 shows some wavefronts of light of frequency 6.0×10^{14} Hz incident on a boundary between the air and some glass. The refractive index of glass is 1.5.

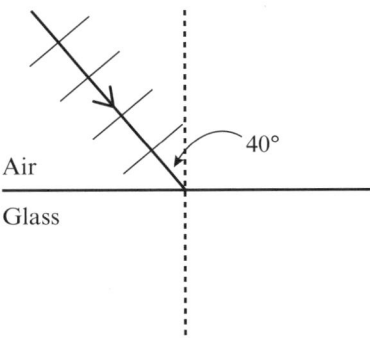

Figure 14.6

- **a** Calculate the angle of refraction of the light.
- **b** Calculate the speed of the light in the glass. (The speed of light in air is 3×10^8 ms^{-1}.)
- **c** Calculate the wavelength of the light in air.
- **d** Calculate the wavelength of the light in the glass.
- **e** What colour is the light in air?
- **f** What colour is the light in the glass?
- **g** Complete the diagram in Figure 14.6 to show the wavefronts being refracted in the glass.
- **h** Indicate on Figure 14.6 the wavelength of the light in the
  - **i** air, λ_{air}.
  - **ii** glass, λ_{glass}.

7 Figure 14.7 shows a ray of light incident on the boundary between some water ($n = 1.33$) and the air ($n = 1.0$).

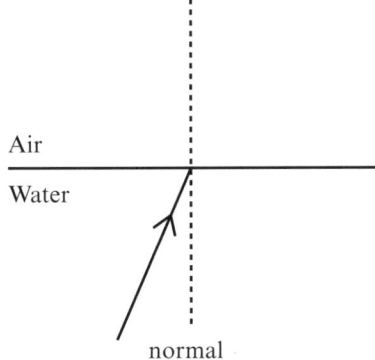

Figure 14.7

a   Complete the diagram to show what happens to the ray of light.

b   As the angle of incidence in the water increases, what happens to the angle of refraction in the air?

c   When the angle of refraction becomes 90°, the ray will travel along the boundary between the water and the air. What will the angle of incidence be for this to happen?

d   What is the name given to this angle of incidence?

e   At angles of incidence greater than the angle you calculated in **part c**, what happens to the ray?

> **TIP**
>
> Use Snell's law and just reverse the direction of the rays.

8   Outline an experiment that could find the refractive index of a rectangular block of glass. Make sure you include

- the equipment required,
- the measurements you need to make (and the instruments you would use to make them) and
- how you would manipulate the data to obtain a reliable value for n.

9   Information is often transmitted using fibre optic cables. Fibre optic cables are made from a glass fibre surrounded by cladding material with an optical refractive index less than that of the glass fibre. An outer covering protects the cladding from exterior damage. Light is transmitted into the cable, in pulses, so that it is incident on the glass fibre–cladding boundary at an angle θ, as shown in Figure 14.8. The pulses of light undergo total internal reflection.

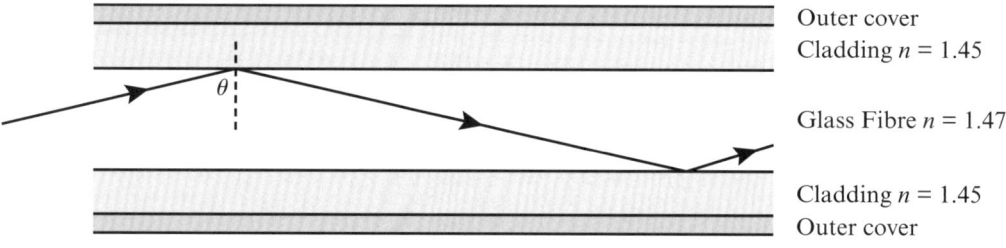

Outer cover
Cladding $n = 1.45$

Glass Fibre $n = 1.47$

Cladding $n = 1.45$
Outer cover

Figure 14.8

a   How would the speed of light in the cladding compare with the speed of light in the glass fibre?

b   Calculate the speed of light in the

   i   glass fibre.

   ii cladding.

c   Determine the minimum value of θ that will allow total internal reflection of the pulses of light to occur.

d   What is the name given to this angle?

e   Hence, calculate the time it would take a pulse of light to travel along a 1.0 km cable at this value of θ.

f   How does the time calculated in **part e** compare to the time it would take light to travel along the glass fibre of a 1.0 km cable if $\theta = 90°$?

g   Suggest some advantages of fibre optic cables over solid copper cables for the transmission of information.

10 In some seismological surveys, longitudinal compression waves (similar to sound waves) of frequency 60 Hz are transmitted downwards through some of the uppermost layers in the Earth's crust. An example of this procedure is shown in Figure 14.9. The speeds at which the compression waves travel through the various layers of the Earth's crust are shown on the right-hand side of each layer.

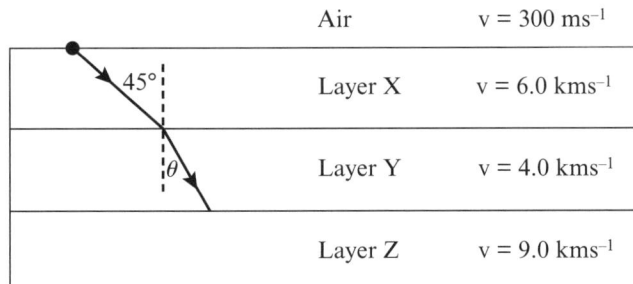

Figure 14.9

a   Use the information in Figure 14.9 to determine the

   i   wavelength of the compression waves in layer X.

   ii angle of refraction, θ, in layer Y.

b   Show that the compression waves will not be transmitted into layer Z.

Exercise 14.2 The principle of superposition

In this section, the questions look at what happens when two or more waves meet at the same place (and time).

Questions 1 and 2 look at a way to model the production of waves and of a linear wavefront.

1   Consider a regular, rectangular tank of water, of constant depth, in which the water's surface is initially still.

   Now consider that you dip the end of a pencil into the water at regular intervals, say once every second, in order to make some transverse waves.

   a   Sketch a diagram to show four wavefronts.

   b   In which direction are the waves travelling?

   c   How does your diagram show that all the wave fronts are travelling at the same speed?

   d   Label on your sketch the wavelength of the waves.

2   Now suppose that waves are produced by a large number of infinitesimally small sources, in a similar way to the waves produced by your pencil dipping into the surface of some water in **question 1**.

   a   What name do physicists give to these hypothetical sources?

   b   Sketch a diagram to show a long line of such sources, all producing identical waves, so that, together, they produce a linear wavefront.

3   Figure 14.10 shows two sources of waves, X and Y, each able to produce identical waves of amplitude A. The point P is equidistant from each of the two sources.

   X •

   • P

   Y •

   Figure 14.10

   Suppose that the two sources produce waves that are *in phase*.

   a   Outline what is meant by the term *in phase*.

   b   Will waves from X and Y arrive at P in phase, out of phase or something in between? Justify your answer.

c With reference to your answer to **part b**, would you expect there to be constructive or destructive interference at point P?

d What would the amplitude of waves be at point P?

4 Look again at Figure 14.10. Suppose that the two sources produce waves that are out of phase with each other.

a Will waves from X and Y arrive at P in phase, out of phase or something in between? Justify your answer.

b With reference to your answer to **part a**, would you expect there to be constructive or destructive interference at point P?

c What would the amplitude of waves be at point P?

5 Figure 14.11 shows two sources of waves, X and Y, each able to produce identical waves, in phase, of wavelength λ and amplitude A. The distance (or path length) from X to P is XP, and the distance (or path length) from Y to P is YP. X, Y and P form a right-angled triangle.

X•   •P

Y•

Figure 14.11

a How is YP–XP usually known?

b What would you expect to observe at P when

  i $YP - XP = \lambda$?

  ii $YP - XP = 2\lambda$?

  iii $YP - XP = n\lambda$, where n is an integer?

c What would you expect to observe at P when

  i $YP - XP = \frac{1}{2}\lambda$?

  ii $YP - XP = \frac{3}{2}\lambda$?

  iii $YP - XP = \left(n + \frac{1}{2}\right)\lambda$?

6 Look again at Figure 14.11. Assume that sources X and Y produce waves of wavelength 1.0 m.

Evaluate whether there would be constructive or destructive interference at P when

  a XP = 4 m and XY = 3 m.

  b XP = 12 m and XY = 5 m.

  c XP = 0.75 m and XY = 1.0 m.

  d XP = 6.5 m and XY = 2.6 m.

  e XP = 1.95 m and XY = 4.0 m.

7 Figure 14.12 shows a pair of hi-fi speakers, each emitting identical sound waves, in phase.

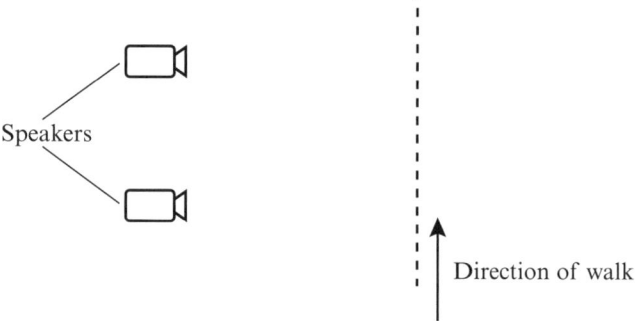

Figure 14.12

A student walks along the dotted line in the direction shown in Figure 14.12 trying to decide where the best place is to listen to the music from the speakers.

  a Describe what the student will hear as she walks along the dotted line.

  b The student decides that the best place to listen to the music is equidistant from the two speakers.

  Justify the student's decision using your knowledge of superposition.

  c The student notices that if she moves her position sideways along the dotted line by only a small distance, the sound she hears is significantly quieter.

  Suggest why the sound is significantly quieter if she moves a small distance sideways.

  d The student also notices that if she moves the two speakers closer together, she can now move sideways a small distance without there being much of a difference in how loud the sound is.

Suggest why the sound is now not significantly quieter when she moves sideways a small distance.

e   Suggest whether it is a good idea or a poor idea to put hi-fi speakers in the corners of a room if you enjoy listening to music.

Exercise 14.3 Diffraction and interference

The questions in this section will help you understand the important ideas of diffraction and interference of waves.

1   Figure 14.13 shows some wavefronts approaching two apertures of different widths.

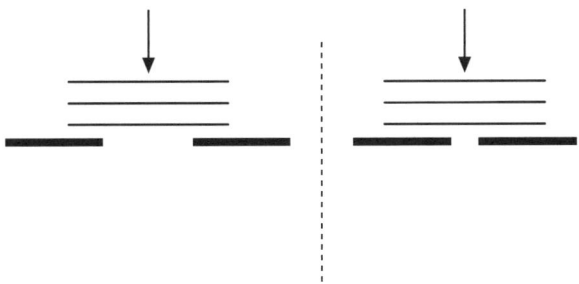

Figure 14.13

a   Complete Figure 14.13 to show what happens to the wavefronts as they pass through the two apertures.

b   What general rule can you apply to the diffraction of waves through apertures of a certain width?

2   Figure 14.14 shows two sets of wavefronts moving alongside similar large objects.

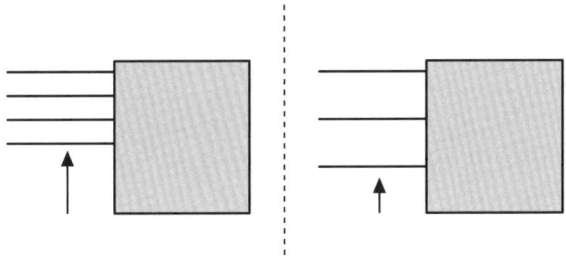

Figure 14.14

a   Complete Figure 14.14 to show what happens as the wavefronts arrive at, and proceed beyond, the edge of the objects.

b   What general rule can you apply to the diffraction of waves, of certain wavelengths, around objects?

3 Coherent green light is incident on a pair of thin slits, as shown in Figure 14.15.

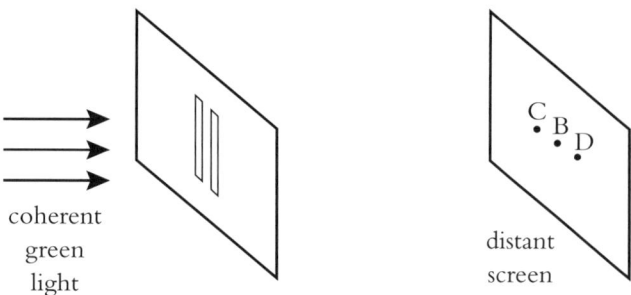

Figure 14.15

a At point B, there is a bright spot of light. Explain how it is produced.

b At point D, there is no light on the screen. Explain why.

c What would you expect to see at point C, which is directly opposite the two slits? Explain your answer.

d If the green light were replaced by red light, what difference or differences, if any, would you expect in the positions of B, C and D?

4 This question derives the relationships for constructive interference at the nth maximum.

Figure 14.16 shows light incident on two slits and a screen, on which an inteference pattern is observed, some distance away from the slits.

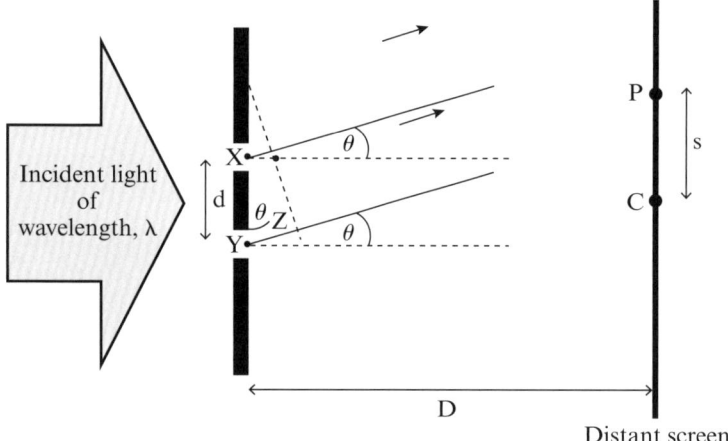

Figure 14.16

Since the screen is a large distance, D, compared to d (and λ), the two rays from points X and Y can be considered to be parallel.

a How much farther does light from Y have to travel than light from X in order to arrive at point P?

- **b** Using geometry, derive an expression for this path difference in terms of d and θ.

- **c** If P is the first maximum away from the central maximum at C, what value must this path difference have?

- **d** Hence, write an equation in terms of d, θ and λ in the form of path difference = condition for constructive interference at first maximum.

- **e** Now suppose that P is the second maximum above C. Rewrite your equation from **part d** for the second maximum.

- **f** Hence, write a general equation for the nth maximum.

5 This question derives an expression for the separation of maxima of the interference pattern on the screen produced by two-slit interference.

- **a** With reference to Figure 14.16, and taking P to be the first maximum, show that $s = D\sin\theta$.

- **b** Hence, write an expression for s in terms of D, λ and d.

- **c** Now suppose that at an angle θ_n, P is the nth maximum. What is the relationship between s, D, λ and d now?

- **d** Repeat **part c** for the $(n + 1)$th maximum.

- **e** Hence, show that the separation of any two consecutive maxima on the interference pattern on the screen is given by $s = \frac{\lambda D}{d}$.

6 A pair of parallel thin slits, 0.15 mm apart, is used to produce an interference pattern on a screen 8 m from the slits. Coherent light of wavelength 450 nm is used.

- **a** Calculate the separation of the bright fringes on the screen.

- **b** Without redoing the calculation completely, how far apart would the bright fringes be if red light of wavelength 675 nm were used?

- **c** If the screen were infinitely wide, determine how many bright fringes would be visible on the screen.

7 White light is incident on a pair of thin Young's slits separated by a distance of 0 2 mm. An interference pattern is observed on a screen placed 5 m from the slits.

- **a** Explain why the central maximum of the interference pattern is white.

- **b** Explain why the maxima on either side of the central maximum are not white.

- **c** Explain why red light is observed on the screen at larger angles than blue light.

- **d** Determine the average separation of maxima on the screen given that green light has a wavelength of about 500 nm.

Exercise 14.4 Single-slit diffraction

The AHL questions in this section examine single slit diffraction in more detail.

1   Waves passing through a single slit produce a single-slit diffraction pattern on a distant screen.

   a   Sketch a diagram to show how the intensity of the waves varies with distance on the screen.

   b   What would happen to this diagram if the

      i   slit width were wider?

      ii wavelength of the waves were larger?

2   Monochromatic light of wavelength 400 nm is incident normally on a single slit of width 5.0 μm.

   a   What colour is the light?

   b   Determine the angular width of the central maximum of the diffraction pattern.

   c   Determine the actual width of the central maximum on a screen that is placed 4.0 m away from the slit.

   d   If the light is replaced by light of wavelength 600 nm, how will your answers to **parts a**, **b** and **c** change?

3   A class of students are waiting for their teacher. As he approaches, his shoes squeak on the corridor at a frequency of 300 Hz. The width of the open classroom door is 0.90 m.

   Using your knowledge of single-slit diffraction, explain why pupils sitting anywhere inside the classroom can hear the teacher approaching. (The speed of sound in air is 330 ms^{-1}.)

4   a   Microwaves of wavelength 2 cm are incident normally on a gap between two thick metal plates. If the width of the gap is 5 cm, calculate the

      i   angle at which the first minimum of the diffraction pattern will occur.

      ii separation of the first-order minimum and the second-order minimum when observed from a distance 1.5 m from the slit.

   b   How many minima are there?

Exercise 14.5 Multiple slits

1   a   Sketch the diffraction pattern that is observed on a screen when light waves of wavelength 500 nm pass through a single slit of width 0.1 mm.

   b   Two such slits are brought together so they are separated by a distance of 0.4 mm. Sketch the interference pattern that will be observed on a screen.

   c   In what way has the single-slit diffraction pattern *modulated* the double-slit interference pattern?

2   a   In the single-slit diffraction pattern, what does the equation $n\lambda = b \sin \theta_n$ tell us?

   b   In the double-slit interference pattern, what does the equation $m\lambda = d \sin \theta_m$ tell us?

   c   In a double-slit interference pattern produced by two slits that are not infinitesimally thin, the value for $\sin \theta_n$ is equal to the value for $\sin \theta_m$. What will the ratio of $\frac{d}{b}$ be?

   d   Which order of maximum of the interference pattern is missing?

   e   How many of the interference maxima will be inside the central maximum of the diffraction pattern?

3   A Young slits interference pattern is observed on a distant screen when monochromatic light passes through two equally narrow slits.

   a   The two slits are replaced by a large number of slits, each of the same width as the originals and each separated by the same distance as before. Sketch a diagram to show how the observations compare to observations for only two slits.

   b   What has happened to the intensity of the maxima? Explain.

   c   What has happened to the spacing of the maxima? Explain.

   d   What has happened to the width of the maxima? Explain.

4   a   Describe what is meant by a *diffraction grating*.

   b   When monochromatic light of wavelength 590 nm illuminates a diffraction grating, a diffraction pattern is observed on a screen some distance away. The light source is replaced by one with a wavelength 450 nm. Suggest two ways in which the observed diffraction pattern on the screen would differ from the original pattern.

   c   Light from a laser of wavelength 630 nm produces an interference pattern when incident on a diffraction grating labelled 600 lines mm^{-1}. Calculate the separation of the central maximum from the first-order maximum on a screen 5 m away.

d Monochromatic light is incident normally on a diffraction grating labelled 600 lines mm^{-1}, producing an interference pattern on a screen that is 8 m away. If the distance between the second-order maximum and the central maximum is 9.5 m, calculate the wavelength of the light.

5 a Low-energy X-rays of wavelength 1.0×10^{-10} m are incident on a diffraction grating labelled 600 lines mm^{-1}. Show that the diffraction grating would not produce an interference pattern that could be observed with an X-ray detector.

b The same low-energy X-rays are now incident on a thin crystal, where the regular lattice spacing of the atoms in the crystal is about 0.3 nm. Show that an interference pattern could now be observed.

c How might such observations as those in **part b** give us useful information about crystals?

EXAM-STYLE QUESTIONS

Multiple-choice questions

1 Red light, of wavelength 600 nm, is shone on a single narrow slit of width, b. A diffraction pattern is observed on a screen nearby with the angle to the first minimum of 9×10^{-3} radians. If the red light is replaced by purple light of wavelength 400 nm, the angle to the first maximum will be

A 3×10^{-3} radians.

B 4×10^{-3} radians.

C 6×10^{-3} radians.

D 1.35×10^{-2} radians.

2 When applied to two sources of waves, the term *coherent* means

A that they both have the same wavelength.

B that they both have the same amplitude.

C that they have a constant phase relationship.

D that they are both plane-polarised.

3 Light waves of wavelength, λ, pass from the air into a medium of refractive index 2.0. Which of the following correctly gives the speed and the wavelength of the waves in the medium?

	Speed	Wavelength
A	C	λ
B	C	½ λ
C	½ C	λ
D	½ C	½ λ

CONTINUED

4. Blue light travels at 3.0×10^8 ms^{-1} in the air. Which one of the following correctly gives its velocity in water, whose refractive index is 1.33?
   A 1.0×10^8 ms^{-1}
   B 2.26×10^8 ms^{-1}
   C 2.33×10^8 ms^{-1}
   D 3.0×10^8 ms^{-1}

5. When light passes from air into water, it experiences a change of
   A speed only.
   B speed and frequency.
   C speed and wavelength.
   D speed, frequency and wavelength.

6. In a Young slits experiment, the two slits are separated by a distance of d and a nearby screen, on which an interference pattern is formed, is a distance D away. If the wavelength of light is λ, the number of maxima per metre in the interference pattern is given by
   A $\frac{d}{\lambda D}$.
   B $\frac{\lambda d}{D}$.
   C $\frac{\lambda D}{d}$.
   D $\frac{dD}{\lambda}$.

7. In a Young slits experiment to demonstrate the interference of light, the slit separation is doubled. In order to keep the spacing of the maxima on the interference pattern the same the distance from the slits to the screen must change to
   A $\frac{1}{2}D$.
   B $\frac{1}{\sqrt{2}}D$.
   C $\sqrt{2}D$.
   D $2D$.

8. When monochromatic light of wavelength λ, is incident on a thin slit of width b, a diffraction pattern is observed on a screen. The spacing of the maxima is x. The light is changed to one with wavelength of 2λ and the width of the slit is reduced to $\frac{b}{2}$. The spacing of the maxima on the new diffraction pattern will be
   A $\frac{x}{4}$.
   B x.
   C $2x$.
   D $4x$.

CONTINUED

9 Monochromatic light incident normally on a pair of slits, each of width b, separated by a distance $4b$, produces an interference pattern on a distant screen. The number of maxima of the interference pattern that occur within the single slit diffraction envelope is

　A　1.
　B　4.
　C　7.
　D　8.

10 Red light of wavelength 650 nm is incident normally on a diffraction grating labelled '600 slits mm^{-1}'. The spacing of the maxima observed on a screen 8.0 m away is about

　A　1 m.
　B　2 m.
　C　3 m.
　D　6 m.

Short-answer questions

11 In a water tank, linear wavefronts with a frequency of 3.0 Hz are incident normally on a boundary between deep water and shallow water. In the deep water, the waves have a wavelength of 60.0 mm. In the shallow water, the waves move with a speed of 12 cms^{-1}.

　a　Define the term *wavefront*. [1]
　b　Calculate
　　i　the speed of the waves in the deep water. [2]
　　ii　the wavelength of the waves in the shallow water. [1]
　　iii　the relative refractive index of the boundary between the deep water and the shallow water. [1]

12 Sound waves of frequency 880 Hz travelling on the air at a speed of 330 ms^{-1} undergo total internal reflection at a boundary between the air and some water when the angle of incidence reaches 13°.

　a　Calculate the wavelength of the sound waves in the air. [1]
　b　Determine
　　i　the speed at which sound waves travel in water. [2]
　　ii　the relative refractive index for sound waves passing from air into water. [1]
　c　Suggest what happens to sound waves incident on the air/water boundary at angles of incidence less than 13°. [1]

13 A ray of light, frequency 6×10^{14} Hz, is incident on a piece of glass at an angle of incidence of 40°. The refractive index of glass is 1.5. Calculate

　a　the angle of refraction of the light. [2]
　b　the speed of the light in the glass. (The speed of light in air is 3×10^8 ms^{-1}.) [1]
　c　the wavelength of the light in air. [1]
　d　the wavelength of the light in the glass. [1]

CONTINUED

14 Red light, of frequency 4.57×10^{14} Hz, from a He-Ne laser is incident normally on a pair of narrow Young slits separated by a distance of 60.0 μm. A series of bright fringes and dark spaces are observed on a screen placed 3.60 m away from the slits.

    a Show that the wavelength of the light is, to three significant figures, 656 nm.
($c = 3.00 \times 10^8$ ms^{-1}) [1]

    b Determine the spacing of the bright fringes on the screen. [2]

    c If the screen is now moved closer to the two slits, suggest **two** changes to the pattern of light and dark spaces that would be observed on the screen. [2]

15 Plane waves of red light are incident normally on a thin slit. A screen placed several metres away from the slit shows an intensity pattern characteristic of single slit diffraction.

    a Sketch a diagram to show how this intensity pattern varies on the screen. [2]

    b Suggest how this intensity pattern would be different if blue light were used instead of red. [1]

    c In what **two** ways would this intensity pattern be different if the width of the slit were smaller? [2]

16 Green light of wavelength 530 nm is incident normally on a single slit of width 0.1 mm. The resulting diffraction pattern is observed on a screen that is 8 m away.

    a Calculate the width of the central maximum of the diffraction pattern. [2]

    b If the light is changed for a red light of wavelength 650 nm, determine the new width of the central maximum. [1]

    c The light is now changed for white light. Suggest how the single-slit diffraction pattern on the screen will change. [2]

17 A diffraction grating is labelled 300 mm^{-1}.

    a Calculate the spacing of the slits. [1]

    b Orange light of wavelength 590 nm is incident normally on the diffraction grating. Calculate the angle between the central maximum and the first-order maximum of the interference pattern produced. [2]

    c Determine what other angles would produce maxima. [2]

18 White light is incident normally on a diffraction grating labelled 500 lines mm^{-1}. If the wavelength of red light is 700 nm and the wavelength of blue light is 467 nm,

    a calculate the angle between the first-order maxima of the pattern observed on a screen of the red light and the blue light. [3]

    b show that the third-order maximum for the blue light will overlap the second-order maximum of the red light. [2]

19 Light of wavelength 550 nm is incident normally on a diffraction grating and the first-order maximum on the interference pattern is observed at an angle of 26.0° with the straight-ahead direction.

    a Calculate

        i the separation of the slits, s. [2]

        ii the number of slits mm^{-1} on the diffraction grating. [1]

    b Determine the wavelength of light that would give a first-order maximum at an angle of 23.5°. [2]

Chapter 15
Standing waves and resonance

CHAPTER OUTLINE

In this chapter, you will:

- differentiate between travelling waves and standing waves in terms of energy transfer.
- identify the nature and formation of standing waves.
- explore nodes, antinodes, amplitude and phase difference of points along a standing wave.
- explore standing waves on strings and in pipes.
- solve problems about standing waves.
- identify the nature of resonance.
- explore how the amplitude of oscillations depends on the natural frequency and on the driving frequency.
- explore how damping affects the amplitude and resonant frequency of oscillations.

KEY TERMS

standing wave: a wave formed by the superposition of two identical travelling waves in opposite directions

travelling wave: a wave that transfers energy from one place to another

node: a point on a standing wave where the displacement is always zero

antinode: a point on a standing wave where the displacement is a maximum (at some instant)

damping: the loss of energy of an oscillating system due to the presence of resistance forces

CONTINUED

driven oscillations: oscillations when an external periodic force acts on the system

driving frequency: the frequency of the external force acting on the system

resonance: the condition when the driving frequency equals the frequency at which the amplitude is a maximum

natural frequency: the frequency of free oscillations of a body

first harmonic: the longest wavelength (and the lowest frequency) at which a standing waveforms; sometimes called the fundamental mode

harmonics: integral multiples of the first harmonic frequency

KEY EQUATIONS

Harmonic wavelengths on a string with nodes at each end or in a pipe with nodes or antinodes at each end:

$\lambda_n = \frac{2l}{n}$,

where λ_n is the wavelength of the nth harmonic on a string, or in a pipe, of length l, $n = 1, 2, 3, \ldots$

Harmonic wavelengths for a pipe with one end closed and the other end open:

$\lambda_n = \frac{4l}{n}$,

where λ_n is the wavelength of the nth harmonic in a pipe of length l, $n = 1, 3, 5, \ldots$.

Note: Standing waves on a string with one end fixed and the other end free are unrealistic and so are not considered here.

Exercise 15.1 Standing waves

The questions in this section will introduce you to what a standing wave is and show you how it is formed.

1 a Figure 15.1 shows a transverse wave on a string moving from left to right. The far right-hand end of the string is attached to a vertical pole.

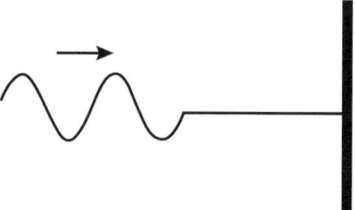

Figure 15.1

Sketch a diagram, similar to Figure 15.1, to show what the string will look like *after* the wave has been reflected from the right-hand end. You may assume that the amplitude of the reflected wave is the same as the amplitude of the incident wave.

b The five diagrams of Figure 15.2 show the displacements for two identical waves, each of amplitude A, travelling in opposite directions along the same string. The wave travelling left to right is drawn as a solid line, and the wave travelling right to left is drawn as a dotted line. Each diagram shows the two waves at small time intervals later than the previous diagram.

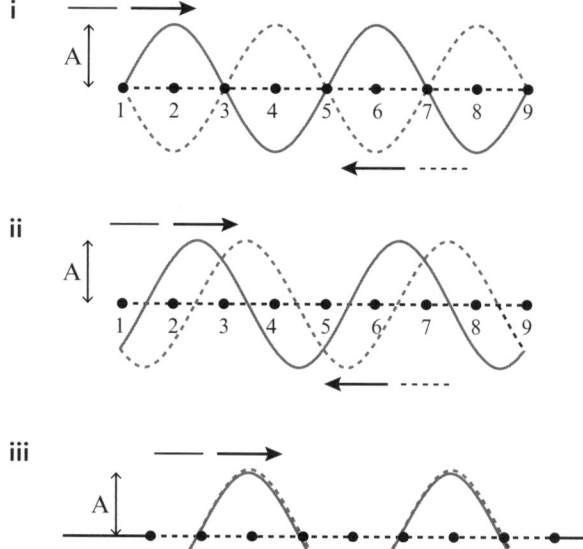

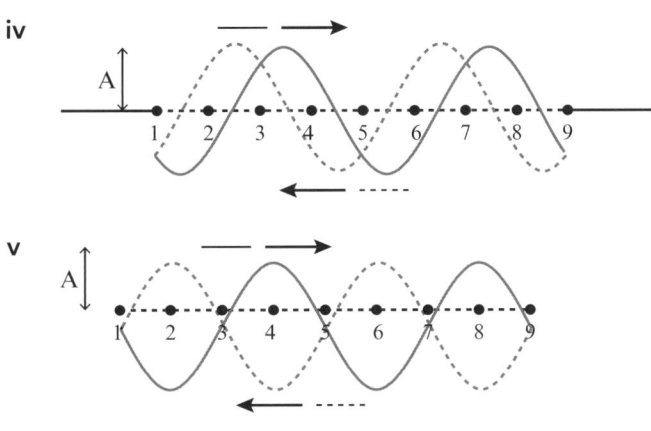

Figure 15.2

Use the five diagrams to complete the table. Each cell shows the net displacement at points 1 through 9 along the string caused by the superposition of the two waves. You should estimate the net displacement in each case, with your values ranging from 0 to ±2A.

		Figure				
		i	ii	iii	iv	v
Point	1					
	2					
	3					
	4					
	5					
	6					
	7					
	8					
	9					

c i With reference to your completed table, what can you say is happening, at all times, at points 2, 4, 6 and 8?

   ii What are these points along the string known as?

d i If four more diagrams, showing further similar progression of the two waves, were used, how would you expect your values in the table to change (if at all)?

   ii What happens at points 1, 3, 5, 7 and 9?

   iii What are these points known as?

e The effect of the superposition of the two oppositely travelling waves is to create a standing wave. How is the separation of the points: 1 and 3, 2 and 4, 3 and 5, 4 and 6, and so on, related to the wavelength of the standing wave?

f Is the standing wave transferring any energy from one place to another, like a progressive wave does?

2 a Outline how a standing wave is formed.

b In what way or ways does a standing wave differ from a progressive wave?

c Can standing waves occur with

  i transverse waves? If so, give an example.

  ii longitudinal waves? If so, give an example.

> **TIP**
> It is really important that you know how to answer this question; it is often asked in exams.

3 A standing wave on a stretched string has successive nodes separated by a distance of 30 cm. The amplitude of the antinodes is 12 cm at a frequency of 8 Hz.

a Outline what is meant by the terms

  i *node*.

  ii *antinode*.

  iii *amplitude*.

  iv *frequency*.

b Determine the average speed of a point on the string that is at a

  i node.

  ii antinode.

c State the average velocity of a point on the string that is at a

  i node.

  ii antinode.

d Determine the wavelength of the standing wave.

e Determine the speed at which waves travel along the stretched string.

Exercise 15.2 Standing waves on strings

These questions look at transverse waves causing standing waves on strings.

1 An elastic string is stretched between two fixed ends, separated by a distance *l*.

a When the string is made to oscillate at a particular frequency, f_o, a standing wave is formed in the *first harmonic mode*.

i   Outline what is meant by the term *first harmonic mode*.

ii Sketch a diagram to show the standing wave in the first harmonic mode.

iii State the wavelength of the standing wave.

b The string is now made to oscillate at a larger frequency, and again, a standing wave is formed, this time as the second harmonic.

i   How is the frequency of the second harmonic related to the frequency of the first harmonic mode?

ii Sketch a diagram to show the standing wave in the second harmonic.

iii What is the wavelength of the standing wave in the second harmonic?

c The string is now made to oscillate at three more, higher frequencies so that standing waves are formed in the third, fourth and fifth harmonics.

i   What will the values of these higher frequencies be compared to that of the first harmonic?

ii Sketch diagrams to show the standing waves in the third, fourth and fifth harmonics.

iii If the number of the harmonic is n, and the speed at which waves travel along the stretched string is v, write general equations for the wavelength and the frequency of the standing wave harmonics.

2 A stretched elastic string of length 1.2 m is held firmly at both ends. It is made to oscillate so that a standing wave is set up in the first harmonic mode at a frequency of 440 Hz.

a Determine the speed at which waves travel along the string. Give your answer to an appropriate number of significant figures.

b What are the wavelengths and frequencies at which the following harmonics will occur?

i   second harmonic

ii third harmonic

iii nth harmonic

c If you listened to the vibrating string, what would the wavelength of the sound be? (The speed of sound in air is 330 ms^{-1}.)

3 Figure 15.3 shows a representation of a standing wave on a string, which is held firmly at both ends.

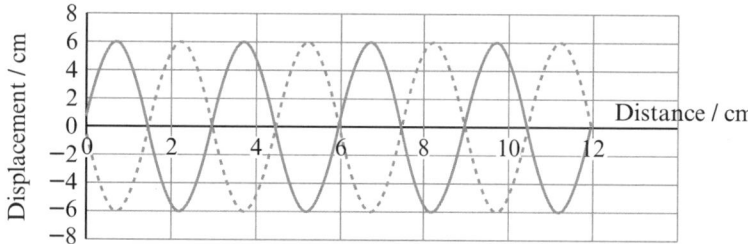

Figure 15.3

Use Figure 15.3 to find the

a amplitude of the standing wave.

b wavelength of the standing wave.

c the harmonic present.

Exercise 15.3 Standing waves in pipes

1 Figure 15.4 shows a pipe of length, l, which is open at one end and closed at the other and which may contain standing waves.

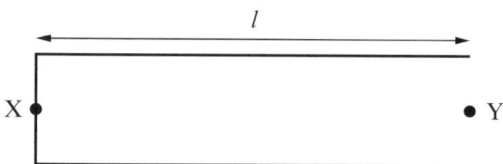

Figure 15.4

a i At point X, will there be a node or an antinode?

   ii At point Y, will there be a node or an antinode?

b Sketch diagrams to show the standing wave in the

   i first harmonic mode.

   ii third harmonic.

   iii fifth harmonic.

c Explain why there cannot be any even-numbered harmonics.

d Write a general equation for the wavelength of the nth harmonic, where n is an odd-numbered integer.

2 Consider a pipe of length *l*, closed at both ends, inside which standing waves can occur.

   a   Will there be nodes, or antinodes, at each end of the pipe?

   b   What will the wavelength of the standing wave in the first harmonic mode be?

   c   Write a general equation for the wavelength of the standing wave in the *n*th harmonic.

3 Now consider a pipe of length *l*, open at both ends, inside which standing waves can occur.

   a   Will there be nodes, or antinodes, at each end of the pipe?

   b   What will the wavelength of the standing wave in the first harmonic mode be?

   c   Write a general equation for the wavelength of the standing wave in the *n*th harmonic.

   d   What do you notice about your answers to **questions 15.3.2 part c** and **15.3.3 part c**?

   e   Is there any restriction on the harmonic number, like there is for a pipe with one open end and one closed end?

4 An organ pipe, both ends of which are open, sustains a standing wave of frequency 220 Hz in its second harmonic mode.

   a   Determine the length of the pipe. (The speed of sound in air is 330 ms^{-1}.)

   b   Calculate the frequency of the third harmonic.

   c   Calculate the wavelength of the fourth harmonic.

   d   Suggest an advantage to having organ pipes that are open at one end and closed at the other end.

5 Figure 15.5 shows a children's toy whistle. The whistle can produce a continuously variable frequency of sound when the piston-like fitting is pushed in or pulled out.

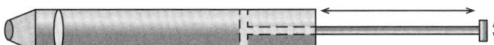

Figure 15.5

Using your knowledge of standing waves,

   a   suggest why pushing the piston inwards causes the sound the whistle makes to be of a higher pitch.

   b   suggest why pulling the piston outwards causes the sound the whistle makes to be of a lower pitch.

Exercise 15.4 Resonance and damping

The questions in this section explore the phenomenon of resonance, how it can be reduced with damping and how it can be hazardous or helpful.

1 Define the following terms:

   a *free oscillations*

   b *forced oscillations*

   c *resonance*

2 a Explain what is meant by *damping*.

   b Suggest why all mechanical systems will suffer damping if they are forced to oscillate by an external force.

   c Outline the difference between an oscillating system being overdamped, underdamped and critically damped.

3 Sketch a graph to show how the amplitude of an oscillator would vary with time if the oscillations are

   • undamped; label this U.

   • critically damped; label this C.

   • over-damped; label this O.

4 A body is being made to oscillate by an externally applied periodic force of varying frequency.

   a Sketch a graph to show how the amplitude of the oscillations of the body will vary with the frequency of the applied periodic force.

   b Add another line to your sketch to show how the amplitude varies if the oscillations are heavily damped.

   c If the body is heavily damped, how will the frequency at which resonance occurs compare with the natural frequency of the body?

   d What is the phase relationship between the forcing oscillations and the oscillations of the body when

      i   the forcing frequency is much less than the natural frequency?

      ii resonance occurs?

      iii the forcing frequency is much greater than the natural frequency?

5 This question examines the roles that resonance plays in some everyday objects and processes.

   a Many music speakers are housed inside wooden or plastic boxes. Sometimes, when music is playing, the box oscillates and produces unwanted noise.

Outline the role that resonance is playing when the box makes this unwanted noise. Suggest how high-quality speaker cabinets may be designed to overcome this problem.

b Microwave ovens heat up food very quickly. Outline how microwave ovens use the phenomenon of resonance.

c In 2000, the Millenium Bridge across the river Thames in London had to be closed two days after it opened. With 2000 people walking on it, the bridge began to oscillate laterally with a dangerously large amplitude. Outline the role that resonance played and how engineers were able to redesign the bridge to avoid such dangerous oscillations.

d Some modern skyscrapers are built in places where there may be an earthquake. Suggest how such skyscrapers might be designed to protect them from the damaging effects of resonance.

e A radio receiver can be 'tuned' to receive different broadcasts from radio stations. Outline the role that resonance plays in a radio receiver.

> **TIP**
> You may need to investigate some of these using the internet. The knowledge gained will be useful because it will illustrate how important resonance and damping are in the world in which we live.

EXAM-STYLE QUESTIONS

Multiple-choice questions

1 A pipe, one end of which is open and the other closed, is 1.2 m long. The air molecules inside the pipe are made to oscillate so that a standing wave in the first harmonic mode is set up.

What is the wavelength of the standing wave?

A 0.3 m

B 0.6 m

C 1.2 m

D 4.8 m

2 The velocity of waves on a stretched string is 72 ms^{-1}. Standing waves occur on the string at a frequency of 288 Hz. Estimate the separation of nodes.

A 0.125 m

B 0.250 m

C 0.500 m

D 2.00 m

CONTINUED

3 Look at Figure 15.6. It shows the side view of a Barton's pendulums set-up. These are often used by physics teachers to demonstrate resonance. The pendulum with the steel bob is displaced sideways. When it's let go, it oscillates freely and forces the other pendulums to oscillate.

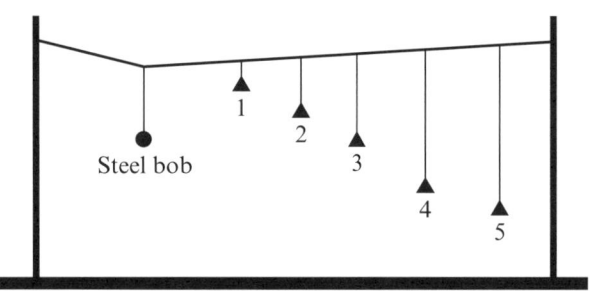

Figure 15.6

Which of the following statements about pendulums 1 through 5 is correct?

A Pendulum 1 will have the largest amplitude oscillation.
B Pendulum 3 will have the largest amplitude oscillation.
C Pendulum 5 will have the largest amplitude oscillation.
D All the pendulums will oscillate with the same amplitude.

4 Look at Figure 15.6. When the steel bob is displaced, which of the following statements is correct?

A Pendulums 1 and 2 will be almost in phase with the steel-bobbed pendulum.
B Pendulum 3 will be in phase with the steel-bobbed pendulum.
C Pendulum 5 will be almost in phase with the steel-bobbed pendulum.
D Pendulums 4 and 5 will lag the steel-bobbed pendulum by $\frac{\pi}{2}$ radians.

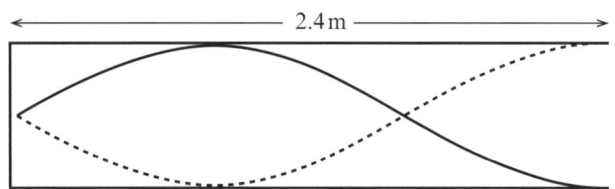

Figure 15.7

5 Look at Figure 15.7. If the speed of sound in air is 330 ms^{-1}, the frequency of the sound is approximately

A 69 Hz.
B 103 Hz.
C 138 Hz.
D 206 Hz.

CONTINUED

6 For a damped oscillating pendulum, the first three oscillations have amplitudes of 56.0 cm, 44.8 cm and 35.8 cm (to 3 s.f.). What amplitude will the fourth oscillation have?
   A 26.9 cm
   B 27.4 cm
   C 28.7 cm
   D 29.2 cm

7 A critically damped oscillator will
   A resonate at a frequency lower than that of a similar undamped oscillator.
   B resonate at the same frequency as that of a similar undamped oscillator.
   C resonate at a frequency larger than that of a similar undamped oscillator.
   D not resonate at all.

8 Air in a pipe, which is open at both ends, is resonating in its first harmonic mode at a frequency of 956 Hz. If the speed of sound in air is 330 ms^{-1}, which of the following will give the length of the pipe, in metres?
   A $\frac{1}{4}\left(\frac{330}{956}\right)$
   B $\frac{1}{2}\left(\frac{330}{956}\right)$
   C $2\left(\frac{330}{956}\right)$
   D $4\left(\frac{330}{956}\right)$

9 A damped oscillator loses 20% of its energy on each oscillation. When the oscillator's energy has been reduced to below 1% of its initial energy, how many oscillations will it have completed?
   A 4
   B 5
   C 21
   D 41

Short-answer questions

10 a In terms of energy transfer, state the difference between a progressive wave and a standing wave. [1]
    b Transverse waves on a stretched string travel at 760 ms^{-1}. Such a string of length 4.0 m, held firmly at both ends, is made to vibrate so that a standing wave forms.
       i   Explain why a standing wave will form only at a number of discrete frequencies. [1]
       ii   Determine the minimum frequency at which the standing wave will form. [2]
       iii State the frequency at which a standing wave will form in its fifth harmonic mode. [1]

11 A string is stretched between two fixed points 24 cm apart. It is made to oscillate up and down, forming a standing wave. The string exhibits *nodes* and *antinodes*. Two consecutive nodes are found to be 8 cm apart.
    a Explain what is meant by the terms *node* and *antinode*. [2]
    b State the wavelength of the waves on the string. [1]
    c Evaluate which harmonic is present. [1]
    d The string is made to oscillate with a higher frequency, again forming a standing wave. Suggest what would happen to the separation of the nodes and antinodes. [1]

CONTINUED

12 Figure 15.8 shows a representation of a stationary sound wave in a pipe of length 3 m.

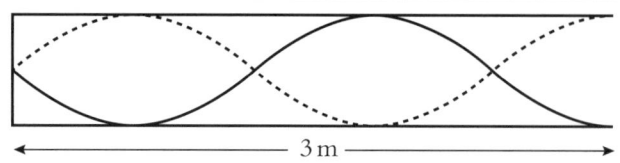

Figure 15.8

Use the diagram to

a calculate the wavelength of the standing wave. [2]

b calculate the frequency of the standing wave. (speed of sound in air = 330 ms⁻¹) [1]

c Determine which harmonic is present. [2]

13 A stretched string held firmly at both ends, 2.4 m apart, exhibits a standing wave in the first harmonic mode.

a Determine the wavelength of the standing wave present. [1]

b If the tension in the string is now doubled, keeping the two ends of the string the same distance apart as before,

  i how will the wavelength of the new standing wave in the first harmonic mode compare to the wavelength of the original standing wave? [1]

  ii how will the frequency of the new standing wave in the first harmonic mode compare to the frequency of the original standing wave? [2]

c For any string stretched between its ends the same distance apart as before, state what aspect of the string, other than the tension it is under, will affect the frequency at which a standing wave in the first harmonic mode occurs. [1]

14 An oscillating body has its oscillations damped so that the amplitude of its oscillations decreases exponentially with time.

a Explain what is meant by the term *exponentially*. [1]

b Outline a simple mathematical test you can do to check whether the amplitude of the oscillations is decreasing exponentially. [2]

c If the amplitude of the oscillations decreases by a factor of 0.9 for each oscillation, how many oscillations will the body undergo before the amplitude of its oscillations has halved? [2]

15 a State how the energy of an oscillator depends on its amplitude. [1]

b Suppose that in a lightly damped oscillator, 10% of the oscillator's energy is lost on each oscillation.

  i Determine how many oscillations it would take for the oscillator to lose 99.9% of its energy. [2]

  ii The Q factor for a damped oscillator is given by the equation
  $$Q = 2\pi \frac{\text{energy stored in a system}}{\text{energy lost per cycle}}.$$

CONTINUED

By calculating the Q factor for the oscillator, suggest how you might describe what the Q factor means in practice. [1]

c State what the maximum value for the Q factor is for a critically damped oscillator. [1]

16 Figure 15.9 shows how the displacement of an oscillator varies with time. The oscillator is subject to damping.

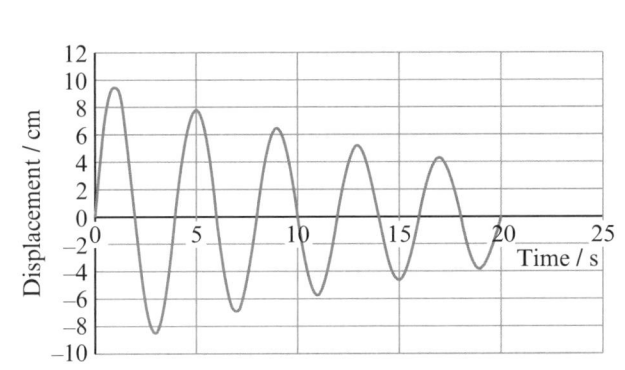

Figure 15.9

a Determine the frequency of the oscillations. [2]
b Outline what is meant by the term *damping*. [1]
c Show that the amplitude of the oscillations is decreasing exponentially. [2]

17 a State what is meant by *resonance*. [1]
b A mass of 400 g is attached to the end of a spring of spring constant 20 Nm⁻¹.
The mass-spring system is forced to oscillate at different frequencies between 0 and 5 Hz.
   i Calculate the frequency at which the mass/spring system will resonate. [2]
   ii Using the axes shown in Figure 15.10, sketch a graph to show how the amplitude of the oscillations of the mass/spring system varies with forcing frequency. [3]

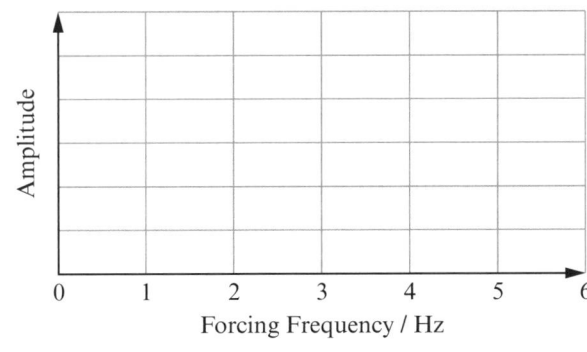

Figure 15.10

Chapter 16
The Doppler effect

CHAPTER OUTLINE

In this chapter, you will:

- explore qualitatively the nature of the Doppler effect.
- use diagrams to illustrate the Doppler effect between sources and observers.
- explore examples of the Doppler effect and its uses.
- examine quantitatively the change in frequency and wavelength of electromagnetic waves due to the Doppler effect.
- examine quantitatively the effect on frequency for sound waves when the relative motion between a source and an observer is an appreciable fraction of the speed of sound waves.

KEY TERMS

Doppler effect: the change in observed frequency when there is relative motion between the source and the observer

blue-shift: the shift in wavelengths towards smaller wavelengths

red-shift: the shift in wavelengths towards larger wavelengths

KEY EQUATIONS

Frequency and wavelength shift when wave speed is much larger than the speed of the source or the observer (usually this means for electromagnetic waves):

$$\frac{\Delta f}{f} \approx \frac{v}{c} \text{ and } \frac{\Delta \lambda}{\lambda} \approx \frac{v}{c},$$

where Δf is the shift (or change) in frequency as observed by the observer, f is the frequency of the source, $\Delta \lambda$ is the shift (or change) in wavelength as observed by the observer, λ is the wavelength of the waves emitted by the source, v is the relative speed of the source and the observer and c is the speed of waves.

Frequency and wavelength shift when wave speed is not significantly larger than the speed of the source or the observer (usually this means for sound and other mechanical waves):

Moving source: $f' = f\left(\frac{v}{v - u_s}\right)$ and $\lambda' = \lambda\left(1 + \frac{u_s}{v}\right)$

> **CONTINUED**
>
> **Moving observer:** $f' = f\left(\dfrac{v + u_o}{v}\right)$ and $\lambda' = \dfrac{v}{f} = \lambda$,
>
> where f' is the frequency observed by the observer, f is the frequency of the source, v is the speed of the waves, u_s is the speed of the source (towards or away from the observer), u_o is the speed of the observer (towards or away from the source), λ' is the wavelength observed by the observer and λ is the wavelength of the waves emitted by the source.

Exercise 16.1 The Doppler effect at low speeds

1. This question will look at what happens when an observer moves towards a stationary source emitting electromagnetic waves of frequency f, and speed c.

   a First consider the observer to be stationary.

   i How many wavefronts will the observer receive in 1 s?

   ii How much time will it take for the next wavefront to arrive at the observer?

   iii How far apart—distance-wise—will the wavefronts be?

   b Now consider the observer moving towards the source at a speed v.

   i Will it take the same time, less time or more time for the observer to receive another wavefront than your answer to **part a ii**?

   ii Justify your answer to **part i**.

   iii So, will the observer now observe waves with the same frequency, a smaller frequency or a larger frequency than before?

   iv And will the observer now observe waves with the same wavelength, a smaller wavelength or a larger wavelength than before?

2. This question repeats the format of the previous question, but this time the observer moves away from the source. Remember that the waves being emitted by the source are electromagnetic waves.

   a First consider the observer to be stationary.

   i How many wavefronts will the observer receive in one second?

   ii How much time will it take for the next wavefront to arrive at the observer?

   iii How far apart—distance-wise—will the wavefronts be?

b Now consider the observer moving away from the source at a speed v.

  i Will it take the same time, less time, or more time for the observer to receive another wavefront than your answer to **part a ii**?

  ii Justify your answer to **part i**.

  iii So, will the observer now observe waves with the same frequency, a smaller frequency or a larger frequency than before?

  iv And will the observer now observe waves with the same wavelength, a smaller wavelength or a larger wavelength than before?

3 This question continues from **questions 1** and **2** by considering a moving source and a stationary observer.

  a From what you should have learnt from Chapter 6: Relativity, will an observer (in their frame of reference) observe any difference between the source moving towards them or their moving towards the source?

  b So,

  i if the source moves away from the stationary observer, will the observer observe the same frequency, a larger frequency or a smaller frequency of waves than those emitted by the source?

  ii if the source moves towards the stationary observer, will the observer observe the same frequency, a larger frequency or a smaller frequency than those emitted by the source?

  iii how will the wavelengths of the waves observed by the observer compare to those emitted by the source for the two cases of relative motion towards or away from each other?

The Doppler effect for light

4 This question develops a quantitive relationship between the frequency and wavelength of electromagnetic waves observed by an observer and the frequency and wavelength of the electromagnetic waves emitted by a source. In this question, we assume that the source (whether it is moving or stationary) emits electromagnetic waves of frequency f, and wavelength λ, that travels at the speed of light, c.

  a First, we will look at the case of a stationary source and an observer moving towards the source with a speed v.

  i How far apart are two successive wavefronts?

  ii How much time does it take for one wavefront to cover the distance of your answer in **part i**?

  iii During this amount of time, how far would a moving observer have moved towards the source?

iv So, write an equation for the distance that the observer observes between successive wavefronts, λ', in terms of λ, v and f.

v Hence, show that $\lambda' = \lambda\left(\frac{1-v}{c}\right)$.

vi Since $\lambda' > \lambda$, we may write $\Delta\lambda = \lambda' - \lambda$. Show that $\frac{\Delta\lambda}{\lambda} = \frac{v}{c}$.

b Now we will look at the case when the observer is moving away from the source at a speed v.

i How far apart are two successive wavefronts?

ii How much time does it take for one wavefront to cover the distance of your answer in **part i**?

iii During this amount of time, how far would a moving observer have moved away the source?

iv So, write an equation for the distance that the observer observes between successive wavefronts, λ', in terms of λ, v and f.

v Hence, show that $\lambda' = \lambda\left(\frac{1+v}{c}\right)$.

vi Now, since $\lambda' < \lambda$, we may write $\Delta\lambda = \lambda - \lambda'$. Show that $\frac{\Delta\lambda}{\lambda} = \frac{v}{c}$.

c Now we will look at the case of a stationary observer and a source moving towards the observer with a speed v.

i How far apart will wavefronts now be?

ii Hence, show that $\frac{\Delta\lambda}{\lambda}$ is given by the same expression as in **parts a vi** and **b vi**.

d Without further analysis, state the expression for $\frac{\Delta\lambda}{\lambda}$, or for $\frac{\Delta f}{f}$, for a source moving away from a stationary observer.

e Now consider if both the observer and the source were moving.
Will the expressions for $\frac{\Delta\lambda}{\lambda}$ and $\frac{\Delta f}{f}$ be any different? Explain.

5 Astronomers and astrophysicists often refer to blue-shift and red-shift.

a Outline what is meant by the terms *blue-shift* and *red-shift* and suggest why they are called as such.

b In what way has our knowledge of the Doppler effect been able to help our understanding of cosmology?

c Light from a distant star is observed using a telescope and a diffraction grating. One spectral line from the star is measured at a wavelength of 580.9 nm, whereas the same spectral line measured in a laboratory has a wavelength of 527.0 nm.

i What can you say about the relative motion of the distant star and the Earth?

ii Calculate the speed at which the distant star is moving relative to the Earth.

6   A motorist, who had driven through a red traffic light, is stopped by police. When questioned, the motorist tells the police that, because of the Doppler effect, he saw the light to be amber-coloured, and so he could drive through the traffic lights legally. The police officer charges the motorist for speeding and reckless driving. If the shortest wavelength of red light is 620 nm and the longest wavelength of amber light is 590 nm, explain, with the use of a Doppler effect calculation, why the policeman charges the motorist.

(Take the speed of light in air to be 3.0×10^8 ms^{-1}.)

7   In some countries, police use a Doppler radar gun to measure the speed of cars travelling along the road.

  a   Outline how the police are able to get an accurate value for the speed of a moving car.

  b   A typical police Doppler radar gun uses electromagnetic waves of frequency 24 GHz.

   i   In which part of the electromagnetic spectrum do such waves occur?

   ii If a police officer measures a frequency change of 2.0 kHz when aiming the radar gun at a receding car, calculate the speed of the car.

  c   Suggest why Doppler radar guns do not use ultrasonic waves instead of microwaves.

Exercise 16.2 The Doppler effect for sound

1   This question looks at what happens when the source of sound waves is moving towards the stationary observer.

Figure 16.1 shows a source of sound waves, S, moving towards an observer with a speed u_s. The sound waves emitted by the source have a wavelength λ; a frequency f; and move through the air with a speed v.

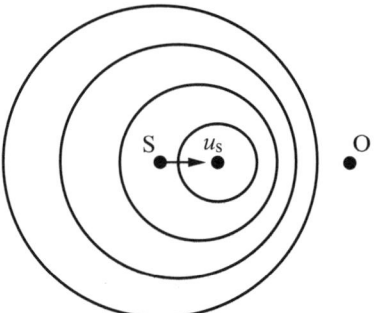

Figure 16.1

a Suppose that it takes a time t for a wavefront to travel from the source to the observer. How far will this wavefront have travelled during the time, t?

b During this time, t, how far will the source have travelled towards the observer?

c How many wavefronts will the source have emitted during the time t?

d In how much distance will these wavefronts be located?

e So, what will the wavelength, λ', of the waves be, as observed by the observer?

f Hence, show that the frequency of the sound waves observed by the observer is given by the expression $f' = f\frac{v}{v - u_s}$.

g So, if the source of the sound waves moves towards the observer, does the observer hear sound waves of the same frequency, larger frequency or smaller frequency compared to the sound waves emitted by the source?

h Does the observer observe the sound waves travelling through the air at speed v? Justify your answer.

i Hence, show that the wavelength of the sound waves observed by the observer is given by $\lambda' = \lambda\left(1 - \frac{u_s}{v}\right)$.

j So, will the observer observe sound waves of the same wavelength, larger wavelength or smaller wavelength than the waves emitted by the source?

2 This question looks at what happens when the source of sound waves is moving away from the stationary observer.

Figure 16.2 shows a source of sound waves, S, moving away from an observer with a speed u_s. The sound waves emitted by the source have a wavelength λ, and a frequency f, and move through the air with a speed v, similar to the case in **questions 1**.

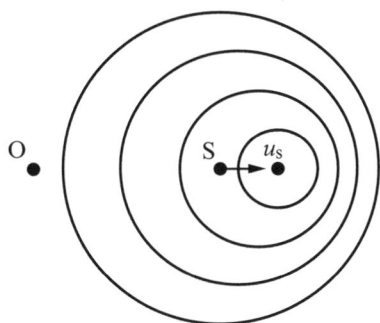

Figure 16.2

a As before, suppose that it takes a time t for a wavefront to travel from the source to the observer. How far will this wavefront have travelled during the time t?

b During this time, t, how far will the source have travelled away from the observer?

c   How many wavefronts will the source have emitted during the time t?

d   In how much distance will these wavefronts be located?

e   So, what will the wavelength, λ', of the waves be, as observed by the observer?

f   Hence, show that the frequency of the sound waves observed by the observer is given by the expression $f' = f \frac{v}{v + u_s}$.

g   So, if the source of the sound waves moves away from the observer, does the observer hear sound waves of the same frequency, larger frequency or smaller frequency compared to the sound waves emitted by the source?

h   Does the observer observe the sound waves travelling through the air at speed v? Justify your answer.

i   Hence, show that the wavelength of the sound waves observed by the observer is given by $\lambda' = \lambda \left(1 + \frac{u_s}{v}\right)$.

j   So, will the observer observe sound waves of the same wavelength, larger wavelength or smaller wavelength than the waves emitted by the source?

3   This question considers what happens when the source of sound waves is stationary and the observer moves towards the source.

Figure 16.3 shows a stationary source of sound waves and an observer moving towards the source with a speed u_o. As before, the source emits sound waves of wavelength λ, and frequency f, which travel through the air at a speed v.

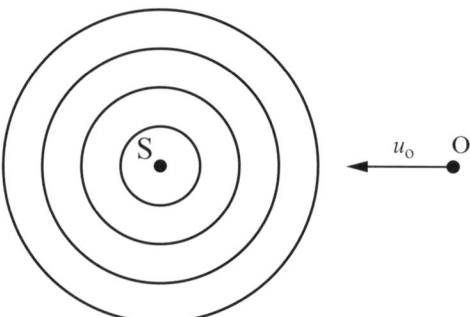

Figure 16.3

a   At what relative speed does the observer observe the sound wavefronts approaching?

b   Does the observer observe the wavelength of the sound waves to be the same, larger or smaller than the wavelength of the sound waves emitted by the source?

c   Hence, show that the frequency of the sound waves observed by the observer is given by the expression $f' = f\left(1 + \frac{u_o}{v}\right)$.

d   So, if the observer moves towards a stationary sound source, does the observer observe the same frequency, a smaller frequency or a larger frequency than that emitted by the source?

16 The Doppler effect

4 Now consider the case of a stationary sound source and an observer moving away from the source at speed u_o.

    a At what relative speed does the observer observe the sound waves approaching?

    b Does the observer observe the wavelength of the sound waves to be the same, larger or smaller than the wavelength of the sound waves emitted by the source?

    c Hence, show that the frequency of the sound waves observed by the observer is given by the expression $f' = f\left(1 - \frac{u_o}{v}\right)$.

    d So, if the observer moves away from a stationary sound source, does the observer observe the same frequency, a smaller frequency or a larger frequency than that emitted by the source?

5 A train moving at a constant speed of 60 ms^{-1} approaches a bridge. The train's whistle blows as it approaches, passes under the bridge and continues along the track. (speed of sound in air = 330 ms^{-1})

    a Describe what a train-spotter standing on the bridge will hear as the train approaches and passes the bridge.

    b If the train's whistle emits a sound of frequency 800 Hz, calculate the frequency of the sound from the train's whistle when the train is

        i approaching the bridge.

        ii travelling away from the bridge.

6 The siren on an ambulance emits sound waves that have a wavelength of 0.500 m as they travel through the air towards you at a speed of 330.0 ms^{-1}.

    a Calculate the frequency of the emitted sound waves.

    b Now calculate the frequency you would expect to hear when

        i the ambulance travels towards you at a speed of 20.0 ms^{-1}.

        ii the ambulance travels away from you at a speed of 20.0 ms^{-1}.

        iii you travel towards the stationary ambulance at a speed of 20.0 ms^{-1}.

        iv you travel away from the stationary ambulance at a speed of 20.0 ms^{-1}.

    c Using your answers to **part b**, what can you conclude about the observed frequencies of a moving source compared to a moving observer?

7 Bats navigate their way through the air by echolocation. They emit sound waves of frequency 40.0 kHz, which reflect off objects. The Doppler-effected frequency they hear can give the bats information about how far away objects are and what their relative speeds are. The speed of sound in air is 300.0 ms^{-1}. You should give your answers to three significant figures.

    a Suggest why it is that humans cannot hear bats as they fly around.

b Suppose a bat flies towards a wall at a speed of 6.00 ms⁻¹.

    i What is the frequency of the sound waves being reflected off the wall?

    ii What frequency does the bat hear from the reflected sound waves?

8 A stationary sound source emits sound waves of frequency 800 Hz. These sound waves are reflected from an observer, O, who is moving towards the source at a speed of 10 ms⁻¹. Another observer, P, standing next to the source hears the sound waves reflected from O and notices that they are of a different frequency to the sound waves he can hear directly from the source. (The speed of sound in air is 330 ms⁻¹.)

Calculate the frequency of

  a the sound waves heard by the moving observer, O.

  b the sound waves reflected from the moving observer, O, and heard by the stationary observer, P.

9 A music student notices that, when a police car with its siren sounding approaches and then recedes from him, the frequency of the siren changes from 480 Hz to 400 Hz. If the speed of sound in air is 330 ms⁻¹,

  a determine the speed at which the police car was travelling.

  b Determine the frequency of the sound emitted by the police car's siren.

> **TIP**
>
> Use the equations for frequency for a moving source and algebraically derive an expression for the speed of the police car. Then use the expression to find u_s.

EXAM-STYLE QUESTIONS

Multiple-choice questions

1 Light from star X is observed to be blue-shifted. Light from star Y is observed to be red-shifted. What is the most likely reason for this?

  A Star X is hotter than star Y.

  B Star Y is hotter than Star X.

  C Star X is moving away from us and star Y is moving towards us.

  D Star X is moving towards us and star Y is moving away from us.

2 A train moving with constant speed towards an observer on a nearby bridge sounds its horn, which emits a sound of frequency f.

As the train approaches the observer, which of the following statements is correct?

  A The observer hears a sound of frequency smaller than f and with a constant intensity.

  B The observer hears a sound of frequency smaller than f and with an increasing intensity.

  C The observer hears a sound of frequency larger than f and with a constant intensity.

  D The observer hears a sound of frequency larger than f and with an increasing intensity.

CONTINUED

3. A motorbike's exhaust pipe emits sound with a frequency of 120 Hz. The motorbike drives directly away from a stationary observer at a speed of 15 ms^{-1}. Which of the following is the best estimate of the frequency of the sound waves from the exhaust pipe detected by the observer? The speed of sound in air is 330 ms^{-1}.

   A 105 Hz
   B 110 Hz
   C 115 Hz
   D 120 Hz

4. A sound wave source, emitting sound waves of frequency f, moves away from a stationary observer at a speed u_s. If the observer detects sound waves with a frequency f', which of the following expressions can be used to calculate, correctly, the speed of sound in air?

   A $v = \dfrac{f' u_s}{f - f'}$

   B $v = \dfrac{f' u_s}{f + f'}$

   C $v = \dfrac{f' - v}{f' u_s}$

   D $v = \dfrac{f' + f}{f' u_s}$

5. Excited hydrogen emits a spectrum of wavelengths in which the hydrogen-alpha line, at a wavelength of 656.28 nm, is a dominant feature. When a distant galaxy is observed from the Earth, the hydrogen-alpha line has a wavelength of 670.0 nm. If c is the speed of light, which of the following best describes the motion of the distant galaxy relative to the Earth?

   A The galaxy is moving towards the Earth with a speed of 2% of c.
   B The galaxy is moving towards the Earth with a speed of 23.7% of c.
   C The galaxy is moving away from the Earth with a speed of 2% of c.
   D The galaxy is moving away from the Earth with a speed of 23.7% of c.

6. A golden eagle dives vertically downwards towards its prey emitting a screech of frequency 870 Hz. If the eagle's prey hears the screech at a frequency of 1025 Hz, the best estimate for the eagle's speed is

   A 46 ms^{-1}.
   B 50 ms^{-1}.
   C 59 ms^{-1}.
   D 63 ms^{-1}.

7. A stationary siren emits sound waves of wavelength 0.40 m, which travel through the air at a speed of 330 ms^{-1}. When a car approaches the siren at a speed of 20 ms^{-1}, the driver of the car hears sound waves with a wavelength of

   A 0.38 m.
   B 0.40 m.
   C 0.42 m.
   D 0.46 m.

CONTINUED

8 Olympic sprinters run at about 10 ms^{-1}. Suppose an Olympic sprinter runs towards a large wall shouting, as he runs, at a frequency of 475 Hz. Which of the following is the best estimate of the frequency that the sprinter hears from the sound reflected from the wall?

   A 475 Hz

   B 489 Hz

   C 505 Hz

   D 512 Hz

Short-answer questions

9 A distant star emits light of wavelength 575 nm. When this light is received at the Earth, its frequency is 4.8×10^{14} Hz. The speed of light through space is 3.0×10^8 ms^{-1}.

   a Calculate the frequency of the light emitted by the star. [1]

   b Determine whether the star is moving towards the Earth or away from the Earth. [2]

   c Calculate the speed of the star relative to the Earth. [2]

10 a Outline what is meant by the Doppler effect. [2]

   b State what two details about a star's motion relative to the Earth can be found from the following statement: 'Light from the star exhibits a red-shift of 5%'. [2]

   c Suggest why light from a hand-held lantern does not exhibit blue-shift if the person holding the lantern is walking towards an observer. [1]

11 Two cars, A and B, are moving towards each other, each having a speed of 20 ms^{-1}. Car A has its horn sounding with an emitted frequency of 200 Hz. The driver of car B hears the horn at a higher frequency than 200 Hz. The speed of sound in air is 330 ms^{-1}.

   a Outline why the driver of car B hears a higher freqency than 200 Hz. [2]

   b Calculate the frequency of the sound from car A's horn heard by the driver of car B. [3]

12 A spacecraft in a science-fiction movie sends a signal to the Earth using radio waves of frequency 5.0 kHz. A scientist on the Earth measures the frequency to be 4.85 kHz. Making the assumption that the Earth is stationary,

   a calculate the wavelength of the signal

      i emitted by the spacecraft (the speed of light through space is 3.0×10^8 ms^{-1}). [1]

      ii received by the scientist. [1]

   b state whether the spacecraft is moving towards the Earth or away from the Earth. [1]

   c determine the speed at which the spacecraft is moving relative to the Earth. [2]

13 A doctor in a hospital is measuring the speed at which blood cells travel along the femoral artery of a patient suspected of having a small blockage in the artery. In a healthy human, the speed of blood cells in the femoral artery can be taken to be 20.0 cms^{-1}. The doctor uses an ultrasonic transmitter of frequency 10.000 Mhz to transmit the waves, which travel through the patient's body at a speed of 1.5 kms^{-1}, directly towards the moving blood cells. If the doctor receives a reflected signal from the blood cells of frequency 10.006 Mhz, and sees that the blood flow rate in the artery is normal, deduce the doctor's conclusion. [5]

CONTINUED

14 At night-time, a house burglar alarm is sounding with a frequency of 1250 Hz. The speed of sound through the night air is 330 ms^{-1}.

   a Calculate the frequency of the burglar alarm's sound that is received by a police car that is travelling at 25 ms^{-1} towards the alarm. [2]

   b Calculate the frequency of the sound from the burglar alarm that a burglar hears when he is running away from the alarm at a speed of 9 ms^{-1}. [2]

   c Suggest how your answers to **parts a** and **b** would change if the alarm had been sounding during the day-time, when the temperature of the air is greater than at night. [1]

15 a State what is meant by the terms

     i *red-shift*. [1]

     ii *blue-shift*. [1]

   b A distant star is observed to emit light with a red-shift. Calculate the change in frequency of emitted light from the star if the star, moving at a speed of 4.5×10^6 ms^{-1} relative to the Earth, emits light of wavelength 620 nm. ($c = 3.0 \times 10^8$ ms^{-1}) [3]

Unit D
Fields

> Chapter 17
Gravitational fields

CHAPTER OUTLINE

In this chapter, you will:

- explore Newton's universal law of gravitation.
- consider when it is appropriate to treat extended masses as point masses.
- explore Kepler's three laws of orbital motion.
- explore gravitational field strength as a vector quantity.
- understand the importance and use of gravitational field lines.

> develop and use the concept of gravitational potential energy as a scalar quantity.

> explore gravitational potential at a point in a gravitational field.

> link gravitational field strength with gravitational potential.

> consider the work done in moving a mass in a gravitational field.

> become familiar with the concept of a gravitational escape speed.

> explore the effect of a small viscous drag on the height and speed of an orbiting object.

KEY TERMS

Newton's universal law of gravitation: an attractive force exists between any two point masses that is proportional to the product of the masses and inversely proportional to the square of their separation. This force is directed along a line joining the two masses.

$$F = -G\frac{M_1 M_2}{R^2},$$

where G is the universal gravitational constant ($G = 6.67 \times 10^{-11}$ Nm^2kg^{-2}), M_1 and M_2 are the masses of the two point masses and R is the separation of the two point masses.

point mass: a theoretical object of no size having mass

gravitational field: a region of space in which a mass experiences a gravitational force

gravitational field strength: the gravitational force per unit mass exerted on a point mass

> **CONTINUED**
>
> **uniform gravitational field:** a gravitational field in which the field strength is constant at all locations
>
> **gravitational field lines:** lines that show the direction of the force exerted on a point mass in a gravitational field
>
> **Kepler's first law:** planets move on ellipses with the Sun at one of the foci of the ellipse
>
> **Kepler's second law:** the line joining a planet and the Sun sweeps equal areas in equal times
>
> **Kepler's third law:** The period of revolution of a planet around the Sun is proportional to the $\frac{3}{2}$ power of the semi-major axis of the ellipse. $T^2 \propto R^3$ or $\frac{T^2}{R^3}$ = constant; $T^2 = \frac{4\pi^2}{GM} R^3$, where T is the orbital period and R is the average orbital radius
>
> **geostationary orbit:** a satellite's orbit around the Earth, above the equator, that has an orbital period of exactly one day so that the satellite remains above the same spot on the Earth's surface
>
> **escape speed:** the minimum speed, v_{esc}, of an object in a gravitational field so that the object reaches infinity with zero kinetic energy

Exercise 17.1 Newton's law of gravitation

The questions in this section introduce you to Newton's law of gravitation, gravitational fields, point masses, gravitational field strength and Kepler's laws of orbital motion.

1. **a** **i** Outline what is meant by the term *gravitational field*.

    ii Outline what is meant by the term *uniform gravitational field*.

    iii Outline qualitatively why we can consider that we all live in a uniform gravitational field.

2. This question will show you why gravitational force is an inverse-square law.

    After analysing a large amount of observational data made by Tycho Brahe in the late 16th century, Johannes Kepler published his third law of planetary orbits, ten years after his first two laws, in 1619. Isaac Newton proposed his law of gravitation 68 years later in 1687.

    a State Kepler's third law.

    b For a planet orbiting the Sun in a circular orbit at a speed v, and at an orbital radius R, state the centripetal acceleration of the planet.

c State the speed, v, of the planet in terms of its orbital radius, R, and its period of orbit, T.

d Hence, show that the acceleration of the planet can be expressed as $a = \frac{4\pi^2 R^3}{T^2} \times \frac{1}{R^2}$.

e Now, using Kepler's third law, show that the gravitational force responsible for the planet's acceleration must be an inverse square relationship with the planet's orbital radius.

3 This question explores the concept of a point mass.

a Outline what is meant by the term *point mass*.

b i What would the density of a point mass be?

ii Suggest why a point mass has to be a theoretical concept. (Refer to your answer to **part i**.)

c Isaac Newton considered the Sun and the planets that orbit around it to behave as point masses.

Suggest **two** reasons why Newton was justified to consider the Sun and its planets to behave as point masses.

4 This question explores the vector nature of gravitational field strength.

a i Write an equation for the gravitational field strength at a point X, which is a distance R from a mass, M.

ii Since gravitational field strength is a vector quantity, in which direction is the gravitational field strength at point X?

b Figure 17.1 shows a similar situation to what you examined in **part a**, but this time, there is another equal mass present.

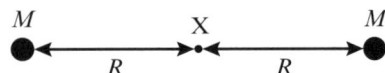

Figure 17.1

Determine the new gravitational field strength at point X.

c Look at Figure 17.2. It shows two equal masses and another point, Y.

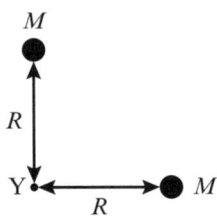

Figure 17.2

Determine the magnitude and the direction of the gravitational field strength at point Y.

5 **a** Explain what is meant by *gravitational field strength*.

  b How is gravitational field strength related to gravitational force?

  c The Earth has a mass of 6×10^{24} kg. Its average radius is 6.4×10^6 m.

   i Calculate the gravitational field strength at the surface of the Earth.

   ii Explain why this gravitational field strength is usually quoted as a *globally averaged* value.

   iii Is the gravitational field strength of the Earth largest at the equator or at the poles? Explain your answer.

6 **a** Calculate the gravitational field strength of the Sun ($M_{Sun} = 2 \times 10^{30}$ kg) at a distance of 1 AU.
(1 AU is the average radial distance of the Earth from the Sun = 1.5×10^{11} m.)

  b Calculate the gravitational field strength of the Moon at a distance equal to the average orbital radius of the moon around the Earth.
(Moon's orbital radius = 3.8×10^8 m.)

  c Comparing your answers to **parts a** and **b**, explain why the Moon has a greater effect on the oceans' tides than the Sun does.

7 The gravitational field strength, g, for the Earth is given by $g = G\dfrac{M}{R^2}$.

  a Assuming that the Earth has a constant density, ρ,

   i show that the gravitational field strength **inside** the Earth is proportional to the distance from the centre of the Earth.

   ii sketch a graph to show how g varies with distance from the centre of the Earth outwards to about three Earth radii.

   iii show that G can be expressed as $G = \dfrac{3g}{4\pi R \rho}$.

  b The average density of the Earth is 5.5×10^3 kgm^{-3}. Calculate the percentage difference between the value of G calculated using $G = \dfrac{3g}{4\pi R \rho}$, and the currently accepted value of 6.67×10^{-11} Nm^{2}kg^{-2}.

8 The Earth orbits the Sun because of the gravitational force of the Sun acting on the Earth.

  a Using your knowledge of centripetal force, write an equation to express this.

  b Show that the speed at which the Earth moves in its orbit is given by the expression, $v = \sqrt{\dfrac{GM_{sun}}{R}}$, where R is the radius of the Earth's orbit.

  c A comedy song from an old movie called *Monty Python's The Meaning of Life* says Earth is orbiting the Sun at 19 miles a second.

Use the expression you derived in **part b** to comment on the accuracy of the song's claim. (A mile is very nearly 1603 metres.)

9   Figure 17.3 shows the Earth and the Moon (not to scale).
They are 3.8×10^8 m apart.

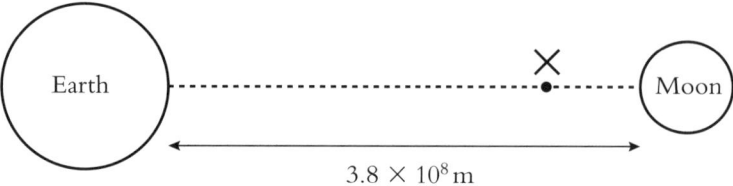

Figure 17.3

a   The Earth's mass is 6×10^{24} kg, and the Moon's mass is 7.3×10^{22} kg. At point X, the gravitational field strength is zero. Calculate how far X is from the Earth.

b   Sketch a graph to show how the gravitational field strength varies with the distance between the Earth and the Moon.

10 a   State Kepler's three laws of orbital motion.

b   Which of Kepler's laws of orbital motion imply

  i   the orbital period of Saturn is larger than the orbital period of Jupiter?

  ii sometimes, the moon appears larger than usual when observed in the sky?

  iii the orbital speed of the Earth is not constant?

11 a   The radius of the Moon's orbit about the Earth is 3.8×10^8 m. Its orbital period is 27.3 days. Show that the mass of the Earth is about 6×10^{24} kg.

b   The gravitational field strength at the surface of Mars is 0.38 of that of the Earth. The radius of Mars is 3400 km. Calculate the mass of Mars.

Exercise 17.2 Gravitational potential and energy

1   This question builds on your previous knowledge of gravitational potential energy.

a   Consider a mass, m, sitting on the surface of the Earth, where the gravitational field strength is a constant value of g.

  i   A physics student wants to pick up the mass vertically and place it on a table. How much force must he apply to pick up the mass?

  ii The student places the mass on a tabletop that is a height, h, above the ground. How much work must the student do?

iii Sketch a graph of the force that the student must apply against the distance it is moved.

iv How can you find the work done by the student on the mass from your graph in **part iii**?

v In terms of energy transfers, what has happened to the work the student has done?

vi Has the mass gained energy; in other words, does the mass now possess more energy than it had when it was on the ground?

b Figure 17.4 shows how the force required to move a mass of 1 kg away from the Earth's surface decreases with distance above the Earth's surface out to an infinite distance away. This is Newton's law of gravitation.

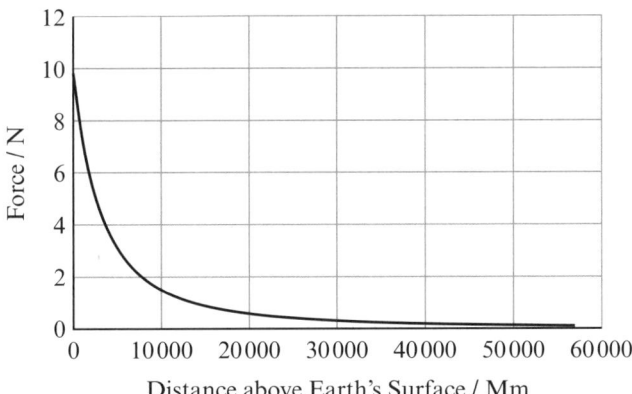

Figure 17.4

i What does the area under the curve in Figure 17.4 represent?

ii *For the more mathematically minded students*:

The mathematical formula for the curve shown in Figure 17.4 is $F = G\frac{Mm}{R^2}$.

($m = 1$ kg, with R in Mm and adjusted so that a value of $R = 0$ indicates the average radius of the Earth.)

Using your answer to **part i**, write a mathematical equation for the area under the curve of Figure 17.4 from $R = 0$ to $R = \infty$ and solve the equation analytically.

Or, for the less mathematically minded students:

Write an equation for the quantity you have indicated in your answer to **part i**.

iii If a 1 kg mass were to be forced away, to an infinite distance, from the Earth's surface, use the data below to calculate how much work would have to be done. ($G = 6.67 \times 10^{-11}$, $M = 6 \times 10^{24}$ and $R = 6400$ km)

    iv Would the 1 kg mass now have more, or less, gravitational potential energy than it had at the Earth's surface?

    v At an infinite distance away from the Earth, the Earth's gravitational field strength is zero (when $R = \infty$, $g = 0$). This means that the gravitational potential energy of a 1 kg mass must be zero too. Given this statement, and your answer to **part iv**, what does this suggest about the value of the gravitational potential energy of the 1 kg mass at the Earth' surface—and above it?

    vi Hence, write an equation for the gravitational potential energy of a mass, m, at a distance, R, from the Earth of mass, M.

> **TIP**
> Remember your answer to **part a vi** earlier.

2 This question builds on the previous question in order to find a formal definition of *gravitational potential energy*.

  a State Newton's law of gravitation in equation form.

  b Sketch a graph of how F varies with R.

  c Now imagine a stationary mass, m, at an infinite distance away from another, very much larger mass, M.

    i When $R = \infty$, how much gravitational force does M exert on m?

    ii Now suppose that m, again initially stationary, is slightly closer to M than an infinite distance away so that M now exerts a gravitational force on m. What will this gravitational force do to the mass, m?

    iii So, what energy transfer is occurring?

    iv Suppose this results in the mass, m, moving a distance closer to the mass M so that m is now at a distance R^* from M. (We can consider that the acceleration of the mass, M, towards the mass, m, is negligible, since $M \gg m$.) What would the area under your graph from **part b**, from $R = \infty$ to $R = R^*$ represent?

    v If we consider that the mass, m, is now at a distance, R^*, from M, how much gravitational potential energy does the mass, m, have?

    vi So, using your answers to **parts iv** and **v**, write a definition for the gravitational potential energy of a mass, m, at a distance R from another mass, M.

> **TIP**
> Think carefully here: where did m start, and where did it end up? Has the distance that the mass has moved been in the direction of the force acting on the mass?

3 **a** **i** Outline briefly what is meant by the term *gravitational potential*, V_g.

    ii How is *gravitational potential* formally defined?

    iii In what units is V_g measured?

    iv Hence, state the mathematical relationship between gravitational potential and gravitational potential energy.

    v Is V_g a scalar or a vector quantity?

b **i** Calculate the gravitational potential at the surface of the Earth caused by the Earth's gravitational field. ($G = 6.67 \times 10^{-11}$ Nm^{2}kg^{-2}, $M = 6 \times 10^{24}$ kg and $R = 6.4 \times 10^6$ m)

ii Now calculate the gravitational potential at a distance of 1.5×10^{11} m from the Sun, whose mass is 2×10^{30} kg.

iii Hence, calculate the total gravitational potential at the surface of the Earth.

iv How much energy would a mass of 5 kg require to leave the Earth's surface and escape entirely from the solar system?

4 This question is about the mathematical relationship between gravitational force, F_g, and gravitational potential energy, E_p.

a **i** Express F in terms of G, M, R and m, where G is the universal gravitational constant, M is the mass of the Earth and R is the distance from the centre of the Earth.

ii Now express the gravitational potential energy of the mass, m, in terms of G, M, R and m.

iii Explain why it would be incorrect to say that $E_p = F_g \times R$.

iv Hence, describe how one can find E_p from the graph of F_g against R.

v Write your answer to **part iv** mathematically.

b **i** Suppose now that you are provided with a graph of E_p against R. For any value of R, how can you use the graph to find F_g?

ii Hence, write your answer to **part i** mathematically.

c Figure 17.5 shows a graph of how the gravitational force, F_g, acting on a mass of 1 kg varies with distance, R, from the Earth's surface. Figure 17.6 shows a graph of how the E_p of a 1 kg mass varies with distance, R, from the Earth's surface.

> **TIP**
> This is an important relationship, one that you should make sure to learn.

> **TIP**
> This is an important relationship too; it is essentially the mathematical inverse to **part a v**. You should make sure to learn this.

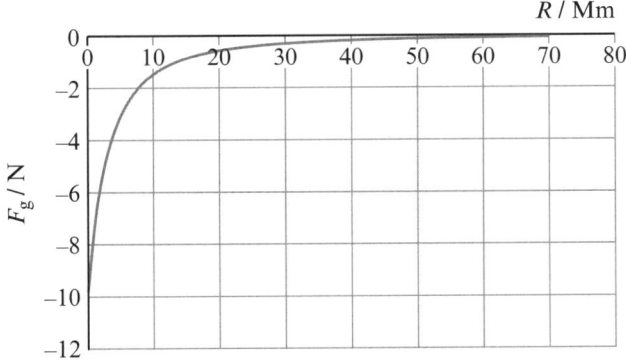

Figure 17.5

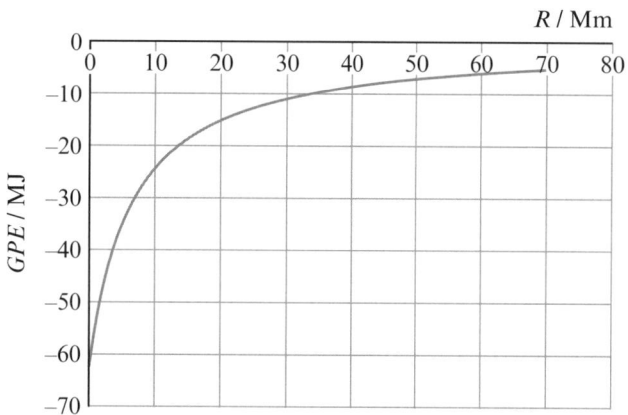

Figure 17.6

    i   Estimate the area under the graph of Figure 17.5 from $R = 10$ Mm out to $R = \infty$. This isn't easy to do, but give it a try!

    ii   Now estimate the E_p possessed by a 1 kg mass at a distance of 10 Mm from the Earth's surface, using Figure 17.6.

    iii   Compare your answers to **parts i** and **ii**.

    vi   Now, again using Figure 17.6, estimate the gradient of the graph at the value of $R = 10$ Mm, and hence, give a value for the gravitational force on the 1 kg mass at a distance 10 Mm from the Earth's surface.

    v   Now, using Figure 17.5, estimate the value of F_g at a value of $R = 10$ Mm.

    vi   Compare your answers to **parts iv** and **v**.

    vii   Have your answers to **part c** confirmed your answers to **parts a** and **b**?

5   This question follows on from **question 4**, using your answers to that question.

    a   In **question 4 part c**, we considered the mass, m, to be 1 kg.

        How might the gravitational force, F_g, acting on the 1 kg mass be referred to?

    b   And how might the E_p of the 1 kg mass be referred to?

    c   So, write down the mathematical relationships between

        i F_g and E_p.

        ii g and V_g.

    d   Explain why the mathematical relationships in your answers to **parts c i** and **c ii** are the same.

6   The observatory in the Burj Khalifa (the tallest building in the world in 2021) is 556 m above the ground. The gravitational field strength in the region just above the Earth's surface is 9.81 Nkg⁻¹.

   a   How much work must be done to take an observer, of mass 60 kg, from the ground floor up to the observatory of the Burj Khalifa?

   b   Given that the mass of the Earth is 6×10^{24} kg and its average radius is 6400 km, what fraction of the observer's E_p at the surface is your answer to **part a**? ($G = 6.67 \times 10^{-11}$ Nm²kg⁻²)

7   Consider a unit mass sitting on a small part of the surface of the Earth, as shown in Figure 17.7. We can consider the field strength, $g \approx 10$ Nkg⁻¹ to 1 significant figure, to be constant for about 20 km or so above the Earth's surface. At the Earth's surface, the gravitational potential is V_g.

Figure 17.7

   a   Draw a line on Figure 17.7 to show all the places where the gravitational potential is $V_g + (1.0 \times 10^4$ Jkg⁻¹). Label this 1.

   b   Now draw four further lines to show all places where the gravitational potential is

   i $V_g + (2.0 \times 10^4$ Jkg⁻¹). Label this 2.

   ii $V_g + (3.0 \times 10^4$ Jkg⁻¹). Label this 3.

   iii $V_g + (4.0 \times 10^4$ Jkg⁻¹). Label this 4.

   vi $V_g + (5.0 \times 10^4$ Jkg⁻¹). Label this 5.

   c   What name is given to each of the lines you have drawn?

   d   How does your diagram show that the Earth's gravitational field strength is constant just above the Earth's surface?

   e   Determine the actual spacing, in metres, of the lines you have drawn.

8   Figure 17.8 shows a planet in deep space, a long way from any other masses. The gravitational potential at the surface of the planet is –80 MJkg⁻¹.

Figure 17.8

a   Add some gravitational field lines to Figure 17.8 to show the direction of the gravitational field that the planet's mass creates.

b   Now add three equipotentials to Figure 17.8 to show the gravitational potential at values of −70 MJkg⁻¹, −60 MJkg⁻¹ and −50 MJkg⁻¹.

c   Outline how your equipotentials show that the gravitational field strength around the planet is decreasing with distance away from it.

d   What geometrical relationship do gravitational field lines have with gravitational equipotentials?

9 Figure 17.9 shows the four quantities that are most important when considering gravitational fields:

- force
- field strength
- potential
- potential energy

Complete the diagram to show

- the equations for each quantity.
- the mathematical relationships between the quantities.

Two mathematical relationships and one equation have been entered for you.

This will provide you with an easy-to-see revision of the main ideas you have met in sections 17.1 and 17.2.

> **TIP**
>
> You should try to make sure that you know all the details on this diagram.

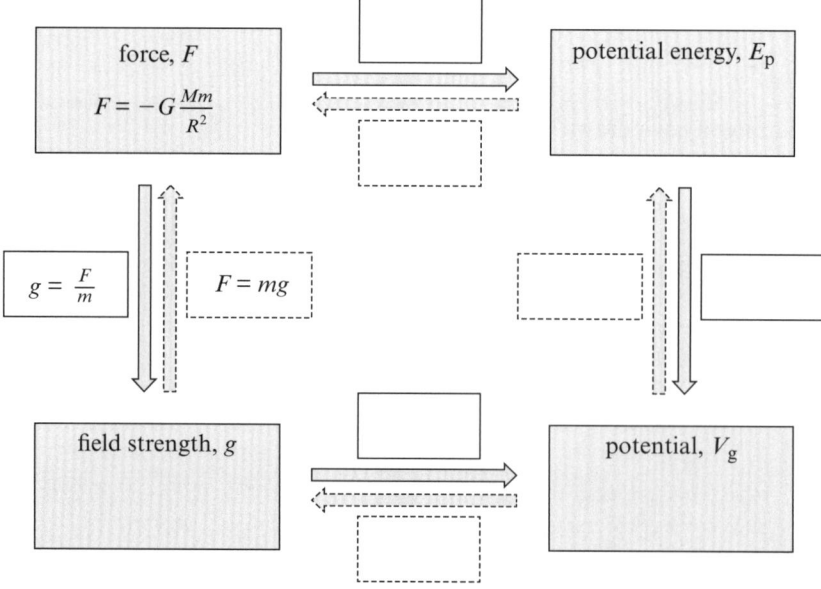

Figure 17.9

Exercise 17.3 Motion in a gravitational field

1   Consider a satellite of mass m, moving through space at a speed v, in a circular orbit around a planet of mass M, at an orbital radius of R.

   a   What force is responsible for providing the centripetal force necessary for the circular motion of the satellite?

   b   By equating the magnitude of this force with the general equation for the centripetal force of a mass m, moving at a speed v, in a circle of radius R, find an expression for the kinetic energy of the satellite in terms of G, M and R.

   c   State the E_p of the satellite in its orbit.

   Hence, derive an expression for the total energy of the satellite in its orbit.

   d   i   The Earth orbits the Sun at an average distance of 1.5×10^{11} m. The mass of the Sun is 2×10^{30} kg, and the mass of the Earth is 6×10^{24} kg. Calculate the total energy of the Earth in its orbit around the Sun.

   ii   The Moon's mass is 7.3×10^{22} kg, and its average orbital radius around the Earth is 3.85×10^8 m. Calculate the total energy of the Moon in its orbit around the Earth.

2   The following table shows the orbital radii of the eight major planets in our solar system.

Planet	Orbital Radius (Gm)	Orbital speed (kms^{-1})
Mercury	58	
Venus	108	
Earth	150	
Mars	228	
Jupiter	779	
Saturn	1434	
Uranus	2873	
Neptune	4495	

   a   Complete the table by calculating, for each planet, its orbital speed.
   ($G = 6.67 \times 10^{-11}$ Nm^{2}kg^{-2} and $M_{Sun} = 2 \times 10^{30}$ kg)

   b   Using your data from the completed table, draw a graph of orbital speed against orbital radius.

c Suppose you were given only the graph you have drawn in **part b**, outline how you could use the graph (together with any other graph you might like to draw) to verify that the mass of the Sun is 2×10^{30} kg.

3 This question looks at a geostationary orbit.

Consider a satellite moving with a speed v, in a circular orbit of radius R, around the Earth and with an orbital period T.

a State v in terms of R and T.

b Express the centripetal acceleration of the satellite in terms of R and T.

c Since this acceleration must be equal to the gravitational field strength of the Earth, of mass M, at a distance R away, derive an expression for R in terms of G, T and M.

d If the orbital period of the satellite is to be exactly 1 day, determine how far above the Earth's surface the satellite must be. ($G = 6.67 \times 10^{-11}$ Nm^{2}kg^{-2}, $M = 6 \times 10^{24}$ kg and the average radius of the Earth is 6.4×10^6 m.)

e If the satellite is to remain exactly over the same part of the Earth's surface, describe briefly the orientation of the satellite's orbit.

f Suggest some uses for such an orbit.

4 The mass of the Sun is 2×10^{30} kg, and at its equator, it rotates on its polar axis once every 25 days.

a Determine how far away from the Sun a planet would have to be in orbit for the planet to have the same orbital period as the equatorial rotational period of the Sun, which is a heliosynchronous orbit. ($G = 6.67 \times 10^{-11}$ Nm^{2}kg^{-2})

b Where would this orbit be compared to the orbits of the other solar system planets?

5 The International Space Station (ISS) has a mass of 4.2×10^5 kg. It was launched in 1998. It still orbits around the Earth at an average height above the Earth's surface of 420 km. It takes 93 minutes to make one complete orbit of the Earth.

The Earth's radius is 6.4×10^6 m.

Determine

a the speed at the which ISS travels in its orbit.

b the value of the Earth's gravitational field strength at the orbital radius of the ISS.

c the mass of the Earth.

d the energy required by the ISS to escape from the Earth's gravitational field completely.

> **TIP**
>
> In questions about orbits, be careful to distinguish between orbital radius and height above the surface.

6 The gravitational potential due to the Earth's gravitational field at the surface of the Earth is -62.5 MJkg^{-1}.

Suppose a large firework rocket contained 62.5 MJ of chemical energy per kilogramme of its mass.

   a Determine the total energy of the rocket at the Earth's surface.

   b Now suppose that, when ignited, the rocket could transform all of its chemical energy into kinetic energy with an efficiency of 100%. Suppose also that there was no friction due to the Earth's atmosphere as it travels upwards.

   As the rocket travels upwards and away from the Earth's surface,

      i what happens to its kinetic energy?

      ii what happens to its gravitational potential energy?

      iii what is the total energy of the rocket at all times during its flight?

      iv what will the eventual fate of the rocket be?

      v calculate the initial speed of the rocket as it blasted off the Earth's surface.

      vi what name can we give to this speed?

      vii suggest what shape the trajectory of the rocket would be.

   c Now suppose that the rocket contained 50 MJ of chemical energy per kilogramme of its mass. Outline any changes you would expect to the journey the rocket would make.

   d Now suppose that the rocket contained 70 MJ of chemical energy per kilogramme of its mass. Outline any changes you would expect to the journey the rocket would make.

7 Consider an astronomical body of mass M, and radius R.

   a Derive an expression, in terms of M and R, for the escape speed of the body.

   b Now suppose that the escape speed of the body was equal to the speed of light; $c = 3.0 \times 10^8$ ms^{-1}. Derive an expression, in terms of M and c, for the radius of such a body. Astrophysicists have named this radius the Schwartzchild radius.

   c Calculate the Schwartzchild radius for the following astronomical bodies:

      i The Sun ($M_{Sun} = 2 \times 10^{30}$ kg)

      ii The Earth ($M_{Earth} = 6 \times 10^{24}$ kg)

      iii Cygnus – X1 ($M = 21.2\ M_{Sun}$)

   ($G = 6.67 \times 10^{-11}$ Nm^{2}kg^{-2})

   d What name do we give to an astronomical body whose escape speed is greater than c?

8 Suppose that a satellite is sent into space with the intention of it orbiting the Earth at a constant orbital radius. Unfortunately, the satellite is not given enough energy and its orbit starts to suffer from frictional forces caused by the upper atmosphere.

   a What effect will the frictional forces, caused by the satellite moving through the upper atmosphere, have on the total energy of the satellite?

   b So, what will happen to the orbital radius of the satellite?

   c So, what will happen to the orbital speed of the satellite?

   d In terms of energy transfers, what is happening?

   e What can you say about the rate at which the effects in **parts b**, **c** and **d** occur?

   f Suggest the likely fate of the satellite.

9 The escape speed from a black hole is greater than the speed of light. (That's why the black hole appears black: no radiation is escaping from it for us to observe.)

   a If the mass of a black hole is 2.4 times the mass of our Sun ($M_{Sun} = 2.0 \times 10^{30}$ kg), calculate the distance from the centre of the black hole to where radiation is just able to escape from the gravitational field.

   b Is the actual 'size' of the black hole likely to be the value you have calculated in **part a** or smaller? Explain your answer.

   c What is the name given to the distance you have calculated?

EXAM-STYLE QUESTIONS

Multiple-choice questions

1 A communications satellite in a geostationary orbit around the Earth is moving at a constant speed. At any moment, the resultant force on the satellite is

   A zero.

   B equal to the gravitational force on the satellite.

   C equal to the vector sum of the gravitational force on the satellite and the centripetal force.

   D equal to the gravitational force on the satellite minus the centripetal force.

2 The gravitational field strength at the surface of the Earth is about 4 times that of Mars. Assuming that the densities of the two planets are the same and that the mass of the Earth is 10 times that of Mars, which of the following is the best estimate of the ratio of Mars's radius to that of the Earth:

   $\dfrac{\text{radius of Mars}}{\text{radius of Earth}}$?

   A 0.40

   B 0.63

   C 1.60

   D 2.50

CONTINUED

3 A star of mass M, and radius R, has a surface gravitational field strength of g. Which of the following expressions correctly gives the ratio of g to G: $\frac{g}{G}$?

A $-\frac{M}{R}$

B $\frac{M}{R}$

C $-\frac{M}{R^2}$

D $\frac{M}{R^2}$

4 The gravitational field strength of the Earth at its surface is g.

If we assume that the Earth is spherical and of constant density, which of the following gives the gravitational field strength halfway from the surface to the centre of the Earth?

A $\frac{g}{2}$

B g

C $2g$

D $4g$

5 The mass of the Sun is about 3.3×10^5 times the mass of the Earth. If the gravitational force exerted by the Earth on the Sun is F, what is the gravitational force exerted by the Sun on the Earth?

A $\frac{F}{3.3 \times 10^5}$

B $-F$

C F

D $3.3 \times 10^5 F$

6 The gravitational field strength of the Earth at a distance equal to the orbital radius of the Moon is very nearly the same value as the orbital centripetal acceleration of the Moon. Which of the following is not a part of the explanation for this?

A The Moon's orbit is not circular.

B The centre of rotation of the Moon's orbit is not at the centre of the Earth.

C The Moon's mass is significantly smaller than the mass of the Earth.

D The Earth does not remain motionless during an orbit of the Moon.

7 An object placed at a distance of twice the Earth's radius, $2R_E$, from the Earth is allowed to fall to the ground. The mass of the Earth is M. In the absence of any frictional forces, which of the following gives the speed at which the object will hit the Earth's surface?

A $\sqrt{\frac{GM}{2R_E}}$

B $\sqrt{\frac{GM}{R_E}}$

C $2\sqrt{\frac{2GM}{R_E}}$

D $2\sqrt{\frac{GM}{R_E}}$

CONTINUED

8 For a planet orbiting a star of mass M, at an orbital radius of R, and with an orbital period T, Kepler's third law states that

A $\dfrac{T^3}{R^2} = \dfrac{GM}{4\pi^2}$.

B $\dfrac{T^3}{R^2} = \dfrac{4\pi^2}{GM}$.

C $\dfrac{T^2}{R^3} = \dfrac{GM}{4\pi^2}$.

D $\dfrac{T^2}{R^3} = \dfrac{4\pi^2}{GM}$.

9 The Earth orbits the Sun at a radial distance of 1 astronomical unit (1 AU) and has an orbital period of 1 year. A planet orbiting the Sun at a radial distance of 100 AU would have an orbital period of

A 100 years.

B 1000 years.

C 10 000 years.

D 100 000 years.

10 For a satellite in orbit around the Earth, which of the following statements is correct?

A The total energy of the satellite is zero.

B The magnitude of the satellite's kinetic energy is greater than the magnitude of the satellite's gravitational potential energy.

C The magnitude of the satellite's kinetic energy is equal to the magnitude of the satellite's gravitational potential energy.

D The total energy of the satellite is less than zero.

11 The Earth orbits the Sun at an average speed of about 30 kms^{-1}. Neptune orbits the Sun with an orbital radius 30 times greater than the Earth's. The best estimate for the orbital speed of Neptune is

A 1.0 kms^{-1}

B 2.7 kms^{-1}

C 5.4 kms^{-1}

D 7.2 kms^{-1}

12 Mars orbits the Sun about 1.5 times further away than the Earth does. The gravitational field strength due to the Sun at the Earth is about

A $\dfrac{1}{1.5}$ times that at Mars.

B $\dfrac{1}{1.5^2}$ times that at Mars.

C 1.5 times that at Mars.

D 1.5^2 times that at Mars.

CONTINUED

13 A satellite initially in orbit around the Earth at an orbital distance R is given energy to move its orbit to a greater orbital distance. Which of the following statements is incorrect:

  A The satellite slows down.
  B The satellite's total energy decreases.
  C The satellite's E_P increases.
  D The satellite's E_K increases.

14 A satellite, of mass m, in orbit around the Earth has an orbital radius of R and a linear speed v. For half of a complete orbit of the Earth, which of the following correctly gives the work done on the satellite by the Earth's gravitational field?

  A 0
  B $\frac{\pi m v^2}{2}$
  C $\pi m v^2$
  D $2\pi m v^2$

15 An orbiting satellite is moved into a new orbit further from the Earth. Which one of the following statements about the satellite's energy is true?

  A Kinetic energy = decreases; Total energy = stays the same
  B Kinetic energy = decreases; Total energy = increases
  C Kinetic energy = increases; Total energy = stays the same
  D Kinetic energy = increases; Total energy = increases

16 Complete this sentence: The gravitational field strength inside a solid sphere is

  A zero.
  B a constant, non-zero value.
  C proportional to the distance from the sphere's centre.
  D inversely proportional to the square of the distance from the sphere's centre.

17 A satellite is orbiting the Earth. Which of the following combinations best describes its kinetic energy (E_K), gravitational potential energy (E_P) and its total energy?

  A $E_K = > 0$; $E_P = > 0$; Total energy $= > 0$
  B $E_K = < 0$; $E_P = 0$; Total energy $= < 0$
  C $E_K = > 0$; $E_P = < 0$; Total energy $= 0$
  D $E_K = > 0$; $E_P = < 0$; Total energy $= < 0$

Short-answer questions

18 a State Newton's universal law of gravitation. [2]

  b Show that the gravitational potential energy of a body of mass m, at the surface of the Earth, of radius R, and mass M, is given by the expression
  $$E_P = -G\frac{Mm}{R}.$$ [2]

  c Hence, show that the gravitational potential at the Earth's surface is 62.5 MJkg^{-1}.
  ($M_{Earth} = 6 \times 10^{24}$, $R = 6.4 \times 10^6$ m, $G = 6.67 \times 10^{-11}$ Nm^{2}kg^{-2}) [2]

CONTINUED

19 The gravitational force between the Sun, of mass $M = 2 \times 10^{30}$ kg, and the Earth, of mass m, is given by Newton's universal law of gravitation

$F = -G\frac{Mm}{R^2}$,

where R is the orbital distance of the Earth ($R = 1.5 \times 10^{11}$ m) and G is the universal gravitational constant, $G = 6.67 \times 10^{-11}$ Nm²kg⁻².

   a State the significance of the minus sign in the equation. [1]

   b Show that the acceleration of the Earth is given by the equation $a = -G\frac{M}{R^2}$. [1]

   c Derive an expression for the orbital speed of the Earth in terms of G, M and R. [2]

   d Hence show that the orbital speed of the Earth is about 30 kms⁻¹. [1]

20 a Define the term *gravitational field strength*. [2]

   b Show that the units for gravitational field strength are the same as those for acceleration. [1]

   c The mass of the Earth is 6×10^{24} kg, and its average radius is 6.4×10^6 m.
   Show that the gravitational field strength at the surface of the Earth is about 9.8 Nkg⁻¹.
   ($G = 6.67 \times 10^{-11}$ Nm²kg⁻²) [2]

21 a State Kepler's three laws of planetary motion. [3]

   b Halley's comet orbits the Sun once every 75.3 years in a hghly elliptical orbit.

   i Suggest how Newton's law of gravitation shows that the speed of Halley's comet is greatest when it is closest to the Sun. [1]

   ii Suggest how Kepler's second law of planetary motion shows that the speed of Halley's comet is greatest when it is closest to the Sun. [1]

22 Figure 17.10 shows a low-orbit satellite in its clockwise circular orbit around the Earth.

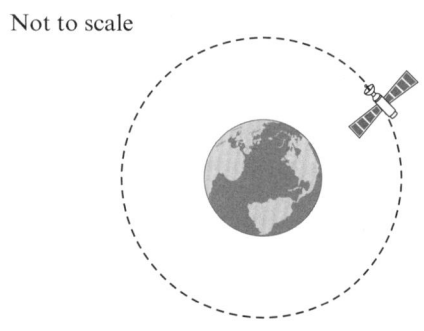

Figure 17.10

   a Add two arrows to the figure to show

   i the instantaneous velocity of the satellite; label this arrow v.

   ii the acceleration of the satellite; label this arrow a. [2]

   b If the orbital radius of the satellite is 6,800 km and the mass of the Earth is 6×10^{24} kg, determine the orbital period of the satellite. ($G = 6.67 \times 10^{-11}$ Nm²kg⁻²) [3]

CONTINUED

23 The following table shows some data for Jupiter's four innermost moons.

Name of moon	Orbital radius / Mm	Time period of orbit / s
Io	422	1.53×10^5
Europa	671	3.07×10^5
Ganymede	1070	6.19×10^5
Callisto	1883	1.44×10^6

    a Draw the graph of (*orbital radius*)^3 against (*time period of orbit*)^2 for these moons of Jupiter. [3]
    b Use your graph to estimate the mass of Jupiter. [2]

24 This question is about Jupiter and Io, one of its moons.
    Io orbits Jupiter at a mean distance of 4.2×10^8 m with an orbital period of 42 hours.
    a Calculate the speed at which Io moves through space in its orbit around Jupiter. [1]
    b Hence, calculate the field strength of Jupiter's gravitational field at Io's orbital radius. [2]
    c Hence, show that the mass of Jupiter is about 1.9×10^{27} kg. [2]

25 a Define the term *escape speed*. [2]
    b The Sun emits charged particles (mostly electrons and protons) from its equatorial regions, in what is referred to as its slow solar wind, at an initial speed of 400 kms^{-1}. By first determining the escape speed of the Sun (of mass 2×10^{30} kg and radius 7.0×10^8 m), suggest whether the slow solar wind particles can escape from the solar system.
       ($G = 6.67 \times 10^{-11}$ Nm^{2}kg^{-2}) [3]

26 The gravitational potential at the surface of the Earth is 62.5 MJkg^{-1}. Jupiter has a mass that is 318 times that of the Earth and its radius is 11.2 times that of the Earth.
    a Define the term *gravitational potential*. [1]
    b Show that the gravitational potential at the surface of Jupiter is about -1.8 GJkg^{-1}. [2]
    c Determine the escape speed from the surface of Jupiter. [2]

27 This question is about a satellite in orbit around the Earth.
    a State the force that provides the necessary centripetal force for the circular motion of the satellite. [1]
    b Show that the speed of the satellite in its orbit is given by $v = \sqrt{\frac{GM_E}{r}}$, where M_E is the mass of the Earth and r is the radius of the satellite's orbit. [2]
    c Geostationary satellites orbiting the Earth have an orbital period of one day. Calculate the radius of the orbit of a geostationary satellite. [2]

› Chapter 18
Electric and magnetic fields

CHAPTER OUTLINE

In this chapter, you will:

- consolidate your understanding of the direction of forces between the types of charge.
- learn Coulomb's law, by treating charged objects as point charges.
- use the principle of conservation of charge.
- use the findings from Millikan's oil drop experiment as evidence of the quantisation of charge.
- learn that charge can be transferred by contact, by friction and by electrostatic induction.
- develop the idea of an electric field as a vector quantity.
- use electric field lines to represent electric fields.
- learn that the density of electric field lines is a measure of field strength.
- learn that the electric field strength between two parallel plates is uniform (though not at the edges).
- consolidate your knowledge of the direction of force between two magnetic poles.
- use magnetic field lines to represent magnetic fields.
- develop an expression for the magnitude and direction of the force on a charge moving in a magnetic field.
- develop an expression for the magnitude and direction of the force on a current-carrying conductor in a magnetic field.

> - understand electrical potential energy in terms of work done.
> - derive an expression for the electrical potential energy of two charged particles.
> - understand that electrical potential is a scalar quantity, with zero defined at an infinite distance away.
> - define *electrical potential*.

CONTINUED

> develop the mathematical relationship between electric field strength and electrical potential.

> solve problems about the work done in moving a charge in an electric field.

> understand, draw and use electrical equipotentials to represent electric fields.

> relate, geometrically, equipotentials with electric field lines.

KEY TERMS

Coulomb's law: the force between two point charges is inversely proportional to the square of the separation and proportional to the product of the charges

$F = k\dfrac{q_1 q_2}{r^2}$

point charge: a charged body of no size

electric field: a region in space in which a charged particle will experience an electrical force

electric field strength: the electrical force acting on a unit positive test point charge

$E = \dfrac{F}{q}$

electric field line: a line showing the direction of electrical force on a positive charge

Millikan's oil drop experiment: the experiment that showed that charge comes in multiples of the charge on an electron, that is that charge is quantised

magnetic field: a region in space in which a magnetic force can act on a moving charge, a current-carrying conductor or a magnetic pole

magnetic flux density, B: the force exerted per metre on a conductor carrying a current of 1 A in a perpendicular magnetic field (B is usually thought of as the strength of the magnetic field.)

magnetic field line: a line showing the direction of force on a magnetic North pole

Fleming's left-hand rule: A way of showing the geometric relationships between the magnetic force (thumb), field (first finger) and current (second finger) for a current-carrying conductor in a magnetic field

amp: An amp is the constant current flowing in two infinitely long, straight, parallel conductors of negligible cross section in a vacuum such that the force between the conductors is 2×10^{-7} Newtons per metre length of the conductors

CONTINUED

electrical potential, Ve: the work done per unit charge to bring a test point positive charge from infinity to where it is in an electrical field

$V_e = k\dfrac{q}{r}$

electrical potential energy: the work done to bring a charged body from infinity to where it is in an electrical field

equipotential: a line or surface on which the electrical potential is the same at all points

KEY EQUATIONS

Electric field strength between two parallel plates: $E = \dfrac{V}{d}$

Magnetic force on a moving charge in a magnetic field: $F = Bqv\sin\theta$

Magnetic force on a current-carrying conductor in a magnetic field:

$F = BIl\sin\theta$

Electrical potential energy between two charged particles: $E_e = k\dfrac{q_1 q_2}{r}$

Electric field strength: $E = -\dfrac{dV_e}{dr}$

Work done in moving a charge, q: work done = $q\Delta V_e$

where k is Coulomb's constant = $\dfrac{1}{4\pi\varepsilon_o}$ = 9×10^9 Nm²C⁻², q_1 and q_2 are the charges on two charged particles, r is the separation of the charged particles, V is the potential difference between two parallel plates, d is the separation of the two parallel plates, B is the magnetic flux density (we can consider this to be the magnetic field strength) in a magnetic field, v is the speed of a moving charged particle, I is the current flowing in the conductor and l is the length of the conductor.

Exercise 18.1 Electric charge, force and field

1. **a** Figure 18.1 shows a small, positively charged sphere. In the region around the sphere, three positions are labelled X, Y and Z.

   Figure 18.1

   i Draw three arrows on Figure 18.1 to represent the force that one coulomb of charge would experience if it were positioned at X, Y and Z. The length of your arrow should represent the magnitude of the force. The direction should represent the direction of the force on the coulomb of charge.

   ii How does the magnitude of the force experienced by the coulomb of charge vary with its distance from the charged sphere?

   b Two small, charged, spheres, A and B, are separated by a distance x.

   When the charge on A is +50 mC and the charge on B is −50 mC, sphere A experiences a force F.

   i In which direction is this force?

   ii Does sphere B experience a force? If so, how big and in which direction is this force?

   iii Which of Newton's laws of motion has helped you to answer **part b ii**?

2. The region of space around a charged object is called an electric field. This electric field exerts a force on any charged particle in it.

   a How does this force depend on

   i the amount of charge on the charged particle in the field?

   ii the amount of charge that the object creating the field has?

   iii the distance between the charged object creating the field and the charged particle in the field?

   b State Coulomb's law in

   i words.

   ii an equation, with explained terms.

c The constant in Coulomb's law, k (usually called the Coulomb constant), has the value 9×10^9 Nm²C⁻² if the space occupied by an electric field is a vacuum or air. Calculate the force between

  i a charge of +50 nC and another charge of −20 nC that are 30 cm apart in air.

  ii a charge of +30 μC and another charge of +20 μC that are 5 mm apart in air.

  iii an electron and a proton that are 100 pm apart in a vacuum.

  iv an alpha particle of charge 6.4×10^{-19} C and a gold nucleus of charge 1.26×10^{-17} C that are 3 fm apart in a vacuum.

3 Using Coulomb's law for this question.

  a Calculate the force experienced by a +50 mC charge and a +20 mC charge that are 2 mm apart in air. Is this force an attractive force or a repulsive force?

  b Calculate the force experienced by a −50 mC charge and a +20 mC charge that are 2 mm apart. Is this force an attractive force or a repulsive force?

  c How does physics convention describe whether a force is attractive or repulsive?

4 Determine the net force acting on the unit positive test charge placed at position X, in the situations **a–d**, shown in Figure 18.2.

TIP

Remember that force is a vector.

a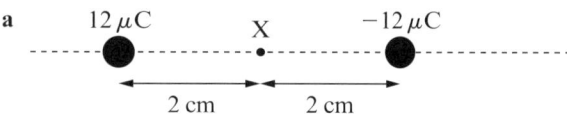

b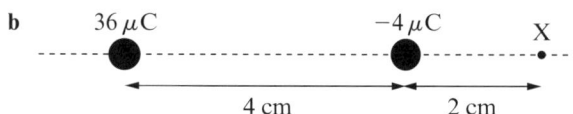

c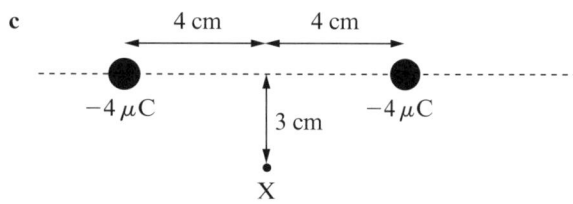

d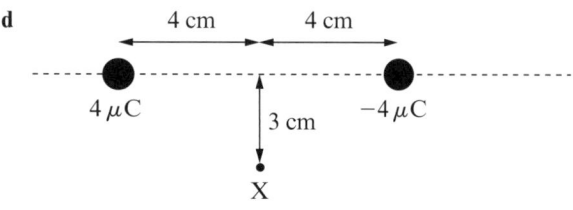

Figure 18.2

5   The magnitude of the force experienced by a charged particle of charge q is proportional to q. So, physicists use the term *field strength* of an electric field, since this is independent of the amount of charge a particle has within the field.

   a   How is electric field strength defined?

   b   What units does electric field strength have?

   c   How is electric field strength related to the force experienced by a charge q, in the field?

6   a   Calculate the electric field strength at a distance of 7×10^{-10} m from a nucleus of carbon.

   b   Calculate the force experienced by an electron at a distance of 7×10^{-10} m from a nucleus of carbon.

   c   If the mass of the electron is 9.1×10^{-31} kg, calculate the acceleration of the electron.

7   Consider a hollow charged sphere, as shown in Figure 18.3.

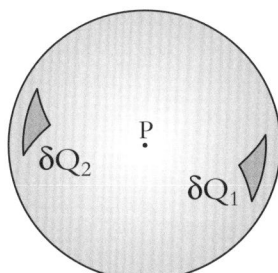

Figure 18.3

   a   Draw an arrow on Figure 18.3 to show the electric field caused by dQ_1 only at point P. Label this arrow 1.

   b   Draw an arrow on Figure 18.3 to show the electric field caused by dQ_2 only at point P. Label this arrow 2.

   c   Imagine you drew more arrows, for all possible places around the surface of the charged sphere. What could you conclude about the electric field strength at point P caused by *all* the charge on *all* the surface of the sphere?

   d   Imagine you changed the position of P to any other place within the hollow sphere, and repeated **parts a**, **b** and **c**. What could you conclude about the electric field strength inside a hollow charged sphere?

8   Imagine Figure 18.3, in the previous question, showed a solid charged sphere, rather than a hollow charged sphere. If you followed the same steps as question 10—but this time drawing arrows at small *volume* sections within the sphere—what would you be able to conclude about the electric field strength inside a solid charged sphere?

9 a Figure 18.4 shows two point charges, each carrying a charge $-q$.

Figure 18.4

The position marked X is equidistant from each of the point charges.

   i   By inspection, what is the electric field strength at the point X?

   ii So, can there be an electric field line at the position X?

   iii Hence, or otherwise, add to Figure 18.6 some electric field lines to show the overall shape of the electric field caused by the two point charges.

   iv How would your diagram differ, if at all, if the two point charges were $+q$ rather than $-q$?

  b Draw another diagram to show the overall electric field caused by two oppositely charged point charges similarly separated to those in Figure 18.4.

  c In any diagram of electric field lines,

   i   can electric field lines intersect?

   ii when the electric field lines are close together, what do you conclude about the electric field strength?

10 Figure 18.5 shows a pair of oppositely charged parallel plates, separated by a distance, d. Each plate is made from a metallic conductor. The potential difference between the two plates is V.

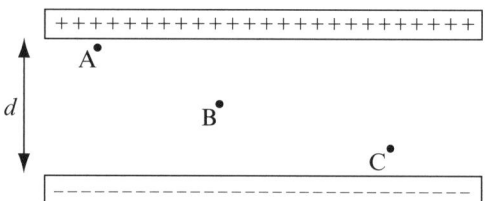

Figure 18.5

  a i   What has happened to the top plate in order to make it positively charged?

     ii What has happened to the bottom plate to make it negatively charged?

  b Explain why the charge density on each plate is uniform all over the plate.

  c Add to Figure 18.5 some electric field lines to show the electric field between the two plates.

  d How does your diagram show that the electric field strength between the two plates is uniform? (You may need to redo your diagram if it doesn't!)

e If a test point charge, q, were to be placed at the points, A, B or C, what can you say about the size and direction of the electric force it would experience?

f Suppose that the magnitude of the force experienced by the test point charge is F.

  i In terms of F and d, how much work would be done if this force moves the point charge from the top plate to the bottom plate, that is through a distance, d?

  ii From what you have already learnt from Chapter 11, give an expression for this work done in terms of V and q.

  iii Hence, show that the electric field strength, E, between the two plates is given by $E = \frac{V}{d}$.

Exercise 18.2 Magnetic field and force

1 Sketch the magnetic field pattern around a bar magnet.

2 One of the effects of a current flowing in a conductor is that a magnetic field is produced around the conductor.

  a Sketch a diagram to show the shape of a magnetic field, produced by a current, around a conductor.

  b How can you know which direction the magnetic field is in?

  c If the current flowing in a conductor is increased, how will your sketch of the magnetic field pattern around the conductor change?

  d There is no magnetic field around a conductor through which no current is flowing. Suggest a likely relationship between the strength of a magnetic field caused by a current and the size of the current.

  e Suggest a relationship between the strength of the magnetic field caused by a current flowing in a conductor and the perpendicular distance away from the conductor.

3 The strength of the magnetic field around a current-carrying wire is given by the equation $B = \mu_0 \frac{I}{2\pi r}$, where B is the magnetic flux density (a measure of the magnetic field strength), μ_0 is the permeability of free space—air or a vacuum—($\mu_0 = 4\pi \times 10^{-7}$ TmA^{-1}) and r is the perpendicular distance from the wire.

  a In what units is B measured?

  b Determine the magnetic field strength in the following situations:

    i 5.0 cm from a current of 120 mA

    ii 8.0 cm from a current of 2 A

    iii 25 cm from a current of 0.5 A

4 a Consider two similar bar magnets, separated by a small distance, with opposite poles facing each other.

Sketch a diagram to show the magnetic field pattern between the two poles of the magnets.

b Figure 18.6 shows the opposite poles of two magnets. There is a perpendicular conductor carrying a current between the magnets.

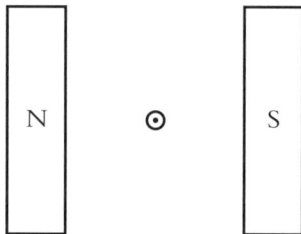

Figure 18.6

   i   In which direction does Figure 18.6 show the current to be flowing, into or out of the page?

   ii How would you show the direction of the current to be opposite to that shown in Figure 18.6?

c i   Copy Figure 18.6 and draw the resulting magnetic field pattern produced by the interaction of the magnetic field from the magnets and the magnetic field from the conductor.

   ii What is this kind of magnetic field usually called?

   iii What effect does this resultant magnetic field have on the conductor?

   iv What *aide memoire* can you use to help you remember this?

   v   Suggest three ways in which this effect could be made larger.

5 a State an equation for the magnetic force, F_{mag}, exerted on a conductor of length l, carrying a current I, at an angle θ, to a magnetic field of strength B.

b A conductor of length 5 cm carries a current of 250 mA and sits perpendicularly in a magnetic field of strength 4.0×10^{-5} T.

   i   Calculate the force experienced by the conductor.

   ii The wire is moved slightly so the direction of the current makes an angle of 30° to the magnetic field. Calculate the force experienced by the wire.

6 How is the magnetic field strength B defined?

7 A copper wire of diameter 2.0 mm and length 8.0 cm is positioned horizontally in a uniform magnetic field of strength 0.2 T perpendicular to the wire. The density of copper is 8900 kgm^{-3}. Calculate the current that needs to flow through the wire so that it is suspended in mid-air. ($g = 9.8$ Nkg^{-1})

8 Suppose that there is a long, vertically orientated wire (it's not necessary to consider the wire's diameter, though we will assume that its diameter is negligibly small) carrying a current, I, upwards.

  a **i** State the equation that gives the magnetic flux density caused by the current in the wire at distance, r, to the right and perpendicular to the wire.

   ii In which direction will B be?

  b Now suppose that there is another, identical wire carrying an identical current at this distance, r, from the first wire.

   i State the equation that gives the magnetic force on this second wire caused by it carrying a current in the magnetic field around the first wire.

   ii Hence, show that the magnetic force on the second wire is given by the expression $F = \mu_0 \frac{I^2 l}{2\pi r}$.

   iii In which direction is this force on the second wire?

  c Newton's third law states that if the second wire experiences a force, then the first wire must also experience an equal, but opposite, force. Using an argument similar to that developed in **parts a** and **b**, show that the first wire does, indeed, experience an equal, but opposite, force to that experienced by the second wire.

9 Two parallel wires, separated by a small distance, each carry a current.

  a If the currents in the two wires are in the same direction, what would you expect to happen to the two wires? Explain your answer.

  b If the currents in the two wires were in opposite directions, what would you expect to happen to the two wires? Explain your answer.

  c How are your answers to **parts a** and **b** relevant to the way in which the S.I. unit of current is defined?

10 Consider a long coil of wire (a solenoid) in which a current flows.

  a Sketch a diagram to show the magnetic field pattern produced by the current flowing in the solenoid.

  b What would happen to the strength of the magnetic field if the coil

   i had more turns per metre length?

   ii carried a larger current?

   iii had a smaller cross-sectional area?

  c State the equation for the magnetic flux density inside a solenoid of length l, with N turns, carrying a current I. Assume that there is only air inside the solenoid.

> PHYSICS FOR THE IB DIPLOMA: WORKBOOK

11 A solenoid of length 20 cm consists of 150 turns of thin wire wrapped around a hollow paper tube. If the solenoid carries a current of 30 mA, calculate the strength of the magnetic field produced at the

   a   centre of the solenoid along the central axis.

   b   edge of the solenoid along the central axis.

12 Suppose a charged particle of charge q moves through a distance l, with a speed v, in a direction that is perpendicular to a uniform magnetic field of strength B.

   a   What will the time it takes for the particle to travel the distance l be?

   b   What is the current caused by the moving charged particle?

   c   Since this current occurs over a length l, show that the force on the moving charged particle in the magnetic field is given by $F = B\,q\,v$.

   d   Now suppose that the charged particle moves at an angle, θ, to the magnetic field. How will the equation for the magnetic force it experiences differ from that given in **part c**?

13 An electron moves in a plane that is perpendicular to a uniform magnetic field of strength 0.5 T.

   a   If the electron moves with a speed of 2×10^6 ms^{-1}, calculate the magnetic force that the electron experiences.

   b   What can you say about the direction of this force?

   c   What will be the subsequent path of the electron?

14 An electron and a proton both travel at the same speed in a direction that is perpendicular to a uniform magnetic field. Suggest

   a   what the subsequent paths of the two particles have in common.

   b   how the two paths will differ.

Exercise 18.3 Electrical potential and electrical potential energy

1 Consider a point charge, Q, in a vacuum—or in air. (We can consider any effect of the air around the point charge to be almost exactly the same as any effect from a vacuum.)

   a   State the equation for the electric field strength E, at a radial distance r, from the point charge.

   b   So, at an inifinite distance from the point charge, what will the electric field strength be?

   Now suppose that we push a unit test charge from infinity towards the point charge Q.

c How does the force we have to apply to the test charge vary as we move the test charge towards the point charge, Q?

d Since we know that work done = force × distance, what is happening to the work we have to do whilst we are moving the test charge towards the point charge, Q?

e If we were to draw a graph of how the force we had to apply varies with distance from the point charge, Q, (i.e. a graph of E against r), what feature of the graph would show how much work we had to do to bring the test charge from infinity to a radial distance r from the point charge?

f Hence, show that the work done to bring a unit test charge from infinity to a distance r from a point charge, Q, is given by the expression work done = $k\frac{Q}{r}$.

g With what you learned from Chapter 17, how do we describe this work done?

h Does the test charge now have more, the same or less energy than it had when it was an infinite distance from Q?

i Suppose now we released the test charge from its position at a radial distance r, from the point charge, what would happen to the test charge?

j Now if we were to repeat the process of pushing a charge from infinity to a distance r from the point charge, but this time we use a charge $+q$, rather than a test charge, how much work must we now do?

k Hence, state the equation for

   i the electrical potential, V_e, at a radial distance, r, from a point charge, Q.

   ii the electrical potential energy, E_p, of a charge, q, at a radial distance, r, from a point charge, Q.

l In which units do we measure

   i electrical potential?

   ii electrical potential energy?

2 A uniform electric field is set with two parallel plates 4 cm apart. The top plate is connected to a supply kept at 50 V. The bottom plate is kept at a potential of 10 V.

   a Suppose a 1 C charge was sitting on the underside surface of the top plate. How much electrical potential energy would it have?

   b Suppose the 1 C charge sat on the upper side of the bottom plate. How much electrical potential energy would it have?

   c How much work would have to be done to move the 1 C charge from the bottom plate to the top plate?

   d In answering part c above, was it necessary to consider the *actual* path along which the 1 C charge would move?

3   a   Describe what is meant by an electrical equipotential.

    b   Figure 18.7 shows two electrical equipotentials in an electric field.

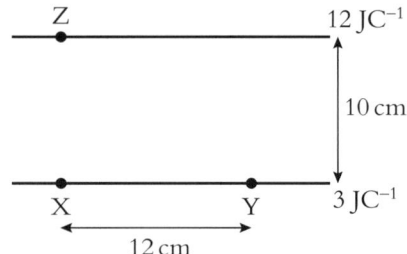

Figure 18.7

How much work must be done to move a 4 μC charge from

    i   point X to point Y.

    ii   point X to point Z.

    iii point Y to point Z.

    c   In **part b**, do your answers depend on

    i   the path taken?

    ii   the way in which the electric field varies (if at all) between the two equipotentials?

4   A small sphere is charged to a potential of −200 V.

    a   Sketch a diagram to show the electric field around the sphere.

    b   How does the electrical potential vary with increasing distance from the sphere?

    c   Add some equipotentials to represent your answer to **part c**.

    d   How does the separation of the equipotential lines relate to the electric field strength?

    e   What geometric relationship do the equipotentials have with the electric field lines?

5   Consider two identically charged spheres separated by a small distance.

    a   Sketch a diagram to show the electric field lines that define the shape of the electric field between and around the two spheres.

    b   Complete the diagram to show some equipotentials.

    c   How does your diagram help you to identify where the electric field strength is smallest?

6 Consider a small, positively charged sphere a small distance above a negatively charged metal plate.

   a Sketch a diagram to show the shape of the electric field between the sphere and the plate.

   b Add some equipotentials. (It is not necessary to give these equipotentials numerical values.)

7 Consider two oppositely charged spheres separated by a small distance. The charge on each sphere has the same magnitude but opposite sign.

   a Sketch a diagram to show the electric field lines that define the shape of the electric field between and around the two spheres.

   b Using your knowledge of the relationship between electric field lines and equipotentials, add some equipotentials to your diagram from **part a**.

   c How does your diagram help you to identify where the electric field strength is greatest?

8 Point X is 5 cm from a small, positively charged sphere of charge 6.0 mC. Point Y is 10 cm from the sphere.

   a Calculate the electrical potential difference between points X and Y.

   b Calculate the work required to move a charge of 2.0 μC from point Y to point X. (Assume that the charged sphere does not move.)

   c Suppose that the 2.0 μC charge has zero kinetic energy when it arrives at point Y. Suggest what will happen to the 2.0 μC charge.

9 a State the equation for the electrical force between a nucleus of charge Q and an electron of charge e, and mass m, about which it orbits at a radius r.

   b Show that the kinetic energy of the electron is $E_K = \frac{kQe}{2r}$.

   c Show that the total energy of the electron in its orbit around the nucleus is less than zero.

   d The total energy of an electron in its ground state in a hydrogen atom is -13.6 eV. Calculate the radius of the electron's orbit around the nucleus.

10 An electron in an excited energy level emits a photon and moves to a different orbit around the nucleus.

   a Has the total energy of the electron increased or decreased?

   b What has happened to the kinetic energy of the electron?

   c What has happened to the electrical potential energy of the electron?

   d Is its new orbit closer to the nucleus or further away from the nucleus?

11 In a radial electric field (such as that occurring around a small charged sphere), what is the relationship between the

   a   force, F, acting on a charge, q, and the field strength, E?

   b   electrical potential, V_E, and the electrical potential energy, E_p for a charge, q?

   c   electric field strength, E, and the electric potential, V_E?

   d   force, F, and the electrical potential energy, E_p?

12 Figure 18.8 shows the four quantities that are most important when considering electric fields:

   - force
   - field strength
   - potential
   - potential energy

Complete the diagram to show

   - the equations for each quantity.
   - the mathematical relationships between the quantities.

Two mathematical relationships and one equation have been entered for you.

This will provide you with an easy-to-see revision of the main ideas you have met in Sections 17.1 and 17.3.

TIP

You should try to make sure that you know all the details on this diagram.

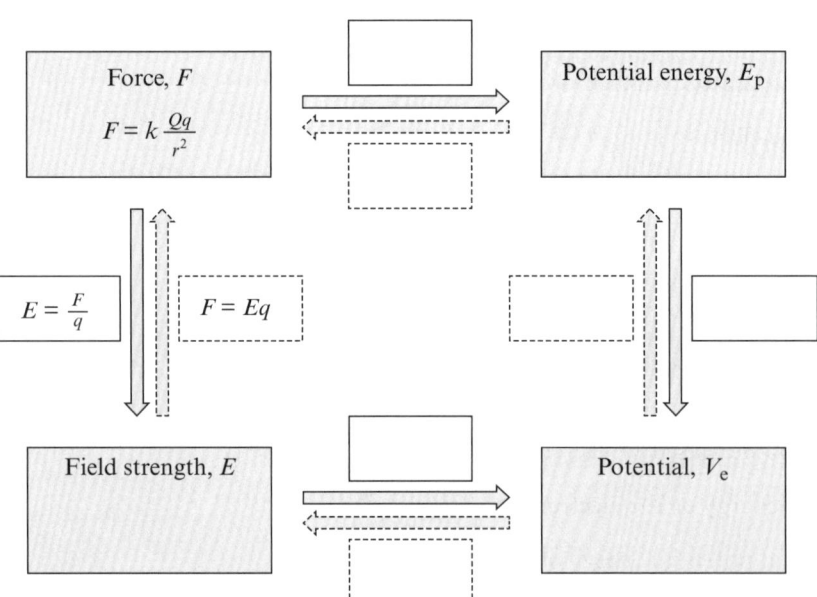

Figure 18.8

18 Electric and magnetic fields

EXAM-STYLE QUESTIONS

Multiple-choice questions

1. Which of the following statements about a charged sphere is true?
   A The electrical potential inside the sphere is zero everywhere.
   B The electrical potential inside the sphere is a non-zero constant everywhere.
   C The electrical potential inside the sphere varies linearly with distance from the centre of the sphere.
   D The electrical potential inside the sphere varies inversely with distance from the centre of the sphere.

2. Which of the following statements about electrical equipotentials is **incorrect**?
   A A charged particle experiences the same force anywhere on an equipotential.
   B An equipotential is always perpendicular to a field line.
   C No work is done against the field when a charged particle moves along an equipotential.
   D A charged particle possesses the same amount of energy anywhere on an equipotential.

3. A test charge is located inside the electric field produced by a pair of oppositely charged metal plates. Which of the following combinations best describes how the force on the test charge and the electrical potential energy (E_p) of the test charge vary with its distance from one of the plates?
   A Force = constant; E_p = constant
   B Force = constant; E_p = proportional to distance from one plate
   C Force = proportional to distance from one plate; E_p = constant
   D Force = proportional to distance from one plate; E_p = proportional to distance from one plate

4. Which of the following descriptions best describes the electrical field strength inside a hollow sphere?
   A The electrical field strength is zero everywhere inside.
   B The electric field strength is proportional to the radial distance from the centre of the sphere.
   C The electrical field strength is a non-zero constant everywhere inside the sphere.
   D The electrical field strength is inversely proportional to the square of the distance from the centre of the sphere.

5. Two identical point charges, each of charge q, are separated by a distance r. When r is decreased, the electrical potential energy between the two charges is doubled. Which of the following correctly gives the change to the repulsive force, F, experienced by each of the point charges?
   A F halves.
   B F stays the same.
   C F doubles.
   D F quadruples.

6. A pair of parallel charged plates have a potential difference between them of 200 V and are separated by a distance of 4.0 cm. A charged particle moving from the top plate to the bottom plate gains 4 nJ of kinetic energy. If the two plates are now moved so that their separation is 6.0 cm, the kinetic energy gained by a similarly charged particle in moving from the top plate to the bottom plate will be
   A 2 nJ.
   B 3 nJ.
   C 4 nJ.
   D 6 nJ.

CONTINUED

7 A horizontal wire of length 40 cm carries a current of 1.5 A. Around the wire is a magnetic field of strength 8×10^{-2} T at right angles to the direction of the current. The wire is suspended in mid-air. Taking $g = 9.81$ Nkg^{-1}, the best estimate of the mass of the wire is

A 3.3×10^{-3} kg.

B 4.9×10^{-3} kg.

C 8.2×10^{-3} kg.

D 12.3×10^{-3} kg.

8 Figure 18.9 shows a positively charged particle approaching the poles of a horseshoe magnet.

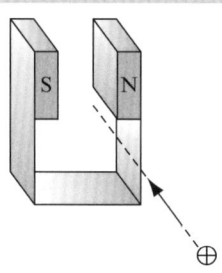

Figure 18.9

When the particle enters the region between the magnetic poles, it will be deflected

A vertically upwards.

B vertically downwards.

C towards the north pole of the magnet.

D towards the south pole of the magnet.

9 A charge, q, is accelerated from one equipotential to another in a time t. If the potential difference between the two equipotentials is V, and they are separated by a distance d, which of the following gives the increase in the particle's kinetic energy?

A qV

B qVd

C $\frac{qVd}{t}$

D $\frac{qV}{d}$

10 A pair of parallel plates, separated by a distance d, are maintained with a potential difference between them of V. A charge, q, placed mid-way between the two plates experiences a force given by

A $\frac{1}{2}qV$.

B qV.

C $\frac{qV}{2d}$.

D $\frac{qV}{d}$.

CONTINUED

11 Which of the following gives an appropriate unit for electric field strength?

   A V
   B NV^{-1}
   C NC^{-1}
   D VC^{-1}

12 Two charged parallel plates, with a constant potential difference between them, are separated by a distance d. Which of the following four graphs correctly shows the relationship between the electric field strength, E, between the two plates and the separation of the plates, d?

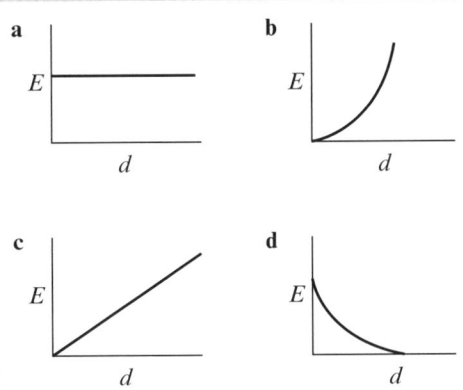

Figure 18.10

Short-answer questions

13 Figure 18.11 shows two charged metal plates, 30 mm apart. The top plate is connected to a supply of +300 V. The bottom plate is earthed (its potential is kept at 0 V).

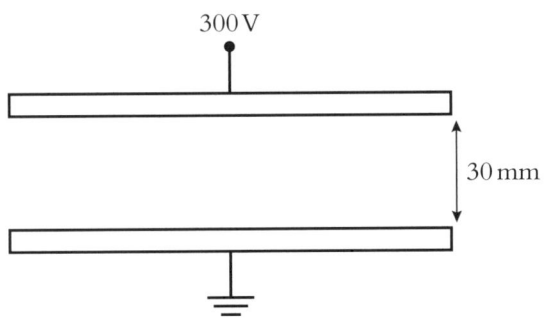

Figure 18.11

   a Calculate the electric field strength between the two plates. [2]
   b Add some electric field lines to show the shape of the electric field between the plates. [1]
   c An electron is placed into the region between the plates. Calculate the force it would experience. [1]
   d In which direction would this force be? [1]

CONTINUED

14 Two parallel metal plates, 20 cm apart, are connected to a power supply. One plate is held at a potential of 100 V. The other is held at a potential of 0 V.

   a Calculate the electric field strength between the two plates. [2]

   b Calculate the electrical force on a charge of 6 μC if it is positioned between the plates. [1]

   c Calculate the work done to move the 6 μC charge from the 0 V plate to the 100 V plate. [2]

15 In a hydrogen atom, an electron orbits around a proton at a radial distance of 5.3×10^{-11} m. (Data: Mass of electron = 9.1×10^{-31} kg; charge on an electron = -1.6×10^{-19} C; charge on a proton = 1.6×10^{-19} C; Coulomb constant, $k = 9 \times 10^9$ Nm^{2}C^{-2})

Calculate

   a the force exerted on the electron by the proton. [2]

   b the centripetal acceleration of the electron. [1]

   c the linear speed of the electron in its orbit. [2]

16 Figure 18.12 shows a unit test charge equally distant from two equally charged point charges, each of charge Q.

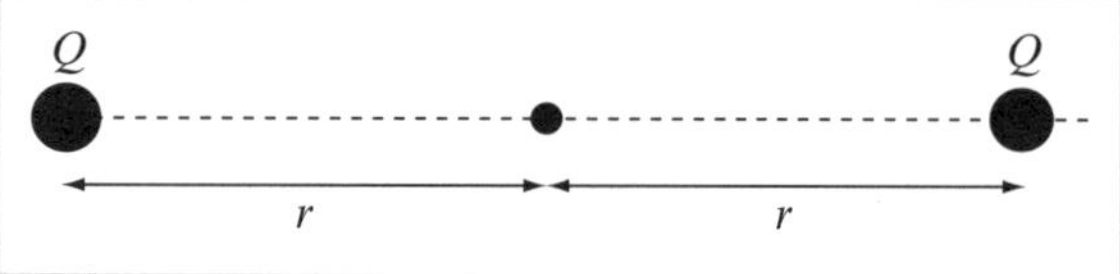

Figure 18.12

   a Show that the net force on the test charge is zero. [2]

   b Determine an expression for the electrical potential, V_e, at the position of the unit charge. [1]

   c If the test charge is now displaced a small distance along the dotted line, discuss what the likely future motion of the test charge will be. [3]

17 A student makes a solenoid from some thin wire by wrapping 20 turns around a hollow paper tube of length 10 cm so that all the paper tube is covered by the wire. The student then attaches the solenoid to a battery which allows a current of 50 mA to flow through the solenoid.

   a Calculate the magnetic field strength inside the centre of the solenoid. [2]

      ($\mu_o = 4\pi \times 10^{-7}$ TmA^{-1})

   b State how the magnetic flux density will differ, if at all, at the two ends of the solenoid, compared to at its centre. [1]

   c The student notices that when the current is flowing in the solenoid, the individual turns of the solenoid move closer together. Explain the student's observation. [2]

CONTINUED

18 A copper conductor of length 1.0 m and cross-sectional area 1.0 mm² carries a current of 1.0 A in a direction that is perpendicular to a magnetic field of flux density 2×10^{-5} T. Electrons carry a charge of -1.6×10^{-19} C, and the free electron number density, n, in copper is 8.4×10^{28} m^{-3}.

  a From the definition of B, state the size of the magnetic force exerted by the magnetic field on the current-carrying conductor. [1]

  b Calculate the total number of free electrons in the copper conductor. [2]

  c If each free electron in the conductor is moving with a speed of 7.44×10^{-5} ms^{-1} along the conductor, show that the total force exerted on all of the electrons in the conductor is equal to the answer to **part a**. [2]

19 Electric field strength, E, and gravitational field strength, g, are both examples of the inverse-square law.

  a Explain what an inverse-square law is. [2]

  b Suggest a simple arithmetic test to check whether two variables, X and Y, are related by an inverse-square law. [2]

  c Measurements of two variables, X and Y, are shown in the table.

X	2.0	4.0	6.0	8.0	10.0	12.0
Y	302	76	34	19	12	8

  Carry out an arithmetic test to see if the two variables are related by an inverse-square law. [2]

> Chapter 19
Motion in electric and magnetic fields

CHAPTER OUTLINE

In this chapter, you will:

- explore the motion of a charged particle in an electric field.

- compare the motion of a charged particle in a uniform electric field with the motion of a mass in a uniform gravitational field.

- solve problems associated with the distance of closest approach.

- explore the motion of a charged particle in an magnetic field.

- consider the path taken by a charged particle in perpendicularly orientated electric and magnetic fields.

KEY TERM

distance of closest approach: the distance at which a charged particle moving directly towards another similarly-charged particle comes to rest (the distance at which the E_K of the charged particle is zero, all its energy being E_P)

Exercise 19.1 Motion in an electric field

1 Consider a pair of parallel plates, separated by a distance of 4.0 cm, across which there is a potential difference of 12 V. A charged particle of charge 4 mC, and mass 1.5×10^{-3} kg, is placed immediately next to one of the plates so that the electric field between the plates will accelerate the point charge towards the other plate.

    a i Calculate the electric field strength between the two plates.

        ii Hence, determine the acceleration of the charged particle.

        iii Hence, determine the time it will take for the charged particle to reach the other plate.

        iv Hence, determine the speed of the charged particle just before it hits the other plate.

        v Hence, determine the kinetic energy of the charged particle just before it hits the other plate.

b **i** How much work will the electric field do on the charged particle in moving it from one plate to the other?

  ii Compare and comment on your answer to **parts a v** and **b i**.

2 Now suppose that a particle of mass m, and charge $+q$, moving with a horizontal velocity v_h, enters a vertically orientated uniform electric field, as shown in Figure 19.1.

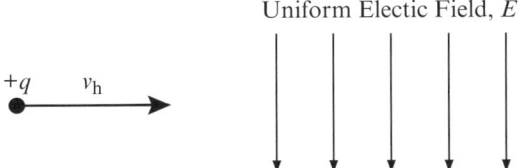

Figure 19.1

a How will v_h be affected when the charged particle enters the electric field? Explain your answer.

b In which direction will the charged particle experience an electric force?

c Write an equation for the vertical velocity of the charged particle, v_v, as a function of time, t, for the time that the charged particle is in the electric field.

d Hence, write an expression for the speed of the charged particle as a function of time, t, for the time that the charged particle is in the electric field.

e Write another expression in vector format (i.e. as two components x and y) for the displacement of the charged particle as a function of time, t, during the time it is in the electric field.

f What shape will the trajectory of the charged particle be during its time in the electric field?

g Discuss the similarity between the motion of the charged particle in the uniform electric field with that of a mass set moving horizontally in a uniform gravitational field.

3 An electron of charge -1.6×10^{-19} C and mass 9.1×10^{-31} kg, moving with a horizontal speed 6.0 Mms^{-1}, approaches a pair of parallel charged plates, of length 30 cm, separated by a distance of 5.0 cm, as shown in Figure 19.2. The potential difference between the two plates is 6 V.

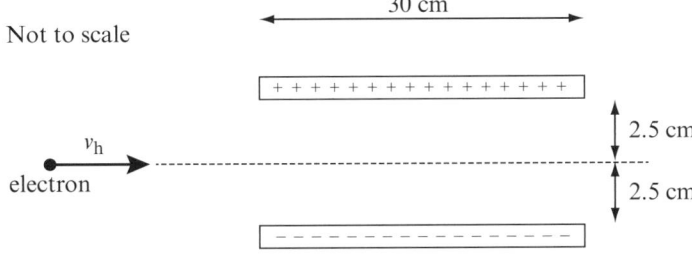

Figure 19.2

Determine whether the electron will be able to pass through the pair of charged parallel plates.

4 Consider a charged particle, q, moving towards another, much larger charged particle, $50q$, with an initial kinetic energy, E_K, as shown in Figure 19.3. The direction along which the q charge is moving is displaced from the horizontal line passing through the centre of the $50q$ charge by a distance, x. In this question, you may assume that the $50q$ charge does not move.

Figure 19.3

a By considering the direction of the electrical force that the $50q$ charge will exert on the q charge, sketch a diagram to show the trajectory of the q charge as it approaches and then recedes from the $50q$ charge. Label this trajectory a.

b Now repeat **part a**, but this time allow the distance, x, to be smaller than it was previously. Label your new trajectory b. Explain your drawings.

c Now consider the case when the value of x is zero; that is the 1 charge is heading directly towards the centre of the $50q$ charge. Sketch the trajectory of the q charge. Label this trajectory c.

d Does what you have drawn for the answers to **parts a–c** remind you of a famous historical physics experiment? Which one?

e Outline what is happening to the kinetic energy of the q charge in each of the **parts a–c**.

f In **part c**, you should have realised that at some position near to the $50q$ charge, the q charge will have zero kinetic energy. What is this position called?

g How would your drawings in **parts a–c** differ, if the initial E_K of the q charge is

   i   smaller?

   ii larger?

5 A proton of charge 1.6×10^{-19} C approaches the nucleus of a nitrogen atom head-on, with an initial kinetic energy of 1.6×10^{-14} J. The charge on the nitrogen nucleus is 1.12×10^{-18} C, $k = 9 \times 10^9$ Nm^{2}C^{-2}.

Calculate the distance of closest approach for the proton and the nitrogen nucleus. Assume that the nitrogen nucleus does not move.

Exercise 19.2 Motion in a magnetic field

1   When a charged particle of mass m, and charge q, moving in a magnetic field of magnetic flux density B, perpendicularly to the direction of the field at a velocity v, the charged particle experiences a magnetic force F_m.

   a   Give the equation for the magnitude of the magnetic force, F_m, in terms of B, v and q.

   b   Give the direction of the magnetic force, F_m, relative to

      i B.

      ii v.

   c   How does your answer to **part b ii** confirm that the charged particle will follow a circular path?

   d   Deduce an expression for the radius, r, of the circular path.

   e   What happens to the radius of the circular path if

      i m increases?

      ii v increases?

      iii B increases?

      iv q increases?

2   A proton (of mass 1.67×10^{-27} kg) and an electron (of mass 9.1×10^{-31} kg) both travelling at 5.0×10^6 ms^{-1} enter a magnetic field at right angles to the field's direction. The proton and the electron have opposite charges of $+1.6 \times 10^{-19}$ C and -1.6×10^{-19} C, respectively. The magnetic field has a magnetic flux density of 4 mT.

   a   Calculate the size of the magnetic force on

      i   the proton.

      ii   the electron.

   b   Hence, calculate the radius of the circular path in the magnetic field that will be followed by

      i   the proton.

      ii   the electron.

   c   Determine the time it takes to make one complete circle for

      i   the proton.

      ii   the electron.

d   In another example, using the same magnetic field as previously, the electron and the proton now enter the magnetic field with a velocity of 1.0×10^7 ms^{-1} (i.e. double their previous velocities).

    i   How will the new magnetic force on each particle differ from previously?

    ii How will the new radii of the two paths differ from previously?

    iii How will the time to make one complete circle for each of the particles differ from before?

    iv Derive an expression for the time taken for one complete circle in terms of B, q and m.

    v   What do you notice about the relationship between v and the time to complete a circle?

3   The idea of a constant time period of circular motion is exploited in a cyclotron, which is a kind of particle accelerator.

Consider Figure 19.4, which shows two semi-circular regions, called 'dees' (shaded in grey) in both of which there is the same-sized, strong, uniform magnetic field, B.

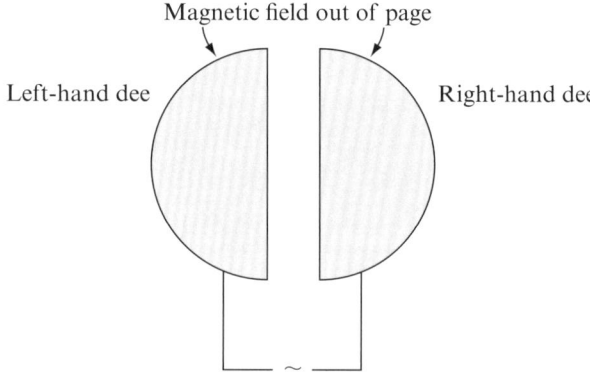

Figure 19.4

a   Suppose that the left-hand dee has an electrical potential of $2V$, and the right-hand dee has an electrical potential of V. If a charged particle of charge q were able to leave the left-hand dee, how much kinetic energy would it gain by the time it arrived at the right-hand dee?

b   Once the charged particle enters the right-hand dee, what shape of path will it follow?

c   After a short time, the charged particle will arrive at the flat edge of the right-hand dee. Suppose that just at this moment, the potentials of the two dees can be swapped over (so that now the left-hand dee has a potential of V and the right-hand dee has a potential of $2V$). What will happen to the charged particle as it leaves the right-hand dee and travels towards the left-hand dee? What has happened to its speed?

d   When the charged particle enters the left-hand dee again, it will, again, follow the same kind of path as it had in the right-hand dee, but what aspect(s) of its path will be different to the path it followed in the right-hand dee?

e   Now, suppose that the processes occurring in **parts a–d** are repeated many times. Describe what the overall shape of the charged particle's path will be as it moves from one dee to the other many times.

f   i   Where, with respect to the two dees, should the charged particle, q, be introduced into the cyclotron?

    ii Once the charged particle has gained the kinetic energy it requires, where, with respect to the two dees, will it be ejected from the cyclotron?

g   The changing of the potentials of the two dees is done by using an alternating voltage supply. Explain briefly why the frequency of such an alternating supply does not need to change as the charged particle travels from one dee to the other many times.

Exercise 19.3 Motion in perpendicularly orientated electric and magnetic fields

1   Consider a charged particle of charge q, moving with speed v, and entering into the electric field produced by a pair of parallel plates, d apart, between which there is a potential difference of V as shown in Figure 19.5.

Figure 19.5

a   i   On a copy of Figure 19.5, add some electric field lines to show the direction and shape of the electric field between the two parallel plates.

    ii Give an expression for the electrical force acting on the charged particle, q.

    iii Explain why this force will not change the horizontal speed, v, of the charged particle.

b   Suppose that in the region between the two parallel plates, there is also a uniform magnetic field, B, that is directed perpendicularly to v.

    i   Give an expression for the magnetic force that will be exerted on the charged particle because of its horizontal motion.

ii Suppose further that this magnetic force acts in the opposite direction to the electric force from **part a ii**. Describe the orientation of the magnetic field necessary to produce such a magnetic force on the charged particle.

c Now suppose that the charged particle is in dynamic equilibrium whilst it is between the two parallel plates.

i Explain what is meant by the term *dynamic equilibrium*.

ii Hence, describe the path that the charged particle will follow whilst between the two parallel plates.

iii Deduce an expression for the strength of the magnetic field, B, required to ensure a dynamic equilibrium of the charged particle.

iv Explain why protons and electrons of the same speed will both be able to travel along the same path through perpendicularly orientated electric and magnetic fields such as in this question.

2 In a region of space, an electric field, produced by a pair of parallel plates attached to a voltage supply, is set up together with a perpendicular magnetic field, such that a charged particle, of mass m and charge q, entering the region, will pass **without** any deflection. This is shown in Figure 19.6.

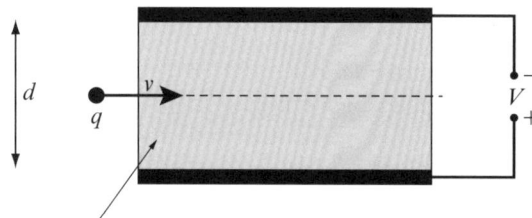

Region of magnetic field, B

Figure 19.6

For each of the following changes to the set-up, state and explain what the resulting deflection (if any) of the charged particle will be:

a V is increased.

b d is increased.

c v is increased.

d q is increased.

e m is increased.

f B is increased.

3 With reference to the experimental set-up shown in Figure 19.6, and using the data given here, determine if the charged particle entering the region of perpendicularly orientated electric and magnetic fields will be undeflected from its initial path.

Data: $V = 80$ V, $v = 4 \times 10^7$ ms^{-1}, $d = 40$ cm and $B = 5.0$ μT

19 Motion in electric and magnetic fields

EXAM-STYLE QUESTIONS

Multiple-choice questions

1. A charged particle enters perpendicularly into a magnetic field, where it will experience a magnetic force. Which of the following quantities will change as a result of the magnetic force acting on the charged particle?
   - A speed of the charged particle
   - B velocity of the charged particle
   - C kinetic energy of the charged particle
   - D all three of the above

2. A moving charged particle enters a magnetic field at right angles to the direction of the field. Which of the following statements about the charged particle's kinetic energy is false?
   - A The E_K remains constant because no work is done on the charged particle by the magnetic field.
   - B The E_K remains constant because the force exerted on the charged particle by the magnetic field is always perpendicular to the velocity.
   - C The E_K remains constant because the speed of the charged particle remains constant.
   - D The E_K remains constant because the velocity of the charged particle remains constant.

3. When a charged particle moves in a circular path within a uniform magnetic field, which of the graphs in Figure 19.7 correctly shows the relationship between the radius, r, of the circular path and p, the momentum of the particle?

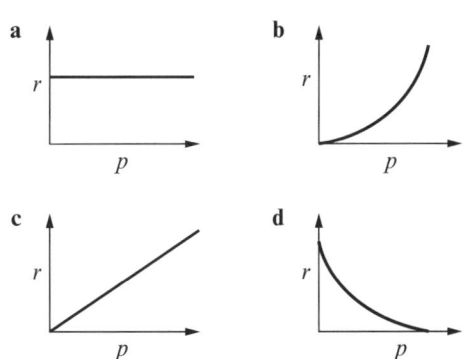

Figure 19.7

4. A charged particle, of mass m and charge q, moving horizontally at a speed v, enters a region between two charged parallel plates of length l, between which there is a uniform electric field of strength E in the vertical direction. Which of the following statements is **not** correct?
   - A It will take a time of $\frac{l}{v}$ for the charged particle to pass through the parallel plates.
   - B Whilst between the parallel plates, the charged particle will have an acceleration of $\frac{Eq}{m}$.
   - C Whilst between the parallel plates, the charged particle will follow a parabolic path.
   - D Whilst between the parallel plates, the angle between the charged particle's velocity and the electric force acting on it is always 90°.

CONTINUED

5   Figure 19.8 shows a charged particle, of charge q and mass m, entering the region between a pair of charged parallel plates at a speed v.

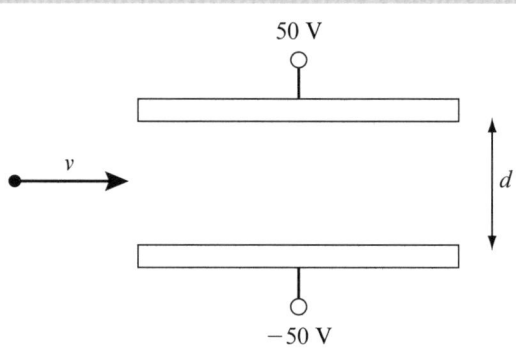

Figure 19.8

Which of the following, by itself, will **not** increase the acceleration of the particle whilst it is between the plates?

A   Increasing v

B   Increasing q

C   Decreasing m

D   Decreasing d

6   A charged particle, of mass m and charge q, moves at a speed v, perpendicular to a magnetic field of magnetic flux density B. Its subsequent path is circular. Which of the following gives the radius, r, of the circular path?

A $\frac{Bqv}{m}$

B $\frac{Bq}{mv}$

C $\frac{mv}{Bq}$

D $\frac{m}{Bqv}$

7   A magnetic field of strength B exerts a force on a charge, q, moving with a speed v, to make the charge move in a circular path of radius r. Which of the following statements about the time it takes for the charge to make one complete circle, T, is true?

A T depends on B, q and m only.

B T depends on B, q, m and v only.

C T depends on B, q, m, v and r.

D T depends on B, v and r only.

CONTINUED

8 Charged particles of mass m and charge q, moving with a speed v, enter a magnetic field of magnetic flux density B, perpendicularly. Inside the magnetic field, the particles move with a circular path of radius r. Which of the following changes would, by itself, increase the radius of the circular path?

- **A** Increasing q
- **B** Increasing m
- **C** Increasing B
- **D** Decreasing v

9 Charged particles enter, perpendicularly, uniform electric and uniform magnetic fields. Which of the following correctly describes the shape of the path taken by the charged particle in the field?

	Uniform electric field	Uniform magnetic field
A	Circular	Circular
B	Circular	Parabolic
C	Parabolic	Circular
D	Parabolic	Parabolic

Short-answer questions

10 Figure 19.9 shows the path of an alpha particle as it passes nearby a gold nucleus.

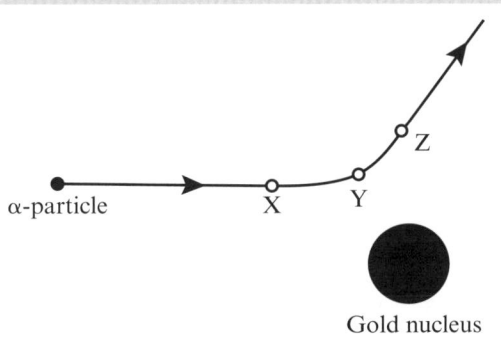

Figure 19.9

- **a** **i** Draw three arrows on Figure 19.9 to show the direction of the electrical force acting on the alpha particle at the positions X, Y and Z. [1]
  - **ii** In which position, X, Y or Z, is the acceleration of the alpha particle greatest? [1]
- **b** Describe what is happening to the speed of the alpha particle as it moves along the path shown. [2]
- **c** Calculate the magnitude of the electrical force exerted on the alpha particle at the position Y if Y is 2.0×10^{-13} m from the gold nucleus. ($q_\alpha = 3.2 \times 10^{-19}$ C, $Q_{au} = 1.26 \times 10^{-17}$ C, $k = 9 \times 10^9$ Nm^{2}C^{-2}) [2]

CONTINUED

11 A solar wind proton of charge 1.6×10^{-19} C moving at 3.0×10^6 ms^{-1} enters perpendicularly into a region of Earth's magnetic field where the value of the magnetic flux density is 4.0×10^{-6} T.

    a Calculate the magnetic force exerted on the proton by the Earth's magnetic field. [2]

    b Calculate the acceleration of the proton. ($m_{proton} = 1.67 \times 10^{-27}$ kg) [1]

    c Calculate the radius of the proton's circular motion. [2]

12 An alpha particle of mass 6.64×10^{-27} kg and charge 3.2×10^{-19} C travels at a speed of 2×10^7 ms^{-1} directly towards the nucleus of a gold atom, of charge 1.26×10^{-17} C.

    a Show that the kinetic energy of the alpha particle is about 8.3 MeV. (1 eV = 1.6×10^{-19} J) [2]

    b Determine the alpha particle's distance of closest approach to the gold nucleus. [3]

13 Figure 19.10 shows an evacuated circular tube inside which protons can be made to travel in circular paths, such as the one shown. The whole of the tube is subject to a uniform magnetic field, which is directed into the page.

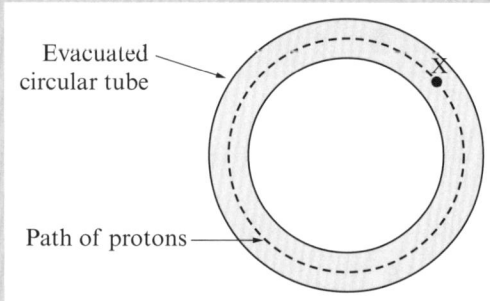

Figure 19.10

    a Add to Figure 19.10 two arrows, one each to show

        i the direction of the instantaneous velocity of a proton at the point X (label this v).

        ii the direction of the magnetic force on the proton (label this F). [2]

    b If the protons move with a speed of 2.88×10^5 ms^{-1} and the magnetic flux density of the field is 3 mT, deduce a value for the specific charge of a proton if the radius of its circular path is 1 m. [2]

    c If the protons were exchanged for electrons moving with the same speed, and with the same magnetic field, state how the radius of the electrons' paths would differ from those of the protons. [1]

CONTINUED

14 A uniform electric field, produced between a pair of parallel plates connected to a voltage supply, is combined with a perpendicular magnetic field, as shown in Figure 19.11. It is observed that when alpha particles, of charge $+3.2 \times 10^{-19}$ C, enter the region, as shown, they are not deflected from their initial paths.

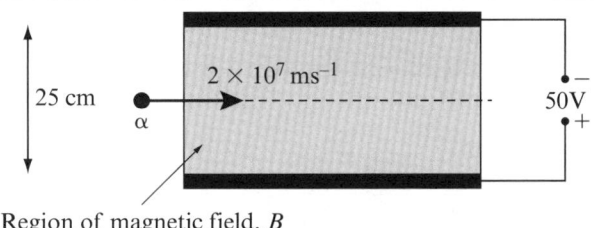

Figure 19.11

a   State the direction of the magnetic field. [1]

b   Show that the electric force acting on the alpha particle is 6.4×10^{-17} N. [2]

c   Hence, determine the strength of the magnetic field required to maintain an undeflected path for the alpha particles. [2]

> Chapter 20
Electromagnetic induction

CHAPTER OUTLINE

In this chapter, you will:

> learn about magnetic flux and magnetic flux linkage.

> identify situations when magnetic flux changes and when an emf can be induced.

> solve problems using Faraday's laws of electromagnetic induction.

> learn Lenz's law and how to apply it in different situations.

> link Lenz's law with the conservation of energy.

> explore the nature of a transformer.

> learn how an alternating current can be produced in a generator.

> consider the effect on an induced emf of changing the frequency of a generator.

KEY TERMS

electromagnetic induction: when the magnetic flux linked to a conductor changes in any way, an electromotive force (emf) is induced in the conductor

magnetic flux, Φ: The product of the magnetic flux density, B, and the perpendicular area, A, through which it passes: $F = BA$

$\Phi = BA \cos \theta$,

where Φ is the magnetic flux, B is the magnetic flux density, A is the area through which the magnetic flux passes and θ is the angle between the magnetic flux density and the normal to the area

magnetic flux linkage: $N\Phi$: the product of the magnetic flux, Φ, and the number of turns, N, of a conductor

Faraday's laws: there are actually two of these, although they are often combined into only one concept:

- an induced emf will occur in any conductor linked with a changing magnetic flux

> **CONTINUED**
>
> - the magnitude of the induced emf is proportional to the rate of change of magnetic flux linkage
>
> $$\varepsilon \propto N \frac{d\Phi}{dt}$$
>
> **Lenz's law:** the direction of the induced emf is such that its effect is to oppose the original magnetic flux change (this shows itself as a minus sign in the equation)
>
> $$\varepsilon = -N \frac{d\Phi}{dt}$$
>
> **alternating voltage:** A time-dependent voltage, which varies between positive and negative values (usually a sinusoidal variation)
>
> **alternating current, AC:** a time-dependent current, which varies between positive and negative values (usually a sinusoidal variation)
>
> **transformer:** an electromagnetic device that is able to change an alternating electrical supply from one potential difference to another; a **step-up** transformer produces a larger potential difference than it is supplied with, and a **step-down** transformer produces a smaller potential difference than it is supplied with
>
> $$\frac{\varepsilon_s}{\varepsilon_p} = \frac{N_s}{N_p} = \frac{I_p}{I_s}$$

Exercise 20.1 Electromagnetic induction

1 A wire, connected to a centre-zero galvanometer, can be moved through a magnetic field, as in Figure 20.1.

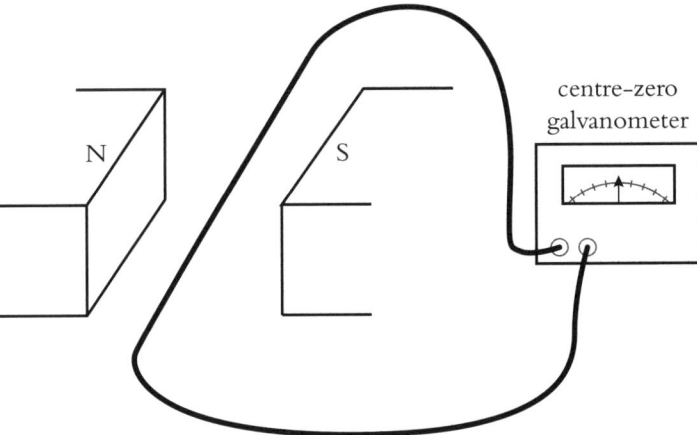

Figure 20.1

a   Describe what you would expect to see on the galvanometer when the wire is moved vertically downwards through the magnetic field.

b   The wire is moved vertically upwards through the magnetic field, at the same speed as in **part a**. Describe what you would see on the galvanometer.

c   Describe what you would expect to see on the galvanometer when the wire is moved horizontally, from left to right, in the magnetic field.

d   How will your answers to **parts a** and **b** differ if the wire is moved more quickly?

e   If the wire remains stationary in the magnetic field, what would you expect to see on the galvanometer?

2   A metal conductor, such as a copper wire, contains a large number of free electrons. The conductor is moved through a magnetic field in a direction perpendicular to the magnetic field lines, as shown in Figure 20.2.

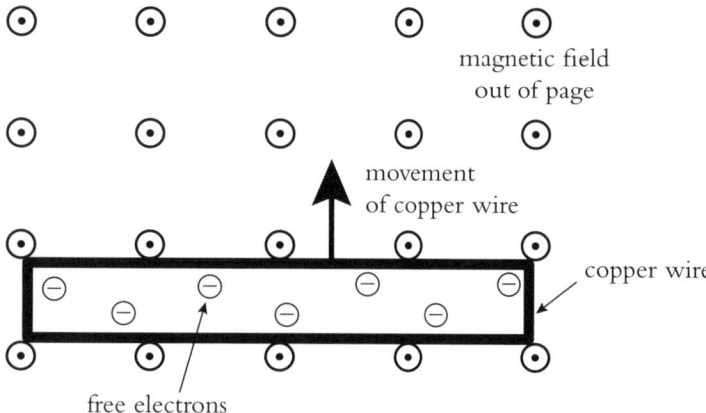

Figure 20.2

a   A force acts on each of the free electrons. In which direction?

b   Since the electrons are free to move, what will happen in the conductor?

c   Will there be an electric field across the ends of the conductor? Explain your answer.

d   When the free electrons in the conductor are in equilibrium, what can you say about the magnetic force and the electrical force acting on them?

e   Derive an equation for the potential difference ΔV across the ends of the conductor, length l.

3   A conductor of length 12 cm is moved perpendicularly through a magnetic field of strength 4.0×10^{-2} T at a speed of 2.0 ms^{-1}. Show that the emf generated across the ends of the conductor is 9.6 mV.

4   Calculate the emf produced when a wire of length 5.0 cm is moved perpendicularly through a magnetic field of strength 0.14 T at a speed of 60 cms^{-1}.

5 A wire of length 25 cm is moved at a speed of 1.5 ms⁻¹ through a magnetic field of strength 0.3 T at an angle θ to the field lines. The emf generated across the ends of the wire is 97 mV. Determine the angle, θ.

6 State what is meant by *magnetic flux* and *magnetic flux linkage*.

7 At the UK Olympic Hockey Centre in London, a hockey pitch measures 91.4 m × 55.0 m. The Earth's magnetic field has strength 4.87×10^{-5} T and is in a direction 24° from the vertical. Calculate the value of the magnetic flux linked with the hockey pitch.

8 Faraday's laws of electromagnetic induction may be expressed by the equation $\varepsilon \propto N \frac{d\Phi}{dt}$.

    a Explain what each of the terms in this equation is.

    b If $\Phi = BA$, expand the equation so that Faraday's laws have two terms for ε.

    c How does this suggest that there are two ways of inducing an emf? Outline these two ways.

9 When a length of wire, connected to a galvanometer, is allowed to fall perpendicularly through a constant horizontal magnetic field, a current flows in the wire.

    a Explain why there is a current in the wire.

    b Current needs energy to flow. Where does the energy come from?

    c What do you think happened to the speed of the wire's movement when it entered the magnetic field?

10 a State Lenz's law.

    b Which of the conservation laws is Lenz's law an example of?

11 A bar magnet moves towards a coil of wire. The ends of the coil of wire are connected to a galvanometer.

    a What happens in the coil as the north pole of the magnet approaches it?

    b The coil behaves like an electromagnet. Which pole, north or south, will the nearest end of the coil to the north pole of the magnet have? Explain your answer using Lenz's law.

12   A solenoid is connected in series to a resistor, a d.c. power supply of negligible internal resistance and a simple switch. An oscilloscope is connected across the resistor so that the current flowing through the solenoid/resistor circuit can be observed as a function of time. The trace observed on the oscilloscope screen is shown in Figure 20.3.

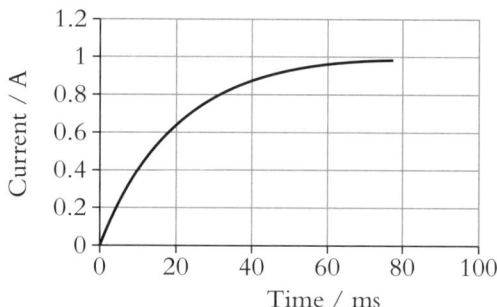

Figure 20.3

a   Suggest why the current flowing through the solenoid does not immediately rise to 1.0 A.

b   If the solenoid is replaced with another solenoid of similar dimensions but twice the number of turns, what would you expect to see on the oscilloscope trace?

13   The 'jumping ring' demonstration consists of a large coil connected to an a.c. supply by a push switch. An iron rod passes through the centre of the coil, protruding upwards. A small aluminium ring is placed over the iron rod, as shown in Figure 20.4.

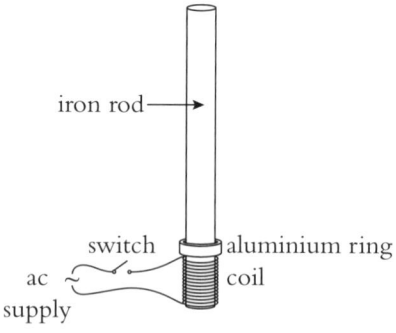

Figure 20.4

When the push switch is pressed, the aluminium ring jumps upwards (1 or 2 m) and leaves the iron rod.

a   What happens to the iron rod when the a.c. supply is switched on?

b   What happens in the aluminium ring when the a.c. supply is switched on?

c   What does Lenz's law suggest will happen?

d Explain why the aluminium ring jumps upwards.

e If the aluminium ring is placed over the iron rod *after* the supply has been switched on, the ring floats mid-way along the iron rod rather than jumping upwards. Suggest why this happens.

f If the aluminium ring is not a complete circle (as in Figure 20.4), what would happen when the supply is switched on?

14 Figure 20.5 shows three examples of a single conducting coil moving relative to a magnetic field.

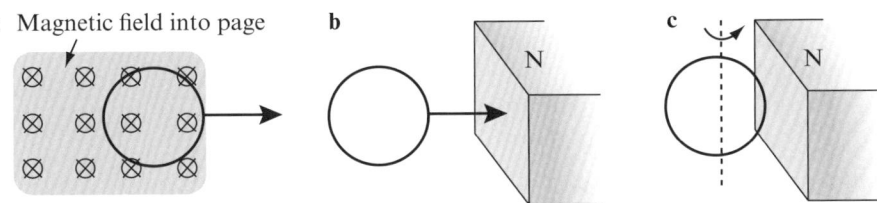

Figure 20.5

For each of the three examples, deduce if there is an induced current in the coil and, if so, the direction of the induced current in the coil.

Exercise 20.2 Generators and alternating current

1 Figure 20.6 shows a single conducting coil, ABCD, in the uniform magnetic field, B, between two opposing poles of similar bar magnets. The coil is free to rotate clockwise about the dotted-line axis, as shown.

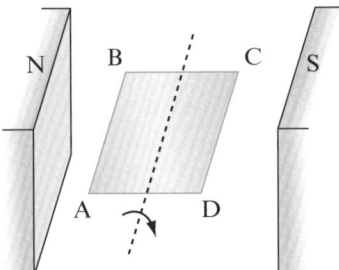

Figure 20.6

a Suppose that the coil starts in the position shown in Figure 20.6 and rotates clockwise 1 complete rotation with a constant angular frequency of ω. Sketch a graph to show how the magnetic flux linked with the coil varies during the rotation.

b If the area enclosed by the coil is A, write an equation for the magnetic flux linkage as a function of time.

c   Because the magnetic flux linked with the coil is changing, an emf will be induced in the coil. For each of the following pairs of points, state whether there is an induced emf and the direction in which this emf will cause a current to flow.

   i   A and B

   ii   B and C

   iii   C and D

   iv   D and A

d   i   Now, using Faraday's law of electromagnetic induction, write an equation for the induced emf in the coil.

   ii   What is the maximum induced emf?

   iii   Using the same time axis as in your answer for **part a**, sketch a graph to show how the induced emf varies with time during the rotation of the coil.

   iv   What is the phase difference between the magnetic flux linkage and the induced emf?

e   How best might one describe this as a generator?

2   A simple a.c. generator produces a sinusoidally varying emf, as shown in Figure 20.7.

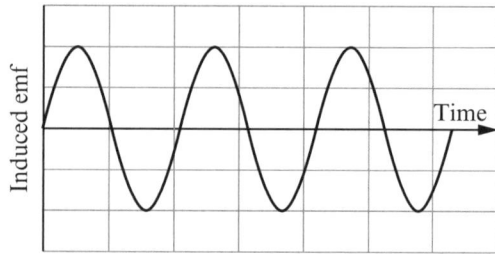

Figure 20.7

Suppose that the generator is now made to rotate with an angular frequency that is double the original rate. On the same axes as those of Figure 20.7, sketch a graph to show how the new emf will vary with time.

3   A peak induced emf of 60 V is generated by rotating a 200-turn coil at an angular frequency of 30π radians s^{-1}. What will the peak induced emf be if the coil

   a   is rotated at an angular frequency of 60π radians s^{-1}.

   b   is replaced by a similar dimension coil with 150 turns?

4 The induced emf, ε, from a rotating coil in a magnetic field can be expressed as $\varepsilon = \varepsilon_0 \sin \omega t$.

If the coil provides a complete path for a current to flow, an induced current, I, is given by $I = I_0 \sin \omega t$.

  a What is the mean voltage being generated?

  b What is the mean current flowing?

  c Give an expression for the power being generated as a function of time.

  d State the mean power being generated.

5 a State what is meant by the term *root-mean-square (RMS) value*, I_{RMS}, of a current, I.

  b How is the RMS current, I_{RMS}, related to the peak current, I_0?

  c In the UK, the RMS voltage of the mains supply is 240 V. Calculate the peak voltage.

6 In a simple dynamo on a child's bicycle, the peak voltage induced is 5.0 V, and the peak current flowing is 600 mA. Calculate the average power dissipated by the dynamo.

7 An a.c. source of peak voltage 18 V is connected to a small device with a resistance of 12 Ω. Calculate the

  a RMS voltage of the source.

  b average power dissipated in the circuit.

8 a Draw a circuit diagram for a transformer.

  b What kind of current is supplied to the primary coil?

  c Explain why the core of the transformer is made of iron.

  d Explain why the iron core is laminated.

  e Outline how the transformer is able to change the voltage across the primary coil into a different voltage across the secondary coil.

9 a Explain what is meant by a *step-up transformer*.

  b Explain what is meant by a *step-down transformer*.

  c Explain what is meant by the term *ideal* when applied to a transformer.

  d Suggest why a transformer might have an equal number of turns on the primary coil as on the secondary coil.

10 An ideal transformer has 360 turns on the primary coil and 45 turns on the secondary coil. The primary coil is supplied with an RMS alternating voltage of 110 V.

  a Is the transformer a step-up or a step-down transformer?

b Calculate the voltage across the secondary coil.

c Suggest a possible use for the transformer in your home.

11 An ideal transformer is used on the output of a small coal-fired power station to step up the voltage from 2 kV to 400 kV.

    a The primary coil of the transformer has 250 turns. How many turns are there on the secondary coil?

    b The current in the primary coil is 150 A. Calculate the

        i power being generated by the power station.

        ii current in the secondary coil.

12 A mobile phone charger uses a step-down transformer, which, for the purposes of this question, may be considered to be 100% efficient. The supply voltage is 240 V. The power rating of the charger is 20 W. The turns ratio of the transformer is $\frac{N_s}{N_p} = 0.05$.

    a Calculate the current in the

        i primary coil.

        ii secondary coil.

    b The mobile phone charges at a constant rate. How much charge will be added in 10 minutes?

13 Explain why power stations use a step-up transformer at the output of the generators to supply the transmission lines with a voltage of about 400 kV.

14 a Figure 20.8 shows a vertically orientated wire in which a constant current can flow when a switch is pressed to make a complete circuit. The rest of the circuit (emf source and connections) is not shown for ease of viewing.

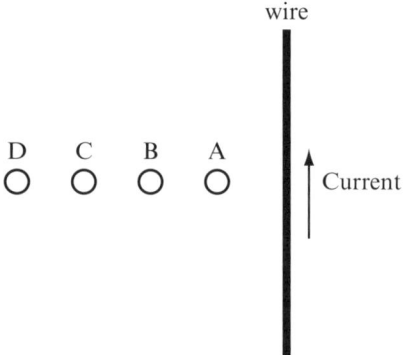

Figure 20.8

Suppose that plotting compasses were to be placed at each of the positions, A to D, shown in Figure 20.8. When the switch is pressed,

    i which of the plotting compasses will align with the magnetic field around the wire first?

- **ii** in which direction will this magnetic field be?
- **iii** which of the plotting compasses will be the last to align with the magnetic field around the wire?
- **iv** what do your answers to **parts i** and **iii** suggest about the magnetic field set up by the current in the wire?
- **v** in which direction is the magnetic field caused by the current in the wire travelling?
- **vi** what geometric relationship is there between your answers to **parts ii** and **v**)?

b Suppose now, the same wire is connected to an alternating supply (instead of the d.c. supply in **part a**) so that the direction of the current keeps reversing.

- **i** What will now be happening to the direction of the magnetic field around the wire?
- **ii** Will the magnetic field still be moving outwards from the wire?
- **iii** If plotting compasses, placed at positions A to D, were observed, each over a period of time, what would an observer see happening?
- **iv** At any of the positions A to D, would there be an electric field? If so, explain briefly why.
- **v** As the varying magnetic field moves outwards from the wire, is it accompanied by a varying electric field? If so, explain briefly why.
- **vi** What geometric relationship is there between the directions of the magnetic field, the electric field and their direction of movement away from the wire?
- **vii** What does your answer to **part v** suggest about the nature of an electromagnetic wave?
- **viii** Sketch a diagram to illustrate your answer to **part vii** above.

EXAM-STYLE QUESTIONS

Multiple-choice questions

1. Which of the following situations will **not** produce an induced emf?
   - A A coil of wire in which an alternating current is flowing
   - B A single wire in which an alternating current is flowing
   - C A coil of wire in a circuit with a battery that is switched on
   - D A coil of wire in a circuit with a constant current flowing

2. In an a.c. generator, a coil of N turns is rotated in a magnetic field of strength, B, at an angular frequency, ω, to produce a peak voltage, V. If the coil's turns are changed to $2N$, the magnetic field strength is changed to $2B$ and the angular frequency is changed to 2ω, what will the peak voltage be?
   - A $\frac{V}{4}$
   - B V
   - C $4V$
   - D $8V$

3. Which of the following combinations is correct for a step-down transformer (note: voltage ratio is $\frac{\text{primary voltage}}{\text{secondary voltage}}$ and current ratio is $\frac{\text{primary current}}{\text{secondary current}}$)?
   - A Voltage ratio = < 1; Current ratio = < 1
   - B Voltage ratio = < 1; Current ratio = > 1
   - C Voltage ratio = > 1; Current ratio = < 1
   - D Voltage ratio = > 1; Current ratio = > 1

4. Figure 20.9 shows how the magnetic flux linkage, $N\Phi$, varies with time for a conducting coil.

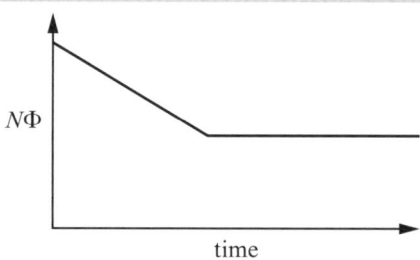

Figure 20.9

Which of the following descriptions correctly describes the induced emf in the coil?
   - A Induced emf is constant for a time and then becomes zero.
   - B Induced emf increases for a time and then becomes zero.
   - C Induced emf decreases for a time and then becomes zero.
   - D Induced emf decreases for a time and then becomes a constant non-zero value.

CONTINUED

5. A passenger aircraft with a wingspan of 70 m flies at a speed of 160 ms^{-1} perpendicularly through the Earth's magnetic field of strength 1.1×10^{-5} T. Which of the following is the best estimate of the emf induced across the aircraft's wings?

   A 1 mV
   B 10 mV
   C 100 mV
   D 1 V

6. During a time of 0.25 s, the magnetic flux linked to a coil of 60 turns varies uniformly from 8.0×10^{-3} T to 4.0×10^{-2} T. Which of the following is the best estimate of the induced emf in the coil?

   A 0.36 V
   B 0.96 V
   C 1.4 V
   D 1.9 V

7. A coil, rotating in a uniform magnetic field, has an induced emf given by the equation $\varepsilon = 20 \cos 60\pi\, t$.

   If the same coil is now rotated in the same magnetic field at twice the original angular frequency, which one of the following equations correctly gives the induced emf in the coil?

   A $\varepsilon = 20 \cos 60\pi\, t$
   B $\varepsilon = 20 \cos 120\pi\, t$
   C $\varepsilon = 40 \cos 60\pi\, t$
   D $\varepsilon = 40 \cos 120\pi\, t$

8. Magnetic flux may be measured in which of the following units?

   A Wbm^2
   B T
   C Tm^2
   D Wbm^{-2}

9. An ideal mains transformer, working with a supply voltage of 240 V, has 2000 turns on its primary coil and 100 turns on its secondary coil. The transformer is used to operate a laptop computer, through which a current of 4 A flows. The best estimate of the current flowing in the primary coil is

   A 2 mA.
   B 20 mA.
   C 200 mA.
   D 2 A.

CONTINUED

Short-answer questions

10 a State Faraday's law of electromagnetic induction. [2]

   b Figure 20.10 shows how the magnetic flux associated with a coil of wire of 200 turns varies with time.

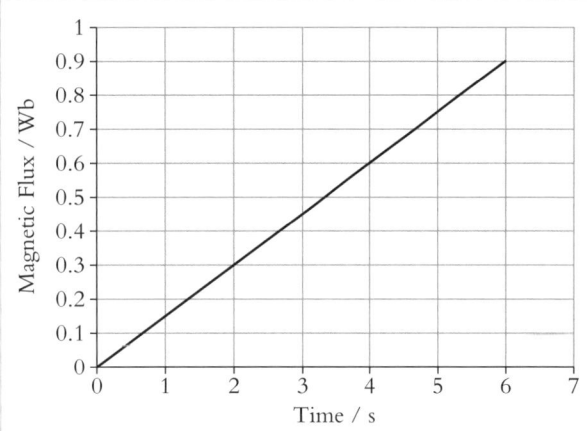

Figure 20.10

Use the graph to calculate the induced emf in the coil. [3]

11 Figure 20.11 shows a magnet falling through a coil of wire attached to an oscilloscope and the resulting oscilloscope trace.

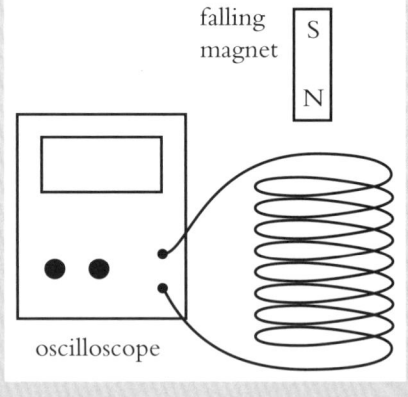 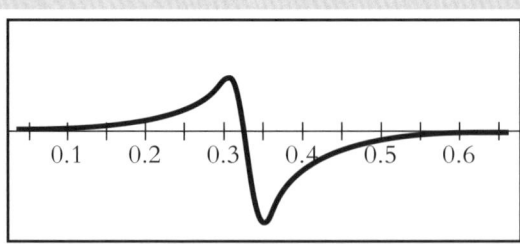

Figure 20.11

   a Explain why the trace shows an increasing voltage from 0 to 0.3 s. [2]
   b Explain why the trace shows a voltage that is negative from 0.35 to 0.6 s. [1]
   c Explain why the maximum negative voltage is greater than the maximum positive voltage. [1]
   d The coil is replaced with another coil of similar dimensions but twice the number of turns. The same magnet is dropped. Describe briefly what you would now see on the oscilloscope trace? [1]

CONTINUED

12 An induced emf is generated by rotating a coil in a magnetic field. State the effect on the induced emf of

    a having a stronger magnetic field strength. [1]

    b having more turns on the coil. [1]

    c having a coil with a smaller area. [2]

    d rotating the coil at a larger angular frequency. [2]

13 Figure 20.12 shows an ideal step down transformer with a constant power supply.

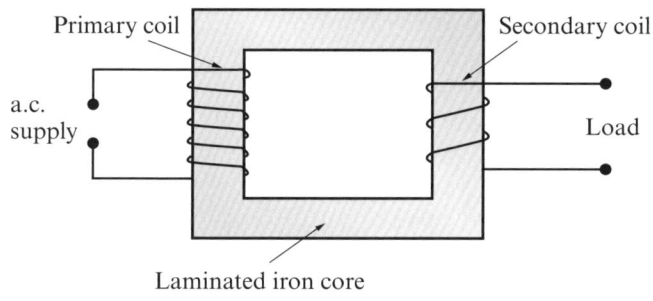

Figure 20.12

Outline

    a what is meant by the term *step down transformer*. [1]

    b why the core of the transformer is made of iron. [1]

    c why the iron core is laminated. [1]

    d why the supply to the primary coil of the transformer has to be an alternating current. [2]

    e why the output current is larger than the input current. [1]

14 Figure 20.13 shows a rectangular coil of 120 turns enclosing an area of 5×10^{-3} m². The coil is in a uniform magnetic field of magnetic flux density 4.0×10^{-3} T (shown as a shaded region) and can rotate about a vertical axis as shown.

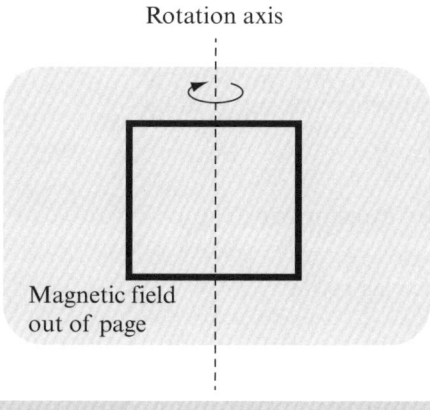

Figure 20.13

CONTINUED

a For the coil in the position shown in Figure 20.13, calculate the magnetic flux linkage. [2]

b When the coil is allowed to rotate about the axis shown, an alternating current is induced in the coil. With reference to the magnetic flux linkage, explain why the induced current is alternating. [2]

c State and explain the effect on the maximum induced current in the coil if the coil is allowed to rotate at twice its original angular frequency. [2]

15 Modern homes frequently use residual current devices (RCDs) instead of old-fashioned fuses, particularly for domestic devices that use large currents, like ovens.

Figure 20.14 shows a typical circuit incorporating an RCD.

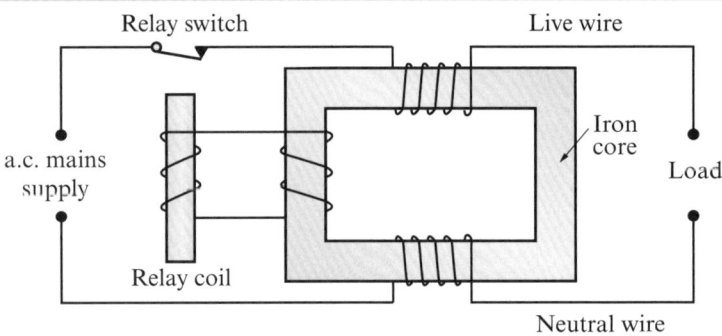

Figure 20.14

a In normal use, there is no net magnetic flux in the iron core. Explain why. [2]

b If there is a problem with the circuit, for example someone is able to touch a bare wire, the currents in the live and neutral wires will not be the same. In this situation, the RCD breaks the circuit making the circuit safe.

With reference to Faraday's law, explain how the RCD is able to break the circuit and make it safe. [4]

16 A very old physics demonstration, called 'Jacob's ladder', used a step-up transformer to produce a voltage between two electrodes that was sufficient to ionise the air between them. The two electrodes were the ends of the secondary coil separated at the base by a distance of 2 cm. When the transformer was switched on, sparks occurred between the two electrodes, which moved vertically upwards, giving the effect of a 'ladder of lightning'. Air will ionise if the potential difference per centimetre is above 30 kVcm^{-1}. The transformer was supplied by a main voltage of 240 V (a.c.) and had 120 turns on its primary coil.

a Outline the main features of a step-up transformer. [2]

b Determine the minimum number of turns that the 'Jacob's ladder' transformer had on its secondary coil. [2]

c Suggest why this physics demonstration is now not allowed in the classroom. [1]

CONTINUED

17 Figure 20.15 shows an electromagnetic wave approaching a vertically orientated conductor.

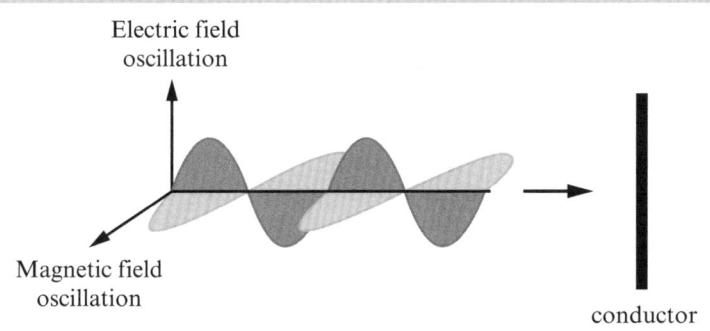

Figure 20.15

a State Faraday's law of electromagnetic induction. [2]

b As the electromagnetic wave passes the conductor, what effect does the varying magnetic field have on the conductor? [1]

c As the electromagnetic wave passes the conductor, what effect does the varying electric field have on the conductor? [1]

d Describe how the conductor behaves like an aerial. [2]

Unit E
Nuclear and quantum physics

> Chapter 21
Atomic physics

CHAPTER OUTLINE

In this chapter, you will:

- explore Rutherford's alpha-particle scattering experiment.

- learn how emission and absorption spectra provide evidence for discrete atomic energy levels.

- use the Bohr model for hydrogen to evaluate energy levels.

- link the energy of a photon with the frequency of the electromagnetic radiation

- see how emission and absorption spectra provide information on chemical composition.

> revise the idea of the distance of closest approach for head-on scattering experiments.

> see how the quantisation of angular momentum leads to quantised energy and orbits.

> link nuclear radius with the nucleon number to explore nuclear densities.

KEY TERMS

emission spectrum: the set of wavelengths (or frequencies) of light emitted by an atom

absorption spectrum: the set of wavelengths (or frequencies) of light absorbed by an atom

photon: the particle of light; massless and moving at the speed of light

ground state: the lowest energy level of an atom

excited state: any atomic energy level with more energy than the ground state

Planck's constant, h: the ratio of a photon's energy to its frequency, $h = 6.63 \times 10^{-34}$ J s

Bohr radius, r_1: the smallest orbital radius in which an electron can exist; $r_1 \approx 0.53 \times 10^{-10}$ m

21 Atomic physics

> **KEY EQUATIONS**
>
> **Bohr's model for hydrogen energy levels:** $E = -\frac{13.6}{n^2}$ eV
>
> **photon energy:** $E = hf = \frac{hc}{\lambda}$
>
> **Bohr's electron orbits:** $mvr = n\frac{h}{2\pi}$
>
> **Bohr radius:** $r_1 = \frac{h^2}{4\pi^2 k e^2 m}$,
>
> where E is energy, n is an integer, h is Planck's constant, f is frequency, m is the mass of an electron, v is the orbital speed of an electron, r is the electron orbital radius, k is the Coulomb constant ($k = 9 \times 10^9$ Nm^{2}C^{-2}) and e is the charge on an electron ($e = -1.6 \times 10^{-19}$ C).
>
> **nuclear radius:** $r = r_o A^{\frac{1}{3}}$,
>
> where r is the nuclear radius, $r_o = 1.2 \times 10^{-15}$ m.

Exercise 21.1 The structure of the atom

1. a J.J. Thomson first suggested the *plum pudding* model of the atom in the late 1870s. Outline the model's main features.

   b Outline Geiger and Marsden's experiment, under the leadership of Lord Rutherford, that led to the demise of the plum pudding model.

   c Outline why the observations made in Geiger and Marsden's experiment were not explainable using J.J. Thompson's plum pudding model.

2. In the now-famous alpha-particle scattering experiment of 1909, two major observations were made. For each observation, state the conclusions made (which led to the Rutherford planetary model of the atom).

Experimental observation	Conclusion
The vast majority of alpha particles passed through the gold foil undeflected.	
Some alpha particles were deflected through such large angles that they bounced backwards.	

3. Suppose that an alpha particle in Geiger and Marsden's experiment had been fired at a gold nucleus head-on and was scattered backwards (through an angle of 180°).

   If the alpha particle began with 5 MeV of kinetic energy, determine the maximum size of a gold nucleus.

Data:

- a gold nucleus has 79 protons
- $k = 9 \times 10^9$ Nm²C⁻², 1 eV = 1.6×10^{-19} J
- the charge on a proton is 1.6×10^{-19} C

> **TIP**
> Look back at questions 6 and 7 from Section 19.1, Chapter 19.

4
  a Explain what is meant by *emission spectrum* when applied to a container of gas at a low pressure.

  b Describe how a student may observe such an emission spectrum in the laboratory.

5 Explain how the emission spectrum from a gas provides empirical evidence for the existence of discrete energy levels of atoms.

6 Consider an electron in an atom of hydrogen.

  a Describe how the planetary model of the atom helps us visualise the electron in the atom.

  b **i** What force keeps the electron in the atom orbiting around the nucleus?

   ii In which direction is this force on the electron acting?

   iii In the planetary model of the atom, is the electron in the hydrogen atom accelerating? Explain your answer.

  c Suggest a reason why modern physicists find the planetary model of the atom flawed.

7 Figure 21.1 shows some of the energy levels possible for a hydrogen atom.

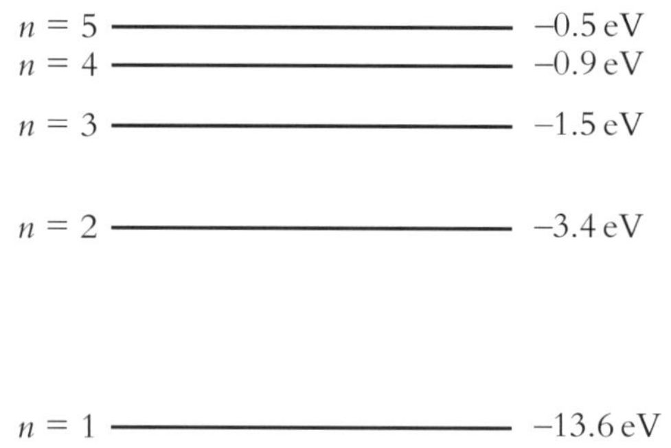

$n = 5$ ——————————— −0.5 eV
$n = 4$ ——————————— −0.9 eV

$n = 3$ ——————————— −1.5 eV

$n = 2$ ——————————— −3.4 eV

$n = 1$ ——————————— −13.6 eV

Figure 21.1

  a Why are all the electron energy levels given negative energy values?

  b Which energy level is usually described as the *ground state*?

  c In a container of hydrogen gas at room temperature, in which energy level would you expect to find most of the electrons in the hydrogen atoms?

d If an electron in the ground state were to gain 10.2 eV, what would you expect the electron to do?

e What name would you give to the process occurring in **part d**?

8 This question is also about the energy levels in a hydrogen atom.

   a For a container of hydrogen gas at a moderate to high temperature, in which energy level or levels might you expect to find electrons in the hydrogen atoms?

   b Explain what is meant by *excited* when applied to electrons in atoms.

   c An excited electron in a hydrogen atom is unlikely to remain excited for more than about 10^{-18} s. What is such an excited electron likely to do?

   d What is the name given to the process in **part c**?

   e As a result of this process, what has happened to the energy of the atom?

9 Bohr showed that the electron energy levels in a hydrogen atom should be given by $E_n = \frac{-13.6\,eV}{n^2}$.

Calculate the total energy that an electron has in level

   a $n = 2$.

   b $n = 3$.

   c $n = 4$.

10 The Einstein–Planck relation for a photon states

$E = hf$.

   a State the meaning of the term *photon*.

   b State what each of the terms in the relation mean and its unit.

   c Show that the Einstein–Planck relation can also be expressed as

   $E = h\frac{c}{\lambda}$.

   d Photon energies are often quoted in electronvolts, eV. Define the term *electronvolt*.

   e Calculate the energy of the following photons; give your answer in Joules and in eV.

   i A red photon of wavelength 630 nm

   ii A green photon of wavelength 532 nm

   iii A blue photon of wavelength 430 nm

11 The visible emission spectrum from a hydrogen atom shows four bright lines: a red line, a turquoise line, a blue line and a violet line.

    a These four lines correspond to transitions between which pairs of energy levels?

    b The red line in the emission spectrum of hydrogen is called the hydrogen alpha line. Its wavelength is 656.3 nm. Show that photons of this wavelength have an energy of 1.9 eV.

    c Which colour emission line is caused by the transition from $n = 4$ to $n = 2$, a change in energy of 2.55 eV?

12 The emission spectrum for hydrogen is sometimes described by five sets of emission lines corresponding to electron transitions that end on energy levels 1 to 5. These sets of emission lines are called 'series':

Series name	Ending energy level	e.m. radiation emitted
Lyman	1	
Balmer	2	
Paschen	3	
Brackett	4	
Pfund	5	

Complete the table to show the regions of the electromagnetic spectrum in which emission lines occur.

13 Describe how the emission spectrum from a filament light bulb is different to the emission spectrum of a gas, such as hydrogen.

14 The emission spectrum of sodium is dominated by two emission lines at 589.0 and 589.6 nm.

    a If these emission lines are the result of transitions from electron energy levels $n = 2$ to $n = 1$, calculate the average energy difference between the electron energy level $n = 2$ and the electron energy level $n = 1$.

    b Suggest a reason why there are two emission lines, at two slightly different wavelengths, from this transition.

15 A typical He-Ne laser in a CD player emits light with a wavelength of 632.8 nm.

    a What colour is this light?

    b This light is the result of electron energy level transitions in the neon atom. Calculate the energy difference between these two levels in

        i Joules.

        ii eV.

16 The emission spectrum of the Sun (actually, also for any star) in the visible region of the electromagnetic spectrum is more or less a continuous spectrum, but it is overlaid with a set of dark lines called Fraunhofer lines.

    a Outline how these dark lines in the solar emission spectrum are formed.

    b Outline how analysis of these lines has allowed astrophysicists to determine the chemical composition of the outer layers of the Sun and other stars.

Exercise 21.2 Quantisation of angular momentum

1   **a** Outline the planetary model for an atom that Rutherford had adapted following the famous alpha-particle scattering experiment.

    b Why did Niels Bohr object to Rutherford's model?

    c What did Bohr propose as a compromise/augmentation of Rutherford's model?

2 Consider the electron property given by the equation mvr, where m is the electron's mass, v its speed and r the radius of its orbit around the nucleus.

    a What units does mvr have?

    b What is this property called?

    c Bohr proposed the idea that the angular momentum of an electron must be quantised.

        i What does the word *quantised* mean?

        ii Bohr's proposal was that angular momentum should be measured in units of $\frac{h}{2\pi}$, where h is Planck's constant, given as $h = 6.63 \times 10^{-23}$ J s. Show that Bohr's proposal is dimensionally consistent.

3 One implication of Bohr's proposal is that electrons can exist only in certain allowable orbits, orbits in which electrons would not radiate electromagnetic radiation. The radii of these orbits were given by the equation

$r_n = n^2 r_1$,

where n is an integer and r_1—called the Bohr radius—is the smallest radius of orbit in which an electron can exist.

    a Using Coulomb's law, show that the Bohr radius, r_1, can be expressed as

$r_1 = k\frac{e^2}{mv^2}$,

where k is the Coulomb constant, e is the charge on the electron (and on the proton), m is the mass of the electron and v is the orbital speed of the electron.

b Using Bohr's idea that the angular momentum of the electron must be quantised in units of $\frac{h}{2\pi}$, show that the Bohr radius can be expressed as
$$r_1 = \frac{h^2}{4\pi^2 k e^2 m},$$
where k is the Coulomb constant.

c Using the following data to show that the Bohr radius is about 0.53×10^{-10} m.

- $h = 6.63 \times 10^{-34}$ J s
- $k = 9 \times 10^9$ Nm²C⁻²
- $e = -1.6 \times 10^{-19}$ C
- $m = 9.1 \times 10^{-31}$ kg

d What will the radii of the orbits be for which $n = 2, 3$ and 4?

4 Consider the single electron in orbit around the nucleus of a hydrogen atom.

a What force keeps the electron in its orbit?

b Write an equation for this force.

c Show that the kinetic energy of the electron in the hydrogen atom can be expressed as
$$E_K = k\frac{e^2}{2r}.$$

d Hence, show that the total energy of the electron is
$$E_{total} = -k\frac{e^2}{2r}.$$

e For a hydrogen atom, show that the total energy of an electron in an orbit with a radius equal to the Bohr radius is -13.6 eV—a result you used in the previous section.

> **TIP**
> You may remember this from Chapters 18 and 19.

5 The size of atomic nuclei is of the order 10^{-15} m, and the size of atoms is of the order 10^{-10} m. The mass of a proton is given as $m_p = 1.67 \times 10^{-27}$ kg, and the rest mass of an electron, m_e, is given as 9.1×10^{-31} kg.

a Calculate the ratio of $\frac{m_p}{m_e}$.

b Is it reasonable to assume that the mass of an atom is very nearly the same as the mass of its nucleus?

c Give an order of magnitude for the ratio of $\frac{\text{volume of an atom}}{\text{volume of a nucleus}}$.

d Hence, state an order of magnitude for the ratio of $\frac{\text{density of a nucleus}}{\text{density of an atom}}$.

e Calculate the density of a proton. ($r_0 = 1.2 \times 10^{-15}$ m)

f The density of diamonds (carbon) is given as 2.3×10^3 kgm⁻³. How does the density of a proton compare with the density of diamonds?

Comment on your answer with reference to **part d**.

6 This question looks at the density of nuclei in a slightly different way.

The radius of an atomic nucleus is given as $r = r_o A^{\frac{1}{3}}$.

    a Give an expression for the volume, V, of a nucleus.

    b Hence, give an expression for the number of nucleons per unit volume in the nucleus.

    c What do you notice? What does this imply about the densities of all nuclei?

    d Hence, calculate the density of a nucleus. You may assume that the average mass of a nucleon is 1.7×10^{-27} kg.

    e Compare your answer to **part d** with your answer to **question 5e**. What can you conclude?

> **TIP**
>
> You may like to solve this question using a spreadsheet.

7 a Complete the following table. Take the average mass of a nucleon to be 1.7×10^{-27} kg.

Nucleus	Nucleon number	Radius ($\times 10^{-15}$ m)	Density
H	1		
He	4		
C	12		
S	32		
Sr	88		
Au	197		
U	238		

    b Does this confirm your answer to **question 21.2.6 part c**?

8 a Estimate the volume of a golf ball.

    b If a golf ball were made from nuclear material, determine its mass.

    c How does your answer to **part b** compare with the regulated mass of a golf ball of 46 grams?

EXAM-STYLE QUESTIONS

Multiple-choice questions

1 Which of the following statements is **not** one of the three assumptions of the Bohr model of the atom?
   A Electrons exist in atoms in discrete energy levels.
   B Electrons exist in atoms as particles that orbit around the nucleus.
   C Electrons may move from one energy level to another by emitting or absorbing electromagnetic radiation.
   D The angular momentum of electrons in atoms is quantised.

2 Complete this sentence: The density of a nucleus is
   A proportional to A, the number of nucleons present.
   B proportional to A^3, the cube of the number of nucleons present.
   C proportional to $A^{1/3}$, the cube-root of the number of nucleons present.
   D independent of the number of nucleons present.

   Questions 3, 4 and 5 refer to Figure 21.2.

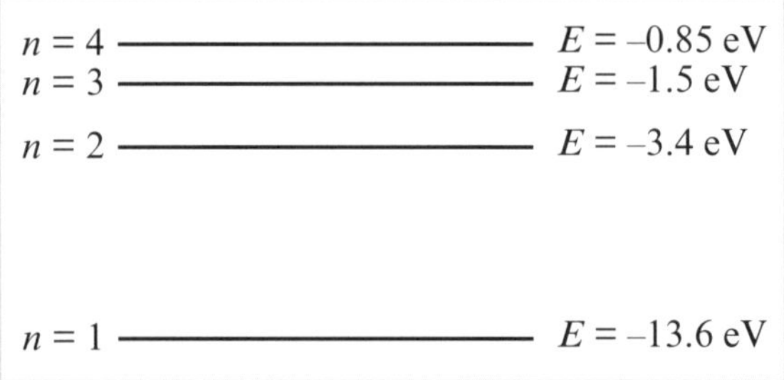

   $n = 4$ ——— $E = -0.85$ eV
   $n = 3$ ——— $E = -1.5$ eV
   $n = 2$ ——— $E = -3.4$ eV

   $n = 1$ ——— $E = -13.6$ eV

   Figure 21.2

3 Which of the following electron transitions will cause the atom to emit a photon of energy 1.9 eV?
   A $n = 2 \rightarrow n = 3$
   B $n = 2 \rightarrow n = 4$
   C $n = 4 \rightarrow n = 2$
   D $n = 3 \rightarrow n = 2$

4 Which of the following electron transitions will cause the atom to emit a photon with the largest wavelength?
   A $n = 4 \rightarrow n = 3$
   B $n = 4 \rightarrow n = 2$
   C $n = 4 \rightarrow n = 1$
   D $n = 2 \rightarrow n = 1$

CONTINUED

5 The most prominent line in the emission spectrum of hydrogen is the hydrogen α-line, which has a frequency of 4.57×10^{14} Hz.

Which of the following electron transitions is responsible for the emission of the hydrogen α-line?

A $n = 4 \to n = 3$
B $n = 4 \to n = 2$
C $n = 3 \to n = 2$
D $n = 3 \to n = 1$

6 Which of the following values is the best estimate of the ratio of the volume of an atom to the volume of a nucleus?

A 10^{-5}
B 10^{5}
C 10^{-15}
D 10^{15}

7 Which of the following series of emission lines from a hydrogen atom does not consist of infrared photons?

A Lyman
B Brackett
C Paschen
D Pfundt

8 Bohr's model of the atom allows electrons to have quantised angular momentum in units of

A $\frac{h}{\pi}$.
B $\frac{h}{2\pi}$.
C $\frac{2h}{\pi}$.
D $\frac{2\pi}{h}$.

9 In a hydrogen atom, the two lowest energy levels for an electron occur for electrons orbiting at speeds of v_1 and v_2, at radii r_1 and r_2, where $r_2 > r_1$. Which of the following correctly predicts the ratio of the orbital speeds, $\frac{v_1}{v_2}$?

A $\frac{1}{4}$
B $\frac{1}{2}$
C 2
D 4

10 For an isotope of uranium, the atomic number is 92 and the nucleon number is 238. The radius of a hydrogen nucleus is 1.2×10^{-15} m. Which of the following is the best estimate for the radius of a nucleus of uranium?

A 5.4×10^{-15} m
B 6.3×10^{-15} m
C 7.4×10^{-15} m
D 8.3×10^{-15} m

CONTINUED

Short-answer questions

11 Figure 21.3 shows some of the energy levels in a hydrogen atom.

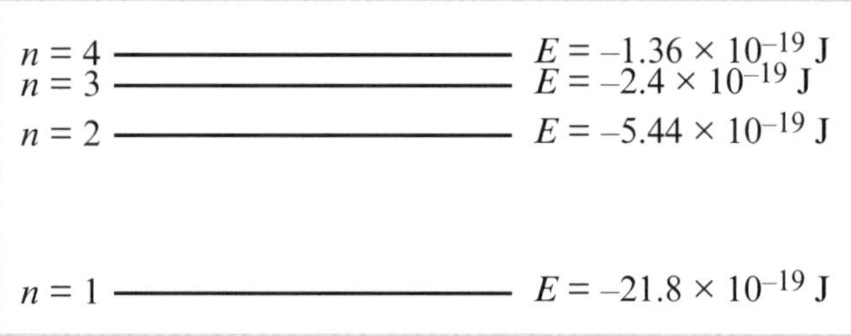

```
n = 4 ─────────── E = –1.36 × 10⁻¹⁹ J
n = 3 ─────────── E = –2.4 × 10⁻¹⁹ J
n = 2 ─────────── E = –5.44 × 10⁻¹⁹ J



n = 1 ─────────── E = –21.8 × 10⁻¹⁹ J
```

Figure 21.3

a Identify the transition responsible for the emission of a photon of frequency 3.08×10^{15} Hz [2]

b In which part of the electromagnetic spectrum does this radiation belong? [1]

c An electron in the ground state is ionised by the absorption of a photon of frequency 4.00×10^{15} Hz. Calculate the kinetic energy of the ionised electron. Give your answer in electronvolts. [2]

12 A free electron colliding with an atom of hydrogen in its ground state can cause the atom to become excited or ionised.

a State the meaning of the following terms:
  i *ground state* [1]
  ii *excited* [1]
  iii *ionised* [1]

b Excited atoms of hydrogen are known to emit several discrete wavelengths of radiation in the visible part of the electromagnetic spectrum. Outline the electron transitions responsible for these emission lines. [2]

13 The four lowest energy levels of a mercury atom are shown in Figure 21.4.

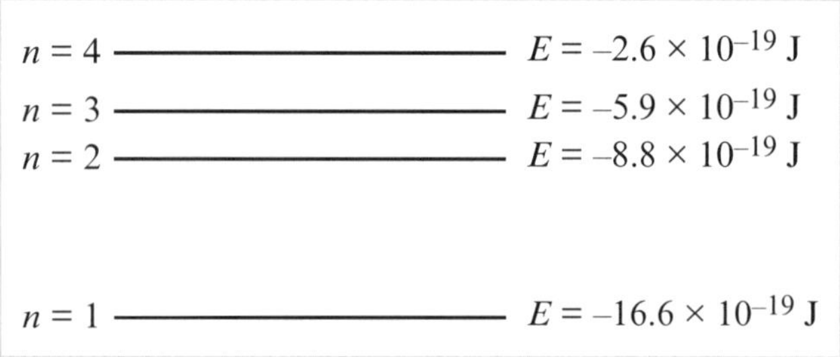

```
n = 4 ─────────── E = –2.6 × 10⁻¹⁹ J
n = 3 ─────────── E = –5.9 × 10⁻¹⁹ J
n = 2 ─────────── E = –8.8 × 10⁻¹⁹ J



n = 1 ─────────── E = –16.6 × 10⁻¹⁹ J
```

Figure 21.4

a An electron in energy level $n = 4$ falls to energy level $n = 2$ and emits a photon. Calculate the wavelength of the emitted photon. [2]

b State the energy level transition that will emit a photon of the longest wavelength. [1]

c State the transitions that will give rise to the emission of a photon of greater frequency than that in **part a**. [2]

CONTINUED

14 The radius of a nucleus is given by the equation
$r = r_o A^{\frac{1}{3}}$, where $r_o = 1.2 \times 10^{-15}$ m.

a Show that the radius of the nucleus of a gold atom, $^{197}_{79}$Au, is about 7×10^{-15} m. [1]

b In the alpha-particle scattering experiment, conducted by Geiger and Marsden under the leadership of Lord Rutherford in 1909, alpha particles were fired at gold atoms.

Figure 21.5 shows the initial trajectories of two equally energetic alpha particles heading towards a nucleus of a gold atom.

Gold nucleus

Figure 21.5

Add to Figure 21.5 to show the full paths of the two alpha-particles. [2]

c If an alpha particle were to get closer than 8 fm (8.0×10^{-15} m) to the gold nucleus, the strong nuclear force would dominate the electrostatic repusion of the Coulomb force. The alpha particle would be absorbed by the nucleus.

Show that the initial kinetic energy an alpha particle would need for it to be absorbed by the gold nucleus is about 28 MeV. [2]

15 A continuous spectrum of light is incident on a cloud of hydrogen gas.
After passing through the gas, it is observed using a spectrometer.

a Explain why the light observed contains dark lines in the continuous spectrum. [2]

b One of the dark lines in the spectrum has a wavelength of 434 nm. Calculate the energy of a photon of light with this wavelength. Give your answer in eV. [2]

c Outline how astronomers can use their observations of the dark lines in the spectra from stars to find information about the composition of the stars. [1]

16 Niels Bohr proposed that the angular momenta of electrons in an atom must be quantised in integer multiples given by the equation
$L = n\frac{h}{2\pi}$.

a On which three quantities, related to the electrons in an atom, does the angular momentum depend? [2]

b An electron in the ground state (principle quantum number, $n = 1$) of a hydrogen atom has an orbiting radius of 0.53×10^{-10} m, called the Bohr radius. If the mass of the electron is given to be 9.1×10^{-31} kg, show that the speed at which the electron is moving in its orbit around the nucleus is about 2.2×10^6 ms^{-1}. [2]

c State the speed at which an electron would be moving in an orbit with principle quantum number 2. [1]

CONTINUED

17 An alpha particle with an initial kinetic energy of 3.50 MeV passes close to the nucleus of a gold atom, as shown in Figure 21.6. (A gold nucleus has 79 protons.)

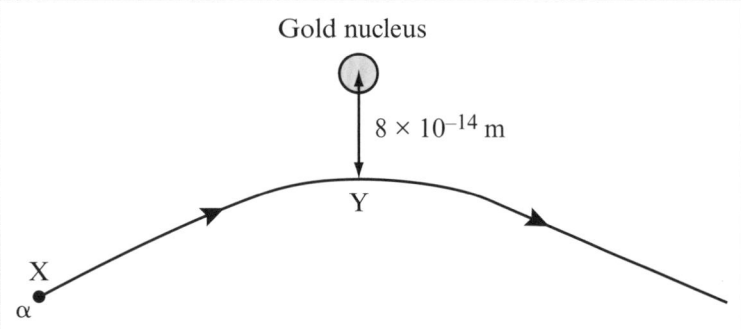

Figure 21.6

- **a** An alpha particle has a mass of 6.64×10^{-27} kg. Calculate the initial speed of the alpha particle. [2]
- **b** Describe how the speed of the alpha particle changes—if at all—as it moves from X to Y. [2]
- **c** Calculate the kinetic energy of the alpha particle at Y. [2]

18 An electron in the ground state (principle quantum number, $n = 1$) of a hydrogen atom requires 13.6 eV for it to escape from the atom, leaving the atom ionised into a positive ion.
- **a** Determine the minimum energy an electron in the ground state requires to become excited into the quantum state $n = 3$ or above. Give your answer in electronvolts. [2]
- **b** At room temperature, T = 20 °C, hydrogen gas does not emit any visible light.
  - **i** Outline the electron energy–level transitions that will cause the emission of visible light photons from hydrogen gas. [1]
  - **ii** Explain why hydrogen gas at room temperature does not emit any visible light. [2]

Chapter 22
Quantum physics

CHAPTER OUTLINE

In this chapter, you will:

> link the photoelectric effect with the particle model of light.

> explore how Einstein explained the photoelectric effect.

> see how the diffraction of particles provides evidence for the wave nature of matter.

> explore the concept of wave–particle duality using de Broglie's equation, $\lambda = \frac{h}{p}$.

KEY TERMS

photoelectric effect: the emission of electrons from a metallic surface when light is incident on the surface

photoelectrons: the electrons emitted in the photoelectric effect

photocurrent: the current produced by the photoelectric effect

stopping voltage: the voltage in the photoelectric effect required to make the current zero

work function: the minimum energy required by an electron to break free of a metal surface

wave–particle duality: the idea that matter can exhibit both wave and particle properties

KEY EQUATIONS

Einstein's photoelectric effect equation: $E_{K_{max}} = hf - \phi$

de Broglie's equation: $\lambda = \frac{h}{p}$,

where $E_{K_{max}}$ is the maximum kinetic energy of the photoelectron, h is Planck's constant, ($= 6.63 \times 10^{-34}$ Js), f is the frequency of the incident photon on the metal surface, ϕ is the work function for the metal, λ is the wavelength of a matter wave and p is the momentum of a particle.

Exercise 22.1 Photons and the photoelectric effect

1. **a** Calculate the energy of the following photons, giving your answers in Joules and electronvolts:

    i A radio wave photon of wavelength 2.5 m

    ii An infrared photon of wavelength 6.0 μm

    iii A visible photon of wavelength 623 nm

    iv An X-ray photon of wavelength 1.5×10^{-10} m

   b A 5-mW laser emits light of wavelength 630 nm. Calculate the

    i energy of a photon of light at this wavelength.

    ii number of photons emitted by the laser in 1 s.

2. Albert Einstein was awarded the Nobel Prize in Physics for his pioneering work on the photoelectric effect.

   a Outline the main conclusion Einstein derived from his work on the photoelectric effect.

   b Why was this work so pioneering?

   c Suggest why the photoelectric effect is such an important topic in physics.

3. Figure 22.1 shows a negatively charged metal plate attached to a gold-leaf electroscope. The metal plate can be illuminated by different wavelengths of light from a variable light source above it.

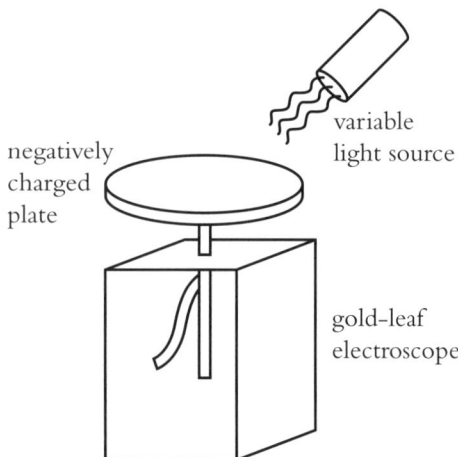

Figure 22.1

a When the metal plate is illuminated with light of wavelength 650 nm, nothing happens to the angle of the gold leaf of the electroscope—even when illuminated for a long time.

   i   Explain this observation.

   ii How does this observation suggest that light is not behaving like a wave?

b When the metal plate is illuminated with light of wavelength 450 nm, the angle of the gold leaf on the electroscope decreases immediately.

   i   Explain this observation.

   ii How does this observation suggest that light is behaving like a stream of particles?

4 A negatively charged zinc plate is attached to a coulombmeter. The zinc plate is illuminated with light of wavelength 440 nm. The coulombmeter shows a decrease in the amount of charge on the zinc plate.

   a What would you expect the coulombmeter to show if the intensity of the illuminating light were increased?

   b Explain your answer to **part a** in terms of light as a stream of discrete particles of energy.

   c Explain what effect, if any, the increase in intensity of the illuminating light will have on the maximum amount of kinetic energy of the photoelectrons.

5 The work function for a particular metal surface is 3.2 eV.

   a Calculate the threshold frequency for the metal surface.

   b What is the longest wavelength of light that could produce photoelectrons from this metal surface?

   c The metal surface is illuminated with ultraviolet light of wavelength 6.5×10^{-8} m. Calculate the maximum kinetic energy of a photoelectron.

6 The work function of a copper surface is 4.2 eV.

   a Determine the threshold frequency for the copper surface.

   b Which part of the electromagnetic spectrum will contain radiation that is just about capable of producing photoelectrons from a copper surface?

   c Calculate the maximum speed at which a photoelectron can leave the copper surface if it is illuminated with radiation of frequency 2.2×10^{15} Hz.

7 Einstein's photoelectric effect equation is often written as $E_{Kmax} = hf - \phi$.

   a State what each of the terms in the equation represents.

   b Sketch a graph of E_{Kmax} (y-axis) against f (x-axis).

   c What information does the gradient of your graph provide?

   d Explain the significance of the intercept on the x-axis.

8   Figure 22.2 shows how the maximum kinetic energy of a photoelectron from a metal surface varies with the frequency of the illuminating radiation.

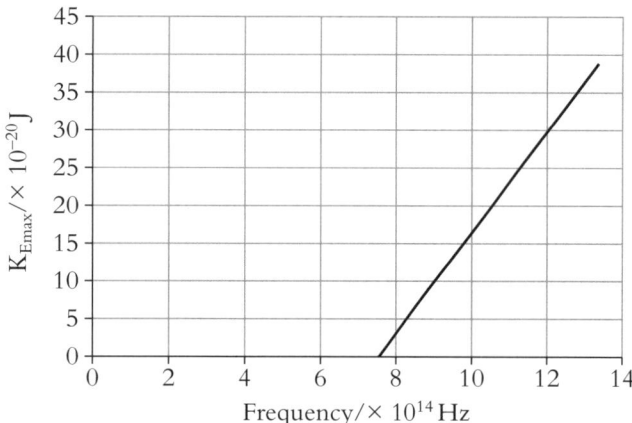

Figure 22.2

a   Use the graph to determine

   i   the work function for the metal surface.

   ii a value for Planck's constant.

b   Sketch the relationship you would expect for the maximum kinetic energy of photoelectrons from a metal surface with a larger work function.

9   Figure 22.3 shows a metal plate, which can be illuminated with light, and a collector, both of which are connected in series with a sensitive ammeter and a variable d.c. power supply. The metal plate and the collector are enclosed in an evacuated glass flask.

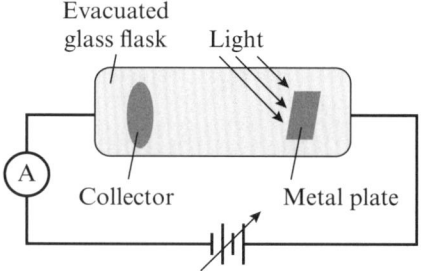

Figure 22.3

a   Give a reason why the metal plate and the collector are enclosed inside an evacuated glass flask.

b   Outline why the ammeter is able to show that a current is flowing.

c   i   Explain what happens to the ammeter reading when the variable voltage supply is increased upwards from zero.

    ii If the voltage supply continues to be increased, explain why, after a particular value of voltage, there is no further change to the reading on the ammeter.

    iii What name is given to this special voltage?

    iv If the incident light is now changed for light of a smaller wavelength, and the same metal plate is used, state and explain what happens to the value of this special voltage.

    v If the incident light is replaced by light that is more intense but of the same wavelength as originally, what will happen to this special voltage now?

Exercise 22.2 Matter waves

1 a When we think of wave behaviour, what two phenomena characterise something behaving like a wave?

   b By the 1920s, Einstein's explanation that light behaved like particles was well accepted by the scientific community. Using an argument based on symmetry, what did Louis de Broglie propose in his PhD thesis of 1923?

   c State the equation proposed by de Broglie that linked the particle property with the wave property for matter.

2 Between 1923 and 1927, Clinton Davisson and Lester Germer experimented with firing accelerated electrons at a crystal of zinc.

   a Why is Davisson and Germer's experiment, first published in the *Franklin Institute Journal* of 1928, considered to be such an important experiment in the history of physics?

   b Describe briefly what Davisson and Germer observed and why it was so relevant to de Broglie's hypothesis.

3 A modern way of demonstrating the wave behaviour of electrons is illustrated in Figure 22.4. You may be lucky enough to have seen this in your physics lessons at school.

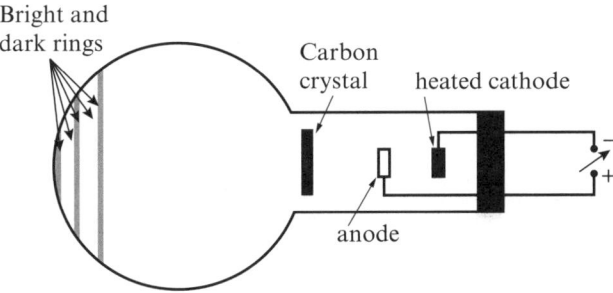

Figure 22.4

Electrons, accelerated by the electron gun inside the evacuated glass flask, are diffracted by the regularly spaced atoms in the carbon crystal, forming a series of bright and dark rings on the inside of the far end of the flask. These rings are easily observed. When the voltage used to accelerate the electrons is increased, the size of the bright and dark rings decreases.

Suppose that in Figure 22.4 the electrons are accelerated through a potential difference of V volts.

    a   How much kinetic energy will the electron gain?

    b   Show that the kinetic energy of the electron can be expressed as $\frac{p^2}{2m}$, where p is the momentum of the electron and m is the electron's mass.

    c   Show that the momentum of the electron can be expressed as $\sqrt{2meV}$.

    d   Using your knowledge of diffraction, how would you expect the radius of the bright and dark rings to depend on the wavelength of the electron waves?

    e   Hence, using de Broglie's equation for the wavelength of an electron wave, justify the observation that increasing the voltage of the electron gun decreases the radius of the bright and dark rings.

4   **a**   Calculate the effective wavelength of

        i   an electron travelling at 2.0×10^7 ms^{-1}. ($m_e = 9.1 \times 10^{-31}$ kg)

        ii   a 160-g cricket ball travelling at 140 kmhour^{-1}.

        iii   a 70-kg human walking at 1.0 ms^{-1}.

    b   **i**   Which of the three examples in **part a** is most likely to behave like a wave?

        ii   How would a human have to move to behave like a wave? How does this help explain why humans behave like particles, not waves?

5   **a**   Calculate the effective wavelength of an electron that has been accelerated through a potential difference of

        i   400 V.

        ii   100 V.

    b   Would the electrons in **part a** show significant signs of diffraction by a crystal lattice with atoms spaced 3.0×10^{-10} m apart?

6   This question looks at the electron in an atom as a wave.

According to de Broglie, electrons in atoms should exhibit wave properties. And according to classical electrodynamics, charged particles that are accelerating must emit electromagnetic radiation. Electrons in orbits of atoms do not emit electromagnetic radiation unless they move from a higher energy level to a lower energy level.

    a   If the electron exists as a wave, what kind of wave must it be for it not to be transferring any energy?

b If the electron wave occupies a length that is equal to the circumference of the electron's orbit, then what possible wavelengths could there be for an electron orbit of radius, r?

c Using Bohr's hypothesis for the quantised angular momentum of an electron, show that the momentum of the electron can be expressed as

$$p = \frac{h}{2\pi n r_1}.$$

d Hence, show that the possible wavelengths of the electron standing waves in the hydrogen atom are given by the expression

$$\lambda = \frac{2\pi r_n}{n}.$$

e For the following electron orbits, corresponding to the principle quantum states $n = 1$, $n = 2$ and $n = 3$, determine the wavelength of the elecron wave and the number of complete waves present in the standing wave:

  i $r_1 \; (= 0.53 \times 10^{-10} \text{ m})$

  ii r_2

  iii r_3

f Hence, state how the principal quantum number is related to the number of complete waves present in the electron standing wave.

7 Figure 22.5 shows a Young slits experiment. In this experiment, electrons are accelerated by an electron gun and then directed at a pair of narrow slits. A fluorescent screen placed some distance away shows where the electrons hit the screen.

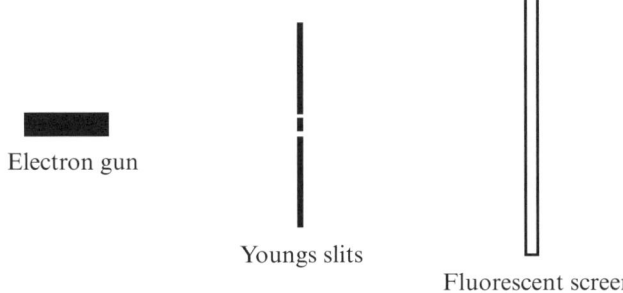

Figure 22.5

a When the experiment is conducted over a period of ten minutes or so, the characteristic interference pattern from a pair of Young slits is observed on the fluorescent screen.

  i Explain why this implies that electrons are exhibiting wave-like properties.

  ii The current from the electron gun is measured to be 4.8 mA. Assuming that 50% of the electrons from the electron gun eventually arrive at the fluorescent sceen, determine the rate at which the electrons produce the classic interference pattern on the fluorescent screen.

iii Explain the effect on the electron's de Broglie wavelength, and on the observed interference pattern on the fluorescent screen, of reducing the accelerating voltage in the electron gun.

b The experiment is now repeated, but, this time, the current from the electron gun is severely reduced, so that the rate at which electrons arrive at the fluorescent screen is only 1 per second.

    i Outline what would be observed on the fluorescent screen.

    ii If the experiment is left to run for a long period of time, and the locations at which the electrons arrive at the fluorescent screen are recorded, what will the eventual result be?

    iii Clearly a single electron cannot interfere with itself. That is, it cannot pass through both slits at the same time, can it? Is it possible to argue that it can?

    iv Outline how Erwin Schrödinger explained the way in which the interference pattern on the fluorescent screen built up over a period of time.

    v Following on from **part iv**, how does Schrödinger's explanation relate to Bohr's model of electrons existing in atoms in discrete orbits?

EXAM-STYLE QUESTIONS

Multiple-choice questions

1 Which of the following statements about the photoelectric effect is incorrect?

    A When a metal plate is illuminated with radiation, photoelectrons are emitted with no time delay.

    B The intensity of incident radiation has no effect on the maximum kinetic energy of emitted photoelectrons

    C Below a certain frequency of illuminating radiation, no photoelectrons are emitted.

    D The maximum kinetic energy of emitted photoelectrons is proportional to the frequency of the illuminating radiation.

2 Which of the following is the best estimate of the order of magnitude of a typical work function of a metal surface?

    A 10^{-21} J

    B 10^{-19} J

    C 10^{-17} J

    D 10^{-13} J

3 In a demonstration of the photoelectric effect, which of the following statements about the stopping voltage is correct?

    A The stopping voltage is independent of the intensity of the illuminating radiation.

    B The stopping voltage is inversely proportional to the intensity of the illuminating radiation.

    C The stopping voltage is proportional to the intensity of the illuminating radiation.

    D The stopping voltage is proportional to the square of the illuminating radiation.

CONTINUED

4 Aidan has a mass of 80 kg and walks along at a speed of 1.5 ms⁻¹. Jennifer has a mass of 60 kg and jogs at a speed of 2.0 ms⁻¹. What is the ratio of their de Broglie wavelengths, $\frac{\lambda_{Aidan}}{\lambda_{Jennifer}}$?

A 0.75
B 1.00
C 1.25
D 1.33

5 Electrons accelerated through a potential difference, V, will acquire a de Broglie wavelength, λ. Which of the following de Broglie wavelengths will electrons acquire if they are accelerated through a potential difference of $4V$?

A $\frac{\lambda}{4}$
B $\frac{\lambda}{2}$
C 2λ
D 4λ

6 Electrons of charge e and mass m that have been accelerated through a potential difference, V, will have a momentum given by which of the following expressions?

A $p = mV$
B $p = \frac{1}{\sqrt{2meV}}$
C $p = \sqrt{2meV}$
D $p = 2meV$

7 A moving electron, of mass m_e, and a moving proton, of mass m_p, both have the same de Broglie wavelength. Which of the following statements about the ratio of the electron's speed to the proton's speed, $\frac{v_{electron}}{v_{proton}}$, is correct?

A $\frac{v_{electron}}{v_{proton}} = \sqrt{\frac{m_p}{m_e}}$
B $\frac{v_{electron}}{v_{proton}} = \sqrt{\frac{m_e}{m_p}}$
C $\frac{v_{electron}}{v_{proton}} = \frac{m_p}{m_e}$
D $\frac{v_{electron}}{v_{proton}} = \frac{m_e}{m_p}$

8 Which of the following correctly gives the momentum of a photon of light of wavelength 300 nm?

A 1.3×10^{-40} kgms⁻¹
B 2.2×10^{-27} kgms⁻¹
C 6.6×10^{-27} kgms⁻¹
D 1.3×10^{-26} kgms⁻¹

CONTINUED

9 Which of the following, all of which are moving at the same speed, has the largest de Broglie wavelength?

   A A proton
   B An a-particle
   C An electron
   D A cricket ball

Short-answer questions

10 When a metal surface is illuminated with ultraviolet light, electrons with a range of kinetic energies are emitted from the metal surface. The metal surface has a work function of 2.2 eV.

   a State what is meant by the term *work function*. [1]
   b Explain why there is a range in the energies of the emitted electrons. [2]
   c Calculate the maximum kinetic energy of an emitted electron if the incident ultraviolet light has a wavelength of 200 nm. [2]

11 A physics teacher wants to teach her class about wave–particle duality.

   a State what is meant by the term *wave–particle duality*. [1]
   b Suggest a demonstration the teacher could use to show that light behaves like
      i   waves. [1]
      ii particles. [1]
   c In order to show her students that particles behave like waves, the teacher chooses to show her students a demonstration of electron diffraction by a crystal of graphite. Outline briefly the main features of her demonstration. [2]

12 Electrons accelerated through a voltage V gain 8.0×10^{-17} J of kinetic energy.

   a Determine the value of the voltage, V. [2]
   b If the mass of an electron is 9.1×10^{-31} kg, show that the de Broglie wavelength of the electrons is about 5.5×10^{-11} m. [2]
   c Explain why we would expect to see diffraction effects from such electrons when they are fired at a crystal with an atomic spacing of 2×10^{-10} m. [2]

13 With reference to the photoelectric effect,

   a state what is meant by *work function for a metal*. [1]
   b explain what is meant by *threshold frequency for a metal surface*. [1]
   c a metal surface is illuminated with light of wavelength 450 nm. The work function of the metal is 1.5 eV. Determine the maximum kinetic energy of the electrons emitted from the metal surface. [2]
   d If the illuminating power in **part c** is 3 W and one electron is emitted from the metal surface for every 8 incident photons, calculate the current produced by the incident radiation. [2]

CONTINUED

14 Figure 22.6 shows a pair of zinc electrodes attached to a variable power supply and a sensitive ammeter. The electrodes each have a work function of 4.25 eV. One of the electrodes is illuminated with ultraviolet light of wavelength 260 nm. The ammeter shows a current flowing in the circuit.

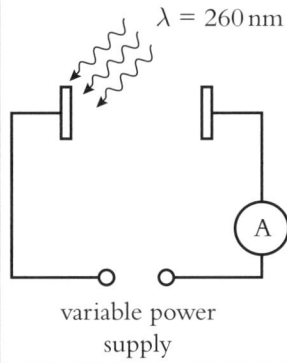

Figure 22.6

- **a** Calculate the maximum kinetic energy, in Joules, of the photoelectrons from the illuminated electrode. [2]
- **b** The variable power supply is adjusted and the current falls to zero. Suggest which terminal on the power supply is negative. [1]
- **c** Determine the minimum terminal voltage required to prevent a current from flowing. [2]

15 Figure 22.7 shows accelerated electrons passing through a thin piece of graphite crystal inside an evacuated tube.

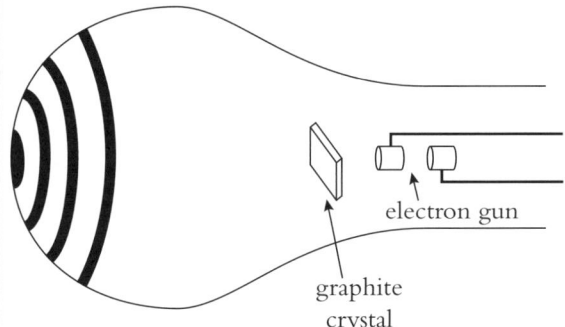

Figure 22.7

- **a** Explain why the tube must be evacuated. [1]
- **b** Explain how the pattern on the fluorescent screen of the tube provides evidence of the wave nature of electrons. [2]
- **c** The distance between the graphite crystal and the fluorescent screen is 20.0 cm. The electrons have been accelerated through a potential difference of 1.0 kV. If the radius of the third observed ring on the fluorescent screen is 3.5 cm, calculate the spacing of the carbon atoms in the graphite crystal. [3]

CONTINUED

16 The graph in Figure 22.8 shows how the stopping potential, in volts, varies with the frequency of incident radiation during a demonstration of the photoelectric effect.

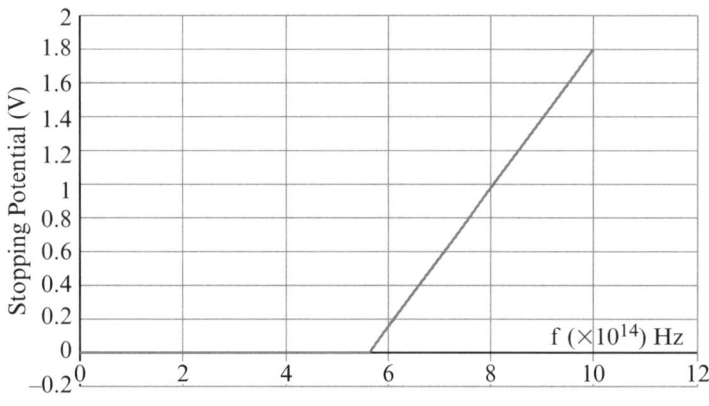

Figure 22.8

Use the graph in Figure 22.8 to estimate
a the threshold frequency, f_o. [1]
b Planck's constant. [2]
c the work function, Φ. [2]

17 Figure 22.9 shows how the maximum kinetic energy of photoelectrons varies with the frequency of incident radiation.

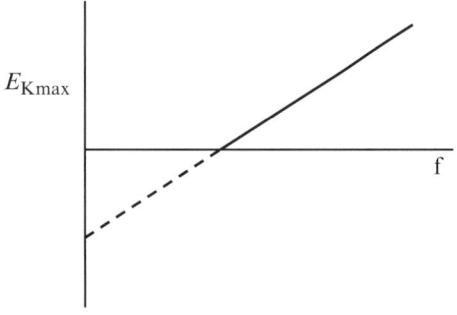

Figure 22.9

a Explain why the graph has a dotted line for negative values of E_{Kmax}. [1]
b State how the graph can be used to find
  i the threshold frequency, f_o. [1]
  ii the value of Planck's constant, h. [1]
  iii the work function, ϕ. [1]
c Add to Figure 22.9 to show how the maximum kinetic energy of photoelectons varies with the frequency of incident radiation for a metal surface with a larger value of work function. [1]

CONTINUED

18 The wave nature of electrons can be used to investigate the structure of protons. Protons have a radius of 1.2×10^{-15} m.

    a Suggest an appropriate de Broglie wavelength for such electrons. [1]

    b Use your answer to **part a** to determine the momentum of the electrons. [2]

    c Suggest, with a suitable calculation, how your answer to **part b** implies that the electron's mass must be larger than its rest mass value of 9.1×10^{-31} kg. [2]

19 A proton and an electron are both moving at the same speed. The de Broglie wavelength of the proton is 2.4×10^{-11} m.

    a Show that the speed of the proton and the electron is about 1.7×10^4 ms^{-1}. [2]

    b Calculate the de Broglie wavelength of the electron. [2]

    c Suggest why demonstrating the wave properties of protons is more difficult than the wave properties of electrons. [1]

> Chapters 23 and 24
Nuclear physics and Nuclear fission

CHAPTER OUTLINE

In this chapter, you will:

- learn—or revise—the notation for nuclides.
- explore nuclear binding energy and the mass defect.
- see how the binding energy per nucleon varies with nucleon number and understand the significance of the shape of the curve.
- use the mass–energy equivalence, $E = mc^2$, to solve nuclear reaction problems.
- explore the strong nuclear force.
- explore radioactive decay as a random process.
- identify the spectra of beta emissions as evidence for the existence of neutrinos and antineutrinos.
- examine the properties of alpha, beta and gamma emissions.
- consider the effects of background radiation.
- understand why some nuclei are stable and others unstable.
- use the spectra of alpha and gamma emissions to provide evidence for discrete nuclear energy levels.
- explore the radioactive decay law and the relationship of the decay constant, λ, to the half-life, $t_{\frac{1}{2}}$.
- solve problems involving activity, count rate and half-life.
- solve problems using the radioactive decay equations.
- examine spontaneous and neutron-induced fission as a process of releasing energy.
- consider the role of chain reactions in nuclear fission.
- examine the roles of control rods, moderators, heat exchangers and shielding in a nuclear power station.
- consider the properties and management of fission products.

KEY TERMS

nucleon: one of the two kinds of particles in the nucleus; a proton or a neutron

atomic number, Z: the number of protons in the nucleus

nucleon number, A: the total number of nucleons in the nucleus

nuclide: a nucleus with a specific number of protons and neutrons

isotope: any nucleus of a given element (i.e. a given number of protons) containing a different number of neutrons

unified atomic mass unit, u: defined exactly as $\frac{1}{12}$ of the mass of a $^{12}_{6}C$ atom. u = 1.661 × 10⁻²⁷ kg

mass defect: the difference between the mass of the nucleons and the mass of the nucleus

binding energy: the minimum energy required to separate all the nucleons of a nucleus

radioactive: a nucleus that is unstable

alpha decay: when an unstable nucleus emits an alpha particle

beta-minus decay: when an unstable nucleus emits an electron and an antineutrino

beta-plus decay: when an unstable nucleus emits a positron and a neutrino

positron: a positively charged electron

gamma decay: when a nucleus in an excited energy state emits a photon of electromagnetic radiation

parent nucleus: the (unstable) nucleus that decays

daughter nucleus: the nucleus formed after a decay process

decay series: a series of decays that shows the progression of an unstable nucleus into a stable nucleus

activity: the number of radioactive decays per second

half-life, $t_{\frac{1}{2}}$: the time it takes for the activity to halve

decay constant, λ: the probability that a decay will occur in the next second

background radiation: radiation from natural sources

radioactive series: a series of decays that leads to a nucleus finally becoming stable (lead or thallium)

nuclear fission: the splitting of an unstable nucleus into two (or more) parts

spontaneous fission: the splitting of an unstable nucleus without absorbing a neutron

> ## CONTINUED
>
> **induced fission:** the splitting of a nucleus after it has absorbed a neutron
>
> **chain reaction:** a continuous series of reactions produced by the products of each reaction
>
> **critical mass:** the smallest mass of nuclear fuel that can sustain a chain reaction
>
> **moderator:** a material used to slow down neutrons by allowing them to collide with atoms of the moderator
>
> **control rod:** a material used to absorb neutrons and so control the rate of fission reactions
>
> **heat exchanger:** a part of a nuclear reactor that removes the thermal energy generated in the moderator
>
> **electromagnetic force:** the interaction mediated by the exchange of photons
>
> **gravitational force:** the interaction mediated by the exchange of gravitons
>
> **weak nuclear force:** the interaction mediated by the exchange of W and Z bosons
>
> **strong nuclear force:** the interaction mediated by the exchange of gluons

KEY EQUATIONS

mass defect, Δm: $\Delta m = ZM_p + (A - Z)M_n - M_{nucleus}$
binding energy, E_B: $E_B = \Delta mc^2$
radioactive decay: $N = N_0 e^{-\lambda t}$ $$\lambda = \frac{\ln 2}{t_{\frac{1}{2}}}$$ $$\frac{dN}{dT} = -\lambda N,$$ where Δm is the mass deficit, Z is the atomic number, M_p is the mass of a proton, A is the nucleon number, M_n is the mass of a neutron, $M_{nucleus}$ is the mass of a nucleus, E_B is the binding energy, c is the speed of light, N is the number of undecayed nuclei, N_0 the number of undecayed nuclei at $t = 0$, λ the decay constant, t is time and $\frac{dN}{dT}$ is the activity or number of decay events per second.

Exercise 23.1 Mass defect and binding energy

1. Explain what is meant by the following terms:

   a *nucleon*

   b *isotope*

   c *nuclide*

2. a Complete the table showing some of the properties of the four fundamental forces.

Name of Force	Acts on	Range	Boson responsible
Electromagnetic			
Gravitational			
Weak force			
Strong nuclear force			

   b Which of the four fundamental forces is responsible for

   i β^--decay?

   ii a black hole not emitting any light?

   iii the movement of a speaker cone?

   iv two protons existing in a nucleus of helium?

   c By considering the different forces that act on nucleons, explain how it is possible for most nuclei to hold their nucleons within the nucleus.

   d With reference to the forces acting in a nucleus, suggest a reason why some nuclei are able to decay by alpha decay.

   e In the early 1900s, Lord Rutherford observed alpha particles being deflected by the nuclei of gold atoms.

   i At low energies, the alpha particles were repelled by the gold nuclei. Use your knowledge of the four fundamental forces to explain why we now expect this to happen.

   ii If the energy of the alpha particles had been substantially higher, the alpha particles may have been absorbed by the gold nuclei. Use your knowledge of the fundamental forces to explain why this can happen.

3   a   Define the terms

    i   *unified atomic mass unit*.

    ii *mass defect, Δm*.

    iii *binding energy*.

   b   Complete this table showing masses of some sub-atomic particles.

Name of particle	Mass / u	Mass / kg
proton	1.00728	
neutron	1.00867	
electron		9.11×10^{-31}

   c   i   The mass of an alpha particle is given as 4.0015 u. Calculate the mass of an alpha particle in kg.

       ii Calculate the total mass of the particles that make up an alpha particle. Give your answer in u.

       iii How do your answers to **parts a** and **b** compare?

       iv Calculate the difference between the mass of the particles that make up the alpha particle and the actual mass of the alpha particle.

       v   Calculate the energy equivalence, in MeV, of the mass defect of the alpha particle.

       vi Hence, show that the binding energy per nucleon for an alpha particle is about 7.1 MeV nucleon^{-1}.

4   Calculate the binding energy per nucleon of the following nuclei:

   a $^{15}_{6}$C (nuclear mass: 15.01060 u)

   b $^{24}_{11}$Na (nuclear mass: 23.99096 u)

   c $^{56}_{26}$Fe (nuclear mass: 55.93494 u)

   d $^{62}_{28}$Ni (nuclear mass: 61.9129 u)

5   a   Sketch a graph to show how the binding energy per nucleon varies with nucleon number for elements up to atomic number 92.

    b   How can you use your graph to indicate which nuclei are the most stable?

    c   Indicate the region where nuclear **fusion** can occur to produce energy.

    d   Suggest why the value for iron is significant.

    e   Indicate the region where nuclear **fission** can occur to produce energy.

23 and 24 Nuclear physics and Nuclear fission

6 Consider the following two nuclear reactions:

$^{47}_{21}Sc \rightarrow ^{47}_{22}Ti + ^{0}_{-1}\beta$ and $^{47}_{21}Sc \rightarrow ^{47}_{20}Ca + ^{0}_{1}\beta^+$

The following data are available:

Particle	Mass in amu
$^{47}_{21}Sc$	46.9524
$^{47}_{20}Ca$	46.9545
$^{47}_{22}Ti$	46.9518
$^{0}_{-1}\beta$ and $^{0}_{1}\beta^+$	0.00055

If the initial $^{47}_{21}Sc$ nucleus is considered to be stationary, both of these equations suggest that the products of the reaction will gain kinetic energy and move away from each other.

a   State the principle of conservation of energy.

b   Explain how the principle of conservation of energy dictates whether the two nuclear reactions can occur.

c   Hence, determine which of the two nuclear reactions can occur and which one cannot.

d   State the principle of conservation of momentum.

e   For the nuclear reaction that can occur,

   i   how much energy is available to be transferred into kinetic energy? Give your answer in keV.

   ii   hence, determine how much kinetic energy each of the reaction products gains.

7 a   Suppose a nuclear reaction were described, in a simplified way, as A → B + C.

   i   What condition must be satisfied for this reaction to occur?

   ii   An example of this kind of reaction might be

   $^{1}_{0}n \rightarrow ^{1}_{1}p + ^{0}_{-1}\beta \; (+^{0}_{0}\bar{\nu})$.

   Suggest why this reaction can occur spontaneously.

   iii   Another example of this kind of reaction is

   $^{1}_{1}p \rightarrow ^{1}_{0}n + ^{0}_{1}\beta(+^{0}_{0}\bar{\nu})$.

   Suggest why this reaction cannot occur spontaneously.

   iv   The reaction in **part iii** does occur, not spontaneously, but from within a nucleus. Suggest how this reaction, within a nucleus, can occur.

b   Now consider a nuclear reaction described by
    A + B → C.

    i   What condition must be satisfied for this reaction to occur?

    ii   List the ways in which this condition can be satisfied.

    iii An example of this kind of reaction is

         $^{2}_{1}H + ^{1}_{1}H \rightarrow ^{3}_{2}He \;(+\gamma),$

         which occurs extensively in the core of the Sun—and other main sequence stars.

         Using the following data, show that this reaction can occur.

         Data: Mass of $^{2}_{1}H$ = 2.01355 u; mass of $^{1}_{1}H$ is 1.00728 u; mass of $^{3}_{2}He$ is 3.01603 u

8   A reaction that occurs naturally is

    $^{233}_{92}U \rightarrow ^{229}_{90}Th + ^{4}_{2}\alpha.$

    The following data are available:

atom	Mass in amu
$^{233}_{92}U$	233.03950
$^{229}_{90}Th$	229.03163
$^{4}_{2}\alpha$	4.001506

    a   Determine the amount of energy available as kinetic energy for the reaction products.

    b   Hence, show that the alpha particle gains 5.83 MeV of kinetic energy.

    c   Calculate the speed of the alpha particle.

Exercise 23.2 Radioactivity

1   Radioactive substances have nuclei that are unstable.

    a   Broadly speaking, there are four reasons why nuclei can be unstable. What are they?

    b   For each of the ways listed in your answer for **part a**, state which radioactive decay process will occur as a result of the nucleus being unstable.

    c   The accepted way of showing the nucleon number (the sum of the protons and neutrons in the nucleus) is to use the letter A. The number of protons in the nucleus (the atomic number) is given the letter Z.

Use A for the nucleon number, Z for the atomic number, and X and Y for nuclides to write the decay equation for the

    i   alpha decay of nuclide X.

    ii   beta-minus-decay of nuclide X.

    iii   beta-plus-decay of nuclide X.

    iv   gamma-decay of nuclide X.

d   Figure 23.1 shows a sketch of how the neutron number, A–Z, is related to the proton number, Z, for those nuclei that are stable. The dotted line shows A–Z = Z.

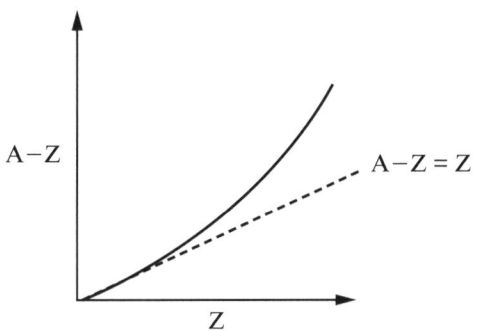

Figure 23.1

Add to Figure 23.1 to show the regions in which nuclei will undergo

    i   α-decay.

    ii   β⁻-decay.

    iii   β⁺-decay.

2   Within a nucleus, the nucleons are subject to two main forces which compete against each other.

a   What are these two forces?

b   Outline how the two forces compete against each other.

c   Generally, that is for the majority of nuclides, which of the two forces remains dominant?

Alpha decay occurs only in the nuclei with the very largest number of nucleons.

d   Explain why the strong force is not always dominant in the nuclides with the largest number of nucleons.

Amercium-241, $^{241}_{95}$Am, an isotope of americium used extensively in classrooms for demonstrating α-decay, decays into neptunium-237.

e Write a nuclear decay equation for the α-decay of americium-241 into neptunium-237.

f The following table shows the nuclear masses, in unified atomic mass units, for americium-241, neptunium-237 and an alpha-particle.

Particle	Mass (amu)
Americium-241	241.004579
Neptunium-237	236.99702
α-particle	4.00151

    i Show that, energetically, this decay is possible.

    ii Hence, calculate the energy released by the decay process.

    iii What fraction of the available energy released would you expect to be taken away as kinetic energy by the α-particle?

    iv In fact, the α-particle carries away 5.49 MeV of kinetic energy. Suggest a reason for this.

g Show that it is not possible for

    i the americium nucleus to emit a proton only.
(Mass of proton = 1.00728 u; mass of $^{240}_{94}$Pu = 240.00211 u)

    ii The americium nucleus to emit a neutron only.
(Mass of neutron = 1.00867 u; mass of americium 240 = 240.00305 u)

h Suggest why it is almost always the case that heavy nuclei decay by alpha-decay and not by emitting a single proton or neutron.

3   **a** When an alpha particle has lost all its energy, what is likely to happen to it?

    b How does your answer to **part a** confirm how Rutherford and Royds, in 1909, were able to demonstrate that alpha particles were the same thing as helium nuclei?

4 An α-particle, emitted from an unstable nucleus, typically has a kinetic energy of a few MeV. With this amount of energy, it can ionise many atoms.

    a Explain what is meant by the term *ionise*.

    b Give three reasons why the α-particle is good at ionising atoms.

    c It takes about 30 eV of the α-particle's energy to ionise an atom. Determine how many atoms an α-particle can ionise.

d Figure 23.2 shows an example of how the number of ionising events an α-particle causes per centimetre of the distance it travels through the air.

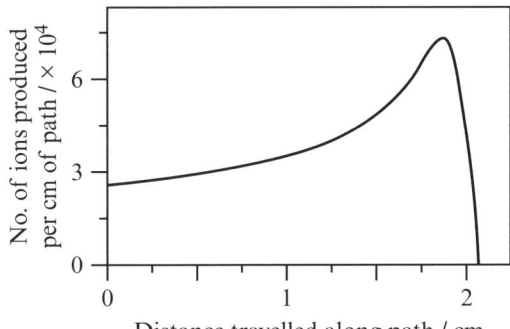

Figure 23.2

   i Explain the shape of the graph.

   ii Use the graph to estimate the number of ion pairs that this α-particle can produce and compare your answer to **part c**.

e A single piece of paper is about 8×10^{-5} m thick. Atoms in a solid are about 2×10^{-10} m apart. Suppose an alpha-particle has 5 MeV of kinetic energy.

   i Calculate how many atoms thick a typical piece of paper is.

   ii Calculate how many ionising events this alpha particle can cause.

   iii Hence, show why alpha-particles are stopped by a piece of paper.

5 Carbon-12, $^{12}_{6}C$, and carbon-14, $^{14}_{6}C$, are two isotopes of carbon. Carbon-12 is stable, but carbon-14 is unstable.

a How many protons and neutrons are there in the nucleus of

   i $^{12}_{6}C$

   ii $^{14}_{6}C$

b Suggest why $^{14}_{6}C$ is unstable.

c How will $^{14}_{6}C$ decay?

d Write a decay equation for the decay of $^{14}_{6}C$.

6 All of the following nuclei are unstable and decay by β^--decay. For each, determine the daughter product nucleus.

   a $^{3}_{1}\text{H}$

   b $^{32}_{15}\text{P}$

   c $^{63}_{28}\text{Ni}$

   d $^{90}_{38}\text{Sr}$

   e $^{209}_{82}\text{Pb}$

7 Some unstable nuclei decay by gamma decay.

   a In what ways is γ-decay different from α-decay and β-decay?

   b Write a general decay equation for γ-decay.

   c With reference to your answer to **part a**, describe what is happening to the nucleus when it undergoes γ-decay.

   d Will a γ-ray be deflected by an electromagnetic field?

   e Typically, how does the energy a γ-ray has compare to the energy a photon has when emitted as a result of an electronic energy–level transition in an atom?

8 Figure 23.3 shows how the intensity of γ-radiation passing through a slab of lead varies with the distance through the lead.

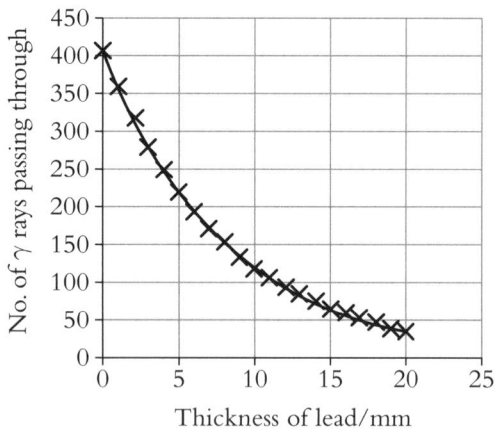

Figure 23.3

   a By taking suitable values from the graph, show that the variation of intensity with distance is exponential.

   b Use the graph to find the thickness of lead required to

      i   halve the intensity.

      ii reduce the intensity by a factor of $1/e$.

TIP

Use the constant ratio rule.

9 Highly energetic γ-photons can sometimes transform their energy, by a process called pair production, into a proton and an anti-proton. The mass of a proton is 938 MeVc^{-2}.

    a Calculate the minimum energy, in joules, of a gamma-ray photon that will be able to produce a proton–anti-proton pair.

    b   **i** Why is it most likely that a proton–anti-proton pair will only be produced by a gamma-ray photon with significantly more energy than your answer to **part a**?

        ii What happens to the extra energy that the photon had if a proton–anti-proton pair is produced?

10 Complete the table listing some of the properties of α, β and γ radiation.

Radiation	What is it?	Charge	Mass(amu)	Ionising ability	Stopped by?	Deflected by em field?
α						
β^-						
β^+						
γ						

11 **a** Outline what is meant by the term *background radiation*.

    b Give some examples of the sources of background radiation.

    c Suggest why, generally, we don't have to worry about the effects of background radiation on our bodies.

    d State what is meant by corrected count.

12 **a** Explain the meaning of the following terms:

        i *half-life*, $t_{\frac{1}{2}}$

        ii *activity*

    b In what SI units is the activity usually measured?

    c Radioactive materials sold for educational purposes often have their activities given in Curies, Ci, or microcuries, μCi. How do 1 Ci and 1 μCi compare to the modern SI unit for activity?

13 A sample of radioactive nuclei has a mass of 160 g. If the half-life of the radioactive isotope is 6 minutes, what mass of radioactive nuclei will remain after

    a 6 minutes?

    b 12 minutes?

    c 24 minutes?

14 Outline an experiment to find the half-life of a sample of radioactive material. You know its half-life is between 10 and 20 minutes. Make sure you include

- the equipment required,
- your method,
- the measurements you need to make and
- how you would manipulate the data to find the half-life.

15 There are three naturally occurring and one artificially induced radioactive series.

    a Explain what is meant by the term *radioactive series*.

    b In one of the radioactive series the unstable nucleus of $^{238}_{92}U$ decays by α-decay. The daughter product produced is also unstable and decays by β^--decay. This continues with the following decays: β^-, α, α, α, α. Even then the nucleus formed is still unstable and the series continues until eventually a nucleus of $^{206}_{82}Pb$ is formed, which is stable.

    Use the grid in Figure 23.4 to map out the series from $^{238}_{92}U$ through the seven decays given. The first decay has been done for you.

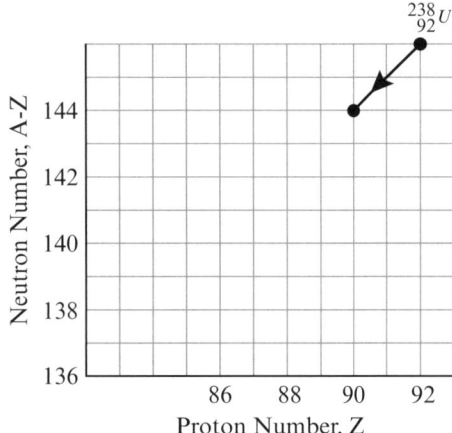

Figure 23.4

    c Identify each of the nuclei in this part of the series by writing nuclear decay equations.

Exercise 23.3 Nuclear properties and the radioactive decay law

1. After Lord Rutherford's highly successful series of experiments with α-particles, other scientists experimented using α-particles of much higher energy. The results they got were not completely in agreement with those Lord Rutherford had found.

   a Outline how the results using much higher-energy α-particles differed from those used by Lord Rutherford.

   b Which of the four fundamental forces was responsible for the disagreement between the two sets of results?

   c How do we now explain what was happening?

2. Carbon-14 is an unstable nucleus that undergoes β^--decay.

   a With reference to Figure 23.1, what is it that makes this nucleus unstable and undergo β^--decay?

   b When the emitted β^--particles are investigated, it is found that their energy spectra look similar to what is shown in Figure 23.5.

   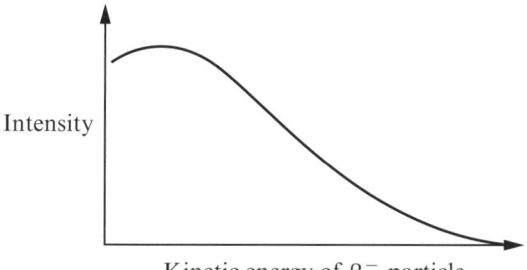

   Figure 23.5

   i Outline how the energy spectrum for β^--particles differs from the energy spectrum for α-particles.

   ii How did Wolfgang Pauli explain the shape of the energy spectrum for β^--particles?

   c Write a decay equation for the β^--decay of carbon-14.

   d i Assuming that the carbon-14 nucleus is stationary, calculate the energy released in the decay process. (Data: mass of $^{14}_{6}C$ = 13.99994 u; mass of $^{14}_{7}N$ = 13.99922; mass of β^--particle = 0.00055 u; mass of $^{0}_{0}\bar{\nu} \approx 0$)

   ii What is the maximum fraction of the available energy that can be taken by the emitted β^--particle?

3   The unstable nucleus of $^{12}_{5}$B decays by β^--decay. When the total kinetic energy of the decay products is investigated it is found that two slightly different β^--decays occur. One of of these decays is accompanied by γ-decay.

   a   Write a general nuclear decay equation for γ-decay.

   b   The energies involved in the two β^--decay events possible are

   - β^- : 9.0 MeV and γ : 4.4 MeV and
   - β^- : 13.4 MeV.

   i   Verify that both of these events release the same amount of energy.

   ii Explain why this must be the case.

   iii Outline how this provides evidence for nuclei to have excited energy states, similar to the excited energy states of electrons in atoms.

4   The α-decay of $^{241}_{95}$Am occurs in three different modes, two of which are accompanied by γ-decay. The energies involved in these three decay modes are

   - α-decay : 5.443 MeV and γ-decay : 0.102 MeV or 0.043 MeV + 0.059 MeV,
   - α-decay : 5.486 MeV and γ-decay : 0.059 MeV and
   - α-decay : 5.545 MeV.

   a   Verify that in these three decay modes, the same amount of total energy is released.

   b   Explain why this must be the case.

   c   On the basis of this information, sketch a simple energy level diagram for the nucleus of a neptunium-237 atom.

   d   How do the magnitudes of the nuclear energy levels compare with those of electron energy levels in atoms?

   e   So, generally, how do the energies of electromagnetic radiations emitted from atoms—as a result of electron energy level transitions—compare with the energies of γ-rays emitted from excited nuclei?

5   In a sample of radioactive nuclei, the number of undecayed nuclei varies with time according to the equation
   $N = N_0 e^{-\lambda t}$.

   a   Show that the half-life of the radioactive nuclei, $t_{\frac{1}{2}}$, is related to the decay constant, λ, by
   $$\lambda = \frac{\ln 2}{t_{\frac{1}{2}}}.$$

b Calculate the decay constant of

  i $^{40}_{19}K$ $(t_{\frac{1}{2}} = 1250$ million years$)$.

  ii $^{13}_{7}N$ $(t_{\frac{1}{2}} = 9.96$ minutes$)$.

  iii $^{60}_{27}Co$ $(t_{\frac{1}{2}} = 5.27$ years$)$.

6 The nuclide $^{24}_{11}Na$ is unstable and has a decay constant of 1.28×10^{-5} s^{-1}.

  a Calculate the half-life of $^{24}_{11}Na$.

  b As a fraction of its initial activity, what would the activity of a sample of $^{24}_{11}Na$ be after

   i 15 hours?

   ii 30 hours?

7 Californium-239 is an artificially produced isotope that is unstable and decays by α-decay with a decay constant of $\lambda = 0.01155$.

  a Calculate the half-life of $^{239}_{98}Cf$.

  b Draw a graph of how the number of undecayed nuclei, N, varies with time for an initial number, $N_o = 600$, of $^{239}_{98}Cf$ nuclei during a period of 10 minutes.

  c Use your graph to

   i determine the initial activity of the sample.

   ii verify your answer to **part a**.

  d Verify your answer to **part c ii** using the relationship between the activity, the decay constant and the number of undecayed nuclei present.

8 a Outline how scientists are able to use radioactive carbon-14 to find the age of fossilised organic material.

  b A sample of 1 g of a growing oak tree will produce a corrected count of 144 in a time of 10 minutes.

   i What uncertainty is there is this corrected count?

   ii The half-life of $^{14}_{6}C$ is 5700 years. How old would a fossilised piece of oak tree be if the corrected count in ten minutes from it was 18?

  c Scientists used radiocarbon dating to determine the amount of $^{14}_{6}C$ in a historic artefact. They found it was 92% of that in living tissue. How old is the artefact?

9 Outline how to determine the half-life of a pure radioactive material for which there is no observable change in the count rate measured by a GM tube.

Exercise 24.1 Nuclear fission

1 Explain what is meant by the following terms:

   a *nuclear fission*

   b *spontaneous nuclear fission*

   c *induced nuclear fission*

2 Nucleii, such as uranium and plutonium, are used to produce energy by nuclear fission.

   a Explain why only the heaviest of nuclei can be used to produce energy by nuclear fission.

   b Stars produce energy by nuclear fusion of small-mass nuclei into larger-mass nuclei. Explain why nuclear fusion releases energy.

   c Which two elements form the boundary between those that can be used for fusion and those that can be used for fission?

3 In a typical nuclear power station, the following nuclear process occurs:

   $^{235}_{92}U + X \rightarrow A + B + nX$, where n is an integer.

   a What type of nuclear process is this?

   b Identify the particles labelled X.

   c What form of energy does this process produce?

4 The following nuclear process is an example of induced fission.

   $^{235}_{92}U + ^{1}_{0}n \rightarrow ^{137}_{55}Cs + ^{95}_{37}Rb + n\,^{1}_{0}n$, where n is an integer.

   a Determine the value of n.

   b Using the data in the table, calculate how much energy is released in this single fission of $^{235}_{92}U$.

Particle	$^{235}_{92}U$	$^{137}_{55}Cs$	$^{95}_{37}Rb$	$^{1}_{0}n$
Mass (amu)	234.994	136.877	94.886	1.0087

   c Data released from the U.K. Atomic Energy Authority and from British Nuclear Fuels Ltd. state that the average energy released by a single fission of $^{235}_{92}U$ is 215 MeV. Suggest why your answer to **part b** is different to this.

5 Uranium mined for power stations contains about 0.6% of the isotope $^{235}_{92}U$; the rest is mostly $^{238}_{92}U$.

   a Suggest why most of the energy production comes from the isotope $^{235}_{92}U$.

   b The specific energy for isotope $^{235}_{92}U$ is about 8.0×10^{13} Jkg^{-1}. How much energy is available from 1 kg of natural uranium?

c The energy produced in a single fission of a $^{235}_{92}$U nucleus is about 200 MeV. Show that the specific energy of $^{235}_{92}$U is about 8×10^{13} Jkg^{-1}.

d How does your answer to **part b** compare with the specific energy of fossil fuels such as coal or oil?

e Modern nuclear power stations use *enriched nuclear fuel*. Explain what the term *enriched nuclear fuel* means, and explain how it aids the overall efficiency of the power station.

6 Modern nuclear power stations use induced fission of $^{235}_{92}$U to release energy. Each fission process typically produces two, three or four fast-moving neutrons.

    a Outline why these fast-moving neutrons

        i are fundamental to the energy production of the nuclear power station.

        ii need to be slowed down.

    b A moderator can facilitate both aspects noted in **part a**. Explain how.

    c In order for the power station to supply a constant amount of energy from the fission processes, a chain reaction is required. Explain what a chain reaction is and why it is necessary.

    d What else is required by the nuclear power station to ensure that a chain reaction is maintained? What function is performed by these?

7 A maintained chain reaction in a nuclear power station requires that the uranium fuel rods each contain a minimum amount of mass of uranium, called the critical mass. Explain why a fuel rod must contain a critical mass of uranium.

8 **a** Outline the energy transformations that take place in a nuclear power station. Begin with the energy form at the start of the process, and end with secondary energy in the form of electrical energy.

    b Outline the main functions of, and the material used for, the

        i moderator.

        ii control rods.

        iii heat exchanger(s).

    c What would you expect to happen to the output of a nuclear power station if you removed the

        i moderator?

        ii control rods?

    d Outline the problems of disposing of nuclear waste from a nuclear power station.

EXAM-STYLE QUESTIONS

Multiple-choice questions

Questions 1 and 2 refer to Figure 23.6

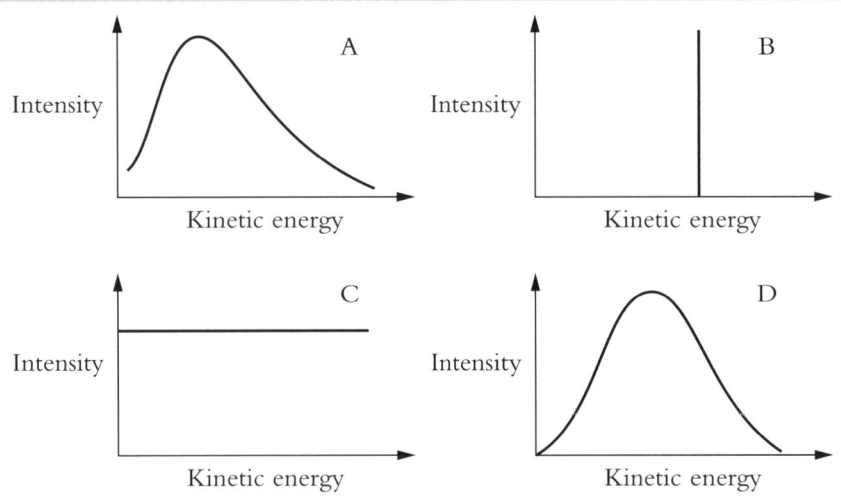

Figure 23.6

1 Figure 23.6 shows four possible emission spectra from radioactive nuclei. Which of the spectra best describes α-decay?

2 Figure 23.6 shows four possible emission spectra from radioactive nuclei. Which of the spectra best describes β^--decay?

3 A physics student wants to find the activity of a sample of radioactive material. To get a corrected value of the activity, the student must

   A subtract the background count from his measured count rate.
   B subtract the background count rate from his measured count rate.
   C subtract the background count from his measured count.
   D subtract the background count rate from his measured count.

4 Cobalt-60 is a radioactive isotope used extensively in physics classrooms. It decays by β^--decay into an isotope of nickel that is stable. After a sample of $^{60}_{27}\text{Co}$ is prepared for use, which one of the following graphs shows how the number of nickel nuclei varies with time?

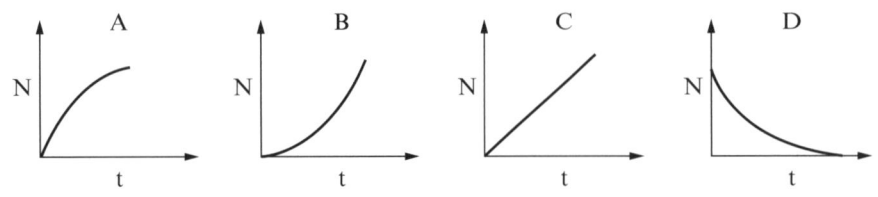

Figure 23.7

CONTINUED

5   Radioactive decay is often described as being spontaneous. This means that
   A the activity of a sample of radioactive material does not follow a mathematical description.
   B any nucleus could decay at any time.
   C in a sample of radioactive nuclei, all of the nuclei will decay after two half-lives.
   D all the nuclei in a sample will decay at the same time.

6   Which of the following gives the correct mathematical relationship between the half-life, $t_{\frac{1}{2}}$, and the decay constant, λ?
   A $t_{\frac{1}{2}} = \frac{1}{\lambda}$
   B $t_{\frac{1}{2}} = \frac{\lambda}{\ln 2}$
   C $t_{\frac{1}{2}} = \frac{\ln 2}{\lambda}$
   D $t_{\frac{1}{2}} = \ln 2 \times \lambda$

7   Nuclear fission and nuclear fusion are both processes that produce energy. Which one of the following statements is true for both of these processes?
   A The conservation of mass-energy is not obeyed.
   B The conservation of momentum is not obeyed.
   C No harmful radiation is released.
   D The binding energy per nucleon increases.

8   The isotope of polonium, $^{214}_{84}\text{Po}$, is unstable and decays by α-decay. Which of the following will be the daughter nucleus after such a decay process?
   A $^{210}_{83}\text{Bi}$
   B $^{218}_{86}\text{Rn}$
   C $^{210}_{82}\text{Pb}$
   D $^{214}_{85}\text{At}$

9   Which of the following graphs best describes the relationship between the activity of a sample of radioactive material and the number of nuclei, N, in the sample?

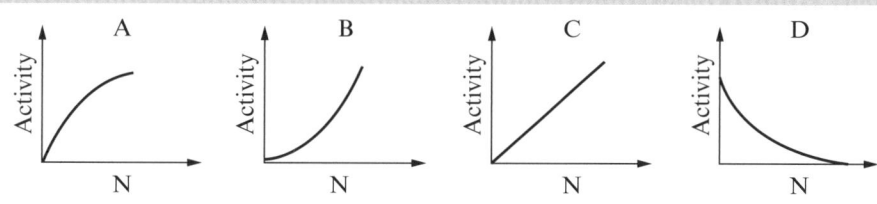

Figure 23.8

CONTINUED

10 Which of the following decay equations is an example of β^--decay?

   A $\quad ^{32}_{15}P \rightarrow \,^{32}_{14}Si + \,^{0}_{-1}\beta^- + \,^{0}_{0}\bar{\nu}$

   B $\quad ^{32}_{15}P \rightarrow \,^{32}_{16}S + \,^{0}_{-1}\beta^- + \,^{0}_{0}\nu$

   C $\quad ^{32}_{15}P \rightarrow \,^{32}_{16}S + \,^{0}_{-1}\beta^- + \,^{0}_{0}\bar{\nu}$

   D $\quad ^{32}_{15}P \rightarrow \,^{32}_{14}Si + \,^{0}_{+1}\beta^+ + \,^{0}_{0}\nu$

11 In a nuclear reactor, the principal function of the control rods is

   A to slow down fast neutrons.

   B to absorb some of the fast neutrons.

   C to remove thermal energy from the fuel rods.

   D to provide neutrons to be absorbed by uranium nucleii.

Short-answer questions

12 The mass of a nucleus of $^{3}_{2}He$ is 3.01603 u.

   a Outline the composition of this nucleus. [1]

   b The mass of a proton is given as 1.007276 u, and the mass of a neutron is 1.008665 u. Calculate the binding energy per nucleon, in MeV, of this nucleus. [3]

   c This kind of nucleus is produced in stars, such as our Sun, by the process of nuclear fusion. Complete the nuclear equation for this fusion process:

   $^{2}_{1}D + \,^{2}_{1}D \rightarrow \,^{3}_{2}He + $ _____ [1]

13 $^{233}_{92}U$ is an unstable nuclide of uranium that decays by α-emission.

   a Write a nuclear decay equation for this decay. [2]

   b The mass difference between the $^{233}_{92}U$ nucleus and the daughter nucleus it decays into is 4.00787 u. The mass of an α-particle is 4.001506 u. Calculate how much energy, in MeV, is available for the α-particle to transfer to E_K. [2]

   c In fact, the α-particle carries away less than this. Suggest what has happened to the remainder of the energy. [1]

14 The following radioactive decay process is observed to occur:

   $^{220}_{86}Rn \rightarrow \,^{216}_{84}Po + \,^{4}_{2}\alpha$.

   a The mass of a $^{220}_{86}Rn$ nucleus is 220.01140 u. The mass of a $^{216}_{84}Po$ nucleus is 216.00192 u. The mass of an α-particle is 4.001506 u. Calculate the mass available to be transferred to E_K during the α-decay process. [1]

   b Calculate the ratio of the E_K of the α-particle to the E_K of the Po nucleus after the decay. [2]

   c Calculate the E_K of the α-particle. [2]

15 The mass of a nucleus of $^{14}_{6}C$ is 14.003241 u. The mass of a nucleus of $^{14}_{7}N$ is 13.999231 u. $^{14}_{6}C$ decays by β^--decay.

   a State the nuclear decay equation for the β^--decay of $^{14}_{6}C$. [2]

   b Calculate the maximum possible E_K of the β^- particle. [2]

   c With reference to your decay equation, explain why β^- particles from the decay of $^{14}_{6}C$ are never observed with this amount of E_K. [1]

CONTINUED

16 A sample of $^{241}_{95}\text{Am}$ (an α-emitter) for use in school physics departments has an activity of 5μCi. (1 Ci = 3.7 × 10¹⁰ Bq.) The half-life of $^{241}_{95}\text{Am}$ is 433 years.

  a Calculate the decay constant for $^{241}_{95}\text{Am}$. [1]

  b Determine the number of $^{241}_{95}\text{Am}$ nuclei in the originally prepared sample. [2]

  c Explain why there isn't likely to be a Trading Standards issue for the samples of $^{241}_{95}\text{Am}$ that are delivered to schools within a year of their preparation. [1]

17 The nuclide $^{90}_{38}\text{Sr}$ is unstable and decays by β^- emission.

  a Write a nuclear decay equation for the decay of $^{90}_{38}\text{Sr}$. [2]

  b Explain why the kinetic energy of the β^- particle can vary from zero up to a maximum value. [2]

  c Explain why the nucleus left behind after the decay process doesn't carry away a significant amount of kinetic energy. [1]

18 A sample of uranium-238 has a mass of 1.0 mg. If the half-life of uranium-238 is 1.42 × 10¹⁷ s, calculate

  a the decay constant, λ. [1]

  b the number of atoms present in the sample. [2]

  c the activity of the sample. [2]

19 A sample of radioactive material is placed in front of a Geiger Muller tube, and its corrected count rate is 470 counts s⁻¹. After 20 minutes, the corrected count rate is 380 counts s⁻¹.

  a Explain what is meant by *corrected count rate*. [1]

  b Determine the decay constant for the radioactive material. [2]

  c Determine the half-life of the radioactive material.

  d Explain why this method of finding the half-life of a radioactive material is inappropriate for a radioactive substance that has a half-life of several million years.

20 Consider the following nuclear reaction:

$^{1}_{1}\text{p} + ^{13}_{6}\text{C} \rightarrow ^{13}_{7}\text{N} + ^{?}_{?}\text{X}$.

  a Show that the particle $^{?}_{?}\text{X}$ must be a neutron. [1]

  b This table shows the masses of the particles involved.

Particle	$^{1}_{1}\text{p}$	$^{13}_{6}\text{C}$	$^{13}_{7}\text{N}$	$^{?}_{?}\text{X}$
Mass (amu)	1.007276	13.000055	13.001889	1.008665

Using the conservation of mass-energy, determine the minimum kinetic energy required by the proton to allow this reaction to occur. [3]

  c Suggest why your answer to **part b** is still insufficient for the reaction to occur. [1]

CONTINUED

21 This equation shows a nuclear process:

$${}^{235}_{92}U + {}^{1}_{0}n \rightarrow {}^{236}_{92}U \rightarrow {}^{144}_{56}Ba + {}^{89}_{36}Kr + 3{}^{1}_{0}n.$$

The masses of the various particles are

${}^{236}_{92}U = 236.0526$ u; ${}^{144}_{56}Ba = 143.92292$ u; ${}^{89}_{36}Kr = 88.91781$ u; ${}^{1}_{0}n = 1.008665$ u.

- **a** State which kind of nuclear process is represented by the equation. [1]
- **b** Calculate the energy released during this process. Give your answer in MeV. [3]
- **c** State the form in which the energy is released. [1]

22 The fission of a ${}^{235}_{92}U$ nucleus produces fast neutrons with about 200 MeV of kinetic energy.

- **a** Calculate the effective 'temperature' of these fast neutrons. [2]
- **b** The neutrons' temperature needs to be about 20 °C to sustain a controlled chain reaction. Calculate the energy, in eV, of a 'thermal' electron at 20 °C. [2]
- **c** Each collision between a fast neutron and the moderator causes the neutron to lose 30% of its kinetic energy. Estimate the number of collisions required for a fast neutron to become a thermal neutron, so a chain reaction is produced. [2]

Chapter 25
Nuclear fusion and stars

CHAPTER OUTLINE

In this chapter, you will:

- explore nuclear fusion processes.
- look at the conditions necessary for fusion to occur.
- solve problems associated with the energy released in fusion reactions.
- identify and use the terms: luminosity and apparent brightness of stars.
- solve problems involving the luminosity and apparent brightness of stars.
- determine the distance to stars using their apparent brightness.
- explore the fusion reactions that occur in the cores of stars.
- explore the proton–proton chain and the energy it releases.
- > explore the carbon–nitrogen–oxygen (CNO) cycle for large mass stars on the main sequence.
- look at main sequence stars on the Hertzsprung–Russell diagram.
- explore the evolution of stars.
- understand the roles of the Chandrasekhar and the Oppenheimer–Volkoff limits in the evolution of stars.
- > examine the nuclear reactions that occur in very massive stars.
- > explore nucleosynthesis in heavy stars.

KEY TERMS

nuclear fusion: the joining of two light nuclei to form a heavier nucleus

nucleosynthesis: the process of producing nuclei by nuclear reactions involving other nuclei

luminosity, L: the total energy emitted by a celestial object per second

$L = \sigma A T^4$,

where σ is the Stefan–Boltzmann constant ($\sigma = 5.67 \times 10^{-8}$ Wm^{-2} K), A is the surface area of the star and T is the absolute temperature of the surface of the star

> **CONTINUED**

apparent brightness, b: the incident power per unit area received at the surface of the Earth from a celestial object. $b = \frac{L}{4\pi d^2}$, where L is luminosity and d is the distance from the Earth to the star

Wien's displacement law: the wavelength of the peak intensity in the emission spectrum of a hot body is inversely proportional to the absolute temperature

proton–proton chain: the sequence of fusion reactions, taking place in the core of main sequence stars, that produce helium from hydrogen

Hertzsprung–Russell diagram: a diagram showing the relationship between the luminosity of stars and their temperatures

main sequence: the stage in a star's life during which it is stable, producing energy in its core by fusing hydrogen into helium

red giant: very large, relatively cool stars with cores hot enough to fuse helium into carbon

planetary nebula: the mass and energy emitted at the end of a red giant's lifetime

supernova: The massive explosion of a red supergiant that sends mass and energy outwards, leaving behind a very dense core

white dwarf: small, hot stars in their final stages of evolution

neutron stars: the very dense, collapsed core of a very massive supergiant star

black hole: a star whose gravitational escape speed is greater than the speed of light

Chandrasekhar limit: the maximum mass of a white dwarf is 1.4 solar masses. Above this mass, the star will collapse into a neutron star

Oppenheimer–Volkoff limit: The maximum mass of a neutron star is about 3.0 solar masses. Above this mass, the star will collapse into a black hole

nucleosynthesis: the process of creating heavier nuclei from lighter ones

s-process: when an unstable isotope decays before it can absorb an additional neutron

r-process: when an unstable isotope absorbs an additional neutron before it has decayed

mass–luminosity relationship for a main sequence star: $L \propto M^{3.5}$, where M is the mass of the star

Exercise 25.1 Nuclear fusion

1   **a**   Outline what is meant by *nuclear fusion*.

   b   Explain why the fusion of light nuclei releases energy.

   c   In what form or forms is the released energy?

2   An example of a simple fusion reaction is

$${}^{1}_{1}H + {}^{1}_{0}n \rightarrow {}^{2}_{1}H + {}^{0}_{0}\gamma.$$

Use the data in this table to determine the amount of energy released in this reaction.

Particle	${}^{1}_{1}H$	${}^{1}_{0}n$	${}^{2}_{1}H$
Mass (amu)	1.007276	1.0088665	2.014102

3   This question looks in detail at the fusion of two protons.

The fusion of two protons to form a deuterium nucleus is given by the equation
$${}^{1}_{1}H + {}^{1}_{1}H \rightarrow {}^{2}_{1}H + {}^{0}_{1}\beta^{+} + {}^{0}_{0}\nu.$$

   a   **i**   Calculate the energy available from this reaction. (Take the mass of the ${}^{0}_{1}\beta^{+}$ to be 0.00055 u and the mass of the ${}^{0}_{0}\nu$ to be 0.)

   ii   Given that the mass of a proton is 1.007276 u and 1 u = 1.66×10^{-27} kg, how many protons are there in 1 kg of hydrogen?

   iii   Hence, determine the energy available from the fusion of 1 kg of hydrogen.

   iv   In fact, the energy available from 1 kg of hydrogen for this reaction is larger than your answer to **part iii**. Suggest what is likely to happen to the ${}^{0}_{1}\beta^{+}$ particle that is produced in the fusion process.

   v   Show that your answer to **part iv** produces an additional 1.02 MeV of energy for each fusion of two protons.

   vi   So, what is the actual total amount of energy that 1 kg of hydrogen can produce via this fusion process?

   vii   How does this compare to the specific energy of anthracite coal, which is about 2.7×10^{7} Jkg^{-1}?

   b   Assume that the protons are moving directly towards each other—head-on—at the same speed.

   i   Why is this a reasonable assumption?

   ii   The radius of a proton is 1.2×10^{-15} m. What is the minimum amount of kinetic energy the protons need in order for them to fuse together?

   iii   If this were the average kinetic energy of a proton, at what temperature would the proton be?

iv   The temperature at the core of the Sun is most likely to be of the order of 10^7 K. Explain how this reaction is possible in the core of the Sun, although the probability of it occurring is rather small.

v   Explain how your answer to **part iv** acts to limit the energy production of a star like the Sun.

4   All stars have to start their production of energy with the fusion reaction from **question 3**. Since this occurs in the core of the star, it gives us information about the conditions that must be satisfied in order for nuclear fusion to take place.

a   The previous question (**question 3**) showed that protons need to have an effective temperature of the order of 10^9 K for the fusion reaction to occur and the core temperatures of stars like the Sun is one or two orders of magnitude lower than this. What process(es) have occurred during the early lifetime of a star to

i   raise the temperature of the core of such a star to such high levels?

ii   increase the density of the core to levels sufficient to maintain thermonuclear fusion of its constituent protons?

b   The probability of the fusion reactions occurring is low. Explain why the very high density of the core of a star

i   makes the proton–proton fusion process viable.

ii   keeps the protons available for the fusion process close enough together for the fusion to occur.

iii   also means that the temperature of the core is kept high enough for the fusion process to occur.

c   Using your answers to **parts b** and **c**, outline why producing nuclear power for domestic use in man-made fusion reactors is still (as of January 2023) seen to be a technological difficulty.

5   It is generally accepted that the first example of the artificial transmutation of elements was performed by Cockcroft and Walton at the Cavendish laboratories in 1932. Protons from an early example of a particle accelerator were fired at lithium atoms producing highly unstable beryllium, which then suffered spontaneous fission into two helium nuclei. The reaction equation for this is
$^1_1H + ^7_3Li \rightarrow ^8_4Be \rightarrow 2^4_2He$.

a   Calculate the overall energy released. (Use the data: Mass of ^7_3Li = 7.016 u, Mass of ^4_2He = 4.0015 u.)

b   Show that each alpha particle gained a kinetic energy of about 1.35×10^{-12} J.

Exercise 25.2 Stellar properties and the Hertzsprung–Russell diagram

1. **a** Sketch the black-body emission spectrum for a star with a
    - **i** very hot surface temperature, such as the star Spica.
    - **ii** low surface temperature, such as the star Betelgeuse.

   b
    - **i** How can you tell the difference between the surface temperatures of two stars by examining their black-body emission spectra?
    - **ii** Which law defines your answer to **part i**? Write this law.
    - **iii** How does the emissivity of a body's surface affect the wavelength at which its radiated energy is greatest?

   c Use Wien's displacement law to calculate the surface temperature of a star whose peak wavelength in its emission spectrum is at 650 nm.
   (Wien's constant = 2.9×10^{-3} m K)

   d Arcturus is a star in the constellation of Bootes. Its surface temperature is about 4300 K.
    - **i** Use Wien's displacement law to calculate the peak wavelength in its emission spectrum.
    - **ii** Suggest why astronomers consider the luminosity of Arcturus to be larger than the calculated value of 110 $L_\odot$.

   e The cosmic microwave background radiation observed from deep space has an emission spectrum with a peak wavelength of 1.063 mm.
   Use Wien's displacement law to calculate the temperature of deep space.

2. **a** When describing stars, state what is meant by the term *luminosity*, L?

   b Assuming a star to be a black-body radiator, with a surface temperature T and a radius R at a distance d from the Earth, write a mathematical expressions for the luminosity, L, of the star.

   c Using the Stefan–Boltzmann constant of $\sigma = 5.67 \times 10^{-8}$ Wm^{-2} K^{-4}, calculate the luminosities of the following stars (you may assume that they are black bodies):
    - **i** Star A, radius 7×10^8 m, surface temperature 5700 K
    - **ii** Star B, radius 8.2×10^{11} m, surface temperature 3500 K.
    - **iii** Star C, radius 4.9×10^{10} m, surface temperature 11 200 K.

   d The luminosity of our Sun is 3.8×10^{26} W. For each of the stars in **part c**, give their luminosities relative to the luminosity of the Sun, $L_\odot$.

3   Solve the following problems involving the luminosity of stars:

   a   Procyon A, a star in the constellation Canis Minor, has a surface temperature of 6530 K and a radius that is twice that of our Sun. If the surface temperature of our Sun is 5700 K, calculate the ratio of their two luminosities, $\frac{L_{Procyon}}{L_\odot}$.

   b   Sirius A, a main sequence star, has a luminosity that is 25.4 times that of our Sun. If the surface temperature of Sirius A is 9940 K and the surface temperature of our Sun is 5700 K, calculate the ratio of the radii of the two stars, $\frac{r_{Sirius\,A}}{r_\odot}$.

4   a   Two stars, X and Y, have luminosities in the ratio $L_X : L_Y = 500$. If the ratio of their surface temperatures $T_X : T_Y = 20$, calculate the ratio of their radii, $R_X : R_Y$.

   b   The star Rigel, in the constellation of Orion, is about 70 times the radius of our Sun. The star Betelgeuse, also in Orion, has a radius about 1100 times that of our Sun. The surface temperature of Rigel is about twice that of our Sun and the surface temperature of Betelgeuse is about three-fifths that of our Sun. Show that the luminosity of Betelgeuse is about twice that of Rigel.

5   a   When describing stars, state what is meant by the term apparent brightness, b?

   b   i   Show that the apparent brightness, $b_\odot$, of our Sun, of luminosity $L_\odot = 3.83 \times 10^{26}$ W, is $b_\odot = 1.4 \times 10^3$ Wm^{-2}. The Sun is 1.5×10^{11} m away from the Earth.

      ii   By what name is this quantity usually known?

   c   Calculate the apparent brightness of a star that has a luminosity of 5.0×10^{28} W if it is four light-years away.

6   Alpha Centauri A, a star in the constellation of Centaurus, has a luminosity that is 1.52 times that of our Sun, and it is 4.3 light-years from the Earth. Our Sun is 8.33 light-minutes from the Earth.

   Calculate the ratio of the apparent brightness of Alpha Centauri to that of our Sun, $\frac{b_a}{b_\odot}$.

7   A charge-coupled device (CCD) attached to a telescope measures the wavelength of the maximum intensity of radiated energy from a star to be 400 nm and the apparent brightness to be 2.8×10^{-10} Wm^{-2}.

   a   Show that the surface temperature of the star is about 7300 K.

   b   At this temperature, the luminosity of the star is determined to be 7.2×10^{27} W.

      Calculate how far away the star is from the Earth. Give your answer in standard form and in light-years.

25 Nuclear fusion and stars

8 a Outline what is meant by *Hertzsprung–Russell diagram*.

 b Sketch a Hertzsprung–Russell (HR) diagram, showing an approximate scale for the two axes.

 c Indicate what is meant by *main sequence*.

 d Indicate where you would expect to find the following stars:

 i Our Sun, $T = 5700$ K

 ii Vega, $T = 9600$ K

 iii Betelgeuse, a red supergiant of $T = 3500$ K

 iv Sirius B, a white dwarf of $T = 25\,000$ K

9 Outline, in terms of their luminosity and their surface temperatures, the main features of a

 a main sequence star.

 b red giant star.

 c supergiant star.

 d white dwarf star.

10 a How is the luminosity of a main sequence star affected by its mass?

 b Show that a main sequence star with a mass 10 times that of our Sun will have a luminosity that is about 3200 times that of our Sun.

 c Use the relationship between luminosity and mass for a star on the main sequence to find the luminosity of a main sequence star that is five times the mass of our Sun. ($L_\odot = 3.8 \times 10^{26}$ W)

 d A main sequence star's luminosity occurs because it transfers mass into energy, via the various nuclear reactions that take place during its time on the main sequence. Suppose that during a star's time on the main sequence a percentage of the star's mass, αM, (where α is the percentage) is converted into energy.

 i Using Einstein's mass–energy conversion, write an expression for the energy converted by a mass of αM.

 ii If the star spends a time, t, on the main sequence, write an expression for t in terms of the luminosity, L, and the energy converted from the mass loss.

 iii Now, using the relationship between the mass, M, of a star and its luminosity, L, determine how the time, t, a star spends on the main sequence depends on its mass.

 iv The value of t for our Sun is about 10 billion years. Calculate the time a star of mass $10 M_\odot$ will spend on the main sequence.

11 a Stars form when large clouds of gas and dust come together to form a concentrated region of matter called a protostar. What is the main energy transformation taking place as this occurs?

  b Once the protostar becomes massive enough to initiate *thermonuclear fusion*, it will become a star, producing energy from its core.

  i What is meant by *thermonuclear fusion*?

  ii What is the end product or products of thermonuclear fusion for a main sequence star?

12 a What happens in the core of a main sequence star to cause it to move off the main sequence?

  b Outline what will happen to a main sequence star (with similar mass to our Sun) after it has moved off the main sequence until it becomes no longer visible.

  c Explain what prevents the gravitational collapse of a white dwarf star into a neutron star.

13 a Outline what will happen to a star that is much heavier than our Sun once it leaves the main sequence.

  b Explain what is meant by the term *Chandrasekhar limit* and why it is important in defining the eventual fate of a heavy main sequence star.

  c What opposes the gravitational force in a neutron star to allow the star to have hydrostatic equilibrium?

  d Explain what is meant by the *Oppenheimer–Volkoff limit* and why it is important in defining the eventual fate of a heavy main sequence star.

14 a Sketch a Hertzsprung–Russell diagram and indicate the path that our Sun will follow during its lifetime.

  b State what happens to the luminosity of the Sun, and what causes the luminosity to change, as it proceeds along this path on the HR diagram.

15 It is not possible to *see* a black hole. What observational evidence *do* astronomers have for their existence?

16 Stars similar to the Sun on the main sequence of the HR diagram fuse protons into helium nuclei in a series of three fusion reactions called the proton–proton chain. The first of these reactions was explored in **question 25.1.3**, where it was found that the energy released was 1.44 MeV.

  a The second of the proton-proton chain reactions is

  $^{1}_{1}H + ^{2}_{1}H \rightarrow ^{3}_{2}He + ^{0}_{0}\gamma$.

  Calculate the energy released in this reaction. (Data: Mass of $^{2}_{1}H$ = 2.013553 u; mass of $^{3}_{2}He$ = 3.01493 u)

b The third of the proton–proton chain reactions is

$${}^3_2\text{He} + {}^3_2\text{He} \rightarrow {}^4_2\text{He} + 2{}^1_1\text{H}.$$

Calculate the energy released in this reaction. (The mass of an alpha particle is 4.001506 u)

c The overall effect of the proton–proton chain is to fuse four protons into a helium nucleus—along with some other particles. Write the nuclear reaction for the overall process of the proton–proton chain.

d By adding up your answers from **parts b** and **c** with the energy released by the first process of the proton–proton chain, show that the total energy released by the fusion of four protons into a helium nucleus in the proton–proton chain is 26.7 MeV.

e The Sun produces energy at a rate of 3.8×10^{26} W. How many proton–proton chain reactions are occurring in the Sun's core every second?

f So how much mass of protons is the Sun losing per second?

g When the Sun began the main sequence about 75% of its mass was hydrogen. If the total mass of the Sun had been 2×10^{30} kg, what mass of hydrogen did it have?

h When the Sun has lost 12% of its hydrogen, it will move away from the main sequence and become a red giant. Determine how much time this will take the Sun to achieve.

i It is estimated that the Sun is already 4.6 billion years old. How long will it be from now before the Sun turns into a red giant?

Exercise 25.3 Stellar evolution extension

1 Stars with a mass much larger than the Sun on the main sequence can produce energy by the carbon–nitrogen–oxygen (CNO) cycle.

  a Complete the following reaction equations that show the complete CNO cycle:

  i ${}^1_1\text{p} + {}^{12}_6\text{C} \rightarrow$ _____ $+ \gamma$

  ii _____ $\rightarrow {}^{13}_6\text{C} +$ _____ $+ {}^0_0\nu$

  iii ${}^1_1\text{p} + {}^{13}_6\text{C} \rightarrow$ _____ $+ \gamma$

  iv ${}^1_1\text{p} +$ _____ $\rightarrow {}^{15}_8\text{O} +$ _____

  v ${}^{15}_8\text{O} \rightarrow {}^{15}_7\text{N} +$ _____ $+$ _____

  vi ${}^1_1\text{p} + {}^{15}_7\text{N} \rightarrow {}^{12}_6\text{C} +$ _____

b Overall, does the CNO cycle have a net production of

  i carbon?

  ii nitrogen?

  iii oxygen?

c So, what is the overall effect of the CNO cycle? In other words, what does it use up, and what does it produce?

d Suggest why stars need to be heavier than the Sun to proceed with the CNO cycle.

2 This question looks, in detail, at the energy released in the CNO cycle.
Use the following data:

Particle	$^{1}_{1}p$	$^{12}_{6}C$	$^{13}_{7}N$	$^{13}_{6}C$	$^{0}_{1}\beta^{+}$	$^{14}_{7}N$	$^{15}_{8}O$	$^{15}_{7}N$	$^{4}_{2}He$
Mass (amu)	1.007276	11.99945	13.00189	13.00006	0.00055	13.99922	14.99867	14.99626	4.001506

a The first of the reactions in the CNO cycle is

$^{1}_{1}p + ^{12}_{6}C \rightarrow ^{13}_{7}N + \gamma$.

Calculate the energy released in this reaction.

b The second of the CNO cycle reactions is

$^{13}_{7}N \rightarrow ^{13}_{6}C + ^{0}_{1}\beta^{+} + ^{0}_{0}\nu$.

Calculate the energy released in this reaction. Remember that a $^{0}_{1}\beta^{+}$ particle will annihilate a $^{0}_{-1}\beta^{-}$ to produce gamma radiation of 1.02 MeV.

c The third of the CNO cycle reactions is

$^{1}_{1}p + ^{13}_{6}C \rightarrow ^{14}_{7}N + \gamma$.

Calculate the energy released in this reaction.

d The fourth of the CNO cycle reactions is

$^{1}_{1}p + ^{14}_{7}N \rightarrow ^{15}_{8}O + \gamma$.

Calculate the energy released in this reaction.

e The fifth of the CNO cycle reactions is

$^{15}_{8}O \rightarrow ^{15}_{7}N + ^{0}_{1}\beta^{+} + ^{0}_{0}\nu$.

Calculate the energy released in this reaction. Remember that a $^{0}_{1}\beta^{+}$ particle will annihilate a $^{0}_{-1}\beta^{-}$ to produce gamma radiation of 1.02 MeV.

f The last of the CNO cycle reactions is

$^{1}_{1}p + ^{15}_{7}N \rightarrow ^{12}_{6}C + ^{4}_{2}He$.

Calculate the energy released in this reaction.

g   Hence, calculate the total energy released in the CNO cycle.

h   Write the nuclear reaction equation for the overall effect of the CNO cycle. Comment on your answer.

i   How does the energy production of the CNO cycle compare to the energy production of the proton–proton chain?

3   Red giant stars with a mass similar to or larger than the Sun will produce energy by the triple-alpha process.

a   Write two nuclear equations to show what the triple-alpha process is.

b   Explain why these two reactions have to occur in very quick succession.

c   Calculate the energy released by this process. (Use data from the table in the previous question.)

d   Outline what is happening to the surface temperature of a star whilst it is undergoing the triple-alpha process.

e   i   What will the eventual fate of a star with a mass less than about 8 solar masses be?

ii   Suggest what the internal structure will be.

iii   Will there be any nuclear reactions occurring in the core?

4   During the giant stage of a star's evolution, nuclei with atomic numbers less than or equal to those of iron and nickel (26 and 28, respectively) can be created by the continual addition of helium nuclei.

a   Explain why this can happen only in stars with a mass greater than about eight solar masses.

b   Explain why this process can create elements only up to iron and nickel.

5   Complete the following table to show how the eventual fate of a star depends on its initial mass.

Initial mass	Eventual fate of star
$M < 0.25 M_\odot$	
$0.25 M_\odot < M < 8 M_\odot$	
$9 M_\odot < M < 12 M_\odot$	
$12 M_\odot < M < 40 M_\odot$	
$M > 40 M_\odot$	

6   Elements with nuclear masses greater than those of iron and nickel can be produced by neutron capture if the availability of neutrons is sufficient.

   a   Explain why neutron capture happens only in highly evolved stars or in supernovae.

   b   An example of neutron capture is

   $^{56}_{26}\text{Fe} + 3\,^1_0\text{n} \rightarrow\,^{59}_{26}\text{Fe} + \,^0_0\gamma$.

   Suggest why this reaction can occur spontaneously. (No calculation required.)

   c   The nuclide $^{56}_{26}\text{Fe}$ is unstable and decays by β^--decay. Write a nuclear reaction equation for this decay and determine the nuclide that is produced.

   d   Suggest how this example shows how even the heaviest of elements can be synthesised during supernovae events.

7   Very heavy stars can produce nuclides up to bismuth-209 by the *slow neutron capture* process, or *s-process*. Explain what this process requires and why it produces nuclides of higher atomic number.

8   Another process involved in the production of heavier elements is the *rapid neutron capture process*, or *r-process*. Explain how this process is different to the s-process and why it can produce heavier isotopes of the same element.

9   Outline how a type 1a supernova occurs and why this implies that they can be used *as standard candles*.

10 Outline how a type 2 supernova occurs and contrast how the relative luminosity of the type 2 supernova is different to that of the type 1a supernova.

EXAM-STYLE QUESTIONS

Multiple-choice questions

1   The r-process and the s-process happen in
   A   main sequence stars.
   B   giants and red giants.
   C   supernovae events.
   D   neutron stars.

2   Of the following, the best definition for *apparent brightness* is
   A   the total energy emitted by a star in 1 s.
   B   the total power per unit area emitted by a star.
   C   the ratio of a star's output power to that of the Sun.
   D   the power per unit area received at the Earth's surface from a star.

CONTINUED

3. The binding energy of a ^2_1H nucleus is 1.1 MeV nucleon^{-1}. The best estimate of the binding energy per nucleon for a ^1_1H nucleus is

   A 0.

   B 0.55 MeV.

   C 1.0 MeV.

   D 1.1 MeV.

4. A star that has a radius twice that of the Sun and a surface temperature half that of the Sun will have a luminosity that is

   A a quarter of the Sun's luminosity.

   B a half of the Sun's luminosity.

   C twice the Sun's luminosity.

   D four times the Sun's luminosity.

5. A star that had an initial mass of $25M_\odot$ will eventually become a

   A white dwarf with a carbon core.

   B black hole.

   C white dwarf with an iron core.

   D neutron star.

6. The Sun's life expectancy on the main sequence is about 10^{10} years. Which of the following is the best estimate of the lifetime of a star on the main sequence of mass 100 times that of the Sun?

   A 10^5 years

   B 10^8 years

   C 10^{12} years

   D 10^{15} years

7. The proton–proton chain is a series of nuclear reactions occurring in stars on the main sequence. One of these reactions is shown here, with one particle missing.

   $^1_1H + ^1_1H \rightarrow ^2_1H + ? + ^0_0\nu$

   Which of the following is the missing particle?

   A $^0_{-1}\beta^-$

   B $^0_1\beta^+$

   C $^0_0\gamma$

   D $^0_0\bar{\nu}$

8. In a white dwarf star, gravitational collapse is prevented by

   A thermal expansion from fusion processes in the core.

   B electron degeneracy pressure.

   C neutron degeneracy pressure.

   D the Oppenheimer–Volkoff limit.

CONTINUED

Short-answer questions

9 This equation shows a nuclear process:

$^2_1D + ^3_1T \rightarrow ^4_2H + ^1_0n$.

The masses of the particles involved are

^2_1D = 2.014102 u; ^3_1T = 3.016050 u; ^4_2He = 4.002604 u; ^1_0n = 1.008665 u.

a State which kind of nuclear process is represented by the equation. [1]

b Calculate the energy released during this process. [3]

c State the form in which the energy is released. [1]

10 In 1987, a supernova in the Large Magellanic Cloud (LMC) galaxy was observed.

a State which region of the HR diagram the star would have been in before it turned into a supernova. [1]

b Suggest whether this star would have been less massive, the same mass or more massive than our Sun. [1]

c State the minimum mass there must be in the core of this star for it to become a neutron star. [1]

d Suggest what might eventually happen to the material that has been ejected from the star during the supernova event. [1]

11 A main sequence star has a luminosity that is 3000 times that of our Sun.

a Using the relationship between the masses and their luminosities for stars on the main sequence, show that the mass of the star is about 10 times the mass of our Sun. [2]

b Outline how this star is most likely to develop after it leaves the main sequence. [3]

12 Figure 25.1 shows an HR diagram. The main sequence is shaded grey. The Sun and three other stars are shown.

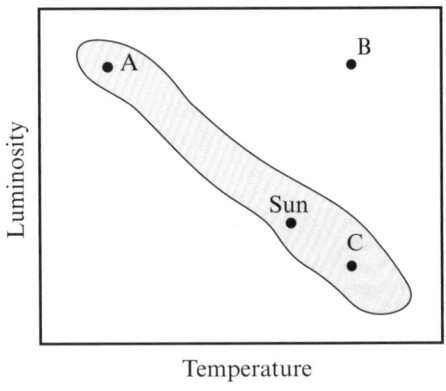

Figure 25.1

a Outline what nuclear reactions may be occurring in stars on the main sequence. [2]

b Explain how the HR diagram indicates that

  i star A is smaller than star B. [2]

  ii star C is smaller than star B. [2]

CONTINUED

13 This question is about the evolution of a star more massive than the Sun by a factor of 20.
   a Outline the stages of evolution for a star with a mass of $20M_\odot$ from its beginnings on the main sequence to its eventual fate. [2]
   b State what is meant by the Oppenheimer–Volkoff limit and how it dictates the eventual fate of a star. [2]
   c Explain why the star will not become a black hole. [2]

14 a State what is meant by the following two terms:
      i   The luminosity of a star [1]
      ii The apparent brightness of a star [1]
   b The apparent brightness of the Sun is about $1.3\ \text{kWm}^{-2}$, and its luminosity is 3.8×10^{26} W. Calculate how far the Sun is from the Earth. [2]
   c Another main sequence star has the same luminosity as the Sun, but its surface temperature is half that of the Sun. Determine the ratio of the radii of the two stars, $\frac{r_\odot}{r_{star}}$. [2]

15 A main sequence star has a surface temperature of 5200 K and a radius of 5×10^8 m.
   a Calculate the wavelength at which the star emits a maximum intensity of radiation. [2]
   b Calculate the luminosity of the star. [2]
   c State what the eventual fate of the star will be. [2]

16 This question is about neutron stars.
   A typical neutron star might have a mass of 3×10^{30} kg.
   a If the density of nuclear material is about $1.8 \times 10^{17}\ \text{kgm}^{-3}$, show that the radius of a typical neutron star is about 16 km. [2]
   b The Sun's mass is 2×10^{30} kg. With reference to the Oppenheimer–Volkoff limit, state why the mass of a typical neutron star cannot be more than 6×10^{30} kg. [2]
   c State what force is preventing the neutron star from collapsing under the effect of gravitational forces. [1]

17 The surface temperature of the Sun is 5778 K, and its radius is 6.96×10^8 m.
   a Show that the luminosity of the Sun is 3.8×10^{26} W. [2]
   b State which process—or processes—are responsible for the generation of energy by the Sun. [1]
   c List the stages in the evolution of the Sun from its present position to its final fate. [3]

Glossary

absolute zero the temperature at which all random motion of molecules stops

absorption spectrum the set of wavelengths (or frequencies) of light absorbed by an atom

acceleration the rate of change of velocity; it is a vector

acceleration of free fall the acceleration, g, due to the pull of the Earth on a body; $g = 9.8$ ms^{-2} near the surface of the Earth

activity the number of radioactive decays per second

albedo the ratio of reflected-to-incident intensity; it has no unit

alpha decay when an unstable nucleus emits an alpha particle

alternating current, AC a time-dependent current, which varies between positive and negative values

alternating voltage a time-dependent voltage, which varies between positive and negative values

ammeter an instrument that measures the electric current through it

amp an amp is the constant current flowing in two infinitely long, straight, parallel conductors of negligible cross section in a vacuum such that the force between the conductors is 2×10^{-7} Newtons per metre length of the conductors

amplitude the maximum displacement from equilibrium

angular acceleration the rate of change of angular speed

angular displacement the angle through which an object has moved during its circular motion/orbit

angular frequency the quantity 2π divided by the period

angular speed the angle through which an object moves per second when following a circular path

angular velocity the rate at which something is rotating: $\overline{\omega} = \frac{\Delta \theta}{\Delta t}$; measured in rads^{-1}

antinode a point on a standing wave where the displacement is a maximum (at some instant)

apparent brightness the incident power per unit area received at the surface of the Earth from a celestial object

Archimedes' principle When a body is wholly or partly immersed in a fluid it experiences an upward bouyant force, F_b, which is equal to the weight of the fluid displaced: $F_b = \rho V g$, where ρ is the density of the fluid being displaced, V the volume of displaced fluid and g the gravitational field strength.

atmosphere a non-SI unit of pressure; equal to the average pressure exerted by the Earth's atmosphere.

atomic number the number of protons in the nucleus

average velocity the displacement divided by the time to achieve that displacement: $\overline{v} = \frac{\Delta s}{\Delta t}$

Avogadro constant the number of particles in one mole

background radiation radiation from natural sources

beta-minus decay when an unstable nucleus emits an electron and an antineutrino

beta-plus decay when an unstable nucleus emits a positron and a neutrino

binding energy the minimum energy required to separate all the nucleons of a nucleus

Bohr radius the smallest orbital radius in which an electron can exist; $r_1 \approx 0.53 \times 10^{-10}$m

black body a theoretical body that absorbs all the radiation incident on it and radiates the maximum possible intensity for a given temperature

black hole a star whose gravitational escape speed is greater than the speed of light

blue-shift the shift in wavelengths towards smaller wavelengths

Boltzmann constant the ratio of the gas constant to Avogadro's number

bouyant force the force acting on an object in a fluid because the object is displacing some of the fluid

Carnot cycle a thermodynamic cycle consisting of two isothermal and two adiabatic curves

centripetal acceleration the rate of change of velocity of a body in orbit; given as $a = \frac{\Delta v}{\Delta t} = \frac{v^2}{r} = r\omega^2 = v\omega$ and is directed towards the centre of the circular orbit

centripetal force a force pointing to the centre of a circular path

chain reaction a continuous series of reactions produced by the products of each reaction

Chandrasekhar limit the maximum mass of a white dwarf is 1.4 solar masses. Above this mass, the star will collapse into a neutron star

closed system a system that can transfer energy, but not matter (mass), into or from its surroundings

coherent A term describing when two or more sources are emitting waves in phase or with a constant phase relationship between them

compression a point where the density of the medium is highest

conductors materials with many free electrons per unit volume, through which thermal energy and electric current can pass easily

coefficient of dynamic friction the ratio of the force of friction to the normal contact force on a body that is sliding along a surface

coefficient of static friction the ratio of the maximum force of friction between two bodies to the normal contact force when an object is at rest

condensation when a vapour changes into a liquid (thermal energy is transferred away from the vapour)

conduction method of thermal energy transfer based on collisions of electrons with atoms

control rod a material used to absorb neutrons and so control the rate of fission reactions

conservation of momentum when the net force on a system is zero, the total momentum of the system remains constant

convection method of thermal energy transfer due to the rising of lower density hot fluids

convection currents motion of a fluid as a result of differences in fluid density

Coulomb's law the force between two point charges is inversely proportional to the square of the separation and proportional to the product of the charges

$F = k \dfrac{q_1 q_2}{r^2}$

critical angle The angle at which the refracted ray (from a more dense medium to a less dense medium) travels along the boundary between the two media;

$\theta_c = \sin^{-1}\left(\dfrac{1}{_1n_2}\right)$

critical mass the smallest mass of nuclear fuel that can sustain a chain reaction

damping the loss of energy of an oscillating system due to the presence of resistance forces

daughter nucleus the nucleus formed after a decay process

decay constant the probability that a decay will occur in the next second

decay series a series of decays that shows the progression of an unstable nucleus into a stable nucleus

diffraction The spreading out of waves as they pass around an object or through an aperture

diffraction grating An assembly of many narrow slits, equally spaced a small distance apart, through which waves can travel

direct current (dc) rate of flow of charge through the cross-sectional area of a conductor

displacement change in position; the vector distance between the oscillator and its equilibrium position

distance length of path followed

distance of closest approach the distance at which a charged particle moving directly towards another similarly charged particle comes to rest

Doppler effect the change in observed frequency when there is relative motion between the source and the observer

drag force the force acting against the motion of an object that is moving through a fluid (gas or liquid)

driven oscillations oscillations when an external periodic force acts on the system

driving frequency the frequency of the external force acting on the system

dynamic friction a force opposing motion when a body moves

efficiency the ratio of useful work or power to input work or power

Einstein's postulates 1. all the laws of physics are the same in all inertial frames; 2. the speed of light in a vacuum is the same for all inertial observers

elastic collision A collision in which the total kinetic energy before the collision equals the total kinetic energy after the collision; that is, E_K is conserved

elastic potential energy the energy stored in a body that has been stretched

electrical potential the work done per unit charge to bring a test point positive charge from infinity to where it is in an electrical field

$V_e = k\dfrac{q}{r}$

electrical potential energy the work done to bring a charged body from infinity to where it is in an electrical field

electrical resistance the ratio of voltage across conductor to the current through it

electric field a region in space in which a charged particle will experience an electrical force

electric field line a line showing the direction of electrical force on a positive charge

electric field strength the electrical force acting on a unit positive test point charge
$E = \dfrac{F}{q}$

electric power the energy per unit time dissipated in a conductor

electromagnetic force the interaction mediated by the exchange of photons

electromagnetic induction when the magnetic flux linked to a conductor changes in any way, an electromotive force (emf) is induced in the conductor

electromagnetic (EM) wave a transverse wave consisting of oscillations of an electric and a magnetic field at right angles to each other

electromotive force the work done per unit charge in moving charge across a battery's terminals

emission spectrum the set of wavelengths (or frequencies) of light emitted by an atom

emissivity the ratio of the intensity radiated by a body to the intensity radiated by a black body of the same temperature

energy balance equation an equation expressing the equality of incoming and outgoing intensities of radiation

enhanced greenhouse effect the augmentation of the greenhouse effect due to human activities

entropy a measure of a system's disorder

equation of state equation relating pressure, volume and temperature of an ideal gas: $PV = nRT$

equilibrium the state when the net force on a system is zero

equipotential a line or surface on which the electrical potential is the same at all points

escape speed the minimum speed, v_{esc}, of an object in a gravitational field so that the object reaches infinity with zero kinetic energy

event something that happens at a particular point in space and time

excited state any atomic energy level with more energy than the ground state

Faraday's laws (of electromagnetic induction) the induced emf is the rate of change of magnetic flux linkage

first harmonic the longest wavelength (and the lowest frequency) at which a standing wave forms; sometimes called the fundamental mode

Fleming's left-hand rule A way of showing the geometric relationships between the magnetic force (thumb), field (first finger) and current (second finger) for a current-carrying conductor in a magnetic field

fluid resistance force a speed-dependent force opposing the motion of a body through a fluid

force the action of one body on a second body; unbalanced forces cause changes in speed, shape or direction

free-body force diagram a diagram showing a body in isolation with all forces acting on it drawn as arrows

freezing when a liquid changes into a solid (thermal energy is transferred away from the liquid)

frequency the number of complete orbits made in one second

gamma decay when a nucleus in an excited energy state emits a photon of electromagnetic radiation

gas constant the constant, R, that appears in the equation of state

geostationary orbit a satellite's orbit around the Earth, above the equator, that has an orbital period of exactly one day so that the satellite remains above the same spot on the Earth's surface

gravitational field a region of space in which a mass experiences a gravitational force

gravitational field strength the gravitational force per unit mass exerted on a point mass

gravitational field lines lines that show the direction of the force exerted on a point mass in a gravitational field

gravitational force the interaction mediated by the exchange of gravitons

gravitational potential energy (E_p) the work done by a force in moving a body to a position above its initial position

gravitational wave a transverse wave, travelling at the speed of light, that stretches and compresses space (by very small amounts)

greenhouse effect the phenomenon in which re-radiated energy from the greenhouse gases returns to earth warming the Earth

greenhouse gases gases in the atmosphere that are capable of absorbing infrared radiation

ground state the lowest energy level of an atom

half-life the time it takes for the activity to halve

Glossary

harmonics   integral multiples of the first harmonic frequency

heat engine   a device that transfers chemical energy to thermal energy and then to mechanical or electrical energy, which can then be used to do mechanical work

heat exchanger   a part of a nuclear reactor that removes the thermal energy generated in the moderator

Hertzsprung–Russell diagram   a diagram showing the relationship between the luminosity of stars and their temperatures

Hooke's law   the tension in a spring is proportional to the extension or compression

ideal gas   a theoretical gas in which the particles do not exert forces on each other except during contact

ideal voltmeter   a voltmeter with infinite resistance (takes no current when connected to a resistor)

impulse   the product of force and the time interval for which the force acts; it equals the change in momentum

induced fission   the splitting of a nucleus after it has absorbed a neutron

inelastic collision   A collision in which the total kinetic energy after a collision is less than the total kinetic energy before the collision; that is, some E_K is lost during the collision.

inertial reference frame   a reference frame in which Newton's first law of motion is obeyed

insulators   materials with few free electrons per unit volume, through which thermal energy and electric current cannot readily pass

instantaneous velocity   the rate of change of position; it is a vector

instantaneous speed   the magnitude of the instantaneous velocity

Intensity   power per unit area

interference   The effect of two or more waves meeting at the same place and time

internal energy   the sum of the random kinetic energy of particles and the inter-particle potential energy

Internal energy   the sum of the total kinetic energy and the total potential energy of all the particles in a system

internal resistance   a resistance in series to the cell due to the chemicals in the cell

isolated system   a system where no thermal energy or matter (mass) can be transferred into or from its surroundings

isothermal curve   a curve on a pressure–volume diagram where all points have the same temperature

isotope   any nucleus of a given element (i.e. a given number of protons) containing a different number of neutrons

Kepler's first law   planets move on ellipses with the Sun at one of the foci of the ellipse

Kepler's second law   the line joining a planet and the Sun sweeps equal areas in equal times

Kepler's third law   The period of revolution of a planet around the Sun is proportional to the $\frac{3}{2}$ power of the semi-major axis of the ellipse.

kinetic energy (E_K)   the energy possessed by a body that is moving

Kirchhoff's first law (the conservation of charge)   the total current flowing into a junction equals the total current flowing out of the junction; $\sum I_{in} = \sum I_{out}$

Kirchoff's second law (the conservation of energy)   The sum of the IR products in any closed loop is equal to the emf supplied in that loop.

length contraction   the length of an object that moves past an observer is shorter than the length of the object in a frame where it is at rest

Lenz's law   the direction of the induced emf is such that its effect is to oppose the original magnetic flux change (this shows itself as a minus sign in the equation)
$\varepsilon = -N\frac{d\Phi}{dt}$

light dependent resistor (LDR)   resistor where resistance decreases as light intensity increases

linear momentum   the product of the mass of a body and its velocity

longitudinal   a wave where the oscillations are parallel to the direction of energy transfer

luminosity   the total energy emitted by a celestial object per second

magnetic field   a region in space in which a magnetic force can act on a moving charge, a current-carrying conductor or a magnetic pole

magnetic field line   a line showing the direction of force on a magnetic North pole

magnetic flux   the product of the component of the magnetic field strength normal to an area

magnetic flux density   the force exerted per metre on a conductor carrying a current of 1 A in a perpendicular magnetic field

magnetic flux linkage the product of the magnetic flux, Φ, and the number of turns, N, of a conductor

main sequence the stage in a star's life during which it is stable, producing energy in its core by fusing hydrogen into helium

mass defect the difference between the mass of the nucleons and the mass of the nucleus

matter wave a wave corresponding to particles whose displacement is related to the probability of finding the particle at a particular position

mechanical wave a disturbance that transfers energy and momentum through oscillations of the particles of a medium

melting when a solid changes to a liquid (thermal energy is transferred to the solid)

Millikan's oil drop experiment the experiment that showed that charge comes in multiples of the charge on an electron; that is, that charge is quantised

moderator a material used to slow down neutrons by allowing them to collide with atoms of the moderator

molar mass the mass in grams of one mole of a substance

mole a quantity of a substance containing as many particles as atoms in 12g of carbon-12; this is equivalent to the Avogadro constant

natural frequency the frequency of free oscillations of a body

net force the one force whose effect is the same as that of a number of forces combined

neutron stars the very dense, collapsed core of a very massive supergiant star

Newton's first law of motion when the net force on a body is zero, the body will move with constant velocity (which may be zero); in other words, it will move on a straight line with constant speed (which may be zero)

Newton's second law of motion the net force on a body of constant mass is proportional to that body's acceleration and is in the same direction as the acceleration)

Newton's third law of motion if body X exerts a force on body Y, then body Y will exert an equal and opposite force on body X

Newton's universal law of gravitation an attractive force exists between any two point masses that is proportional to the product of the masses and inversely proportional to the square of their separation. This force is directed along a line joining the two masses.
$F = -G \frac{M_1 M_2}{R^2}$

node a point on a standing wave where the displacement is always zero

normal contact force the force between two touching bodies that is perpendicular to the touching surface

nuclear fission the splitting of an unstable nucleus into two (or more) parts

nuclear fusion the joining of two light nuclei to form a heavier nucleus

nucleon one of the two kinds of particles in the nucleus; a proton or a neutron

nucleon number the total number of nucleons in the nucleus

nucleosynthesis the process of producing nuclei by nuclear reactions involving other nuclei

nuclide a nucleus with a specific number of protons and neutrons

Ohm's law at a constant temperature, the current through a metallic conductor is proportional to the voltage across the conductor

Oppenheimer–Volkoff limit The maximum mass of a neutron star is about 3.0 solar masses. Above this mass, the star will collapse into a black hole

parallel connection resistors connected so that they have the same potential difference across them

parent nucleus the (unstable) nucleus that decays

peak wavelength the wavelength corresponding to the peak of the black body spectrum curve

period the time for one full oscillation

period the time to create one full wave

phase the state of a substance depending on the separation of its molecules; we consider the solid, liquid and vapour phase in this course

phase angle the angle that appears in the formula for displacement, determined by the initial position and velocity

phase difference $\Delta \phi = \frac{\Delta t}{T} \times 2\pi$, where T is the period and Δt is the time difference between two neighbouring peaks

photocurrent the current produced by the photoelectric effect

photoelectrons the electrons emitted in the photoelectric effect

photoelectric effect the emission of electrons from a metallic surface when light is incident on the surface

photon the particle of light; massless and moving at the speed of light

Glossary

Planck's constant   the ratio of a photon's energy to its frequency

planetary nebula   the mass and energy emitted at the end of a red giant's lifetime

point charge   a charged body of no size

point mass   a theoretical object of no size having mass

position   the coordinate on the number line

position vector   the vector from the origin of a coordinate system to the position of a particle

positron   a positively charged electron

potential difference   the work done per unit charge in moving the charge from one point to another

power   the rate at which work is being done (or energy is being dissipated)

pressure   the normal force on an area per unit area

proper length   the length of an object measured by an observer in a frame of reference in which the object is stationary with respect to the observer

proper time interval   the time interval between two events that occur in a reference frame in which both events occur at the same position

proton–proton chain   the sequence of fusion reactions, taking place in the core of main sequence stars, that produce helium from hydrogen

radioactive   a nucleus that is unstable

radioactive series   a series of decays that leads to a nucleus finally becoming stable (lead or thallium)

radiation   method of thermal energy transfer through the emission of electromagnetic waves from a hot surface

rarefaction   a point where the density of the medium is lowest

ray diagram   A diagram showing the path, or paths, of waves

real gas   a gas obeying the gas laws approximately for limited ranges of pressures, volumes and temperatures

red giant   very large, relatively cool stars with cores hot enough to fuse helium into carbon

red-shift   the shift in wavelengths towards larger wavelengths

reference frame   a set of coordinate axes and a set of clocks at every point in space

reflection   When a wave meets a boundary between two different media, some, or all, of the wave may not pass beyond the boundary and will 'bounce off'. This is called reflection.

refraction   The change in speed (and sometimes direction) when waves pass from one medium into a different medium

refractive index   The ratio of the speed of electromagnetic waves in a vacuum to the speed of the same wave in a different medium; $n = \frac{v_{vacuum}}{v_{medium}} = \frac{c}{v}$

resistivity   the resistance of a conductor of unit length and unit cross-sectional area

resonance   the condition when the driving frequency equals the frequency at which the amplitude is a maximum

series connection   resistors connected one after the other so they take the same current

simple harmonic motion (SHM)   oscillations in which the acceleration is opposite and proportional to the displacement

simultaneity   events that take place at the same time are said to be simultaneous

Snell's law $_1n_2 = \frac{\sin \theta_1}{\sin \theta_2}$

solar constant   the intensity received in the upper atmosphere of the Earth

spacetime diagram   a graph in which the y-axis represents time (although it is more usually given as ct), and the x-axis represents position, x; single events are then shown by a dot on the diagram

specific heat capacity   the energy required to change the temperature of a unit mass by one degree

specific latent heat of fusion   the energy needed to change a unit mass from the solid to the liquid phase at a constant temperature

specific latent heat of vaporisation   the energy needed to change a unit mass from the liquid to the vapour phase at a constant temperature

spontaneous fission   the splitting of an unstable nucleus without absorbing a neutron

standing wave   a wave formed by the superposition of two identical travelling waves in opposite directions

state of a gas   a gas with a specific value of pressure, volume, temperature and number of moles

states of matter   matter can exist in one of three states: solid, liquid or gaseous form

static friction   a force opposing the tendency to motion when a body is at rest

stopping voltage   the voltage in the photoelectric effect required to make the current zero

Stefan–Boltzmann law the radiated intensity is proportional to the fourth power of the kelvin temperature

strong nuclear force the interaction mediated by the exchange of gluons

supernova The massive explosion of a red supergiant that sends mass and energy outwards, leaving behind a very dense core

superposition When two or more waves meet at the same place and time

temperature a measure of the average random kinetic energy of particles

tension the force arising when a body is being stretched or compressed

terminal speed the constant speed attained when the resistance force becomes equal to the force pushing the body

Thermistor temperature-dependent resistor where resistance decreases as temperature increases

The first law of thermodynamics When an amount of heat Q is given to a gas, the gas will absorb that energy and use it to change its internal energy and/or to do work.

the wave equation $v = f\lambda$, where v is the wave speed, f is the frequency of the wave and λ is the wavelength of the wave

time dilation an observer with respect to whom a clock moves, measures a longer time interval between the ticks of the clock than the observer at rest relative to that clock

time period the time it takes for an orbiting object to make one complete orbit

total mechanical energy the sum of the kinetic energy, gravitational potential energy and elastic potential energy of a body

transfer of thermal energy the transfer of energy from one body to another as a result of a temperature difference

transformer an electromagnetic device that is able to change an alternating electrical supply from one potential difference to another

transverse a wave where the oscillations are at right angles to the direction of energy transfer

travelling wave a wave that transfers energy from one place to another

unified atomic mass unit defined exactly as $\frac{1}{12}$ of the mass of a $^{12}_{6}C$ atom. u = 1.661×10^{-27} kg

uniform gravitational field a gravitational field in which the field strength is constant at all locations

uniform motion motion with constant velocity

vaporisation when a liquid changes into vapour (thermal energy is transferred to the liquid)

voltage the potential difference across a conductor

voltmeter an instrument that measures the potential difference across its ends

wavefront A line, or surface, showing parts of a wave that are of the same phase as each other (usually shown as wave peaks)

wavelength the length of one full wave

wave–particle duality the idea that matter can exhibit both wave and particle properties

weak nuclear force the interaction mediated by the exchange of W and Z bosons

weight the force of attraction between the mass of a planet and a body

white dwarf small, hot stars in their final stages of evolution

Wien's displacement law the wavelength of the peak intensity in the emission spectrum of a hot body is inversely proportional to the absolute temperature

work done the product of the force in the direction of the displacement multiplied by the distance travelled

work–energy principle the net work done on a system is equal to the change in kinetic energy of the system

work function the minimum energy required by an electron to break free of a metal surface

worldline a line on a spacetime diagram relating a sequence of events, the angle of which is related to the speed at which something is moving